Thank you so m[uch] your [...]

ADVANCE PRAISE FOR
Who's Reporting Africa Now? *Clare*

"This is a unique book that goes beyond any other in exploring how journalists and NGOs produce knowledge about Africa in today's multimedia environment. With a sharp eye on the changing contexts and interactions of all relevant actors, it gives an illuminating account of the 'moral economies' of journalism about Africa, animating the complex struggles of media producers and reflecting on what these may mean for the ways we learn about and understand Africa today. A valuable read."

—Lilie Chouliaraki, Chair in Media and Communications,
London School of Economics

"*Who's Reporting Africa Now?* traces the increasingly influential role of NGOs in shaping the story about Africa in global media. Kate Wright draws on her own extensive experience as a journalist as well as empirical research into a range of media, from legacy platforms to online outlets, to provide a persuasive account of the interactions between journalists and NGOs and the moral and political economies underpinning these complex relationships. The book breaks new ground in exploring political and ethical questions at the heart of global journalism in a changing media landscape, and in so doing, it contributes to the building of theory about journalism in and about Africa."

—Herman Wasserman, Professor of Media Studies, University of Cape Town

"Journalism is a much more complex, mixed, and altogether messy form of media work than it is generally made out to be. Kate Wright offers a critical yet respectful view of what this means in both theory and practice. What a great read!"

—Mark Deuze, Professor of Media Studies, University of Amsterdam

"*Who's Reporting Africa Now?* is a fascinating journey behind the scenes of the production of contemporary representations of Africa. Thanks to Kate Wright's unique access and understanding of the news industry, the book unravels a captivating media ecology where NGOs and journalists engage in complicated exchanges, not only with each other but also with freelancers, private foundations, and PR agencies and social media participants. In so doing, Wright offers compelling evidence to understand how NGOs have come to play such a central role in the production of visual images of Africa. With tremendous energy, the book successfully articulates and combines a wide range of debates and literature from African studies, international development, media studies, and cultural and creative industries. The book will be a terrific opportunity for African studies readers to reconsider the key debates over Africa's image in an increasingly mediatized world."

—Toussaint Nothias, Lecturer in African Studies, Stanford University

Who's Reporting Africa Now?

This book is part of the Peter Lang Media and Communication list.
Every volume is peer reviewed and meets
the highest quality standards for content and production.

PETER LANG
New York • Bern • Berlin
Brussels • Vienna • Oxford • Warsaw

Kate Wright

Who's Reporting Africa Now?

Non-Governmental Organizations, Journalists, and Multimedia

PETER LANG
New York • Bern • Berlin
Brussels • Vienna • Oxford • Warsaw

Library of Congress Cataloging-in-Publication Data
Names: Wright, Kate, author.
Title: Who's reporting Africa now?: non-governmental organizations,
journalists, and multimedia / Kate Wright.
Description: New York: Peter Lang, 2018.
Includes bibliographical references and index.
Identifiers: LCCN 2017056633 | ISBN 978-1-4331-5104-0 (hardback: alk. paper)
ISBN 978-1-4331-5103-3 (paperback: alk. paper) | ISBN 978-1-4331-5105-7 (ebook pdf)
ISBN 978-1-4331-5106-4 (epub) | ISBN 978-1-4331-5107-1 (mobi)
Subjects: LCSH: Africa—Press coverage. | Africa—In mass media.
Reporters and reporting—Africa. | Journalism—Objectivity.
Africa—Foreign public opinion. | Non-governmental organizations—Africa—Influence.
Non-governmental organizations—Public relations.
Classification: LCC P96.A37 W75 2018 | DDC 070.44996—dc23
LC record available at https://lccn.loc.gov/2017056633
DOI 10.3726/b12613

Bibliographic information published by **Die Deutsche Nationalbibliothek.**
Die Deutsche Nationalbibliothek lists this publication in the "Deutsche
Nationalbibliografie"; detailed bibliographic data are available
on the Internet at http://dnb.d-nb.de/.

The paper in this book meets the guidelines for permanence and durability
of the Committee on Production Guidelines for Book Longevity
of the Council of Library Resources.

TABLE OF CONTENTS

ILLUSTRATIONS

PREFACE

I remember vividly the day I first used multimedia from a Non-Governmental Organization. It was back in 2003, when I was a journalist working on *Newshour*, the English-language flagship for BBC World Service Radio. My editor was emphatically not a morning person. He was slumped at his desk, mainlining strong coffee and trying to make it through the pre-dawn editorial meeting with at least a modicum of courtesy. "The thing is Kate", he explained in a long-suffering manner, "war in the Congo is not new. Millions of people have been dying there for seven bloody years, so why cover it today? What's *new?*"

He had me there. One more militia attack, however vicious, was just one more militia attack, even to our engaged global audience. I didn't even have a correspondent on the ground to help me develop a sharper, more unusual news line. He was over a thousand kilometers away covering an important political rally. But the accounts coming through on the wires were enough to make me blink away tears. The civilian death toll was just getting higher and higher. Eye witnesses described seeing piles of mutilated bodies, including those of children. Surely the world should know about this? Surely it was important, precisely because the violence showed no signs of stopping?

As a journalist with nearly a decade of experience under my belt, I was well aware that news coverage didn't always bring about a political response.

But I also knew from my in-box that many top diplomats listened to the program, so I thought it was worth a shot. At the back of my mind was the genocide which had occurred just over the Congolese border in Rwanda, less than a decade earlier. Like many other international journalists, I was haunted by the possibility that maybe the world's media could have done more, could have shouted louder and more persistently, could have done *something* to provoke an international response, before it was too late. Maybe, maybe.

The editor, with whom I had been working for some time, looked at me and rolled his eyes. "I know, Kate, I *know*. War is bad and it kills babies. But I do not need your bleeding heart at 6am. I need some f*****g *news*." Then I noticed an e-alert from Human Rights Watch in my in-box. Pygmies living in the Ituri region of eastern Congo had not only been massacred by the attacking militia, their bodies had been eaten. Their press officer had eye-witness accounts of these acts of cannibalism on tape—would the program like them biked over?

"*Pygmy-eating?*" my editor visibly perked up. "Well, that's *different*. We haven't had *pygmy-eating* before!" A ripple of uneasy laughter went around the room. "Alright then," he conceded. "Get them to send the tapes over, and *if* they are strong enough—I mean if I actually *care* when I hear them—I'll let you do the piece." So that was the first time I used audio provided by an NGO in a news program.

I wasn't alone. My colleagues at World Service also found that the material provided by NGOs helped them get around recalcitrant editors: enabling them to generate better news angles and add human interest, as well as supplying that all-important factor—colorful and engaging audio. Journalists working on the overnight program, which went out every half-hour, were especially happy to accept audio from NGOs because it helped them to diversify their geographic coverage of sub-Saharan Africa. It was also remarkably handy in helping them cope with the "dead zone", which occurred in the early hours of the morning when yesterday's material was far too old to use, but little new material had yet been filed from the field.

However, within a few months, the Head of English language programs at World Service put a stop to it. She sent us an email reminding us that the BBC was statutorily obliged to remain impartial and that the World Service operated in the most politically sensitive areas of the globe. That meant that we had a particular responsibility to be seen to be neutral. Understandably, she argued, NGOs had their own agendas. So it was perfectly ok to discuss their reports and so on, but we should not allow those reports to set our news agenda. From then on, we could not use their audio without her personal authorization.

That managerial ruling sparked a heated internal debate. On one side, were journalists concerned that refusing to use NGO material would lead to less frequent coverage of poor Southern countries and non-elite issues, which they thought undermined the Corporation's commitment to provide diverse forms of international news coverage. Meanwhile, others argued that even if absolute impartiality was unachievable, the Corporation needed to keep its critical distance from NGOs, which were increasingly powerful.

Although I was one of those who wanted to be able to use NGO-provided material on occasion, I saw the validity of the points made by my opponents. Since then, I have often wondered what I should advise my own students to do if they find themselves faced with similar situations in future. Indeed, after I left journalism in 2006, widespread cost-cutting carried out within the news industry has made journalists' use of NGO material far more common. This book is therefore my answer to my students' (and my own) questions about the effects of NGOs' production of international news about Africa.

ACKNOWLEDGEMENTS

My deep gratitude goes to all of the people who participated in this study: who trusted me enough to tell me so much about the challenging and sometimes worrying aspects of their work. I appreciate your candor and hope I have repaid your trust in me by writing up a fair, respectful and well-contextualized critique.

My hearty thanks go to my friends and colleagues at the Department of Geography, Media and Communication at Karlstad University in Sweden, who showed me such amazing hospitality as a Visiting Scholar at their Ander Center for Research on News and Opinion in the Digital Era. I am so grateful for your encouragement, companionship and endlessly thought-provoking conversations. Particularly big thanks go to Henrik Örnebring, Michael Karlsson and Johan Lindell for their constructive feedback on early chapter drafts. May we keep discussing big ideas for many years to come!

My deep thanks also go to Santander, whose Global Research fund helped pay for the interpretation and transcription work needed to complete the study on which this book is based. I have also benefited hugely from being awarded a Chancellor's Fellowship at the University of Edinburgh, which gave me the time and space I needed to develop an early draft of this book into a manuscript which was ready for submission

But I would have struggled to make the journey from practice to research at all without the support and guidance of Natalie Fenton and Aeron Davis, who served as my doctoral supervisors at Goldsmiths. I've also learned so much from the fabulous all-female reading group on humanitarianism, human rights and media at LSE. Lilie Chouliaraki, Monika Krause, Ella McPherson, Mirca Madianou, Kate Nash and Shani Orgad: together, you comprise the most wonderfully rigorous, critical "hive mind."

Thanks also to all my peers, friends and fellow researchers who have enriched my thoughts by taking time to talk or correspond with me, who fed back on early ideas or drafts, and just cheered me on along the way. I'm looking at you: Stuart Allan, Mel Bunce, Glenda Cooper, David Hesmondhalgh, Flor Enghel, Suzanne Franks, Tobias Kelly, Ben Jones, Fiona Mackay, Toussaint Nothias, Chris Paterson, Matthew Powers, and Martin Scott.

Finally, I want to thank my fabulous husband, Brendan Paddy, who always has my back. I don't know what I would do without you.

· 1 ·

INTRODUCTION

Are Non-Governmental Organizations the new reporters of news about Africa? Many of the largest and wealthiest are regularly involved in the production of international news about poor, sub-Saharan countries. This involves NGO-workers checking facts and conducting extensive, on-the ground interviewing in locations where correspondents and news bureaux have been cut (Powers 2015, 2016). NGO-workers may also write news stories and features for placement in mainstream newspapers or websites (Cooper 2007, 2016). But most frequently of all, NGO-workers produce, commission and verify multimedia—including audio, but more often, video or photography (Abbott 2015; Frontline Club 2008, 2011, 2015; Hallas 2012).[1]

NGO-workers regularly offer this multimedia, free of charge to major news organizations—most of which are still based in Europe and North America (Cottle and Nolan 2007; Fenton 2010a). But this book shows that NGO multimedia also arrives at news outlets via more indirect routes. These include freelancers pitching material originally commissioned by NGOs to news outlets, and interns picking up material circulated through social media. These indirect routes make it less likely that journalists will attribute material to an NGO. Indeed, I found that half of the news items which contained NGO-provided material in my sample did not indicate this clearly to audiences.

The lack of any clear distinction between the production and dissemination of non-governmental and mainstream news reporting means that some critics have stopped discussing the relationship between NGO-work and journalism—and started talking about "NGO journalism" instead (McPherson 2015a; Zuckerman 2010). Such statements indicate that important changes are occurring in the boundaries between NGO-work and journalism (Carlson and Lewis 2015; Powers 2015). But these changes are highly controversial, with many critics fearing that they threaten the critical independence of journalism and/or the alterity of NGO work (Cottle and Nolan 2007; Fenton 2010a; Franks 2013; Seaton 2010). However, more optimistic practitioners and scholars see journalists' use of NGO-provided material as having the potential to be far more progressive: enhancing the dynamism, inclusivity and social engagement of journalism, and developing NGOs' ability to engage in mediated advocacy (Beckett 2008; Frontline Club 2008, 2011, 2015).

This book is part of a new wave of criticism which consists of researchers who argue that we should move beyond over-generalized "boon or bane" arguments about the complex effects of NGOs' shift into news-making (Powers 2017; see also Waisbord 2011). In particular, I interrogate the effects of journalists' use of NGO-provided multimedia in the news about Africa which is offered to UK audiences. This is the kind of international coverage which occurs most frequently in industry and academic debates on the subject (Beckett 2008; Franks 2010; Frontline Club 2008, 2015; Lugo-Ocando and Malaoulu 2014). Yet it has never been subject to any kind of systematic analysis.

Moreover, I argue that in order to evaluate NGOs' involvement in the production of news about sub-Saharan countries, it is necessary to understand why and how their involvement has come about, in ways which address the motivations, perspectives and practices of all of the media producers who were involved. This moves us beyond a narrow binary approach to journalist-NGO relations: enabling us to consider the often crucial roles played by other kinds of actors. These include fieldworkers, senior managers, freelancers, interns, social media participants, PR and advertising creatives, and business people working on Corporate Social Responsibility Schemes. Such complex exchange systems cut across geographic boundaries, as well as spanning many different fields of activity. They also tend to construct the "trust" needed to facilitate exchanges in ways which are not only shaped by the confluence of different political economies, but also by new combinations of normative values.

Indeed, the most notable feature of this kind of news-work is its strongly normative character. That is to say, that media producers are usually convinced that they are personally doing "good work", at the same time as reshaping collective understandings of what constitutes appropriate conduct in their respective fields. These normative shifts were found to have profound effects not only on the framing of news texts, but also on the collective ethos of news organizations and NGOs. So it is somewhat surprising that previous studies in this area haven't really explored actors' agentive reflections about normative issues in much detail.

In order to do this, I take an interdisciplinary approach: drawing from literature on African Studies, International Development, Media Studies, Sociology and the Cultural and Creative Industries. In particular, I develop theory about moral economies in order to analyze how and why particular political economies interact with the normative values of multiple actors. I focus on the ways in which media producers use their interactions with one another to renegotiate tensions between their ideals of creative autonomy, and their understandings of their responsibilities or obligations to others. Moral economy theory is also used to develop less ethnocentric ways of evaluating these new exchange systems, by attending to which and whose capabilities are enhanced in production processes, and the effects of this on the construction of mediated knowledge about "Africa".

Causal factors: geographic and visual specialism

Although previous work in this area hasn't tended to explore actors' renegotiation of normative values in much detail, some causal factors shaping NGOs' move into news production have been discussed before. After all, at first glance, it seems rather puzzling that NGO-workers should wish to spend their precious resources on news production. It is very difficult for them to get multimedia accepted by news outlets and it costs a lot of money to purchase, and continually update, communications technology (Fenton 2010a; Powers 2014). In order to construct and pitch multimedia successfully to journalists, large and wealthy NGOs also tend to hire former journalists who understand and can reproduce the requirements of specific news outlets (Fenton 2010a; Powers 2014). So news-making is by no means an easy enterprise: it takes considerable time, money, effort and skill, which has serious implications for the staffing and resourcing of an NGO.

Fundraising has long been assumed to be a particularly powerful factor driving these changes because there is a very strong correlation between the amount of news coverage an NGO obtains, and the amount of money it is able to raise from the public (Cooper 2015; Franks 2013). The NGO field is now so crowded that getting news coverage is believed to be extremely important for NGOs' financial survival (Cottle and Nolan 2007). Indeed, serious questions have been raised about the extent to which fundraising imperatives shape NGO-workers' perpetuation of rescue narratives about Africa which position Northerners as the saviors of the continent, in order to prompt more donations (Franks 2013; Lugo-Ocando and Malaolu 2014).

However, NGOs don't just engage in journalistic production to raise money: they also claim to use news to bring about social change through mediated forms of advocacy (Keck and Sikkink 1998; Reese 2015; Yanacopulos 2015). Yet "advocacy" is a bit of a fuzzy term, which is used by NGO-workers to refer to a host of different objectives and strategies (Yanacopulos 2015). These include conducting mass education campaigns, placing pressure on policy-makers and giving "voice" to the disempowered (Dogra 2012; Orgad 2013; Powers 2014; Wright 2018).

NGOs' claims to engage in mediated advocacy may also serve as a means of legitimizing their own intervention in poor, African countries (Lugo-Ocando and Malaolu 2014). These interventions have been viewed by many as having questionable effects, not least because of NGOs' lack of democratic accountability. As *The Economist* so famously put it, "who elected Oxfam?" (2000, discussed in Slim 2002).

Thus there are a variety of reasons why NGOs might choose to provide multimedia to news outlets. But why might journalists accept it? Journalists' own advocacy objectives appear to have played some role in their growing use of NGO material (Abbott 2015; Wright 2016a, 2016b). However, changes in the political economy of the mainstream news industry are usually regarded as being much more powerful causal factors. These changes include the dramatic fall in financial income faced by most major news organizations, caused by the sharp drop in circulation and the shift of advertising online, where it is worth far less (Brock 2013). News outlets also face increased competition for income, brought about by deregulation and digitization (Boyd-Barrett 2010). Meanwhile, public service media organizations have experienced a reduction in state subsidies (Hendy 2013; Sehl *et al.* 2016).

To make matters worse: at the same time as news organizations' income has been falling, the costs of news production have been rising. Newspapers have attempted to woo remaining print consumers and advertisers by producing glossy magazines and supplements (Moore 2010; Phillips 2010). But far bigger, ongoing costs stem from news organizations' development of new modes of multi-platform delivery, which are necessary to respond to changing patterns of news consumption (Fenton 2010b).

This combination of falling income and rising costs has led to widespread cost-cutting in major news organizations (Fenton 2010b; Örnebring 2016). As well as severe reductions in the numbers of foreign news bureaux and correspondent posts, there have been repeated cuts in staffing and travel budgets, which limit journalists' ability to leave the head offices of their news organizations (Beckett 2008; Franks 2010). As poor sub-Saharan countries tend to be regarded as less newsworthy than wealthier, elite countries (Galtung and Ruge 1965; Harcup and O'Neill 2016), such cost-cutting has had a disproportionate impact on African news.

Nevertheless, offering a wide range of international coverage is widely held to be "an integral part of any serious news offer" (Sambrook 2010, 66). In the UK, where this study was undertaken, international news is held to be of such importance that public service broadcasters have specific legal obligations relating to it (e.g. Communications Act 2003), which are overseen by the Office of Communications (known as OFCOM). Offering a wide geographic range of news coverage is also commercially important, as overseas audiences are often attracted to British-based satellite and online news outlets because of the quality of their international coverage (Wall and Bicket 2009; Hamilton 2010; Newman and Levy 2012).

Thus I see the changes in the political economy of journalism as producing a kind of Catch 22 for journalists, wherein they are expected to produce a wide geographic range of international news, but are less and less able to do so because of cuts in resourcing. This Catch 22 is exacerbated by journalists' lack of time, which makes it difficult for them to construct news stories in other ways. The increasing dominance of online output in news organizations means that journalists are expected to produce far more content than they used to, and this needs to be constantly updated (Paterson 2007; Redden and Witschge 2010). So journalists have experienced a dramatic speeding-up of the news cycle, which seriously impedes their ability to engage in traditional forms of newsgathering and verification (Redden and Witschge 2010; Sambrook 2010).

Another important change in the political economy of journalism which I argue shapes the adoption of NGO content pertains to the difficulties which journalists now face in accessing sufficient visual images. Producing online news is particularly labor-intensive because it contains a lot of photographs

and video, as well as written text (Barnhurst 2010). Arresting images are used
to grab the attention of online users, who are likely to be flicking rapidly
between news and other websites or social media, many of whom now arrive
at news sites using search engines or news aggregators (Newman and Levy
2014). Visual images are also used to create interactive genres, such as photo
slideshows, which are thought to enhance the "stickiness" of news sites: persuading news users to stay for longer and explore more of the site (Caple and
Knox 2012; Scott 2005). So visual imagery has become increasingly important in enhancing numbers of unique users and improving clickstream data:
both of which are vital to news organizations trying to attract greater revenue
from advertisers and sponsors (Currah 2009; Newman and Levy 2014).

Finally, visual images help to construct relationships between a news organization's brand and value-laden notions of globality, in ways which are
believed to encourage consumer loyalty (Newman and Levy 2014; Roosvall
2013). So visual media is believed to be of vital commercial importance to
most major news outlets. Yet visual specialists, such as photojournalists and
picture editors, have been disproportionately affected by successive waves of
redundancies at news organizations (Anderson 2013; Argles 2013; Bardan
2015; Klein-Avraham and Reich 2016). This is because these cuts have often
been enacted as role-merging and multiskilling, with managers often citing
the ability of new editing software to enable visual media production by non-
specialists (Klein-Avraham and Reich 2016). Thus at the very time when
highly visual forms of online media have come to dominate news-making because of growth in online news, news organizations have lost their access to
their in-house visual expertise, knowledge and craftsmanship.

Therefore I argue that journalists face not one, but two, dilemmas. How
can they meet the demand for increased volumes of striking and distinctive
visual media, when they don't have many in-house visual experts? And how
can they provide a wide range of international news coverage when so many
foreign bureaux and correspondent posts have been cut, especially in sub-
Saharan Africa? In short, how can journalists compensate for the loss of visual
and geographic specialism?

NGOs appear to be well placed to step in to supply the necessary geographic
expertise because their extensive local and cross-border networks mean that
they now have far more in-country staff than mainstream news organizations
in the Global South (Otto and Meyer 2012; Powers 2016). For instance, the
think-tank, the International Crisis Group now has more locally based analysts
than *The New York Times*, the *Financial Times* or CNN—most of which are in

sub-Saharan Africa (Wright 2014). But NGOs also have a strong, historical tradition of producing, curating and redistributing visual media, especially photography (Denčik and Allan 2017; Fehrenbach and Rodogno 2015; McLagan and McKee 2012). So large, wealthy international NGOs (known as INGOs) not only recruit former journalists familiar with the needs of specific news outlets (Cottle and Nolan 2007; Fenton 2010a), they also recruit picture editors driven out of mainstream news organizations, and regularly commission freelance photojournalists (Hallas 2012; Wright 2014, 2016a).

For all of these reasons, NGO-work and journalism have begun to dovetail into one another, in ways which may have important political effects on North/South relations. For although media audiences can (and do) resist the messages encoded in media texts (Seu and Orgad 2017), international news coverage has the potential to invite media audiences to construct imagined relations with distant others in particular ways (Chouliaraki 2006; Doty 1996; Mody 2010). International news texts may therefore encourage and/or inhibit particular kinds of audience response (Chouliaraki 2006; Dunn 2003; Spurr 1993). They are even believed to have the potential to influence foreign and aid policy when politicians have yet to decide upon strategy (Franks 2015).

Analyzing the effects of NGOs' shift into international news production is especially important at a time of rapidly escalating global need. A combination of climate change, economic globalization and a sharp spike in violent conflict mean that far more of the world's population are expected to be living in fragile situations by 2030 (Office for the Coordination of Humanitarian Affairs 2015; Organization for Economic Co-operation and Development 2015). Yet the poorest countries in the world still receive the least international aid, and far too little attention is paid to long-term development, including addressing gross disparities in wealth (UN High Level Panel on Humanitarian Financing 2016).

Negative constructions of "Africa"

When academics, journalists and NGO workers talk about NGOs' involvement in news-making, they keep returning to questions about whether NGOs can improve the coverage of Africa (Beckett 2008; Franks 2010; Frontline Club 2008, 2015; Lugo-Ocando and Malaolu 2014). This is because Northern news organizations are believed to represent sub-Saharan countries exceptionally badly: offering only sporadic or patchy coverage of events; selecting

only negative events to cover; and then failing to explain the causes or con-
texts of those crises adequately to news audiences (Franks 2013; Philo 1993).
Thus disasters, military crises and epidemics seem to "just happen" in Africa
(Rieff 2005; see also Nauta and Stavinoha 2012).

Indeed, Northern journalists have been accused of promoting Afropessimism by measuring sub-Saharan countries' progress in an ethnocentric manner and using the coverage of specific crises to make dire predictions about
the future of the whole continent (De B'Béri and Louw 2011; Nothias 2013a).
Such homogenizing, negative and racist forms of news are often claimed to in-
flict serious harm on African people: undermining their self-esteem (Opuku-
Owusu 2003) and preventing international recognition of their diverse political systems and cultures (de Beer 2010a, 2010b; Ogazi 2010). Poor Northern
news coverage of Africa has even been charged with perpetuating the un-
derdevelopment of the continent by discouraging international investment,
trade and tourism (Marthoz 2007; Schorr 2011).

The critical thinking underpinning these arguments owes much to Mudimbe's work about Europeans' invention and imposition of the concept of
"Africa" (1988, 1994). Visual imagery disseminated through news journalism is thought to play a vital role in such constructions, Othering Africans
through different forms of imperial gaze (Palmberg 2001; Pratt 1992; Vokes
2012). Journalists have long been seen as complicit in this (Spurr 1993), and
are still criticized for refusing work from sub-Saharan photojournalists and
other media producers unless it complies with the "expected [negative] stereotypes" (Jayawardane 2017; see also Richardson 2017). Indeed, the use of
stereotypes in news reports about Africa is seen as so common that it has been
satirized by the Kenyan journalist and writer, Binyavanga Wainaina, in a now
famous essay entitled, "How to Write about Africa" (2005).

One of the stock characters which academic critics discuss is the lone,
suffering child, whose image evokes innocence by drawing on Christian visual
traditions (Seaton 2005). Images of a single mother and baby are believed to
perform a similar function, given their strong connotative links to the iconography of the Madonna and Child (Höijer 2004; Seaton 2005). Such images
have been found to dominate news coverage of sub-Saharan famines, from the
Biafra in the 1960s onwards (Burman 1994; Duffield 1996; Fair 1993; Franks
2013). However, these kinds of images are now used by British newspapers to
indicate the innocence of those suffering in other kinds of situations, including flood victims in Mozambique in 2000 (Okere 2004) and refugees fleeing
fighting in the Sudanese region of Darfur in 2004 (Campbell 2007). Silent,

nameless, black African victims and white Northern "helpers" have also been seen to dominate recent North American TV coverage of the ebola epidemic in Liberia (French 2017): echoing earlier news representations about the spread of HIV-AIDS (Nauta and Stavinoha 2012).

Such imagery may stimulate Northerners' desire to help by indicating victims' worthiness, but it tends to focus viewers' attention on subject's bodies, rather than their thoughts, opinions and activities (Seaton 2005). It therefore tends to portray African people as passive and devoid of cultural and political engagement (Höijer 2004; Franks 2010; Philo 1993). As a result, these forms of media representation are often seen as exploitative and even pornographic: stripping African peoples' personhood down to their corporeality and exposing the undignified details of their bodily suffering to the camera's gaze, in order to position Northern media audiences as powerful and morally superior saviors (Burman 1994; Fair 1993; Franks 2013).

Some critics claim that NGOs have the ability to challenge these stereotypes by enabling sub-Saharan people to produce and disseminate more empowering and diverse representations of the continent (Beckett 2008; Beckett and Mansell 2008). But others see NGOs as perpetuating the problematic representation of the continent because it serves their financial and political interests to portray "Africans" as requiring their benevolent intervention (Franks 2013; Lugo-Ocando and Malaolu 2014; Philo 1993). In particular, international aid agencies based in the US and UK have been criticized for steering journalists towards decontextualized and stereotypical images of "ideal" victims, in order to raise as much money as possible for their organizations (Duffield 1996; Kennedy 2009; Manzo 2006, 2008; Van der Gaag and Nash 1987).

Aid organizations have responded to these criticisms by engaging in sophisticated debates, culminating in the production of several batches of image guidelines by individual organizations and umbrella bodies (Dogra 2012, 2015; Lidichi 1999). But a report on the coverage of the East African drought of 2011, found that "inconsistency and double standards" still existed within international aid organizations, given the "fundraising logic" of portraying "a crying emaciated baby on the ground" (Seu et al. 2012, 4; see also Magee 2011).

However, aid agencies are not the only INGOs accused of reinforcing imperialistic representations of sub-Saharan Africa. Human rights organizations have also been criticized for decontextualizing military conflicts and dehumanizing those suspected of war crimes: utilizing a savages-victims-savior triad in order to amass moral/political support to press for their prosecution (Mutua 2001; see also Douzinas 2007). Thus human rights INGOs have been accused of perpetuating Northern journalists' tendency to represent sub-Saharan conflicts as a battle between good and evil (Ibelema 1992). This involves Othering combatants by portraying them as "barbaric", "wild", "evil" "mad" or "savage", as occurred in American newspaper representations of armed groups in the Somali conflict of 1992–1993 and the Rwandan genocide of 1994–1995 (Brookes 1995; Carruthers 2004; Marthoz 2007; McNulty 1999). In such portrayals, the political causes and contexts shaping conflict are marginalized or erased, with the grievances of combatants often being portrayed as largely "tribal" in nature (Ibelema 1992, 2014; Marthoz 2007).

The depiction of African child soldiers has tended to be more mixed, since it straddles two representational traditions: the portrayal of children as passive victims in need of rescuing and the portrayal of combatants as savage, deranged or diabolical. So, it is argued, young combatants tend to be portrayed as either deviant aberrations or as traumatized, passive victims in need of rescue (Coundouriotis 2010; Linfield 2010). A notable example of INGOs' engagement in the latter was *Kony 2012*, a video created by the US-based INGO, Invisible Children Inc., which went viral in 2012. This video repeatedly used the motif of innocent children in order to press for the arrest of the former Ugandan rebel commander, Joseph Kony, who is still wanted by the International Criminal Court on a variety of charges, including the forced recruitment of child soldiers (Akena 2014; Gregory 2012; Nothias 2013b).

However, Scott (2017) has recently performed a comprehensive scoping review which challenges commonly held beliefs about the ways in which Northern news organizations represent Africa. He studied Anglophone research about US and UK news representations of "Africa" published between 1990 and 2014. He concluded that scholars have constructed a "myth" about "media" representations of "Africa" on the basis of research about a very narrow range of media, countries and topics. Specifically, Scott (2017) found that the vast majority of academic research and grey literature focused on print newspapers, news magazines and television, with very few analyzing internet representations, and only one focusing on radio (Wright 2012). These studies also tended to focus on only six out of 56 African countries: South Africa, Rwanda, Sudan, Kenya, Sierra Leone and Somalia. Finally, the range of media topics analyzed in academic studies was also very small: with the majority of writers analyzing media coverage of extreme, negative events, such as the Rwandan genocide of 1994 or the Darfur crisis of 2003–2009.

So it seems that we may actually know far less about how Africa has been represented in Northern news coverage than we thought we did. Indeed, in a recent study of French and British broadsheets, inspired by Scott's work, Nothias (2016), found that the coverage of Africa between 2007 and 2012 was far more nuanced than previous critics had anticipated. Although journalists did tend to conflate different African countries, they rarely mentioned "tribalism" or "darkness", and quoted significant numbers of African speakers, although these participants tended to be framed in subtly disempowering ways. Therefore, academic researchers need to pay more detailed, systemic attention to how journalists actually represent Africa, rather than making over-generalized assumptions on the basis of limited empirical evidence.

What is clear is that the ways in which Africa is reported are changing. Claims about the sporadic and overwhelmingly negative nature of international news about sub-Saharan Africa have long been linked to "fire-fighting" reporting practices, wherein journalists were flown in and expected "to deliver something within days if not hours" (Franks 2005, 132). Such practices were widely seen as problematic because "firefighting" journalists were poorly equipped to explain the complex causes and contexts of crises to media audiences. "Firefighting" approaches to news reporting also involved challenging newsgathering logistics, particularly when the locations in question were expensive and time-consuming for reporters to visit from the main hubs of news production in Nairobi or Johannesburg (Franks 2010). In particular, travelling in some parts of rural Africa involves negotiating patchy travel and communications infrastructure; bureaucratic difficulties in obtaining visas and permits; as well as different languages, cultural traditions, political and military allegiances (Carruthers 2004; Franks 2005; Marthoz 2007).

For these reasons, international aid agencies have long sought to influence news coverage by facilitating journalists' visits to crisis zones. This has included booking them onto UN flights, arranging other kinds of transport, finding accommodation for them, and arranging access to case studies, as well as "fixers" or interpreters (Cooper 2016). Indeed, journalists may be completely "embedded" journalists with aid agencies on foreign trips (Cooper 2016; Cottle and Nolan 2007; Franks 2010, 2013). So some critics view the incorporation of NGO multimedia into mainstream news as an extension of this pre-existing, symbiotic relationship (Cooper 2009; Franks 2013). However, declining news audiences, dwindling advertising revenue, and reduced newsroom budgets make it harder for journalists to justify even these kinds of "assisted" trips to their managers (Kimberley Dozier, CBS reporter, speaking at Frontline Club 2008). In addition, previous rationales for covering African news, such as the movement of previous colonies towards independence and the Cold War, have vanished (Franks 2010).

This means that contemporary news about sub-Saharan countries is now much more likely to be produced by relatively low-paid freelancers (Bunce 2010, 2015) or by journalists working remotely in the headquarters of news organizations (Franks 2010). However, freelancers may feel pressurized into conforming with dominant news norms in order to get commissions from news outlets (Bunce 2010) and remote reporting potentially increases the risk that journalists will seriously misunderstand situations on the ground (Carruthers 2004; Franks 2010; Marthoz 2007). Thus it may be that using content from INGOs with longstanding and extensive local networks can help international news outlets to contextualize faraway events more effectively and/or give more alternative voices and perspectives an airing (Beckett 2008; Powers 2017; Reese 2015). But we need much more empirical research to evaluate whether this is the case.

Away from crisis-driven research, towards heterogeneity

Much like studies about the media representation of Africa, studies of journalists' use of NGO material have tended to involve "negative cherry-picking" (Scott 2014a): focusing on highly negative events, such as hurricanes, tsunamis and famines (e.g. Cooper 2007, 2009, 2011, 2016; Cottle and Nolan 2007; Franks 2013). This is problematic because these kinds of news-making periods are highly likely to be dominated by particular kinds of narrative frames involving "emergency imaginaries", which portray crises as sudden ruptures in an otherwise stable world order (Calhoun 2010). This is because of longstanding representational traditions, but also because of agreements between news organizations and international aid agencies which come into effect at such times.

In the UK, the 13 international aid agencies which are members of the UK's Disasters Emergency Committee (DEC) have an agreement with British-based broadcasters to launch a joint appeal when three criteria are met. These are firstly, that there is a disaster of such scale and urgency that swift international humanitarian assistance is required. Agencies must also be in a position to give such assistance, but there must also be reasonable grounds to expect that a public appeal would be successful, which involves gauging public sympathy (DEC, n.d.). The first signatory to this agreement was the BBC, which agreed to engage in joint appeals with DEC in 1966, following a Turkish earthquake (Franks 2013). Since then, a number of other UK-based broadcasters have joined them, including ITV/ITN, Channel 4, Channel 5, and Sky News. Al Jazeera English, which is based in London, has not formally signed the DEC agreement but has carried DEC appeals on an *ad hoc* basis (interview with Brendan Paddy, DEC Head of Communications, July 6, 2016).

Specifically, these broadcasters allow DEC members to broadcast pre-recorded messages, which are often fronted by celebrities, at peak times (Franks 2013; Sambrook 2015). Although broadcasters may refuse to participate: for example, the BBC did not take part in the Gaza Appeal of 2009, because managers felt that doing so would breach the Corporation's statutory obligations regarding impartiality. But the most important thing about the DEC agreement is that it tends to be interpreted quite broadly by broadcasters, with ITV and ITN often giving aid agencies additional air-time during mainstream programming as well (interview with Brendan Paddy, DEC Head of Communications, July 6, 2016).

Such norms and practices may have ramifications for news-making far beyond the UK, given that the international aid agencies and news organizations involved in the DEC are major, global players, and given that journalists habitually monitor and respond to their competitors' coverage. The DEC is also part of the Emergency Appeals Alliance, which includes sister organizations in nine other countries, including Canada, Germany, Sweden and Japan. These organizations have historically followed the DEC's lead on any joint appeal, although their participation is increasingly shaped by their own members and/or agreements with news media in their own countries. Moreover, at the time of writing in 2017, seven aid agencies in the US had just launched a joint fundraising appeal under the banner of the Global Emergency Response Coalition, following consultations with the DEC. So far, this umbrella group doesn't have a formal agreement with any mainstream news organizations, but it does pitch material to journalists and has partnerships with Google and Twitter.

Franks (2013) is the only scholar to have addressed the effects of the agreements between aid agencies and news organizations in any detail. She analyzes the relationship between DEC and the BBC: using archival evidence and interviews with key actors to demonstrate that the two organizations became much closer during the 1984 Ethiopian famine and the televised music concert, Live Aid. Although this appeal was a financial success, raising millions of pounds to fund a massive relief effort, Franks argues that its effects were deeply problematic. Specifically, she views the appeal as enabling humanitarian agencies to frame news stories about the Ethiopian famine in ways which excluded important political and military contexts. As a result, she concludes, collective responses were poorly judged, missing the epicenter of suffering and delivering aid in ways which inadvertently perpetuated conflict (see also Philo 1993; Rieff 2005).

However, Franks then goes one step further: asserting that the DEC agreement has encouraged journalists to develop an uncritical trust in international aid agencies, which means they continue to privilege aid-workers' interpretations of events—especially in the coverage of sub-Saharan Africa (2008a, 2008b, 2010, 2013). It is an interesting hypothesis, but until now, there wasn't much evidence to prove or disprove it. This was because no one has previously undertaken a study of how and why journalists engage with international aid agencies, or any other NGOs, outside of joint fundraising appeals.

Academic studies have been lacking in this area because it is often very difficult for academics to obtain research access to major news organizations. Managers can be reluctant to expose their organizations to reputational risk, and journalists are often unwilling to speak with researchers. This lack of willingness is shaped to some extent by time pressure, but also by anger and frustration with researchers who regularly condemn news about Africa, without understanding the pressures and constraints involved in news production (Wrong 2017). Yet the lack of research into journalists' uses of NGO material creates a vicious circle, as the absence of data about journalistic perspectives and practices means that academic understanding of these kinds of news production remains partial, fragmented and poorly contextualized. As a former journalist with a background in African news production, I am in a better position than most to gain the research access needed to gather this missing empirical data.

Analyzing journalists' responses to aid agencies outside of joint appeals is also important if we want to explore how the differences between these INGOs may impact upon news-making. Both Powers (2014) and Orgad (2013, 2015) stress the need to avoid over-generalizing about aid agencies' approach. Instead, they advise scholars to acknowledge the ways in which aid agencies' approach to mediation is constantly re/shaped by multiple tensions, which exist within and between such humanitarian organizations.

In particular, Orgad (2013) discusses the differences between "chemical" aid agencies, which seek to prioritize immediate humanitarian relief and "alchemical" agencies, which prioritize exposing and challenging the structural causes of suffering. Both Orgad (2013) and Powers (2014) then discuss the necessity of attending to internal tensions within aid agencies, including conflicts between INGOs' advocacy and fundraising teams. They therefore conclude that aid agencies' media strategies tend to emerge from complicated internal conflicts, negotiations and compromises, which aren't always visible to outsiders.

In addition, examining journalists' use of NGO-provided multimedia outside of major appeal periods offers us a better opportunity to examine journalists' interactions with other kinds of NGOs. This is important because Powers' work on US-based INGOs (2013, 2014) provides evidence to suggest that INGOs have different media strategies. Specifically, he argues that human rights organizations tend to target elite news outlets in order to try and influence policy-makers via the niche media they consume (2013, 2014). In contrast, he argues, international aid agencies tend to target popular news outlets in order to engage in public fundraising, as well as fulfilling advocacy goals relating to mass education (Powers 2013, 2014).

Moreover, examining a quiet news period makes it more likely that we will find examples of journalists' engagement with other kinds of NGOs, which may be more diverse and potentially more time-consuming to contact— including sub-Saharan NGOs. This is important because research conducted in Latin America suggests that NGO-journalist coalitions there can be much more heterogeneous: having complex, and often mixed, effects (McPherson 2015a, 2015b; Waisbord 2011). Certainly, a number of sub-Saharan INGOs are active in news-making, like the Treatment Action Campaign, an HIV advocacy group based in South Africa, and AMREF, a health development organization, which has offices in Ethiopia, Kenya, South Sudan, Tanzania and Uganda (Davies 2013; Jones 2017). Scores of smaller local and national NGOs are also springing up all the time in sub-Saharan countries: covering issues as diverse as the environment, disability, microfinance and social entrepreneurship (Davies 2013; Igoe and Kelsall 2005).

Furthermore, analyzing a quiet news period gives us an opportunity to interrogate whether other kinds of normative values shape the interactions between journalists and NGOs. This is important because of the stress which many journalists and NGO-workers place on their desire to improve news about Africa. So their exchanges with one another seem not to only be driven by economic imperatives, but also by normative ideas about what constitutes "good" news coverage of the continent. This then relates to my final point: that is, that avoiding sampling during joint appeal periods helps us to ascertain whether NGOs really do promote endlessly negative depictions of Africa through the news (Hawk 1992; Lugo-Ocando and Malaolu 2014), or whether they help to create different, more inclusive and/or progressive narratives about sub-Saharan countries.

There is some evidence to suggest that some NGOs are already engaging in some forms of deliberate positivism (Dogra 2012). For example, Oxfam's "See Africa Differently" campaign, highlighted the beauty of different African landscapes (Scott 2014b). Other positivistic campaigns run by INGOs have stressed the agency and "dignity" of African people, as well as expressing hope for the future of the continent (Scott 2014b; Yanacopulos 2015). But although such campaigns may appear to be a refreshing change, these INGOs have been accused of using positive stereotypes and over-generalized statements about Africa in order to generate feel-good marketing campaigns aimed at jaded international donors (Dogra 2012).

Such NGO campaigns also appear to have been influenced by the deliberately positive "Africa Rising" narratives disseminated in more recent forms of international news (Bunce et al. 2017; Nothias 2014). Much like positivistic INGO campaigns, these kinds of news representations appear to oppose Afro-pessimism by concentrating on economic growth, self-help, refugees returning after the end of civil war, and the rapid spread of mobile phones and social media (Nothias 2014). But "Africa Rising" news narratives have been criticized as the flip-side of Afro-pessimism. This is because they may appear to be more progressive and empowering, but they still use racist stereotypes and totalizing strategies in order to measure sub-Saharan countries' "progress" in terms of their acceptance of Northern neoliberal economic policies (Nothias 2014).

The emergence of seemingly "positive" news and NGO representations of sub-Saharan countries do not appear to have led to the death of Afro-pessimism in news coverage. Instead, research suggests that both news and NGO media output now contain a mixture of positive, negative and neutral frames (Bunce 2017; Dogra 2012; Ojo 2014). But a critical alertness to NGOs' involvement in the creation of "Africa Rising" narratives prompts us to look for the presence of NGO material in different kinds of news stories about sub-Saharan countries—not just reports about disasters and other crises.

In addition, more recent work on "Africa Rising" narratives helps to move us away from binary conceptualizations of NGO-journalist relations and towards an analysis of the multidirectional flows of influence shaping newsmaking about the continent. For in addition to INGOs and NGOs, multinational businesses, private foundations, diasporic media, freelancers and social media participants have all been found to play important roles in shaping the creation and dissemination of more "positive" news representations of "Africa" (Bunce *et al.* 2017; Grayson 2014; Ogunyemi 2017).

Finally, there is some evidence to suggest that the correspondents, freelancers and semi-freelance stringers who work for Northern news organizations engage in dialogue with sub-Saharan actors via social media. This includes them taking more participatory approaches to news production and responding to others' criticisms of the overly negative or stereotypical coverage of Africa (Nothias 2014, 2017; Vicente 2013, 2017). The most famous example of this was when Kenyans objected *en masse* to a series of reports broadcast by CNN, including one which called their country a "hotbed of terror", using the Twitter hashtag, #SomeoneTellCNN (Bunce 2010; Nothias 2017; Nyabola 2017).

For these reasons, I didn't begin this book by assuming that I would find uniform, negative constructions of "Africa" imposed on sub-Saharan people by Northern journalists (Mudimbe 1988, 1994). Nor did I assume that media representations produced by sub-Saharan actors would necessarily pose a more positive, liberatory or "authentic" alternative (Mengara 2001), given the relational, and often contested, nature of mediated discourse (Gallagher 2015). Instead, I intended to explore the various roles played by multiple media producers within and outside of sub-Saharan countries; interrogating the kinds of collaboration and struggle shaping their mutual engagement in the production of international news about "Africa".

This book

In order to do this, I asked a number of questions. Why do mainstream journalists use multimedia provided by NGOs in the news coverage of sub-Saharan countries? Why do NGOs produce, commission or curate it? How does this material reach journalists? How is it incorporated into news coverage? And finally, what are the effects of these exchanges on journalism, NGO-work and the mediated representations of "Africa" made available to UK audiences?

Undertaking a comprehensive study of the coverage of all sub-Saharan studies would clearly be beyond the scope of one book. So instead, I discuss five contrasting case studies about the production of different items about Chad, the Democratic Republic of Congo (DRC), Kenya, Mali and South Sudan. These media items were published by different kinds of news organizations in different genres, contained within different sorts of media, yet they all contained photos or video produced by different sorts of NGOs, including major INGOs and one sub-Saharan NGO. They were drawn from a bigger sample of 23 items about sub-Saharan Africa which contained NGO-provided multimedia: all of which appeared in the broadcast, online and print news made available to UK audiences.

To avoid replicating a critical focus on the joint fundraising appeals studied by other researchers, I chose a different kind of sampling period. This was a relatively "quiet" news week (13–19 August 2012), which fell between the London Olympic and Paralympic Games, and outside of any joint fundraising appeals, parliamentary sessions, major international summits or conferences. A variety of checks were used to identify poorly-attributed items and straplines and/or the on-air attribution of journalists were then used to trace back and conduct 57 semi-structured interviews with those who took key decisions shaping the production of these news items. These included European and North American journalists, NGO-workers, managers and freelancers. Most of these participants have agreed to be named, so acknowledging the importance of their personal agency. But I have anonymized some participants at their request or because of risks to their security or livelihoods.

This extraordinary access was enabled by my contacts in NGO-work and my "insider" status within journalism. Indeed, this book contains the first major study about the ways in which journalists use NGO content at major Northern news organizations. However, in order to avoid excluding the perspectives and labor of those working in sub-Saharan countries (Mosco and Lavin 2009; Shome and Hegde 2002), I also sought out actors based in these countries who played important roles Thus I have conducted the first study which tracks such production processes from the perspectives of multiple actors in the Global North and the South.

I minimized the risk that I would inadvertently shape the emergence of post-hoc rationales by triangulating actors' accounts of each other's deliberations, decisions and actions at the time. I also triangulated interview data with written internal reports, personal correspondence, trip briefs and editing notes, as well as relevant staffing and financial figures, which were given to me by these participants. Finally, I conducted multimodal analyses of the texts themselves: interrogating how journalists' and NGO-workers' framing of their relationship/s with each other related to the ways in which sub-Saharan "Africa" is constructed in news texts (Caple and Knox 2012, 2015; Entman 1993; Goffman 1986; Stones 2014, 2015). In this way, I have sought to address Scott's complaints (2017): namely that research about news coverage of "Africa" tends to divorce textual analysis from production studies, as well focusing on an overly narrow range of media, countries and extreme, negative events.

I found that during "quiet" news periods, journalists used the photos and video produced, commissioned or curated by NGOs to represent a wide variety of different sub-Saharan countries. These news texts also differed from the ones previously studied, which were news leads about major famines, hurricanes and other disasters (Cooper 20-16; Cottle and Nolan 2007; Franks 2013). Instead, the texts I found were lower-ranking items, including relatively long-form investigative news reports, as well as photo-slideshows, blogs and soft, upbeat features.

This book also differs from other studies as NGOs' exchanges with journalists were found to be far more complex and varied than they were previously believed to be. This was because NGOs did not always pitch material directly to news outlets (Fenton 2010a; Franks 2013: Powers 2014). Instead, NGO material tended to arrive at news outlets via indirect routes involving third parties, such as social media participants, interns, and, most importantly, freelancers.

Unlike in other studies, the freelancers in this book were not based within the continent, nor were they from sub-Saharan countries themselves (Bunce 2010, 2015). Instead, they were all European or North American, and were well-respected by those working for INGOs and news outlets because of their specialism in particular geographic areas, or particular media—either photography or film-making. Most worked on commission for both INGOs and news outlets: sometimes taking commissions in quick succession and sometimes running them concurrently. This tended to involve them reversioning material commissioned for NGOs for news outlets. But they could also syndicate multimedia back and forth between news outlets and INGOs at a much later date (Wright 2016a, 2016b).

However, other kinds of actors were also important in shaping NGO-journalist interactions, including private foundations and trusts, social media participants and commercial advertising and PR agencies. For these reasons, this book engages critically with the often complex economies which shaped these heterogeneous forms of production. Yet an attention to the political economies of these exchanges was not sufficient to explain their characteristics or effects. This was because different kinds of powerful, normative values were a prominent feature of these forms of news-making, and these were usually embedded in actors' understandings of their obligations to others.

Some of these obligations were formal: for instance, journalists working for Public Service Broadcasters often discussed their use of NGOs' material in relation to their statutory responsibilities. Some NGOs also commissioned multimedia to meet the project reporting requirements of their donors. Media producers with full-time jobs in NGOs and news outlets also had numerous organizational responsibilities: to their managers, colleagues, and audiences. But all of these media producers also engaged in exchanges with one another because of their moral, political and professional values. These were imbricated in actors' informal, but often passionately felt, understandings of their obligations to others—and to their sense of moral conscience.

The normative values underpinning actors' understandings of their responsibilities often pertained to broader ideas about what constituted good journalism, good NGO-work and appropriate representations of Africa. Such normative values were tremendously important in actors' decision-making processes. Sometimes normative values even modified economic imperatives to work faster and more cheaply, albeit in ways which tended to feed back into branding and market positioning. Normative values were also found to be vital in constructing the trust needed to facilitate exchanges. Although this trust was sometimes constructed indirectly via third parties in ways which allowed both journalists and NGO-workers to disavow too close a connection with one another.

Finally, changes in actors' normative values—which frequently occurred after their exchanges with one another—were found to play a vital role in the renegotiation of boundaries. This boundary work involved the construction of imagined relations of concern across geographic boundaries, as well as the renegotiation of boundaries between the fields of NGO-work, journalism and other fields of activity (Carlson and Lewis 2015; Powers 2015). For these reasons, I talk about the interlinked moral economies, as well as the political economies, of these kinds of news-making practices: viewing the recursive relationships between the two as having profound implications for NGO-work, journalism and mediated knowledge about Africa.

Chapter map

The next chapter begins by defining NGOs and outlining the key arguments for and against using NGO content in mainstream news. I'll look first at critical arguments about its impact on journalism before turning to debates about its influence on NGO-work. I'll then outline more recent research on the homologies between NGOs and journalists, as well as discussing NGOs' and journalists' mutual engagement in the construction of different journalistic logics. Finally, I will move beyond organizationally-bounded approaches to discuss how we think about the involvement of multiple actors, including freelancers.

In so doing, I identify many of the theoretical concepts which shaped my critical approach, criticizing and refining them where appropriate. This discussion then leads into the Chapter 3, which deals with the thorny issue of how to ground normative evaluation in post-colonial contexts, before embarking on an explanation of what moral economy theory is, and how it relates to this study in more detail. The following five chapters discuss the case studies themselves: beginning with those found in legacy media, produced primarily for domestic audiences, before turning to online outlets which were geared towards international audiences.

Chapter 4 focuses on a double page spread on a hunger crisis in Mali, which was published as a "World News" article in the British broadsheet, *The Independent on Sunday*. This was a lengthy report, written entirely by the Head of Media at the international aid agency, Christian Aid, who had previously been the editor of another British Sunday broadsheet. It also contained a number of pictures, taken by an experienced freelance photojournalist who had been hired by the INGO, but who had previously been a member of staff at *The Independent*.

In particular, this chapter discusses how and why the production process involved collaboration between highly experienced "old hands" in print journalism, who were employed variously in the news outlet, as a freelancer, and for the INGO. Together, these "old hands" tried to uphold normative ideas about professionalism and the progressive potential of photojournalism, despite severe financial difficulties. These difficulties were caused by serious drops in income at both organizations, which managers responded to by making redundancies and organizational restructuring. Staff at both organizations were also seriously concerned with questions of branding and market posi-

tioning, as well as minimizing risks to their personal and organizational reputations at a time of great insecurity.

Chapter 5 then discusses a different case, involving a report which cam-
paigned for the arrest of a Congolese rebel commander, wanted for war crimes
by the International Criminal Court. This report was broadcast by the TV
program, *Channel 4 News* and included a short clip of video footage which
the US-based INGO, Human Rights Watch, bought from two freelancers.
This clip was pitched to *Channel 4 News* by a third freelancer, who obtained
commissions from both the INGO and the news program. The contribution
made by the INGO was not attributed in the piece, which was also indirectly
influenced by Amnesty International and Invisible Children Inc., the makers
of *Kony 2012*.

So this chapter discusses how and why the norms of multiple human rights
INGOs interacted with ideas of witnessing in mainstream news. In so doing,
it highlights the relevance of participants' reflections about their extensive
experiences of reporting on deeply unequal wars, as well as the normative synergies between their organizations. In particular, it demonstrates how journalists came to conceptualize public service news as "human rights journalism",
whilst INGO-workers' perceived themselves as engaging in "proper reporting", which was not commercially driven and which had important public
purposes. However, the chapter also attends to journalists' and NGO-workers'
efforts to deny too close a relationship with one another: using freelancing as
a means of sustaining claims about their independence.

The following chapters discuss journalists' use of INGO-provided photos
in the creation of online genres for international news audiences. Chapter 6
is about the production of a "human interest" audio slideshow published by
BBC News Online. This was about a former child soldier in South Sudan,
who had returned to his village after the civil war appeared to have ended.
The slideshow was constructed through a collaborative production process,
which involved photos provided by a media producer employed as a member
of staff by the international aid organization, Save the Children UK. Whilst
the audio was provided by a BBC journalist embedded with the INGO on a
trip to a rural area.

In particular, this case study attends to the ways in which production
processes were shaped by ideas about the relationship of mediation to education, as well as highly commercialized practices of "promoting" or "selling in"
stories. It focuses on the pronounced tensions which characterized this production process, which involved members of the INGO's press office coopting

more radical approaches present elsewhere in aid agency. But it also details the argument that took place between representatives of the INGO and BBC journalists. In so doing, this chapter illuminates tensions between different approaches to humanitarianism within Save the Children, as well as the efforts of BBC staff to produce visually distinctive, "clickable" images, without contravening the Corporation's editorial guidelines regarding impartiality.

Next, Chapter 7 analyzes the production of a blog which was published by *The Guardian* website about a group of radio stations in Chad, which were run for refugees from the Darfur conflict by the US-based INGO, Internews. The INGO claims to foster independent media and access to information, so its senior managers thought it was appropriate to hire two freelancers to produce a quasi-journalistic report for institutional donors about the project. This was a "legacy report" which celebrated what the project had achieved, even though donors had withdrawn their funding. However, freelancers reversioned this material for a blog, published in the Global Development section of *The Guardian's* website.

As Internews and the Global Development site are both funded by the Bill and Melinda Gates Foundation, this chapter analyzes how and why a relatively closed system of meaning was created and justified in relation to ideas about transparency, participation and the creation of digital, dialogic communities. In this way, it highlights how financial incentives work together with normative ideas to entrench particular, dominant approaches to "international development", despite the lack of any conspiracy to this effect.

Finally, Chapter 8 discusses an example of journalists' use of NGO content in uplifting features about African people appearing to "help themselves" through the power of social media. It focuses on the production of a photo taken as part of a fundraising campaign for a small sub-Saharan NGO called the Kenyan Paraplegic Organization. This image was reproduced by many different news outlets, including Al Jazeera, the BBC, the *Washington Post* and Kenya's *The Nation*. However, this chapter focuses on journalists working at the Sunday version of *The Guardian* newspaper, *The Observer*, as well as on the website *Guardian.co.uk*, as this coverage fell within the week sampled.

This case is particularly interesting because journalists assumed that using material from an African NGO would be more progressive and empowering than using material produced by one of the big "commercialized" INGOs. But the concerns of lower-ranking NGO members were marginalized in production processes, which were dominated by leading figures in the NGO and expat creatives working for multinational advertising, marketing and PR agencies. This was because the campaign was created under the auspices of a Corporate Social Responsibility program, run by Safaricom, a multinational telecommunications company which wanted to promote its cash transfer platform, M-PESA, and improve its public image after a major international fraud scandal. So together, Kenyan and expat elites created a campaign heavily influenced by forms of commercial nationalism which appealed to Northern journalists keen to avoid negative stereotypes about passive, African victims, and sympathetic to "Africa Rising" narratives.

Therefore this book moves away from a binary approach to NGO-journalist relations, interrogating heterogeneous and often complex moral economies, which involved multiple ideas of the good, just or simply appropriate. Such moral economies focused on the production of particular kinds of visual imagery which had decidedly mixed effects. But before I go on to discuss what these were, I need to explain how I define NGOs, and why I think that moral economy theory is better suited to interrogating their engagement in news-making than existing theoretical models.

Note

1. The Frontline Club is an influential, members-only society for media practitioners interested in international news, which is based in London, but sometimes holds events in New York.

References

Abbott, Kimberly. "NGO Communications in the New Media Ecology: How NGOs Became the 'New(s) Reporters.'" In *Humanitarianism, Communications and Change*, edited by Simon Cottle and Glenda Cooper, 183–93. New York: Peter Lang, 2015.

Akena, Francis Adyanga. "Pornography and the Entrenchment of Western Hegemony: Deconstructing the Kony 2012 Video." *Socialist Studies/Études Socialistes* 10, no. 1 (2014): 50–66.

Anderson, Monica. "At Newspapers, Photographers Feel the Brunt of Job Cuts". *Pew Research Center*, November 11, 2013.

http://www.pewresearch.org/fact-tank/2013/11/11/at-newspapers-photographers-feel-the-brunt-of-job-cuts/.

Argles, Martin. "The Future of Photography." Speech given at meeting of National Union of Journalists' London Photographer's Branch, June 15, 2013.

Bardan, Alexandra. "The Dual Model of the Digital Photo Journalist: A Case Study on Romanian Photojournalism beyond the Economic Crisis." *Journal of Media Research* 8, no. 1 (2015): 19–40.

Barnhurst, Kevin G. "The Form of Reports on US Newspaper Internet Sites, an Update." *Journalism Studies* 11, no. 4 (2010): 555–66.

Beckett, Charlie. *SuperMedia: Saving Journalism so It Can Save the World*. London: Blackwell, 2008.

Beckett, Charlie, and Robin Mansell. "Crossing Boundaries: New Media and Networked Journalism." *Communication, Culture and Critique* 1, no. 1 (2008): 92–104.

Beer, Arnold S. de. "Looking for Journalism Education Scholarship in Some Unusual Places: The Case of Africa." *Communicatio: South African Journal for Communication Theory and Research* 36, no. 2 (2010a): 213–26.

———. "News from and in 'the Dark Continent': Afro-Pessimism, News Flows, Global Journalism and Media Regimes." *Journalism Studies* 11, no. 4 (2010b): 596–609.

Boyd-Barrett, Oliver. "National News Agencies in the Turbulent Era of the Internet." In *National News Agencies in the Turbulent Era of the Internet*, edited by Oliver Boyd-Barrett, 16–44. Barcelona: Government of Catalonia, 2010.

Brock, George. *Out of Print: Newspapers, Journalism and the Business of News in the Digital Age*. London, New York: Kogan Page Publishers, 2013.

Brookes, Heather Jean. "Suit, Tie and a Touch of Juju'—the Ideological Construction of Africa: A Critical Discourse Analysis of News on Africa in the British Press." *Discourse & Society* 6, no. 4 (1995): 461–94.

Bunce, Mel. "'This Place Used to Be a White British Boys' Club': Reporting Dynamics and Cultural Clash at an International News Bureau in Nairobi." *The Round Table* 99, no. 410 (2010): 515–28.

———. "Africa's Media Image: New Storytellers, New Narratives?" In *Images of Africa: Creation, Negotiation and Subversion*, edited by Julia Gallagher, 42–62. Manchester: Manchester University Press, 2015.

———. "The International News Coverage of Africa: Beyond the 'Single Story'." In *Africa's Media Image in the 21st Century: From the "Heart of Darkness" to "Africa Rising,"* edited by Mel Bunce, Suzanne Franks, and Chris Paterson, 17–29. Abingdon, Oxon: Routledge, 2017.

Bunce, Mel, Suzanne Franks, and Chris Paterson. *Africa's Media Image in the 21st Century: From the "Heart of Darkness" to "Africa Rising."* Abingdon, Oxon: Routledge, 2017.

Burman, Erica. "Innocents Abroad: Western Fantasies of Childhood and the Iconography of Emergencies." *Disasters* 18, no. 3 (1994): 238–53.

Calhoun, Craig. *The Idea of Emergency: Humanitarian Action and Global (dis) Order*. New York: Zone Books, 2010.

Campbell, David. "Geopolitics and Visuality: Sighting the Darfur Conflict." *Political Geography* 26, no. 4 (2007): 357–82.

Caple, Helen, and John S. Knox. "Online News Galleries, Photojournalism and the Photo Essay." *Visual Communication* 11, no. 2 (2012): 207–36.

———. "A Framework for the Multimodal Analysis of Online News Galleries: What Makes a 'Good' Picture Gallery?" *Social Semiotics* 25, no. 3 (2015): 292–321.

Carlson, Matt, and Seth C. Lewis, eds. *Boundaries of Journalism: Professionalism, Practices and Participation*. London, New York: Routledge, 2015.

Carruthers, Susan. "Tribalism and Tribulation: Media Constructions of 'African Savagery' and Western Humanitarianism in the 1990s." In *Reporting War: Journalism in Wartime*, edited by Stuart Allan and Barbie Zelizer, 155–73. Oxford: Routledge, 2004.

Chouliaraki, Lilie. *The Spectatorship of Suffering*. London: Sage, 2006.

Cooper, Glenda. "From Their Own Correspondent." *The Guardian*, 5 November 2007.

———. "When the Lines between NGO and News Organization Blur'. Special Report: NGOs and the News." *Nieman Journalism Lab*, December 21, 2009. http://www.niemanlab.org/2009/12/glenda-cooper-when-lines-between-ngo-and-news-organization-blur/.

———. *From Their Own Correspondent? New Media and the Changes in Disaster Coverage: Lessons to Be Learned*. Oxford: Reuters Institute for the Study of Journalism, 2011.

———. "'Give Us Your F***ing Money': A Critical Appraisal of TV and the Cash Nexus." In *Humanitarianism, Communications and Change*, edited by Simon Cottle and Glenda Cooper, 67–78. New York: Peter Lang, 2015.

———. "From Our Own Correspondents? How User Generated Content Has Altered Power Dynamics in Reporting Humanitarian Disasters." City University, 2016.

Cottle, Simon, and David Nolan. "Global Humanitarianism and the Changing Aid-Media Field: Everyone Was Dying for Footage." *Journalism Studies* 8, no. 6 (2007): 862–78.

Coundouriotis, Eleni. "The Child Soldier Narrative and the Problem of Arrested Historicization." *Journal of Human Rights* 9, no. 2 (2010): 191–206.

Currah, Andrew. *What's Happening to Our News: An Investigation into the Likely Impact of the Digital Revolution on the Economics of News Publishing in the UK*. Oxford: Reuters Institute for the Study of Journalism, 2009.

De B'béri, Boulou Ebanda de, and P. Eric Louw. "Afropessimism: A Genealogy of Discourse." *Critical Arts* 25, no. 3 (2011): 335–46.

Davies, Thomas. *NGOs: A New History of Transnational Civil Society*. London: Hurst and Company, 2013.

Denčik, Lina and Stuart Allan. "In/visible conflicts: NGO and the visual politics of humanitarian photography." *Media, Culture and Society* (2017) Online First doi:10.1177/0163443717726865

Disasters Emergency Committee. "Appeal Criteria." *Disasters Emergency Committee*, n.d. https://www.dec.org.uk/article/when-we-launch-an-appeal.

Dogra, Nandita. *Representations of Global Poverty: Aid, Development and International NGOs*. Library of Development Studies, vol. 6. London, New York: I.B. Tauris; Palgrave Macmillan, 2012.

———. "International NGOs, Global Poverty, and the Representations of Children." In *Humanitarianism, Communications and Change*, edited by Simon Cottle and Glenda Cooper, 103–16. New York: Peter Lang, 2015.

Doty, Roxanne Lynn. *Imperial Encounters: The Politics of Representation in North-South Relations*. Vol. 5. Minneapolis, MN: University of Minnesota Press, 1996.

Douzinas, Costas. *Human Rights and Empire: The Political Philosophy of Cosmopolitanism*. London: Routledge-Cavendish, 2007.

Duffield, Mark. "The Symphony of the Damned: Racial Discourse, Complex Political Emergencies and Humanitarian Aid." *Disasters* 20, no. 3 (1996): 173–93.

Dunn, Kevin. *Imagining the Congo: The International Relations of Identity.* New York: Palgrave Macmillan, 2003.

Entman, Robert M. "Framing: Toward Clarification of a Fractured Paradigm." *Journal of Communication* 43, no. 4 (1993): 51–58.

Fair, Jo Ellen. "War, Famine, and Poverty: Race in the Construction of Africa's Media Image." *Journal of Communication Inquiry* 17, no. 2 (1993): 5–22.

Fehrenbach, Heide, and Davide Rodogno, eds. *Humanitarian Photography: A History.* Cambridge: Cambridge University Press, 2015.

Fenton, Natalie. "NGOs, New Media and the Mainstream News: News from Everywhere." In *New Media, Old News: Journalism & Democracy in the Digital Age*, edited by Natalie Fenton, 153–68. London: Sage, 2010a.

———. *New Media, Old News.* London: Sage, 2010b.

Franks, Suzanne. "Reporting Africa: Problems and Perspectives." *Westminster Papers in Communication.* November (2005): 129–134

———. "Aid Agencies: Are We Trusting Too Much?" *The Political Quarterly* 79, no. 3 (2008a): 316–18.

———. "Getting into Bed with Charity." *British Journalism Review* 19, no. 3 (2008b): 27–32.

———. "The Neglect of Africa and the Power of Aid." *Communication Gazette* 72, no. 1 (2010): 71–84.

———. *Reporting Disasters: Famine, Aid, Politics and the Media.* London: Hurst Publishers, 2013.

———. "From Pictures to Policy: How Does Humanitarian Reporting Have an Influence?" In *Humanitarianism, Communications and Change*, edited by Simon Cottle and Glenda Cooper, 153–66. New York: Peter Lang, 2015.

French, Howard. "Media Perspectives: How Does Africa Get Reported? A Letter of Concern to 60 Minutes." In *Africa's Media Image in the Twenty-First Century: From the Heart of Darkness to Africa Rising*, edited by Mel Bunce, Suzanne Franks, and Chris Paterson, 38–39. Abingdon, Oxon: Routledge, 2017.

Frontline Club. *The News Carers: Are Aid Groups Doing Too Much Real Newsgathering?* New York, 28 February 2008. https://www.frontlineclub.com/the_news_carers_are_aid_groups_doing_too_much_real_newsgathering_-_new_york_-_fully_booked/

———. *Aid and the Media.* London. January 26, 2011. https://www.frontlineclub.com/aid_and_the_media_a_troubled_relationship/

———. *Embedding with Aid Agencies: Editorial Integrity and Security Risks.* London, February 10, 2015. https://www.frontlineclub.com/embedding-with-aid-agencies-editorial-integrity-and-security-risks/

Gallagher, Julia. "Theorising Image—A Relational Approach." In *Images of Africa: Creation, Negotiation and Subversion*, edited by Julia Gallagher, 1–20. Manchester, UK: Manchester University Press, 2015.

Galtung, Johan, and Mari Holmboe Ruge. "The Structure of Foreign News the Presentation of the Congo, Cuba and Cyprus Crises in Four Norwegian Newspapers." *Journal of Peace Research* 2, no. 1 (1965): 64–90.

Goffman, Erving. *Frame Analysis: An Essay on the Organization of Experience*. Boston, MA: Northeastern University Press, 1986.

Grayson, Louise. "The Role of Non-Government Organisations (NGOS) in Practising Editorial Photography in a Globalised Media Environment." *Journalism Practice* 8, no. 5 (2014): 632–45.

Gregory, Sam. "Kony 2012 through a Prism of Video Advocacy Practices and Trends." *Journal of Human Rights Practice* 4, no. 3 (2012): 463–68.

Hallas, Roger. "Photojournalism, NGOs and the New Media Ecology." In *Sensible Politics: The Visual Culture of Nongovernmental Activism*, edited by Meg McLagan and Yates McKee. New York: Zone Books, 2012.

Hamilton, James T. "The (many) Markets for International News: How News from Abroad Sells at Home." *Journalism Studies* 11, no. 5 (2010): 650–66.

Harcup, Tony, and O'Neill, Deirdre. "What Is News? News Values Revisited (Again)." *Journalism Studies* 2, no. 2 (2016): 1–19.

Hawk, Beverly G. *Africa's Media Image*. New York, Westport, CT, London: Praeger, 1992.

Hendy, David. *Public Service Broadcasting*. New York: Palgrave Macmillan, 2013.

Höijer, Birgitta. "The Discourse of Global Compassion: The Audience and Media Reporting of Human Suffering." *Media, Culture & Society* 26, no. 4 (2004): 513–31.

Ibelema, Minabere. "Tribes and Prejudice: Coverage of the Nigerian Civil War." In *Africa's Media Image*, edited by Beverly Hawk G., 77–93. New York, Westport, CT, London: Praeger, 1992.

———. "Tribal Fixation' and Africa's Otherness Changes and Resilience in News Coverage." *Journalism & Communication Monographs* 16, no. 3 (2014): 162–217.

Igoe, Jim, and Tim Kelsall. *Between a Rock and a Hard Place: African NGOs, Donors and the State*. Durham, NC: Carolina Academic Press, 2005.

Jayawardane, M. Neelika. "Problem with Photojournalism and Africa." *Al Jazeera.com*, January 18, 2017.http://www.aljazeera.com/indepth/opinion/2017/01/problem-photojournalism-africa-170118085814572.html

Jones, Ben. "Looking Good: Mediatisation and International NGOs." *European Journal of Development Research* 29, no. 1 (2017): 176–91.

Keck, Margaret E., and Kathryn Sikkink. *Activists beyond Borders: Advocacy Networks in International Politics*. Ithaca, NY: Cornell University Press, 1998.

Kennedy, Denis. "Selling the Distant Other: Humanitarianism and Imagery—Ethical Dilemmas of Humanitarian Action." *The Journal of Humanitarian Assistance* 28 (2009). https://sites.tufts.edu/jha/archives/411

Klein-Avraham, Inbal, and Zvi Reich. "Out of the Frame: A Longitudinal Perspective on Digitization and Professional Photojournalism." *New Media & Society* 18, no. 3 (2016): 429–46.

Lidichi, Helen. "Finding the Right Image: British Development NGOs and the Regulation of Imagery." In *Culture and Global Change*, edited by Tim Skelton and Tracey Allen, 87–101. London: Routledge, 1999.

Linfield, Susie. *The Cruel Radiance: Photography and Political Violence*. Chicago, IL: University of Chicago Press, 2010.

Lugo-Ocando, Jairo, and Patrick O. Malaolu. "Africa—That Scar on Our Face." In *Blaming the Victim: How Global Journalism Fails Those in Poverty*, Jairo Lugo-Ocando, 85–103. London: Pluto Press, 2014.

Magee, Helen. *The East African Famine: Did the Media Get It Right?* London: International Broadcasting Trust, 2011.

Manzo, Kate. "An Extension of Colonialism? Development Education, Images and the Media." *Development Education Journal* 12, no. 2 (2006): 9–12.

———. "Imaging Humanitarianism: NGO Identity and the Iconography of Childhood." *Antipode* 40, no. 4 (2008): 632–57.

Marthoz, Jean-Paul. "African Conflicts in the Global Media." In *The Media and Conflicts in Central Africa*, edited by Marie-Soleil Frère, 221–39. Boulder, CO: Lynne Rienner, 2007.

McLagan, Meg, and Yates McKee. "Introduction." In *Sensible Politics: The Visual Culture of Nongovernmental Activism*, edited by Meg McLagan and Yates McKee, 9–26. New York: Zone Books, 2012.

McNulty, Mel. "Media Ethnicization and the International Response to War and Genocide in Rwanda." In *The Media of Conflict: War Reporting and Representations of Ethnic Violence*, edited by Tim Allen and Jean Seaton, 268–286. London: Zed Books, 1999.

McPherson, Ella. "Advocacy Organizations' Evaluation of Social Media Information for NGO Journalism—The Evidence and Engagement Models." *American Behavioral Scientist* 59, no. 1 (2015a): 124–48.

———. "Surmounting the Verification Barrier Between the Field of Professional Human Rights Fact-Finding and the Non-Field of Digital Civilian Witnessing," 2015b. https://www.repository.cam.ac.uk/handle/1810/248302.

Mengara, Daniel M. *Images of Africa*. Trenton, NJ: Africa World Press, 2001.

Mody, Bella. *The Geopolitics of Representation in Foreign News: Explaining Darfur*. Plymouth: Lexington Books, 2010.

Moore, Martin. *Shrinking World: The Decline of International Reporting in the British Press 1979–2009*. London: Media Standards Trust, 2010.

Mosco, Vincent, and David O. Lavin. "The Labouring of International Communication." In *Internationalizing Media Studies*, edited by Daya K. Thussu, 147–62. London: Routledge, 2009.

Mudimbe, V. Y. *The Invention of Africa: Gnosis, Philosophy, and the Order of Knowledge*. Bloomington, IN: Indiana University Press, 1988.

———. *The Idea of Africa*. Bloomington, IN: Indiana Press, 1994.

Mutua, Makau W. "Savages, Victims, and Saviors: The Metaphor of Human Rights." *Harvard International Law Journal* 42, no. 1 (2001): 201–45.

Nauta, Wiebe, and Ludek Stavinoha. "Framing AIDS in Times of Global Crisis: 'Wasting' Africa Yet Again?" *Globalizations* 9, no. 5 (2012): 695–711.

Newman, Nic, and David Levy. *Reuters Institute Digital News Report 2012*. Oxford: Reuters Institute for the Study of Journalism, 2012.

Newman, Nic, David Levy, and Rasmus K. Nielsen. *Reuters Institute Digital News Report 2015*. Oxford: Reuters Institute for the Study of Journalism, 2014.

Nothias, Toussaint. "Definition and Scope of Afro-Pessimism: Mapping the Concept and Its Usefulness for Analysing News Media Coverage of Africa." *Leeds African Studies Bulletin* 75 (2013a): 54–62.

———. "'It's Struck a Chord We Have Never Managed to Strike': Frames, Perspectives and Remediation Strategies in the International News Coverage of Kony2012." *Ecquid Novi: African Journalism Studies* 34, no. 1 (2013b): 123–29.

———. "'Rising', 'Hopeful', 'New': Visualizing Africa in the Age of Globalization." *Visual Communication* 13, no. 3 (2014): 323–39.

———. "How Western Journalists Actually Write about Africa." *Journalism Studies* (2016): 1–22. DOI:10.1080/1461670X.2016.1262748.

———. "Mediating the Distant Other for the Distant Audience: How Do Western Correspondents in East and Southern Africa Perceive Their Audience?" In *Africa's Media Image in the Twenty-First Century: From the Heart of Darkness to Africa Rising*, edited by Mel Bunce, Suzanne Franks, and Chris Paterson, 73–82. Abingdon, Oxon: Routledge, 2017.

Nyabola, H. Nanjala. "Media Perspectives: Social Media and New Narratives: Kenyans Tweet Back." In *Africa's Media Image in the Twenty-First Century: From the Heart of Darkness to Africa Rising*, edited by Mel Bunce, Suzanne Franks, and Chris Paterson, 113–15. Abingdon, Oxon: Routledge, 2017.

Office for the Coordination of Humanitarian Affairs. "Global Humanitarian Overview." Geneva, UN, 2015.

http://reliefweb.int/sites/reliefweb.int/files/resources/GHO-FINAL-web.pdf.

Ogazi L. Emeka. *African Development and the Influence of Western Media*. Bloomington, IN: XLibris, 2010.

Ogunyemi Olatunji. "The Image of Africa from the Perspectives of the Africa Diasporic Press in the UK." In *Africa's Media Image in the Twenty-First Century: From the Heart of Darkness to Africa Rising*, edited by Mel Bunce, Suzanne Franks, and Chris Paterson, 61–71. Abingdon, Oxon: Routledge, 2017.

Ojo, Tokunbo. "Africa in the Canadian Media: The Globe and Mail's Coverage of Africa from 2003 to 2012." *Ecquid Novi: African Journalism Studies* 35, no. 1 (2014): 43–57.

Okere, Linus Chukwuemeka. "International Media and Disaster Relief: British Press Reporting of the Mozambique Floods, 2000." *International Studies* 41, no. 2 (2004): 219–28.

Opuku-Owusu, Stella. *What Can the African Diaspora Do to Challenge Distorted Media Perceptions about Africa?* London: African Foundation for Development, 2003.

Orgad, Shani. "Visualizers of Solidarity: Organizational Politics in Humanitarian and International Development NGOs." *Visual Communication* 12, no. 3 (2013): 295–314.

———. "Underline, Celebrate, Mitigate, Erase: Humanitarian NGOs' Strategies of Communicating Difference." In *Humanitarianism, Communications and Change*, edited by Simon Cottle and Glenda Cooper, 117–32. New York: Peter Lang, 2015.

Organization for Economic Cooperation and Development. *States of Fragility: Meeting Post-2015 Ambitions*. Paris: Organization for Economic Cooperation and Development, 2015. http://www.keepeek.com/Digital-Asset-Management/oecd/development/states-of-fragility-2015_9789264227699-en#.V491g_krKUk#page1.

Örnebring, Henrik. *Newsworkers: A Comparative European Perspective*. London: Bloomsbury Publishing, 2016.

Otto, Florian and Christoph Meyer, C."Missing the Story?—Changes in Foreign News Reporting and Their Implications for Conflict Prevention." *Media, War and Conflict* 5, no.3 (2012):205–221.

Palmberg, Mai, ed. *Encounter Images in the Meetings between Africa and Europe*. Uppsala, Sweden: The Nordic Africa Institute, 2001.

Paterson, Chris. "International News on the Internet: Why More Is Less." *Ethical Space: The International Journal of Communication Ethics* 4, no. 1/2 (2007): 57–66.

Phillips, Angela. "Old Sources, New Bottles." In *New Media, Old News: Journalism and Democracy in the Digital Age*, edited by Natalie Fenton, 87–101. London: Sage, 2010.

Philo, Greg. "From Buerk to Band Aid." In *Getting the Message: News Truth and Power*, edited by Glasgow Media Group, 104–25. London: Routledge, 1993.

Powers, Matthew. "Humanity's Publics: NGOs, journalists and the international public sphere." New York University, 2013

———. "The Structural Organization of NGO Publicity Work: Explaining Divergent Publicity Strategies at Humanitarian and Human Rights Organizations." *International Journal of Communication* 8 (2014): 18.

———. "NGOs as Journalistic Entities: The Possibilities, Promises and Limits of Boundary Crossing." In *Boundaries of Journalism: Professionalism, Practice and Participation*, edited by Matt Carlson and Seth Lewis C., 186–200. London: New York, 2015.

———. "The New Boots on the Ground: NGOs in the Changing Landscape of International News." *Journalism* 17, no. 4 (2016): 401–16.

———."Beyond Boon or Bane: Using Normative Theories to Evaluate the News-Making Efforts of NGOs." *Journalism Studies* 18 no. 9 (2017): 1070–86.

Pratt, Mary Louise. *Imperial Eyes: Travel Writing and Transculturation*. London, New York: Routledge, 1992.

Redden, Joanna, and Tamara Witschge. "A New News Order? Online News Content Examined." In *New Media, Old News*, edited by Natalie Fenton, 171–86. London: Sage, 2010.

Reese, Stephen D. "Globalization of Mediated Spaces: The Case of Transnational Environmentalism in China." *International Journal of Communication* 9 (2015): 2263–81.

Richardson, Whitney. "Who Is Telling Africa's Stories?" *The New York Times*, January 10, 2017. https://lens.blogs.nytimes.com/2017/01/10/who-is-telling-africas-stories/

Rieff, David. "Dangerous Pity." *Prospect Magazine*, July 23, 2005. http://www.prospectmagazine.co.uk/features/dangerouspity.

Roosvall, Anna. "The Identity Politics of World News: Oneness, Particularity, Identity and Status in Online Slideshows." *International Journal of Cultural Studies* 17, no. 1 (2013): 55–74.

Sambrook, Richard. *Are Foreign Correspondents Redundant?* Oxford: Reuters Institute for the Study of Journalism, 2010.

————. "From Buerk to Ushahidi: Changes in TV Reporting." In *Humanitarianism, Communications and Change*, edited by Simon Cottle and Glenda Cooper, 53–59. New York: Peter Lang, 2015.

Schorr, Victoria. "Economics of Afro-pessimism: The Economics of Perception in African Foreign Direct Investment." *Nokoko*, 2

https://carleton.ca/africanstudies/wp-content/uploads/Nokoko-Fall-2011-2-Schorr.pdf

Scott, Ben. "A Contemporary History of Digital Journalism." *Television & New Media* 6, no. 1 (2005): 89–126.

Scott, Martin. "Introduction to the DSA Media and Development Study Group." London, 2014a.

————. *Media and Development: Development Matters.* London: Zed Books, 2014b.

————. "The Myth of Representations of Africa." *Journalism Studies* 18, no. 2 (2017): 191–210. Doi:10.1080/1461670X.2015.1044557.

Seaton, Jean. *Carnage and the Media: The Making and Breaking of News about Violence.* London: Allen Lane, 2005.

————. "Global Understanding." In *Power without Responsibility: Press, Broadcasting and the Internet in Britain*, edited by James Curran and Jean Seaton, 311–25. London: Routledge, 2010.

Sehl, Annika, Alessio Cornia, and Rasmus K. Nielsen. "Public Service News and Digital Media." *Reuters Institute Reports*, 2016. http://papers.ssrn.com/sol3/papers.cfm?abstract_id=2771076.

Seu, Irene Bruna, and Shani Orgad (eds.). *Caring in Crisis? Humanitarianism, the Public and NGOs.* London, New York: Palgrave Macmillan, 2017.

Seu, Irene Bruna, Shani Orgad, and Frances Flanagan. *Knowing about and Acting in Relation to Distant Suffering: Mind the Gap!* London: POLIS, London School of Economics, 2012. http://www2.lse.ac.uk/media@lse/POLIS/documents/Polis%20papers/12_0196-POLIS-Report-INNER-V12.pdf.

Shome, Raka, and Rhadha S. Hegde. "Postcolonial Approaches to Communication: Charting the Terrain, Engaging the Intersections." *Communication Theory* 12, no.3 (2002): 249–27

Slim, Hugo. "By What Authority? The Legitimacy and Accountability of Non-governmental Organisations." *The Journal of Humanitarian Assistance* 10 (2002).

https://www.gdrc.org/ngo/accountability/by-what-authority.html

Spurr, David. *The Rhetoric of Empire: Colonial Discourse in Journalism, Travel Writing, and Imperial Administration.* Post-Contemporary Interventions. Durham, NC: Duke University Press, 1993.

Stones, Rob. "Social Theory and Current Affairs: A Framework for Greater Intellectual Engagement." *British Journal of Sociology* 65, no. 2 (2014): 293–316.

————. *Why Current Affairs Needs Social Theory.* London, New York: Bloomsbury, 2015.

UK Government. Communications Act, 2003. http://www.legislation.gov.uk/ukpga/2003/21/contents.

UN High Level Panel on Humanitarian Financing. "Too Important to Fail- Addressing the Humanitarian Financing Gap: Report to the Secretary General," January 2016. http://reliefweb.

int/sites/reliefweb.int/files/resources/%5BHLP%20Report%5D%20Too%20important%20
to%20fail%E2%80%94addressing%20the%20humanitarian%20financing%20gap.pdf.

Van der Gaag, Nikki, and Cathy Nash. *Images of Africa: The UK Report*. Oxford: Oxfam, 1987.

Vicente, Paulo. "Foreign Correspondence from Sub-Saharan Africa: An Evolving Communi-
cational Paradigm Shift." *Index Communicacion* 3, no. 2 (2013): 13–35.

———. "Foreign Correspondents in Sub-Saharan Africa: Their Demographics and Professional Culture." In *Africa's Media Image in the Twenty-First Century: From the Heart of Darkness
to Africa Rising*, edited by Mel Bunce, Suzanne Franks, and Chris Paterson, 86–95. Abingdon, Oxon: Routledge, 2017.

Vokes, Richard. "Introduction." In *Photography in Africa: Ethnographic Perspectives*, edited by
Richard Vokes. Rochester, NY: James Currey, 2012.

Wainaina, Binyavanga. "How to Write About Africa," Vol. 92. Granta Publications, 91–95.
London, New York: Granta, 2005.

Waisbord, Silvio. "Can NGOs Change the News?" *International Journal of Communication* 5
(2011): 142–65.

Wall, Melissa, and David Bicket. "Window on the Wider World': The Rise of British News in
the United States." *Journalism Practice* 2, no. 2 (2009): 163–78.

Wright, Kate. "Listening to Suffering: What Might 'Proper Distance' have to do with Radio
News?" *Journalism* 13 no. 3 (2012): 284–302.

———. "A Quiet Revolution: The Moral Economies Shaping the Use of NGO-Provided Multimedia in Mainstream News about Africa." Goldsmiths College, University of London,
2014.

———. "'These Grey Areas' How and Why Freelance Work Blurs INGOs and News Organizations." *Journalism Studies* 17, no. 8 (2016a): 989–1009.

———. "Moral Economies: Interrogating the Interactions of Nongovernmental Organizations,
Journalists and Freelancers." *International Journal of Communication* 10 (2016b): 1510–29.

———. "'Helping Our Beneficiaries Tell Their Own Stories?' International Aid Agencies, the
Politics of Voice and the Pitfalls of Interpretation within News Production." *Global Media
and Communication*, 2018 Online First DOI: 10.1177/1742766518759795.

Wrong, Michaela. "Media Perspectives: In Defence of Western Journalists in Africa." In *Africa's Media Image in the Twenty-First Century: From the Heart of Darkness to Africa Rising*,
edited by Mel Bunce, Suzanne Franks, and Chris Paterson, 30–32. Abingdon, Oxon: Routledge, 2017.

Yanacopulos, Helen. *International NGO Engagement, Advocacy, Activism: The Faces and Spaces
of Change*. Non-Governmental Public Action Series. Houndmills, Basingstoke: Palgrave
MacMillan, 2015.

Zuckerman, Ethan. "Advocacy, Agenda and Attention: Unpacking Unstated Motives in NGO
Journalism." *Nieman Journalism Lab*, January 19, 2010. http://www.niemanlab.org/2010/01/
ethan-zuckerman-advocacy-agenda-and-attention-unpacking-unstated-motives-in-ngo-
journalism/.

· 2 ·

NGOS, NEWS ORGANIZATIONS, AND FREELANCERS

An Overview

Although trust in all public institutions is falling, NGOs are still the most trusted kinds of institutions in the world (Edelman 2017). Some are huge and phenomenally wealthy: the largest International NGOs (INGOs) work in scores of countries and have budgets bigger than the governments of many developing nations (Yanacopulos 2015). There are also more than 30,000 local and national NGOs whose work has an international focus—and new NGOs are being created all the time (Union of International Associations 2015). Yet it is notoriously difficult to define what an NGO actually is.

Most academics take a broad, negative approach, defining NGOs as "formal, non-statutory and non-profit-making organizations" (Deacon 2003, 99). This is an approach which has been strongly shaped by documents published by the United Nations or UN. But the UN's first attempt at defining NGOs was nothing more than a hastily inserted clause in its Charter (1945), which mentions private groups who wished to be consulted in intergovernmental processes, but which are not inter-governmental agencies (Article 71, discussed in Lang 2013). Subsequent UN documents have continued to take a broad, negative approach: stating that organizations may be called NGOs if they do not use violent means, or seek to replace an existing government.

This therefore excludes political parties, national liberation and guerrilla organizations, as well as animal rights and Pro-Life organizations which use violent means (Martens 2003; Willetts 1999). However, violent acts designed to break and enter—or even destroy—property do not seem to have prevented environmental groups, such as Greenpeace, from being considered as NGOs by the UN or others (Howell and Pearce 2002). Thus the UN's top-down approach to defining NGOs has been moderated to some extent by bottom-up or populist approaches (Davies 2013).

A similar pattern of interaction between official and unofficial approaches has shaped understandings of the purpose and scope of NGO-work. In order to claim consultative status with the UN, NGOs have to work in areas which support the aims of the UN's Economic and Social Council (United Nations Economic and Social Council (ECOSOC) Resolution 1296, 1968). But Eastern and Southern governments have often expressed concern about NGOs' potential engagement in political activities, viewing this as undermining their statehood (Götz 2008; Willetts 2006). So a raft of conditions were prepared to reassure Cold War adversaries and newly independent sub-Saharan states, which were worried that NGOs might act as spies or agitators for foreign powers (Götz 2008; Willetts 2006). These conditions restricted NGOs' ability to intervene politically by withdrawing NGOs' consultative status if they engaged in politically motivated acts against member states, as well as obliging NGOs to derive the majority of their funding from voluntary contributions (ECOSOC Resolution 1296 (1968), discussed by Götz 2008; Korey 1999).

Nevertheless, NGOs have since become involved in a wide range of political activities, such as environmental and human rights activism, which involve explicitly criticizing national governments (Davies 2013; Lang 2013). For example, the Treatment Action Campaign famously sued the South African government over its refusal to allow retroviral drugs to be given to pregnant women in order to prevent the transmission of HIV to unborn children (Nauta and Stavinoha 2012). Moreover, NGOs have now become involved in a number of activities which were previously the preserve of nation states, and which have important political ramifications. The most obvious example of this is when international aid agencies act as "mobile sovereignties" (Appadurai 1996, discussed in Pandolfi 2003, 369). This involves NGOs taking on "the *de facto* status of government through the act of administering welfare services", including running large networks of schools and medical clinics (McLagan and McKee 2012, 11).

Other INGOs and NGOs have been involved in brokering peace talks (Dudouet 2010; Ramsbotham *et al.* 2005) and in monitoring compliance with international protocols, such as those on the environment (Cameron 1996; Gulbrandsen and Andersen 2004). INGOs may even help to draw up international treaties, like that which banned anti-personnel landmines (Chandhoke 2002; Rutherford 2000); that which established the International Criminal Court (Glasius 2010; Korey 1999); and that which controls the arms trade (Isbister and O'Farrell 2013). So although they are called "non-governmental", NGOs are deeply imbricated in the processes of global governance (Yanacopulos 2005). Indeed, they have even been described as comprising the "fifth estate of the new world order" (Seaton 2007, 46).

NGOs' growing political influence has come about, in part, because of broader changes in the political field. Sometimes this has involved internal changes or struggles within countries: for example, intra-elite arguments over US foreign policy in the 1970s shaped the emergence of major human rights organizations (Powers 2015). But NGOs' political influence has been even more powerfully shaped by their ability to maneuver effectively within and between the transnational centers of power which proliferated after the end of the Cold War (Davies 2013; Djelic and Sahlin-Andersson 2006). A key factor which enabled NGOs' maneuverability has been the increasingly mediatized nature of politics: that is, the ways in which the power-relations are saturated with, shaped by, and enacted through, digital media (Davis 2007; Esser and Strömbäck 2014).

The chain of causality between news coverage, audience attention and social change is neither simple nor uncontested (Couldry *et al.* 2010; Gilboa 2005; Koch-Baumgarten and Voltmer 2010). But there are strong correlations between the amount of media coverage which aid agencies receive, the amount of money they are able to raise, and the scale of a humanitarian relief operation (Cooper 2011, 2015; Franks 2015). There is also some evidence to suggest that the narrative frames used in news coverage may influence governmental policy when there is no pre-existing political strategy (Franks 2013, 2015).

Moreover, the portrayal of NGOs as "experts" in mainstream journalism tends to position them as voices of authority on particular geographic areas or themes (Ecker-Erhardt 2010). These kinds of media consecration are known to have helped NGOs to influence political processes from which they would otherwise have been debarred. For example, when human rights activists were not given places on the working parties for international treaties in the 1990s, they used their reputation as "experts"—constructed, in part, via the media—to access early, informal discussions, so helping to frame the debate from the beginning (Willetts 1999). One famous instance of this was when the official working group convened to begin drafting the Protocol to the Convention against Torture: they arrived to find that a draft had already been compiled by politicians working with Amnesty International and Human Rights Watch (Joachim and Locher 2008).

INGOs have also been known to use mainstream media coverage in order to overcome the obstacles to political participation experienced by local and national NGOs. For example, when China tried to block the access of human rights NGOs to the World Conference on Women in Beijing in 1995, INGO workers positioned within governmental delegations as "experts" gave so many interviews to the mainstream media, and reported back frequently to informal, open NGO caucuses. So the boundary between private and open sessions—and the access allowed to different kinds of NGOs—became thoroughly eroded (Clarke 1998; McDougall 2004). Indeed, many INGOs routinely target mainstream news outlets at precisely the same time as engaging in more direct forms of political participation, in what are sometimes seen as closely related forms of global governance (Yanacopulos 2005).

Thus mainstream news has played a key role in constructing the transnational power of NGOs, even though it is not easy for them to gain news coverage (Powers 2016). In particular, NGOs have become well known for their sophisticated production of multimedia, using visual images to try and shape new kinds of collective identity, public knowledge and/or joint action (Denčik and Allan 2017; McLagan and McKee 2012). Such activity has a long history. As early as the turn of the twentieth century, the transatlantic pressure group, the Congo Reform Association was involved in placing photos taken by its supporters in mainstream newspapers, as well as publishing them in the paper set up by its founder, the *West African Mail* (Fehrenbach and Rodogno 2015; Hochschild 2006; Sliwinski 2006). But how should we conceptualize NGOs' contemporary engagement in media-making and its effects on journalism and NGO-work?

Networked journalism

Critical debates about the effects of NGOs' engagement in journalism have tended to be both generalized and polarized. Those studying journalism have tended to treat NGOs' engagement in news-making as either a "boon" which enhances the diversity and geographic reach of journalism, or as a "bane" which dangerously undermines its critical and political independence (Powers 2017). Those in the "boon" camp often position NGOs' engagement in journalistic production as part of a broader shift towards more open, dialogic and socially-engaged forms of "networked journalism" (Beckett 2008; Beckett and Mansell 2008; Lück *et al.* 2016; Sambrook 2010).

Earlier work in this area not only drew from Castells' ideas about the networked society (2000; see also Deuze 2007, 2008; Jarvis 2006; van der Haak *et al.* 2012) but also from Gillmor's book, *We the Media* (2006). So it takes a strongly normative approach: viewing networked journalism as involving more collaborative, inclusive and empowering approaches to news production. For example, Beckett and Mansell recommend that journalists retain the responsibility to "report, analyze and comment" but surrender their monopoly over newsgathering (2008, 93). Instead, they see journalists as facilitating news-making by filtering, editing and contextualizing material from a variety of different sources, through a process of constant and interactive dialogue with others. Such a shift in journalistic practice, Beckett and Mansell claim, would not only be more cost-effective, but would also be more politically progressive and "ethical" (2008, 99). Indeed, they argue that adopting such an approach would allow journalism to move beyond the dichotomies of "North" and "South", "information rich" and "information poor", "hegemonic" and "indigenous" knowledge, towards a new, not yet completely understood, "alternative" (Beckett and Mansell 2008, 99).

In some ways, these writers have a point: the extensive local and cross-border networks of NGOs do have the potential to "bring something of the global conversation to particular local settings" (Reese 2015, 2277; see also Yanacopulos 2015). For instance, they may be able to give news organizations early warnings about the emergence of localized or more fluid forms of political activity (Livingston and Asmolov 2010). The model of networked journalism also has some critical advantages: enabling us to acknowledge the multiplicity of actors and practices which are potentially involved in news production, without precluding actors' commitments to particular values or political agendas. In so doing, it encourages us to address multidirectional flows of influence. Thus the model of networked journalism initially seems well-suited to a study of the kinds of journalism explored in this book, which involved complex exchanges between NGOs, news outlets and others, such as freelancers, social media participants, businesses or private foundations.

However, earlier work on networked journalism (Beckett 2008; Beckett and Mansell 2008) risks minimizing the problems caused by deep-seated inequalities. In particular, it is important to stress that the much-cited spread of mobile phones in sub-Saharan Africa (Pew Research Center 2015) has not necessarily led to more inclusive forms of media participation. This is because smartphones, which are capable of accessing the internet and shooting photos or video, remain an expensive luxury enjoyed by wealthy, urban professionals (Winsor 2015). Data is also very expensive in sub-Saharan countries and charging a mobile phone can be costly, sometimes even necessitating a visit to a special booth (Akpabile 2015; *The Economist* 2016). Indeed, getting a mobile signal at all can be challenging, particularly in rural areas (*The Economist* 2016). As a result, only eighteen per cent of African households have access to the internet (International Telecommunications Union 2017)

Participating in networked journalism also requires large amounts of cultural capital. Even major INGOs find that they need to recruit former journalists, picture and video editors to accomplish this, as well as spending considerable amounts on continually updating their communications kit and related software (Fenton 2010; Wright 2014). Moreover, the internet tends to be dominated by fluency in the English language (Curran *et al.* 2012). These obstacles, together with other social factors, seriously constrain the ability of some groups to participate in mediation. One particularly noticeable pattern is the exclusion of women (Gurumurthy 2016). Indeed, the gender gap is actually widening in Africa, with twenty-five per cent fewer women than men able to access the internet (International Telecommunications Union 2017). But early research which utilizes the model of networked journalism doesn't really follow that line of thought through, in order to examine who is excluded from international news production as a result.

Even if non-traditional participants do find ways to contribute to mainstream news production in the Global North, the experience may be far from empowering. Their self-representation may be appropriated and reshaped by powerful elites (Ogunyemi 2011), and engagement in digital mediation can expose actors to political and economic surveillance (Morozov 2011). This is a particularly important problem to acknowledge in sub-Saharan Africa because only seven sub-Saharan states have any data protection laws (Gurumurthy 2016). Moreover, many critics have argued that the spread of communications technology and international news is bound up with the growing power of transnational businesses on the continent, effectively entrenching the world-views of cosmopolitan elites (e.g. Herman and McChesney 1997; Murdock and Golding 2010; Saleh 2010).

Later work on NGOs' and journalists' engagement in "networks of coproduction" (Lück *et al.* 2016) is far more sophisticated: dropping the techno-optimistic rhetoric of some earlier work in favour of examining the mutually enabling aspects of such journalistic practices. In so doing, it helps to draw a more differentiated picture of collaborations between NGOs and news outlets: illuminating how and why different kinds of news outlets and NGOs influence and adjust to each other during international conferences. In particular, Lück *et al.* (2016) explain how different kinds of journalist-NGO collaborations are shaped by multiple causal factors, especially different kinds of news beat, media, target audience/s and strategic orientations. However, even this nuanced work fails to deal with the assumption which underpins all approaches to networked journalism: that is, the belief that it is possible to shift aspects of journalistic production to others without fundamentally undermining the integrity of international news (Örnebring 2016).

PR, information subsidies, and churnalism

This assumption is challenged by researchers who contextualize journalists' use of NGO material in terms of their growing reliance on external sources, including PR and wire agency material. Indeed, those adopting this kind of approach have even accused the early advocates of networked journalism of making optimistic "prophecies" about how journalism could be—rather than analyzing how it actually is (Curran 2009). Such skeptics often begin by highlighting the strong historical correlation between cost-cutting in major news organizations and the amount of PR and wire agency material found in news output.

In particular, scholars point to the deregulation of the news industry in the 1980s and the global economic downturn of 2007–2009 as key events prompting increases in journalists' use of PR and wire agency material (Boyd-Barrett 2010; Curran and Seaton 2003; Davis 2003). The shift toward online journalism which occurred in 2005–2010 is then seen as exacerbating this trend: triggering a sharp increase in journalists' use of PR and wire agency content, because news outlets now have much less money and time to invest in traditional news-gathering and fact-checking tasks (Lewis *et al.* 2006, 2008a, 2008b). Rather than leading to greater inclusivity and diversity, these studies find that news is becoming more and more homogenous: with online news journalists becoming the most heavily dependent of all on reversioning material from external sources (Paterson 2007, 2010; Redden and Witschge 2010).

For all of these reasons, skeptical scholars see journalists' use of NGO material as far more of a "bane" than a "boon" for journalism (Powers 2017). These more skeptical critics tend to draw on different theoretical models, such as Gandy's "information subsidies" (1982). This term refers to the time and financial savings which PR specialists give to journalists, by providing them with ready-made forms of newsworthy material (discussed in Franklin 2011; Verčič and Verčič 2016). In return, PR specialists gain strategic advantages within mediated discourse, including framing problems, their causes and proposed solutions, in ways which reflect their world-views and serve their strategic interests. Thus the increased structural dependence of news outlets on NGOs is viewed by these critics as deeply harmful to news: systematically undermining journalists' critical independence, and privileging powerful and wealthy organizations which can afford to employ teams of PR experts.

Perhaps the best-known skeptic is the freelance journalist, Nick Davies. In his book, *Flat Earth News*, he argues that journalists have become "passive processors of whatever material comes their way, churning out stories, whether real events, PR artifice, important or trivial" (Davies 2008, 59). Indeed, Davies asserts, journalists have become complicit in reproducing a single dominant world-view: repeatedly privileging the accounts given by what Hall *et al.* called "primary definers" (1978, 58). As he puts it, "By favoring facts and ideas which are safe, especially those which are supported by official sources, the news factory tends to recycle a view of the world which reflects the status quo" (Davies 2008, 192).

Davies views INGOs as highly complicit in this: citing instances when major charities and campaigning groups have used the influence of PR professionals and/or wire agencies to gain media acceptance for exaggerated or poorly contextualized "facts" which furthered their organizations' own interests, so "distorting" public political discourse (2008, 186–92). He therefore sees news organizations' reliance upon NGO-provided material as damaging journalists' ability to scrutinize the activities and claims of those in power, as well as narrowing the range of perspectives included within mediated debates. This, Davies claims, harms citizens' ability to make informed decisions about their participation in national, and transnational, politics.

Davies' ideas have gained so much traction in the news industry that the British journalism pressure group, The Media Standards Trust, developed its own "churnalism" search engine, Churnalism.com. But Davies reaches some-what different conclusions to the Cardiff researchers, on whose study his book is based (Lewis *et al.* 2006). This is because the Cardiff researchers did not see journalists as passive dupes, reproducing a single worldview. Instead, they drew on the work of Gans (1979) to argue that journalists are willing and active participants in many different "dances" with their sources—although they conceded that these sources were increasingly leading the way (Lewis et al 2008a, 8)

Franks (2008a, 2008b, 2013) builds upon these ideas by arguing that BBC journalists' active eagerness to beat their competitors to a "scoop" led to them becoming embedded with international aid agencies during the Ethiopian famine of 1984. She then provides detailed evidence to suggest that this practice shaped journalists' adoption of aid agencies' understandings of the nature of the crisis, and the kinds of solutions which were needed. These interpretative frames marginalized local, political and military contexts in ways which, Franks and others argue, prompted misguided forms of collective action (2013). In particular, these writers argue that international relief was delivered in ways which missed the epicenter of suffering and inadvertently perpetuated conflict in the country.

Moreover, Franks asserts, journalists' collaboration with aid agencies in joint fundraising efforts, and their ongoing editorial exchanges with these organizations, have led to the emergence of warm, uncritical forms of "trust", which erodes journalists' ability to scrutinize INGOs' claims (2008a, 2008b, 2013; see also Seaton 2010). However, Cooper (2015, 2016) argues that international aid agencies' trusting symbiosis with news outlets has not gone unchallenged. She asserts that the growth of User Generated Content posed a profound threat to aid agencies' privileged relationship to news outlets, as it appeared to offer journalists more immediate and seemingly authentic forms of digital witnessing.

Cooper (2015, 2016) then argues that this threat was one of the factors motivating INGOs to begin producing their own multimedia, in order to woo back mainstream news outlets. Although aid agencies have also begun to address media audiences directly, by cloning social media forms, such as blogs, Tweets and Facebook posts (Cooper 2015). Thus Cooper's work starts to move us away from a fixed, binary understanding of the trust between NGOs and journalists and towards multidirectional models of influence which are much more dynamic and potentially unstable. In so doing, she highlights the importance of attending to important tensions between journalists and NGO-workers, as well as trusting forms of collaboration.

A report conducted by the industry think-tank, the International Broadcasting Trust, supports this latter point (Magee 2014). This is because it explores the concerns of journalists anxious that aid agencies have become so commercialized and powerful that using their material risks allowing news to be used as a vehicle for NGO branding and marketing. However, what none of the work on PR really deals with is the lack of NGO intentionality which characterized most of the cases in this book: with media commissioned or produced by NGOs regularly turning up in news outlets which NGO-workers had not targeted or approached. Indeed, some NGO-commissioned multimedia was even incorporated into news output when it had not been intended for use in mainstream news at all, but was instead commissioned as part of a donor report.

NGO advocacy, media logic, and news cloning

What are the implications of this for NGO-work? Much like early proponents of networked journalism, scholars who see NGOs as engaging in mediated advocacy regard their shift into journalistic production as characterized by dynamic and pluralistic dialogue enabled through new media practices (Keck and Sikkink 1998; Reese 2015; Yanacopulos 2015). Some of this work aims to "speak back" to critics who contextualize NGOs' role in journalism in relation to PR. For example, McPherson (2015a, 2015b) explores how human rights INGOs engage in time-consuming and skilled verification of video evidence of atrocities committed in Syria disseminated via social media, before notifying the national and international press. She goes on to argue that such practices prove that NGO-provided "information subsidies" (Gandy 1982) can have progressive effects: constituting "verification subsidies", which strengthen journalism, whilst also enabling NGOs to act as advocates for victims seeking justice.

Other research stresses how social media enables far more fluid, dialogic links between INGOs, local activists and news outlets. For example, Reese (2015) analyzes the ways in which bloggers and social media networks spread evidence found by local Greenpeace researchers about a major oil tanker spill in China, so enabling news of the environmental damage to reach Chinese and international news outlets. Although such studies stress the role of new media, they can also be contextualized in relation to older work about the multidirectional and dialogic nature of media communication during transnational advocacy campaigns. For instance, in the Jubilee 2000 campaign, local Ugandan NGOs began talks with their government about debt relief options whilst supported by Northern INGOs (Edwards 2001). The results of this dialogue then informed the content and direction of the transnational advocacy campaign led by those INGOs, which included mainstream news coverage (Edwards 2001).

These kinds of transnational advocacy campaigns relate closely to Northern INGOs' efforts to enhance their legitimacy via their "partnerships" with local NGOs, following widespread criticisms of their claims to speak for the poor and disempowered in the Global South (Slim 2002; Zadek 1996). However, an empirical study found that twenty-one out of twenty-three did not consult their Southern "partners" about advocacy objectives and media strategies, let alone involve them in detailed decision-making processes about the production of multimedia (Anderson 2007). A study of the "Make Poverty History" campaign of 2005 also found that there were marked tensions between the advocacy objectives and media strategies of Northern INGOs, smaller NGOs and the other activists who took participated (Sireau and Davis 2007). All of these hinged upon the extent to which actors were willing to compromise with the agendas of mainstream news outlets (Sireau and Davis 2007).

Since then, numerous critics have stressed that producing, commissioning or verifying multimedia for mainstream news outlets tends to have unintended effects, reshaping what is done and valued within INGOs. In particular, Cottle and Nolan have argued that "media logic" has spread to international aid agencies, so that their press officers have become overly preoccupied with tailoring media content precisely to the requirements of news outlets (Altheide and Snow 1979, cited in Cottle and Nolan 2007, 863). Specifically, these authors argue that aid-workers have begun to prioritize acquiring celebrity appearances, staging pseudo-events, and personalizing political issues for the press , over empowering local people (Cottle and Nolan 2007). Indeed, Cottle and Nolan claim that the spread of this media logic is so pervasive that even international aid-workers who are not press officers have come to interpret the world, and their concerns within it, in conformity with mainstream news culture.

Fenton's work (2010) builds upon that of Cottle and Nolan (2007), but she looks at the activities of a far broader range of INGOs and NGOs. She argues that, in order to successfully place media in mainstream news, NGOs need to commit to spending large amounts of money purchasing and constantly updating communications kit, as well as recruiting former journalists. Fenton argues that these former journalists continue to see themselves as journalists, and as news staff are now too time-poor to spend time at events, NGO press officers effectively "clone" news items for them, which they can download at "the click of a button" (2010, 164). Fenton stresses that such practices lead to smaller NGOs being pushed out of mediated discourse, and marginalize actors within NGO-work with alternative role-perceptions and values. Thus, she concludes, news cloning undermines INGOs' alternative working cultures, enabling them to become successful in placing their material in news outlets, whilst capitulating to dominant news criteria (Fenton 2010, 158).

Even when NGOs work with journalists on longer-term projects, which don't involve news coverage, this may still damage the alterity of NGO-work, as Jones (2017) shows in his anthropological study. He analyzes the production of a multimedia project run by AMREF Health Africa, in collaboration with *The Guardian* website. This involved the multimedia representation of the progress of a development program in the Ugandan village of Katine. But Jones found that the INGO's involvement in this project caused NGO-workers to reconceptualize and operationalize accountability in media-oriented ways. These were largely directed upwards at Northern donors; rather than downwards towards the INGO's supposed beneficiaries. As a result, Jones concludes, media teams became much more powerful within AMREF; indeed the whole organization shifted to become far more like a media, rather than non-governmental, organization.

So this cluster of studies help us understand some of the normative claims made about NGOs' engagement in journalistic production and some of their positive and negative effects, including their unintended consequences. However, these approaches to NGOs' engagement in news-making lack precision. Ideas relating to mediated advocacy are the most obviously problematic, as advocacy can involve many different media strategies and objectives, and self-interested, as well as altruistic, motives. But there are also many different kinds of media logic and multiple news values. These may be in tension with one another, so how should we analyze actors' privileging of some approaches over others? Moreover, which kinds of mediatization affect which kinds of accountability in which non-governmental contexts? Finally, how do we conceptualize the struggles between NGO-workers with different kinds of values and approaches, including the former journalists now working as NGO press officers?

Structural homologies and journalistic logic

Powers' work begins to address some of these questions (2013, 2014, 2016). Like Jones (2017) and Cottle and Nolan (2007), he notes the increasing tendency of INGOs to conceptualize success in terms of achieving mainstream news coverage. But he also uses institutional theory to analyze what he calls the "path dependence" of INGOs on mainstream news outlets: marshaling empirical data to demonstrate that INGO-workers believe that institutional donors and other political actors evaluate their effectiveness in terms of their ability to shape news discourse (2016a). Without empirical data from policy-makers, it is hard to speculate about the extent to which INGOs really do acquire these kinds of political legitimacy. But the fact that they perceive themselves to do so is illuminating, particularly in conjunction with Powers' earlier research about the multiple factors shaping the heterogeneous, but patterned, interactions between NGOs and news outlets (2013, 2014).

Specifically, Powers (2013) argues that NGOs' media strategies are shaped by their funding, relationship to government, organizational dynamics, target audiences, and strategic objectives. Broadly speaking, he suggests that U.S. based international aid agencies tend to target populist news outlets because of their need to fundraise from the general public, and because of the value they place on mass awareness-raising and public education (2013, 2014). In contrast, he argues, international human rights organizations enjoy generous grants from private donors, so have no need to engage in mass fundraising: thus they tend to try and pressurize policy-makers via the kinds of elite, niche media they consume (Powers 2013, 2014).

In order to make this argument, Powers (2013) builds upon Benson and Neveu's seminal work about the application of Bourdeusian field theory to journalism (2005). Specifically he develops Bourdieu's concept of structural homologies (1996), explaining that these are the

...correspondences between actors across different fields of actions [which] are structural because they express the objective tendencies of specific positions within a field, and [which] help give rise to patterned interactions with actors in different fields of comparable position. (Powers 2013, 75)

So, Powers argues, NGOs and news outlets are more likely to interact closely with one another when they have complementary forms of positioning in relation to the political and economic fields, as well synergies between their internal organizational structures. But their interactions with one another are also likely to involve negotiating tensions within and between their respective fields of activity, because a field is

> ...a structured social space, a field of forces, a force field. It contains people who dominate and people who are dominated. Constant permanent relationships of inequality operate inside this space which at the same time becomes a space in which various actors struggle for the transformation or preservation of the field. All the individuals in this universe bring to the competition all the (relative) power at their disposal. It is this power that defines their position in the field and as a result their strategies. (Bourdieu 1998, 40–1)

Such a critical approach has the advantage of allowing us to address actors' potentially complex position-taking strategies (Bourdieu and Wacquant 1992). These involve the relative distribution of financial capital, the forms of cultural and social capital specific to each field, as well as their own socio-economic positioning. However, the kinds of position-taking strategies permitted in each field are limited by what Bourdieu calls *doxa*: that is, the norms or rules structuring a particular field of activity. *Doxa*, is in turn, closely linked to actors' *illusio*: that is, their value-laden convictions about why the activity is worth engaging in at all. Both *doxa* and *illusio* are shaped—but not wholly determined—by actors' *habitus*: that is, the socio-economic setting wherein they acquired their habits, skills, normative and aesthetic predispositions (Bourdieu 1984, 1998; Bourdieu and Wacquant 1992).

Thus Powers' (2013) use of Bourdieu opens up the possibility that journalists' and NGO-workers' position-taking strategies may involve normative values and aesthetic tastes, which relate to the socio-economic positioning of media producers and target audiences. Such ideas resonate with Waisbord's research because he discusses the ways in which different kinds of "journalistic logic" (2011, 149) shape heterogeneous (and often tense) sets of relations between NGOs and journalists. These logics, he goes on, are shaped by particular news values and media formats, as well as labor conditions and editorial positions. Waisbord's alertness to media genre, in particular, has been invaluable in this study, as was his attentiveness to forms of editorial positioning, which are not necessarily bounded by organizations or fields.

Yet Waisbord's work (2011) prompts us to recognize a problem with the Bourdieusian framework proposed by Powers (2013). For Bourdieu's work on journalism was published long before the advent of social media and the widespread casualization of media production, including the rapid growth in freelancing, which is such a dominant theme in this book. So his field theory isn't designed to explain what happens when media actors move in and out of different fields, or occupy positions multiple positions in different fields at the same time. Such practices have important implications for renegotiating the boundaries between fields, so deserve far more critical attention.

Freelancers and outsourcing

As I have discussed in previous work, freelancers often play pivotal roles in mediating between NGOs and news outlets (Wright 2016a, 2016b). In many ways, freelancing can be seen as blurring the boundaries between mainstream journalism and NGO-work (Cooper 2009, 2016; Wright 2016a). International aid agencies pay for the flights, accommodation and trip costs of freelancers working for news outlets far more frequently than those of staff journalists (Cooper 2016). INGOs may also pay freelancers a day rate, even when they are producing a piece for a news organization (Cooper 2016). Yet there is relatively little scrutiny of such practices by the editorial staff of news organizations (Cooper 2016).

Many INGOs use this to their advantage. For example, the Head of News at Médecins sans Frontières recently told an industry forum that she regularly asked the freelancers who worked for her to pitch material to news outlets as "independent journalists", because she knew this eased their acceptance of NGO material (Polly Markandya, speaking at Frontline Club 2015). None of the freelancers in this book was asked to pitch in this way and they sometimes took INGOs by surprise when they asked for permission to do so. Nevertheless, they relied on others' perceptions of them as independent freelancers to engage in a number of liminal or boundary-crossing practices. These included working alternately for NGOs and news organizations, and syndicating multimedia back and forth between the two at a later date (Wright 2016a, 2016b). However, INGOs' hiring of freelancers has tended to be ignored in the most well cited studies about their engagement in news-making, with the majority of scholars focusing on INGOs' recruitment of former journalists as staff (e.g. Cottle and Nolan 2007; Fenton 2010).

So it is worth attending to the efforts of Örnebring et al. (in print) to rework Bourdieusian field theory in ways which address the growth in casual labor, as well as well social media. These authors stress that fields are spaces which actors may move into, around, and out of in a mobile fashion (Örnebring *et al.* in print). Indeed, they stress that prior to the twentieth century, it was normal for those producing journalism to be engaged in other occupations as well. But this does not mean that the boundaries of journalism are unimportant. Instead, Örnebring *et al.* (in print) argue that contests over the definition of what is—and what is not—journalism continue to be crucial for actors' acquisition of symbolic and material capital.

In order to address these issues, Örnebring *et al.* (in print) recommend that we move away from a classic Bourdieusian map, structured according to the twin poles of financial and cultural capital. Instead, they recommend adopting a three-dimensional model comprising three axes: *journalistic capital, access to resources* and *material security.* The first axis, *journalistic capital,* involves the extent to which actors have accumulated cultural capital within the journalistic field, which shapes the respect or status they are accorded. In contrast, the second axis involves the *material resources* which the organization/s which actors work for put at their disposal. However, this is different to the third axis, which pertains to the extent to which actors obtain *material security* from their employment. This includes whether they are paid a regular salary and have a stable, long-term contractual arrangement with their employer/s.

This analytical model speaks powerfully to the factors shaping freelancers' work for both NGOs and news outlets. The experienced European and North American freelancers in this book had high journalistic capital because they were well-known and well-respected by others in the news industry as geographic or visual specialists. But, like many other freelancers, they struggled with low material security, so had decided to work for other clients as well as news organizations (Deuze 2007; Frölich *et al.* 2013; Ladendorf 2013; Obermaier and Koch 2015). The financial pressure upon them had become more pronounced in recent years because news organizations were giving out fewer commissions, and freelance fees had not risen in line with inflation (Brown 2010). To make things even worse, established freelancers were facing increased competition from new freelancers, joining the market following repeated rounds of redundancies at news organizations (Brown 2010).

But these freelancers enjoyed and valued the kinds of specialized work they did. So their primary concern was not simply about making ends meet as a freelancer, but about how to continue to engage in their chosen area of specialist work. In particular, these freelancers struggled to access the resources they needed to pursue their specialist interests: fees were often not so much the problem as funding lengthy field trips. Securing these resources was difficult because news managers were increasingly reluctant to commission them to go on long trips, especially in hostile environments, which necessitated not only steep financial costs, but also necessitated completing large amounts of paperwork relating to health and safety risk assessments. So the decrease in news commissions for these kinds of freelancers has not only been shaped by cost-cutting in news organizations, but by news managers' time poverty and reluctance to take risks, particularly after the recent deaths of a number of well-known journalists, including the veteran war correspondent, Marie Colvin (Cooper 2016; Pendry 2015).

INGOs were much more willing to provide freelancers with the material resources they needed to go on lengthy field trips, including to logistically difficult and/or dangerous areas (Campbell 2007; Conrad 2015; Grayson 2014). In part, this was shaped by the nature of INGO funding, as INGOs found it far easier to commission freelancers than to recruit new communications staff. This is because most NGO funding is restricted to particular projects or appeals, so even the wealthiest struggle to pay for ongoing costs, including the salaries of staff members.

But this does not mean that INGOs were cavalier with freelancers' safety. Indeed, the freelancers in this book commented warmly on how well INGOs "looked after" them: engaging in extensive risk-prevention procedures before trips and often sending staff to accompany them to ensure their well-being and access to subjects. This sense of support was especially important to photojournalists: after all, ninety per cent of those who responded to a recent global survey said that they are regularly exposed to the risk of physical injury in the course of their work (Hadland et al. 2015).

In many ways, this resonates with research about news organizations' outsourcing of health and safety security risks, as well as time and financial costs to others (e.g. Örnebring and Ferrer-Connill 2016, 207; see also Jaakkola 2015; Palmer 2015). In particular, I see the increasing use of NGO-provided material as relating closely to Örnebring's (2016) work on the ways in which such outsourcing forms part of a broader reorganization of journalistic work. He argues that this involves technical tasks, such as publication, being folded back into journalists' daily workload; whilst time-consuming, expensive and specialized forms of editorial activity have been passed on to external parties.

However, "outsourcing" has serious limitations as a theoretical model. Its strict division between inside/outside isn't well suited to addressing these grey areas of freelancing, which were neither wholly inside nor wholly outside of NGOs and news organizations (Wright 2016a). In addition, outsourcing doesn't do much to help us to explore the complex relationships between parties who have been "outsourced" to. So it doesn't provide us with the critical tools we need to investigate the relationships between NGOs and freelancers. Nor does it allow us to consider the influence of other actors, like private foundations and other NGOs, which did not contribute material to news output, but which nonetheless had a powerful influence on news production processes.

Finally, outsourcing does not allow us to get at the profoundly normative dimensions of these kinds of work. In particular, I want to stress that freelancers' legitimization of these liminal or boundary-crossing practices did not involve a straightforward shift from professional ethics to individual morality, as some have suggested (Ladendorf 2013). Instead, freelancers' boundary-crossing activities involved complex mixtures of moral, political, religious and professional ethics, which were closely linked to freelancers' understandings of their responsibilities to others.

However, it is important to stress freelancers' understandings of their normative responsibilities did not include any obligation to remain impartial (Wright 2016a). Some freelancers had always seen themselves as campaigning journalists. Whilst others gradually moved towards abandoning impartiality, following a long period of being posted in a particular place (Wright 2016a). Still others experienced a particular moment of epiphany: the most dramatic of which involved one helping a prisoner of conscience to escape from jail by disguising him in women's clothing.

Nevertheless, freelancers did see their moral and political responsibilities as relating to ideas about their creative autonomy or independence (Hesmondhalgh and Baker 2011). Unfortunately, freelancers—and others—tended to seriously overestimate this (Wright 2016a, 2016b). This meant that freelancers cross-fertilized aesthetic and normative values, as well as interpretative frames, as they moved back and forth between the news and non-governmental organizations they worked for, in ways which were largely unacknowledged and unimpeded (Wright 2016a, 2016b). Indeed, payments to "independent" freelancers enabled INGOs and news outlets to minimize risk to their organizational reputations by allowing both to claim to do direct deals with trusted freelancers, rather than with each other.

There were interpersonal dimensions to journalists' trust in these freelancers as many were social contacts, friends, or even former colleagues, of news staff. But even when freelancers were not known personally to journalists, they tended to trust their reputation for specialist expertise and high ethical standards. However, this reassurance could also operate the other way. That is to say, that staff at news outlets with experience of freelancers faking multimedia were sometimes reassured by the idea that well-known and trusted INGOs were supervising and checking freelancers' work. This trust was built on other kinds of social connections, including journalists' personal experience of volunteering to help with press work during DEC appeals, but also the organizational reputations of wealthy and longstanding NGOs. Either way, journalists thought that their use of material commissioned from freelancers by INGOs was far less risky that using User Generated Content (UGC), as they believed that the latter required extensive checking in order to avoid news organizations damaging their reputations by inadvertently publishing faked material.

Thus the three dimensional Bourdeusian framework proposed by Örnebring *et al.* (in print), together with other publications by Örnebring (2016) and Örnebring and Ferrer-Connill (2016), does much to illuminate how and why specialized freelancers chose to work for INGOs and news organizations. But it doesn't help us interrogate the effects of these liminal forms of freelancing on the boundaries of NGO-work and journalism, including perceptions of what constitutes "good work" within each organization and field. In order to do this, we need an overarching theoretical model which brings together the critical insights contained in this chapter.

Such a model needs to enable us to analyze the effects of actors' exchanges with one another in terms of their collective renegotiation of tensions between autonomy and responsibility, risk and trust, struggle and co-operation across multiple fields. Finally, if this model is to enable us to assess the mixed effects of such exchanges, it needs to ground our own engagement in normative evaluation in ways which don't proceed from either an optimistic or a pessimistic standpoint. But finding ways to do this which are not ethnocentric is no easy task, as the next chapter explains.

References

Akpabile, Paul-Miki. "Rural Africa is the Most Expensive Place on Earth to Charge a Phone." *Fusion*, March 6, 2015.
http://fusion.net/story/59726/rural-africa-is-the-most-expensive-place-on-earth-to-charge-a-phone/.
Anderson, I. "Global Action: International NGOs and Advocacy." In *NGOs as Advocates for Development in a Globalising World*, edited by Barbara Rugendyke, 71–95. London: Routledge, 2007.

Beckett, Charlie. *SuperMedia: Saving Journalism so It Can Save the World.* London: Blackwell, 2008.

Beckett, Charlie, and Robin Mansell. "Crossing Boundaries: New Media and Networked Journalism." *Communication, Culture and Critique* 1, no. 1 (2008): 92–104.

Benson, Rodney Dean, and Erik Neveu, eds. *Bourdieu and the Journalistic Field.* Cambridge, Malden, MA: Polity, 2005.

Brown, Maggie. "Why Freelancing is now a Dead Loss." *British Journalism Review* 21, no. 1 (2010):61–5

Bourdieu, Pierre. *Distinction: A Social Critique of the Judgement of Taste.* Cambridge, MA: Harvard University Press, 1984.

———. *The Rules of Art: Genesis and Structure of the Literary Field.* Stanford, CA: Stanford University Press, 1996.

———. *On Television and Journalism.* London: Pluto Press, 1998.

Bourdieu, Pierre, and Loïc J. D. Wacquant. *An Invitation to Reflexive Sociology.* Cambridge: Polity, 1992.

Boyd-Barrett, Oliver. "National News Agencies in the Turbulent Era of the Internet." In *National News Agencies in the Turbulent Era of the Internet,* edited by Oliver Boyd-Barrett, 16–44. Barcelona: Government of Catalonia, 2010.

Cameron, James. "Compliance, Citizens and NGOs." In *Improving Compliance with International Environmental Law,* edited by Jacob Werksman, James Cameron, and Peter Roderick, 29–42. London, New York: Routledge, 1996.

Campbell, David. "Geopolitics and Visuality: Sighting the Darfur Conflict." *Political Geography* 26, no. 4 (2007): 357–82.

Castells, Manuel. *The Rise of the Network Society.* 2nd ed. Information Age, vol. 1. Oxford: Blackwell, 2000.

Chandhoke, Neera. "The Limits of Global Civil Society." In *Global Civil Society 2002 Yearbook.,* edited by Marlies Glasius, Mary Kaldor, and Helmut Anheier,35–53. London: The Centre for Global Governance, London School of Economics, 2002.

Clarke, Gerard. "Non-Governmental Organizations (NGOs) and Politics in the Developing World." *Political Studies* 46, no. 1 (1998): 36–52.

Conrad, David. "The Freelancer–NGO Alliance: What a Story of Kenyan Waste Reveals about Contemporary Foreign News Production." *Journalism Studies* 16, no. 2 (2015): 275–88.

Cooper, Glenda. "When the Lines between NGO and News Organization Blur'. Special Report: NGOs and the News." *Nieman Journalism Lab,* December 21, 2009. http://www.niemanlab.org/2009/12/glenda-cooper-when-lines-between-ngo-and-news-organization-blur/.

———. *From Their Own Correspondent? New Media and the Changes in Disaster Coverage: Lessons to Be Learned.* Oxford: Reuters Institute for the Study of Journalism, 2011.

———. "Hurricanes and Hashtags: How the Media and NGOs Treat Citizens' Voices Online in Humanitarian Emergencies." *Interactions: Studies in Communication & Culture* 6, no. 2 (2015): 233–44.

———. "From Our Own Correspondents? How User Generated Content Has Altered Power Dynamics in Reporting Humanitarian Disasters." City University, 2016.

Cottle, Simon, and David Nolan. "Global Humanitarianism and the Changing Aid-Media Field: Everyone Was Dying for Footage." *Journalism Studies* 8, no. 6 (2007): 862–78.

Couldry, Nick, Sonia M. Livingstone, and Tim Markham. *Media Consumption and Public Engagement: Beyond the Presumption of Attention*. Revised and updated edition. Basingstoke, New York: Palgrave Macmillan, 2010.

Curran, James. "Prophecy and Journalism Studies." *Journalism: Theory, Practice and Criticism* 10, no. 3 (2009): 312–14.

Curran, James, Natalie Fenton, and Des Freedman. *Misunderstanding the Internet*. Communication and Society. London: Routledge, 2012.

Curran, James, and Jean Seaton. *Power without Responsibility: The Press, Broadcasting and New Media in Britain*. 6th ed. London: Routledge, 2003.

Davies, Nick. *Flat Earth News: An Award-Winning Reporter Exposes Falsehood, Distortion and Propaganda in the Global Media*. London: Chatto and Windus, 2008.

Davies, Thomas. *NGOs: A New History of Transnational Civil Society*. London: Hurst and Company, 2013.

Davis, Aeron. "Public Relations and News Sources.' In *News, Public Relations and Power*, edited by Simon Cottle, 27–42. London: Sage, 2003.

———. *The Mediation of Power: A Critical Introduction*. London: Routledge, 2007.

Deacon, D. "Non-Governmental Organisations and the Media." In *News, Public Relations and Power*, edited by Simon Cottle, 99–115. Thousand Oaks, CA: Sage, 2003.

Denčik, Lina and Stuart Allan. "In/visible conflicts: NGO and the visual politics of humanitarian photography." *Media, Culture and Society* (2017) DOI 10.1177/0163443717726865

Deuze, Mark. *Media Work*. Cambridge: Polity, 2007.

———. "The Professional Identity of Journalists in the Context of Convergence Culture." *Observatorio (Obs*)* 2, no. 4 (2008): 103–117.

Djelic, Maire-Laure, and Kerstin Sahlin-Andersson. *Transnational Governance: Institutional Dynamics of Regulation*. Cambridge: Cambridge University Press, 2006.

Dudouet, Veronique. "Mediating Peace with Proscribed Armed Groups." Special Report. Washington, DC: US Institute of Peace, May 2010.

Ecker-Erhardt, Mathias. "Aid Organisations, Governments and the Media: The Critical Role of Journalists in Signaling Authority Recognition." In *Public Policy and the Mass Media: The Interplay of Mass Communication and Political Decision Making*, edited by Sigrid Koch-Baumgarten and Katrin Voltmer, 106–124. Abingdon, Oxon: Routledge, 2010.

Edelman. Edelman Trust Barometer, 2017.
https://www.edelman.com/trust2017/.

Edwards, Michael. "Global Civil Society and Community Exchanges: A Different Form of Movement." *Environment and Urbanization* 13, no. 2 (2001): 145–49.

Esser, Frank, and Jesper Strömbäck, eds. *The Mediatization of Politics: Understanding the Transformation of Western Democracies*. New York: Palgrave Macmillan, 2014.

Fehrenbach, Heide, and Davide Rodogno, eds. *Humanitarian Photography: A History*. Cambridge: Cambridge University Press, 2015.

Fenton, Natalie. "NGOs, New Media and the Mainstream News: News from Everywhere." In *New Media, Old News: Journalism & Democracy in the Digital Age*, edited by Natalie Fenton, 153–68. London: Sage, 2010.

Franklin, Bob. "Sources, Credibility and the Continuing Crisis in UK Journalism." In *Journalists, Sources and Credibility: New Perspectives*, edited by Bob Franklin and Matt Carlson, 90–106. London: Routledge, 2011.

Franks, Suzanne. "Aid Agencies: Are We Trusting Too Much?" *The Political Quarterly* 79, no. 3 (2008a): 316–18.

———. "Getting into Bed with Charity." *British Journalism Review* 19, no. 3 (2008b): 27–32.

———. *Reporting Disasters: Famine, Aid, Politics and the Media.* London: Hurst Publishers, 2013.

"From Pictures to Policy: How Does Humanitarian Reporting Have an Influence?" In *Humanitarianism, Communications and Change*, edited by Simon Cottle and Glenda Cooper, 153–66. New York: Peter Lang, 2015.

Frölich, Romy, Thomas Koch, and Magdalena Obermaier. "What's the Harm in Moonlighting? A Qualitative Survey on the Role Conflicts of Freelance Journalists with Secondary Employment in the Field of PR." *Media Culture and Society* 35, no. 7 (2013): 809–29.

Frontline Club. *Embedding with Aid Agencies: Editorial Integrity and Security Risks.* London, 10 February, 2015. https://www.frontlineclub.com/embedding-with-aid-agencies-editorial-integrity-and-security-risks/.

Gandy, Oscar H. *Beyond Agenda Setting: Information Subsidies and Public Policy.* Norwood, NJ: Ablex, 1982.

Gans, Herbert J. *Deciding What's News: A Study of CBS Evening News, NBC Nightly News, Newsweek, and Time.* Northwestern University Press: Evanston, ILL., 1979.

Gilboa, Eytan. "Global Television News and Foreign Policy: Debating the CNN Effect." *International Studies Perspectives* 6, no. 3 (2005): 325–41.

Gillmor, Dan. *We the Media: Grassroots Journalism by the People, for the People.* Beijing: O'Reilly, 2006.

Glasius, Marlies. *Expertise in the Cause of Justice: Global Civil Society Influence on the Statute for an International Criminal Court.* Oxford: Oxford University Press, 2010.

Götz, N. "Reframing NGOs: The Identity of an International Relations Non-Starter." *European Journal of International Relations* 14, no. 2 (2008): 231–58.

Grayson, Louise. "The Role of Non-Government Organisations (NGOS) in Practising Editorial Photography in a Globalised Media Environment." *Journalism Practice* 8, no. 5 (2014): 632–45.

Gulbrandsen, Lars, and Steinar Andersen. "NGO Influence in the Implementation of the Kyoto Protocol: Compliance, Flexibility Mechanisms and Sinks." *Global Environmental Politics* 4, no. 4 (2004): 54–75.

Gurumurthy, Anita. "Gender and Communications Rights." Paper given to the *International Association for Media and Communication Research* conference, University of Leicester, Leicester, 27-31 July, 2016.

Hadland, Adrian, David Campbell, and Paul Lambert. *The State of News Photography: The Lives and Livelihoods of Photojournalists in the Digital Age*. Oxford: Reuters Institute for Journalism, Oxford University, September 22, 2015.

Hall, Stuart, Chas Critcher, Tony Jefferson, John Clarke, and Brian Roberts. *Policing the Crisis – Mugging, the State, and Law and Order. London: Macmillan*. London: Macmillan, 1978.

Herman, Edward S., and Robert Waterman McChesney. *The Global Media: The New Missionaries of Corporate Capitalism*. London, Washington, DC: Cassell, 1997.

Hesmondhalgh, David, and Sarah Baker. *Creative Labour: Media Work in Three Cultural Industries*. Culture, Economy and the Social. London: Routledge, 2011.

Hochschild, Adam. *King Leopold's Ghost: A Story of Greed, Terror, and Heroism in Colonial Africa*. London: Pan Books, 2006.

Howell, Jude, and Jenny Pearce. *Civil Society and Development: A Critical Exploration*. Boulder, CO; London: Lynne Rienner Publishers, 2002.

International Telecommunications Union. "ICT Facts and Figures," 2017. http://www.itu.int/en/ITU-D/Statistics/Documents/facts/ICTFactsFigures2017.pdf.

Isbister, Roy, and Kloe Tricot O'Farrell. "Lessons Learned: How NGOs Contributed to the ATT Success." *SaferWorld*, June 4, 2013. http://www.saferworld.org.uk/news-and-views/comment/97-lessons-learned-how-ngos-contributed-to-the-att-success.

Jaakkola, Maarit. "Outsourcing Views, Developing News: Changes in Art Criticism in Finnish Dailies, 1978–2008." *Journalism Studies* 16, no. 3 (2015): 383–402.

Jarvis, Jeff. "Networked Journalism." *BuzzMachine*, July 5, 2006. http://buzzmachine.com/2006/07/05/networked-journalism/.

Joachim, Jutta, and Birgit Locher. *Transnational Activism in the UN and the EU: A Comparative Study*. 1st ed. New York: Routledge, 2008.

Jones, Ben. "Looking Good: Mediatisation and International NGOs." *The European Journal of Development Research* 29, no. 1 (2017): 176–91.

Keck, Margaret E., and Kathryn Sikkink. *Activists beyond Borders: Advocacy Networks in International Politics*. Ithaca, NY: Cornell University Press, 1998.

Koch-Baumgarten, Sigrid, and Katrin Voltmer. *Public Policy and the Mass Media: The Interplay of Mass Communication and Political Decision Making*. London: Routledge, 2010.

Korey, William. "Human Rights NGOs: The Power of Persuasion." *Ethics & International Affairs* 13 (1999): 151–74.

Ladendorf, Martina. "Freelance Journalists' Ethical Boundary Settings in Information Work." *Nordicom Review* 33, no. 1 (2013): 83–98.

Lang, Sabine. *NGOs, Civil Society, and the Public Sphere*. Cambridge: Cambridge University Press, 2013.

Lewis, Justin, Andrew Williams, and Bob Franklin. "A Compromised Fourth Estate?" *Journalism Studies* 9, no. 1 (2008a): 1–20.

———. "Four Rumours and an Explanation." *Journalism Practice* 2, no. 1 (2008b): 27–45.

Lewis, Justin, Andrew Williams, Bob Franklin, James Thomas, and Nick Mosdell. "The Quality and Independence of British Journalism: Tracking the Changes over 20 Years." Cardiff: Cardiff University, 2006. http://www.cardiff.ac.uk/jomec/resources/QualityIndependence ofBritishJournalism.pdf.

Livingston, Steven, and Gregory Asmolov. "Networks and the Future of Foreign Affairs Reporting." *Journalism Studies* 11, no. 5 (2010): 745–60.

Lück, Julia, Antal Wozniak, and Hartmut Wessler. "Networks of Coproduction How Journalists and Environmental NGOs Create Common Interpretations of the UN Climate Change Conferences." *The International Journal of Press/Politics* 21, no. 1 (January 1, 2016): 25–47.

Magee, Helen. *The Aid Industry—What Journalists Really Think*. London: International Broadcasting Trust, 2014.

Martens, Kerstin. "Mission Impossible? Defining Nongovernmental Organizations." *Voluntas: International Journal of Voluntary and Nonprofit Organisations* 13, no. 3 (2002): 271–85.

McDougall, Gay J. "A Decade in Human Rights Law: Decade of NGO Struggle." *Human Rights Brief* 11 (2004): 12–67.

McLagan, Meg, and Yates McKee. "Introduction." In *Sensible Politics: The Visual Culture of Nongovernmental Activism*, edited by Meg McLagan and Yates McKee, 9–26. New York: Zone Books, 2012.

McPherson, Ella. "Advocacy Organizations' Evaluation of Social Media Information for NGO Journalism: The Evidence and Engagement Models." *American Behavioral Scientist* 59, no. 1 (2015a): 124–48.

———. "Surmounting the Verification Barrier Between the Field of Professional Human Rights Fact-Finding and the Non-Field of Digital Civilian Witnessing," 2015b. https://www.repository.cam.ac.uk/handle/1810/248302.

Morozov, Evgeny. *The Net Delusion: How Not to Liberate the World*. London: Penguin, 2011.

Murdock, Graham, and Peter Golding. "Introduction." In *Digital Dynamics: Engagements and Disconnections*, edited by Graham Murdock and Peter Golding, i–xviii. Cresskill, NJ: Hampton Press, 2010.

Nauta, Wiebe, and Ludek Stavinoha. "Framing AIDS in Times of Global Crisis: 'Wasting' Africa Yet Again?" *Globalizations* 9, no. 5 (2012): 695–711.

Obermaier, Magdalena, and Thomas Koch. "Mind the Gap: Consequences of Inter-Role Conflicts of Freelance Journalists with Secondary Employment in the Field of Public Relations." *Journalism*, 16, no. 5 (2015): 615–29.

Ogunyemi, Olatunji. "Representation of Africa Online: Sourcing Practice and Frames of Reference." *Journal of Black Studies*, 42 no. 3 (2011): 457–78.

Örnebring, Henrik. *Newsworkers: A Comparative European Perspective*. London: Bloomsbury Publishing, 2016.

Örnebring, Henrik, and Raul Ferrer-Connill. "Outsourcing Newswork." In *The Sage Handbook of Digital Journalism*, edited by Tamara Witschge, C.W. Anderson, David Domingo, and Alfred Hermida, 207–21. London, Thousand Oaks, CA: Sage, 2016.

Örnebring, Henrik, Michael Karlsson, Karin Fast, and Johan Lindell. "The Space of Journalistic Work." *Communication Theory*, in print.

Palmer, Lindsay. "Outsourcing Authority in the Digital Age: Television News Networks and Freelance War Correspondents." *Critical Studies in Media Communication* 32, no. 4 (2015): 225–39.

Pandolfi, Mariella. "Contract of Mutual (in)difference: Governance and the Humanitarian Apparatus in Contemporary Albania and Kosovo." *Indiana Journal of Global Legal Studies* 10, no. 1 (2003): 369–81.

Paterson, Chris. "International News on the Internet: Why More Is Less." *Ethical Space: The International Journal of Communication Ethics* 4, no. 1/2 (2007): 57–66.

Paterson, Chris. "Changing Times: The Move Online and the UK's Press Association." In *National News Agencies in the Turbulent Era of the Internet. Barcelona*, edited by Oliver Boyd-Barrett, 225–43. Barcelona: Government of Catalonia, 2010.

Pendry, Richard. "Reporter Power: News Organisations, Duty of Care and the Use of Locally-Hired News Gatherers in Syria." *Ethical Space* 12, no. 2 (2015): 4–13.

Pew Research Center. "Cell Phones in Africa: Communication Lifeline." *Pew Research Center's Global Attitudes Project*, April 15, 2015. http://www.pewglobal.org/2015/04/15/cell-phones-in-africa-communication-lifeline/.

Powers, Matthew. "Humanity's Publics: NGOs, Journalism, and the International Public Sphere." New York University, 2013. http://gradworks.umi.com/35/67/3567326.html.

———. "The Structural Organization of NGO Publicity Work: Explaining Divergent Publicity Strategies at Humanitarian and Human Rights Organizations." *International Journal of Communication* 8 (2014): 90–107.

———. "NGOs as Journalistic Entities: The Possibilities, Promises and Limits of Boundary Crossing." In *Boundaries of Journalism: Professionalism, Practice and Participation*, edited by Matt Carlson and Seth C. Lewis, 186–200. London, New York: Routledge, 2015.

———. "NGO Publicity and Reinforcing Path Dependencies: Explaining the Persistence of Media-Centered Publicity Strategies." *International Journal of Press/Politics* 21, no. 4 (2016): 490–507.

———. "Beyond Boon or Bane: Using Normative Theories to Evaluate the News-Making Efforts of NGOs." *Journalism Studies*, 18, no. 9 (2017): 1070–86.

Ramsbotham, Oliver, Tom Woodhouse, and Hugh Miall. *Contemporary Conflict Resolution: The Prevention, Management and Transformation of Deadly Conflicts.* 2nd ed. Cambridge, Malden, MA: Polity, 2005.

Redden, Joanna, and Tamara Witschge. "A New News Order? Online News Content Examined." In *New Media, Old News*, edited by Natalie Fenton, 171–86. London: Sage, 2010.

Reese, Stephen D. "Globalization of Mediated Spaces: The Case of Transnational Environmentalism in China." *International Journal of Communication* 9 (2015): 2263–81.

Rutherford, Kenneth R. "The Evolving Arms Control Agenda: Implications of the Role of NGOs in Banning Antipersonnel Landmines." *World Politics* 53, no. 1 (2000): 74–114.

Saleh, Nivien. *Third World Citizens and the Information Technology Revolution.* New York: Palgrave Macmillan, 2010.

Sambrook, Richard. *Are Foreign Correspondents Redundant?* Oxford: Reuters Institute for the Study of Journalism, 2010.

Seaton, Jean. "Being Objective; Changing the World." In *Global Voices: Britain's Future in International Broadcasting*, edited by Richard Sambrook, 40–55. London: Premium Publishing, 2007.

————. "Global Understanding." In *Power without Responsibility: Press, Broadcasting and the Internet in Britain*, edited by James Curran and Jean Seaton, 311–25. London: Routledge, 2010.

Sireau, Nick, and Aeron Davis. "Interest Groups and Mediated Mobilisation: Communication in the Make Poverty History Campaign." In *The Mediation of Power: A Critical Introduction*, edited by Aeron Davis, 131–50. London: Routledge, 2007.

Slim, Hugo. "By What Authority? The Legitimacy and Accountability of Non-Governmental Organisations." *The Journal of Humanitarian Assistance* 10 (2002). https://www.gdrc.org/ngo/accountability/by-what-authority.html

Sliwinski, Sharon. "The Childhood of Human Rights: The Kodak on the Congo." *Journal of Visual Culture* 5, no. 3 (2006): 333–63.

The Economist. "Continental Disconnect: Mobile Phones Are Transforming Africa." *The Economist*, December 10, 2016. https://www.economist.com/news/middle-east-and-africa/21711511-mobile-phones-are-transforming-africa-where-they-can-get-signal-mobile-phones.

Union of International Associations. *The Yearbook of International Organisations*. Brussels, Belgium: Union of International Associations, 2015.

United Nations. Charter of the United Nations | United Nations (1945). http://www.un.org/en/charter-united-nations/.

United Nations Economic and Social Council. Resolution 1296 (XLIV) (1968). https://www.globalpolicy.org/component/content/article/177/31832.html.

Van der Haak, Bregtje, Michael Parks, and Manuel Castells. "The Future of Journalism: Networked Journalism." *International Journal of Communication* 6 (2012): 2923–38.

Verčič, D, and A. T. Verčič. "The New Publicity: From Reflexive to Reflective Mediatisation." *Public Relations Review*, 42, no. 4 (2016): 493–498

Waisbord, Silvio. "Can NGOs Change the News?" *International Journal of Communication* 5 (2011): 142–65.

Willetts, Peter. "The Rules of the Game: The United Nations and Civil Society." In *Whose World Is It Anyway? Civil Society, the United Nations and the Multilateral Future*, edited by John Foster and Anita Anand, 247–84. Ottawa: United Nations Association, 1999.

————. "What Is a Non-Governmental Organization?" Output from the Research Project on Civil Society Networks in Global Governance, 2006. http://www.staff.city.ac.uk/p.willetts/CS-NTWKS/NGO-ART.HTM.

Winsor, Morgan. "Mobile Phones in Africa: Subscriber Growth to Slow Sharply as Companies Struggle to Reach Rural Populations and Offer Faster, Cheaper Services." *International Business Times*, October 15, 2015. http://www.ibtimes.com/mobile-phones-africa-subscriber-growth-slow-sharply-companies-struggle-reach-rural-2140044.

Wright, Kate. "A Quiet Revolution: The Moral Economies Shaping the Use of NGO-Provided Multimedia in Mainstream News about Africa." Goldsmiths College, University of London, 2014. http://research.gold.ac.uk/11854/

———. "'These Grey Areas' How and Why Freelance Work Blurs INGOs and News Organizations." *Journalism Studies* 17, no. 8 (2016a): 989–1009.

———. "Moral Economies: Interrogating the Interactions of Nongovernmental Organizations, Journalists and Freelancers." *International Journal of Communication* 10 (2016b): 1510–29.

Yanacopulos, Helen. "Patterns of Governance: The Rise of Transnational Coalitions of NGOs." *Global Society* 19, no. 3 (2005): 247–66.

———. "*International NGO Engagement, Advocacy, Activism: The Faces and Spaces of Change.* Non-Governmental Public Action Series. Houndmills, Basingstoke: Palgrave MacMillan, 2015.

Zadek, Simon. "Interlude: Looking Back from 2010." In *Compassion and Calculation. The Business of Private Foreign Aid.*, edited by David Sogge, 24–35. London: Pluto Press, 1996.

· 3 ·

"GOOD" JOURNALISM AND MORAL ECONOMIES

Critical arguments about NGOs' increased involvement in news production revolve around normative evaluations: that is, ideas about what is good or bad, just or just, appropriate or inappropriate. To recap: some argue that using NGO material can improve journalism (Beckett 2008; Frontline Club 2008, 2015), whilst others assert that this undermines its critical independence (Franks 2013; Lugo-Ocando and Malaoulu 2014). Similar arguments are made about the effects of journalistic production on NGO-work. One group of critics conceptualize it as enabling progressive, transnational dialogue and/ or mediated advocacy (McLagan and McKee 2012; Reese 2015; Yanacopulos 2015). But others see the spread of media logic and related forms of news cloning as undermining NGOs' alternative values, perspectives and working cultures (Cottle and Nolan 2007; Fenton 2010; Jones 2017).

These arguments are important because international news is widely regarded as having a significant potential to harm, through its transmission of content to millions (Couldry 2006). Most evaluations of NGOs' engagement in news-making tend to rest on the assumption that international news about sub-Saharan Africa is pretty dreadful to start with: involving overly sporadic, negative and Othering representations of the continent and its people (Hawk 1992). Critical debates about NGOs' engagement in the production of news about Africa therefore tend to be framed in terms of whether such interventions will improve the poor state of international news about Africa—or make it even worse. Yet scholarly assumptions about the dire state of African news have recently been challenged by Scott (2017), who demonstrated that academic researchers have themselves been guilty of engaging in overly negative selection: studying only a narrow range of items about African famines, wars and genocide.

In addition, previous studies tend not to analyze the frameworks scholars use to make their normative evaluations. But this is essential, otherwise how can readers judge the validity of academic critiques? I mentioned earlier, that the analytical and evaluative approach I would be taking involved moral economy theory. However, this isn't used much in media studies (Hesmondhalgh 2017; Wright 2016a), and is used in very different ways in other disciplines in the social and political sciences. So it deserves much more thorough discussion, before we go on to the findings chapters.

Finally, if we are going to talk about normative evaluation we need to tackle some of the trickiest philosophical questions in media studies: that is, whether normative evaluation is desirable at all, and if so, how to engage in it without lapsing into ethnocentricity. Assessing any form of international news production is particularly difficult because such processes involve many different countries, so it cannot be assessed in relation to a single media system (Hallin and Mancini 2004, 2012).

In addition, most normative theory about journalism is produced by academics working in Europe and North America (Rao and Wasserman 2007; Wasserman 2010). This situation has been shaped by the legacy of empire and is perpetuated by the nature of the existing studies available to those working within the field, and the unequal distribution of research grants (de Beer 2010; Khiabany 2011). The languages which dominate academic publication and the geographic location of academic publishing houses also make it much harder for African scholars to disseminate their work (Mano 2009).

For these reasons, one of the leading scholars in journalism studies, Barbie Zelizer, has argued that critics should refrain from making their own normative judgements: treating all normative perspectives equally as a "critical strategy" to counteract the dominance of European and North American theory, and "reinvigorate the debate about the purpose/s of journalism" within the academy (2004, 3–6). One way of doing this, Zelizer suggests (1993, 2011), might involve critics analyzing immanent journalistic ethics as they are embedded within specific interpretative communities, shaped by multiple political, cultural and economic contexts.

However, international news production not only spans (and intersects) multiple interpretative communities, but also it does so in ways which involve very unequal flows of people, ideas and resources (Appadurai 1996; Massey 1993). Analyzing these unequal flows highlights how actors' moral values, political claims, and cultural identities are often premised in ways which are at the expense of others (Fraser 1997). So it is logically impossible to treat all approaches to international journalism equally (Fraser 1997).

The same is also true of different forms of media production which take place within a single country. For example, those interested in committing acts of ethnic violence and genocide are well-known to spread hatred through journalism (Somerville 2012; Thompson 2006). The example of hate media may be extreme, but it helps to demonstrate a further critical point: that is, that it is not only illogical, it is also grossly irresponsible to consider all normative approaches to journalism as if they were of equal worth. I therefore argue that Zelizer's approach (2004) creates more analytical and ethical problems than it solves.

Indeed, the irony is that Zelizer advocates trying to withhold normative judgement for profoundly normative reasons, which have to do with notions of progressiveness, justice and emancipation. This highlights what, for me, is the final, unarguable point: that is, that refraining from making normative judgments is impossible in academic research because deciding which phenomena it is important to know more about, and which kind/s of knowledge it is desirable to have, are all profoundly value-laden activities (Wright 2011).

So I would argue that when scholars refrain from making explicit normative judgements, what they risk doing is pushing their normative approaches underground, where they are far less available for critical interrogation. I think that researchers must accept that there is no "pure" ground to retreat to, which is untainted either by normative judgements, or by the unequal structures shaping normative theorization (Nolan 2008). Indeed, attempting such a retreat seems likely to fatally undermine our ability to deliver effective critiques.

A critically alert commitment to normative evaluation is particularly important if journalism theory is to talk to news practice in a meaningful manner (Phillips 2005; Skinner et al. 2001). This is because newspaper pages and television or radio air-time, as well as journalists' resources and audiences' time, are all finite, so journalists have to prioritize the coverage of some events, people, places and narrative accounts over others (Hafez 2007; Wright 2014). So normative judgement underpins journalistic practice, especially in news production, which depends quite explicitly on notions of what, who and where audiences should know about (Gasher 2009; Gasher and Klein 2008; Schudson 2003).

No matter how developed individual journalists become as "reflective practitioners" (Schön 1991) this kind of decision-making must always relate to broader collectivities, including the editorial teams and news organizations in which they work, as well as their sources, audiences and advertisers. So although we may criticize dominant news values (Harcup and O'Neill 2017; Ogunyemi 2011), some shared normative frameworks are necessary to shape journalists' engagement with their colleagues, and with others outside of journalism.

Journalists' need for shared normative frameworks becomes particularly acute when they are located within the kinds of massive, complex media organizations whose work dominates the provision of international news, and which are strongly associated with the uptake of NGO multimedia. Such massive news organizations broadcast and/or publish material electronically on a 24/7 basis. So in these organizationally complex contexts, there have to be shared ethical guidelines and related routines and structures, otherwise confusion and conflict could easily lead to organizational paralysis (Wright 2014).

Thus attempting to avoid explicit normative evaluation would not only prevent media scholarship from informing ideas about "good" (or "better") journalistic practice, but would also hold us back from engaging in debates about how news organizations, and indeed the news industry, should be structured, funded and regulated. This would put media scholars in a ridiculous position: obliging them to metaphorically sit on their hands during important political debates, even though they are in a position to make unique and valuable contributions, informed by years of research. So although grounding normative evaluation in ways which minimize the risk of ethnocentricity is difficult, it is necessary for anyone seriously committed to universities having a wider, public function (Bailey and Freedman 2011).

The problems with democratic theory

What evaluative frameworks are available to us? Journalism is often assessed in relation to democracy: indeed, it is almost the default setting for media scholars reluctant to pass moral judgements about what is good or bad. However, the Cameroonian critic, Francis Nyamnjoh, has urged media scholars to be wary of using democratic theory: remembering there is no "One-Best-Way of being and doing to which Africans must be converted and be converted in the name of modernity and civilization" (2005a, 3). In particular, Nyamnjoh objects to the dominance of liberal democratic theory, which privileges Enlightenment values of journalistic balance and impartiality (2005b). These kinds of norms, he argues, could drive some African journalists' pronounced political, ethnic and local affiliations underground, rather than out into the open, where they could contribute to democratic practice by helping to form a more pluralistic media.

Nyamnjoh's argument here is that representative democratic theories originate from Europe or North America, and are inextricably linked to forms of democratic practice valued in these countries (Berger 2002; Mafeje 1995; Mak' Ochieng 1996; Mwangi 2010). Unfortunately, very little democratic theory has emerged from sub-Saharan Africa (Mafeje 1995; Mwangi 2010), despite the fact that almost all of the constitutions upon which independent African states were founded include statements regarding their democratic aspirations (Anyang' Nyong'o 1995). What we do know is that the democratic practices and institutions in Africa vary tremendously from country to country, as well as from North American and European countries (personal email from Manager for Governance at the Electoral Institute for Sustainable Democracy in Africa, November 12, 2012).

However, the Cultures of Journalism project found that journalists across the world tend to say that they value impartiality (Hanitzsch et al. 2011). It isn't possible to use this study to generalize too much about African journalism, as the project only included one sub-Saharan country—Uganda. Yet in contrast to arguments made by Nyamnjoh (2005b), Ugandan journalists said that they valued impartiality even more than some journalists in Europe and North America (Hanitzsch et al. 2012, 484). Although researchers found that journalists from Uganda and elsewhere in the Global South differed from their European and American counterparts on matters relating to interventionism and objectivism, situational ethics, and the importance of separating facts from opinion (Hanitzsch et al. 2011). So perhaps we need to think again about democratic theory, employing a more flexible approach, which takes into account variations in local democratic practice. This includes acknowledging the constraints on journalistic activity imposed by severe financial difficulties, political censorship and security threats (Lodamo and Skjerdal 2009; Mabweazara 2010; Ndangam 2009).

Powers (2017) argues that representative liberal theory can be used to develop more nuanced, flexible evaluations of NGO-journalist relations, as long as critics are sensitive to the different strands contained within it. These include attending to the ways in which NGOs may assist deliberative processes via a commitment to accurate, detailed investigation and specialist expertise (Schudson 2010, discussed in Powers 2017). But Powers argues that more radical traditions within liberal representative theory permit greater partiality, so they enable critics to value more partisan NGOs which address social peripheries, rather than mass audiences or elites.

Such a critical/political approach may seem appropriate because the United Nations only allows NGOs to have consultative status if they can prove their representative function. Indeed, this is why UN officials claim that NGOs act as invaluable "bridges between the general public and the intergovernmental process" (UN report A/53/170, cited in Rugendyke 2007, 10). However, using any form of democratic theory in normative evaluation carries a high risk of ethnocentricity, automatically privileging democratic over other political approaches. In addition, using democratic theory to assess NGOs' involvement in news-making risks undermining our ability to interrogate its contribution to global governance in a broader sense.

Firstly, the use of democratic theory as an evaluative tool risks masking issues to do with the securitization of international aid, and the promotion of wealthy countries' political interests. This is because the 9/11 attacks on the World Trade Center in New York, the 7/11 Tube bombings in London and the Bali nightclub bombings have all prompted US, UK and Australian governments to privilege support for NGOs which promote democratic practice recognized in donor countries (Howell 2014; Howell and Lind 2009). Such donors tend to link the promotion of these forms of democratic practice to "good governance" and social stability: so by funding pro-democracy NGOs donors believe that they are "undermining the conditions that terrorist organizations seek to exploit" (Howell and Lind 2009, 1286).

Secondly, using democratic theory in normative evaluation risks marginalizing more fundamental arguments about the ways in which NGOs may undermine local political structures and practices in Africa because of their imbrication in the roll-back of the nation state. For instance, the Tanzanian critic, Issa Shivji (2007), has argued that international NGOs' engagement in international, mediated politics effectively shifts debates about poor African peoples' rights and development away from the local and national spheres which they might have been able to influence. Sub-Saharan governments have also been very vocal about their fears that NGOs undermine their national sovereignty, spreading foreign ideologies and even acting as agitators for foreign powers (Götz 2008; Willetts 2006).

Meanwhile, other critics have pointed out that international NGOs may erode the feedback loop of accountability in African democracies by delivering essential public services instead of newly independent sub-Saharan states (Cooley and Ron 2002; Turner and Hulme 1997). Indeed, some scholars have even seen NGOs as complicit in the spread of neo-liberalism: carrying out privatized and globalized solutions to national and local problems, in ways which detract attention from deep-seated structural inequalities, and which may even be driven by self-interested profiteering (de Waal 1997; Hancock 1991).

Finally, some scholars from sub-Saharan countries have argued that liberal democratic theory is fundamentally antipathetic to indigenous African worldviews (Mafeje 1995; Sesanti 2010; Shaw 2009). In particular, these critics object to the ways in which such theory depends upon individualistic conceptions of personhood and agency rather than the more collective approaches within their own cultural/normative traditions. For these reasons, they reject liberal democratic theory as part of their broader critical/political efforts to "decolonize the mind" (Ngũgĩ 1986).

Indigenous ethics, global ethics, and media effects

The most famous of these Afrocentric critics is the Zambian professor, Francis Kasoma (1994, 1996). He advocated a communitarian "Afriethics", which involved respecting respect for policy-makers and fostering support for state policies, as an alternative to what he saw as journalists' scurrilous muck-raking. But Kasoma and others have been criticized for romanticizing, homogenizing and essentializing African culture in ways which are dangerous, rather than liberating (Banda 2009; Nyamnjoh 2005a; Tomaselli 2003). In particular, Fourie (2008) has argued that Kasoma's Afriethics is vulnerable to being appropriated and misused by elites in order to legitimize repressive regimes and tightly controlled media systems—effectively suppressing media criticism, difference and dissent within sub-Saharan countries.

Banda (2009), Gallagher (2015) and Tomaselli (2003) have also stressed the difficulty of identifying any indigenous culture which has been untouched by colonialism and contemporary globalization, let alone a single "African" culture. For these reasons, later scholars have tended to emphasize the multiplicity of indigenous normative frameworks at play in sub-Saharan Africa, including the Southern African philosophy of *ubuntuism*, which entails the notion that "a person is a person through other people" (Christians 2004, 241). Using indigenous normative approaches may help to unsettle the individualism underpinning dominant normative theory from Europe and North America (Christians 2004; Rao and Wasserman 2007). But, as it is impossible to draw a hard and fast line between "African" and European or North American approaches to journalism, such critical approaches still involve reconstructing an idealized approach to traditional value-systems (Fourie 2007, 2008).

Thus indigenous approaches cannot be seen as standing outside unequal power structures—rather, they are a (limited, but still significant) critical/political response to them. It is worth underlining the broader philosophical implications of this: that is, that normative approaches to journalism are constantly reworked by different social groups, as they renegotiate their relationships to one another, within unequal socio-economic power structures (Khiabany 2011). These unequal power structures have intersecting local, national and international dimensions. So it seems wise to shift towards an evaluative approach which is alert to the ways in which people, values, media texts and practices cross physical, political, economic and social borders, whilst simultaneously recognizing the importance of attending to different kinds of contexts and constraints.

In recent years, several scholars have tried to respond to these challenges by constructing more responsive forms of global journalism ethics (Ward 2010) or even global media ethics, in recognition of the increasing interaction between social and mass media (Christians *et al.* 2008; Couldry 2012; Rao 2010; Silverstone 2007; Wasserman 2006). Such scholars tend to draw from postcolonial research about hybridity (e.g. Appadurai 1996; Bhabha 1994), in order to try and move beyond the dichotomy between Eurocentric, Universalist frameworks and indigenous exceptionalism (Christians *et al.* 2008). They therefore view local and/or indigenous traditions as complementing, speaking with, and/or modifying Northern philosophical traditions. So, for example, Couldry (2012) and Ward (2010, 2011, 2015) have sought to rework Aristotelian ideas about wellbeing or flourishing, whilst Christians (2007) has revised dialogic duty ethics.

However, the search for a global journalism ethics or a global media ethics is not without its own problems. To begin with, how possible it is to establish a global journalism ethics? How can critics engage with local and chronological variation in normative values without lapsing into cultural relativism? One could cope with this problem by emphasizing the existence of very broad, Universalist "protonorms", such as truth-telling, the sacredness of life, and non-violence (Christians and Nordenstreng 2004; Christians and Traber 1997). But this easily slips into over-generalized abstractions, and doesn't really allow us to engage with the richness of media ethics within local contexts.

Another approach, which may or may not involve building on universal protonorms, involves recasting global media ethics as an open, dialogic field (Ward and Wasserman 2015). This includes dialogue between normative theorizing and empirical evidence about "glocalized" ethics, as these are embedded in everyday media practices: so gaining a much "thicker" and more detailed understanding of media ethics (Rao and Wasserman 2015). This is more convincing, but I am still unsure about the desirability of pursuing a study about global journalism or global media ethics, even in this more dynamic, dialogic sense. That is because the most important question for me is about how useful such frameworks are in enabling us to make detailed evaluations of specific sorts of transnational news-making. Such a utilitarian approach is somewhat at odds with many of the other scholars working in this area (Wright 2014). However, I have been very influenced by these global ethicists' attention to the recursive relationships between international journalism and people's multiple capabilities (Nussbaum 2001, 2003; Sen 1999, 2010, discussed in Couldry 2012; Rao and Wasserman 2015; Ward 2010).

Specifically, I draw on Sen's suggestions about the ways in which journalism may enhance the capabilities which make public reasoning possible (2010). This involves news coverage promoting free speech and disseminating knowledge which enables critical scrutiny—although Sen does not see this as precluding the expression of emotion or vested interests. Sen also suggests that news coverage may "give voice" to those who are neglected and disadvantaged in other forms of mediated discourse: thereby serving a protective function and aiding more open and inclusive forms of communication and argument. Crucially, he sees these debates as involving discussions about different approaches to what is good or just (Sen 2010, 336). In this way, Sen avoids the essentialism of much of Nussbaum's work (2001, 2003).

But how do we identify which and whose capabilities are enabled and/or constrained by exchanges between NGOs, journalists and others, in order to make such an evaluation possible? Pinpointing media effects is another notoriously thorny problem in journalism studies. Early discussions of NGOs' engagement in news-making tended to assume that if media audiences could be encouraged to reimagine their relationships to distant others, this would trigger progressive forms of social and political change (De Jong *et al.* 2005; Gaber and Wynne Wilson 2005). But we now know that although news texts can be structured in ways which invite audiences to respond in particular ways (Chouliaraki 2006), they may not do so. Instead, audience members' responses are shaped by "unique and intersecting repertoires of thoughts and emotions, identity commitments and situated biographies" (Livingstone 2017, 65–66). Indeed, audiences often employ a range of strategies to neutralize and deny the calls to action contained in media texts, including those issued by NGOs (Scott 2015; Seu 2010, 2011, 2013; Seu and Orgad 2017).

Policy-makers may also use the international news coverage of Africa to justify strategies that they have already decided upon, rather than experiencing any change of heart (Graybill 2004; Hawkins 2002; Natsios 2002). Some evidence exists which suggests that on occasions when policy has not already been determined, news coverage may have some impact (Gowing 1994; Livingston 1997, discussed in Franks 2015). But these studies were conducted two decades ago, long before the growth in online journalism and social media. So it is not clear if these findings are still relevant. All we can say is that there don't seem to be straightforward links between media representation, audience attention and policy change (Couldry *et al.* 2010; Koch-Baumgarten and Voltmer 2010).

Thus in this book, I evaluate the effects of international news production in a much more limited sense: attending in detail to the effects of news-making on media producers themselves, and on the kinds of news texts they produce. In order to do this, I utilize moral economy theory. I argue that such a critical framework is well-suited to engaging with the intensely normative nature of such work. Its interdisciplinary nature and responsiveness to post-colonial concerns also enable it to address economic exchanges which cut across different organizations, countries and fields of activity, which involve complex and multidirectional forms of normative and economic influence.

But the term "moral economy" is used to mean different things in the various social sciences, as well as in the arts and humanities (Siméant 2015). So in order to avoid any confusion, I want to take a moment here to outline how three bodies of moral economy research informed the critical approach used in this book. These involve i/the analysis of poor and/or subaltern actors' exchanges with others, in order to try and prevent intolerable suffering; ii/ transnational forms of not-for-profit activity, including NGO-work; and iii/

work within the cultural and creative industries. I will then go on to explain how I used moral economy theory to pinpoint specific kinds of effects, and to flesh out my approach to normative evaluation in more detail.

Introducing moral economy theory: suffering, resistance, and post-colonialism

The first body of research which influenced my approach to this book portrays a "moral economy" as a network of economic exchanges founded in emotionally charged obligations to preserve others' ability to obtain subsistence. So these kinds of "moral economies" are seen as challenging extractive or free market economic approaches. In particular, this body of research focuses on the limited, but still significant, agency of poor and/or subaltern groups as they interact with powerful elites: examining how and why their economic need interacts with their ideas about good or bad, just or unjust, tolerable or intolerable social relations. It therefore approaches the effects of such exchanges in terms of pinpointing how and why compliance and cooperation may tip over into unrest and resistance. Thus socio-economic dominance is conceptualized as depending upon complex and relational notions of legitimacy, which are reproduced in a dynamic fashion through everyday socio-economic exchanges.

This approach was founded by Thompson (1971), who coined the phrase "moral economy" in his study of bread riots in eighteenth century England. He argued that these revolts were caused by a complex mixture of causal factors, including urbanization, legal changes and hunger, but also by poor English people's normative judgements about practices such as price-hiking and flour adulteration. Specifically, Thompson asserts that the poor were outraged that their social superiors had stopped fulfilling their customary, paternalistic responsibilities to protect their ability to obtain subsistence, and were demanding a return to the previous *status quo*. The free market model, which replaced the previous system, was indeed "demoralized" in the sense of being "disinfested of intrusive moral imperatives" (Thompson 1971, 90). Nevertheless, Thompson demonstrates that it still relied upon normative values: with free marketeers arguing that people would be better able to obtain the means of subsistence if markets were allowed to find their own level.

Scott (1976) expanded upon Thompson's ideas in post-colonial contexts in his book about farmers in Burma and Vietnam in the 1930s. Scott argues that the combined intervention of international capitalism and the colonial state seriously undermined the moral economies of local agricultural communities. Whilst these groups accepted their oppression in some ways, he argues that they resisted it in other, everyday ways. This resistance included their adherence to a "subsistence ethic", exercised as reciprocal gift-giving between kin during food crises. In this way, Thompson argues, farmers continued to exercise their traditional responsibilities to protect the capabilities of the vulnerable and preserve social stability during times of hardship. Thus Scott's work (1976) develops moral economy theory far beyond the scope envisaged by Thompson (1971): using it to examine the effects of intersecting exchanges at local, national and transnational levels.

Although this strand of moral economy theory was developed by two British scholars, it allows researchers to analyze the complex interplay of compliance and resistance in the normative/economic exchanges between multiple, unequally positioned groups. For these reasons, it has been widely adopted and developed by researchers from Asia, the Middle East and Africa. Many of these studies focus on short-term crises within colonial and post-colonial societies, such as industrial strikes, labor protests, and armed rebellions (Abdullah 1994; Lonsdale 1992; Lubeck 1985; Posusney 1993; Zeleza 1995). However, following a transnational research project on African Moral Economies hosted by the University of Dar es Salaam, other scholars started to analyze how sub-Saharan groups cope with the threats to subsistence posed by economic globalization, and related forms of environmental and/or climate change (Kimambo *et al.* 2008).

Thus more recent work in African Studies tends not to treat moral economies as involving the traditional, pre-capitalist and homogenous exchange systems within indigenous groups. Instead, it seeks to use moral economy theory to understand how different sub-Saharan communities respond to contemporary threats to their communal well-being by renegotiating their value-laden responsibilities to each other, to outsiders, and to their environment. This critical approach has influenced my decision to include the perspectives of local aid-workers and media producers, alongside their European and North American actors: moving beyond most studies of NGO-journalist interactions which focus on newsrooms and press offices in the Global North.

Indeed, my initial intention had been to include interviews with those represented in the news, alongside other local, national and international actors. Unfortunately, this proved impossible as so many had been displaced by conflict, and one was an indicted war criminal, recently extradited to the

International Criminal Court at The Hague. So unfortunately, I could not address the practices and perspectives of those who were represented, including their understandings of the capabilities which mediation might afford to them, and the economic values and normative responsibilities shaping their decision to participate. This is a regrettable limitation of this study, but what I did discover was sufficient to make me wary of positioning local groups' moral economies as challenging or opposing imperialistic/market norms. Indeed, I see such an approach as over-simplifying and romanticizing the norms of sub-Saharan groups.

Finally, I found that this body of moral economy research tended to focus so much on communities positioned in particular geographic locales that it didn't lend itself well to an analysis of transnational exchanges. One of the consequences of this was that the interventions of transnational actors, such as INGOs, were not analyzed in detail. Instead they were positioned in rather simplistic ways: as supporting the traditional moral economies of the poor and vulnerable (e.g. Maghimbi 2008), or as opposing these moral economies because of their commitment to international development as modernization (e.g. Frouville 2008). Such a simplistic and polarized approach to normative evaluation doesn't really help us to interrogate the ambivalent and contested positioning of NGO-work globally. So I rely more heavily on the critical approaches to "moral economies" found in the following bodies of research.

The moral economies of NGO-work

The second body of research which influenced my approach to this book moves away from a narrow focus on people's ability to obtain subsistence to broader questions of "vulnerability and survival" (Friberg and Götz 2015, 143). In particular, it interrogates forms of transnational exchange which are not for profit, but which claim to enhance the capabilities of vulnerable, but distant others, including through NGO-work. Such work tends to draw upon sociological approaches to gift-giving as a means of creating and sustaining the reciprocal ties which constitute community (e.g. Mauss 1990). But scholars then tend to blend this with understandings derived from Sayer (2000a, 2000b, 2001, 2003, 2004, 2007, 2010, 2011), who was influenced by Granovetter (1992) and Polanyi (2001), both of whom wrote about the social embedding of all economic activity.

Specifically, Sayer argues that all exchange relations are "moral economies", in the sense that they are embedded within a complex web of value-laden rights and responsibilities, which include legal, organizational, and other social obligations. These responsibilities constitute the trust necessary to form and sustain exchange relations, by shaping collective ideas about acceptable practice, including the appropriate division of labor (Sayer 2007). But Sayer also argues that moral economies shape actors' response to external events by placing them within particular interpretative frames which relate social meanings to value-judgments (2007, 2011). Such moral economies are not fixed, but dynamic: continually shaping, and being shaped by, actors' agentive renegotiation of their own and others' capabilities in the context of changing political economies (Sayer 2007, 2011). These recursive processes often involve contestation, as well as being emotionally charged, because they depend upon actors' (re)assessments "of behaviors and situations in relation to well-being" (Sayer 2007, 267).

International humanitarian aid is most commonly studied in relation to these kinds of moral economy theory (Friberg 2015; Ivarsson 2015; Lindström 2016; Shutt 2012). These researchers not only attend to the centrality of normative values in aid-workers' construction of their professional identities and role-perceptions, but also interrogate the roles played by normative values in defining what humanitarian aid is (Lindström 2016; Shutt 2012). Such scholars note that there are many normative values at play in humanitarianism, including notions of "value for money", charity, and rights, and that these values and related goals may be in conflict with one another (Shutt 2012). So the aims of humanitarian assistance, the principles which should shape it and its boundaries relative to other fields are all subject to continual contestation by aid-workers, donors and recipients (Friberg 2015; Ivarsson 2015; Shutt 2012).

Whilst research about the moral economies of INGO-work rarely mention Bourdieu's field theory (1984, 1998; Bourdieu and Wacquant 1992), such studies appear to have been heavily influenced by it. For instance, Lindström argues that one of the key functions of a moral economy is to "define what an economic practice is and the norms that surround it, thus guiding action by defining what is appropriate, doable, and conceivable in a specific context" (2016, 7). But moral economy adds two important things to field theory. Firstly, it enables us to analyze how and why actors' efforts to negotiate "the multitude of moral considerations involved in the economics of humanitarian assistance" (Friberg 2015, 254) are not only linked to the struggle for greater differentiation and autonomy, but also to forms of trust and cooperation grounded in notions of accountability.

Secondly, moral economy theory allows us to interrogate what happens when exchanges cut across countries and fields in much more detail. This is most obvious in research about the ways in which other kinds of NGOs participate in broader moral economies with many different kinds of actors. For example, Goodman (2004) uses moral economy theory to examine how coalitions of INGOs, commercial businesses and consumers comprise "fair trade" networks, which, she says, re/construct a "spatial dynamics of concern" which purports to "span the North/South divide" (Goodman 2004, 891). Meanwhile, Mostafanezhad and Hannam (2016) use moral economy theory to discuss the moral economies of ecotourism, which involves exchanges between environmental NGOs, Northern consumers, Southern governments, specialist tourism companies and national tourism boards.

So this body of research explains how moral economies are involved in renegotiating relations between social groups located distantly from one another, as well as relations between state and non-state actors, commercial and not-for-profit activity. Indeed, one of the strongest findings to emerge from this work is the way in which such transnational exchanges are not necessarily positioned closer to either the poles of cultural or economic capital (Bourdieu 1984, 1998; Bourdieu and Wacquant 1992). Instead, they may be positioned in ways which are simultaneously "in and against the market" (Goodman 2004, 893). That is to say, they can involve exchanges between actors who stand against unfettered market imperatives, stressing instead their value-laden obligations to others. Yet at the same time, these actors may use normative values and related notions of responsibility to better brand and market their products to consumers.

But despite all this boundary-crossing activity, moral economies can also be used to re/construct symbolic boundaries. Indeed, Rajak's work (2010) on the related area of Corporate Social Responsibility (CSR) shows that sometimes, the more common boundary-crossing becomes in a practical, every-day sense, the more important these symbolic boundaries become. I have found that similar principles apply to the boundary-crossing practices of freelancers, who work alternately for NGOs and news organizations, or who syndicate multimedia back and forth between the two (Wright 2016a, 2016b). However, most of the work about freelancing and digital production is located in another body of moral economy research: that which is about the creative and cultural industries.

Moral economies in the cultural and creative industries

This third body of moral economy research draws from the work of Keat (2000, 2004), who applied Booth's (1994) point that "every economy is a moral economy" to the notion of cultural goods. Such studies concentrate on how actors in the cultural and creative industries negotiate tensions between their desire for greater creative independence or autonomy, and their responsibilities to others in their communities. In order to do this, these scholars rework Sayer's arguments about the impossibility of wholly disembedding economic exchanges from socio-economic structures (2001, 2007 discussed in Wright 2016a).

Specifically, Sayer argues that actors' normative values may modify the economic values involved in exchange relations, causing them to behave in ways that are not always in their self-interest (2001, 2007). But normative values may also be "influenced, modified or overridden by economic forces" (Sayer 2003, 1), amending actors' normative values in ways which legitimize "entrenched power relations" (Sayer 2000b, 80). For these reasons, Sayer (2001) sees exchange relations as having the potential to develop a momentum and characteristics of their own; becoming partially disembedded from the institutions and lifeworlds in which they originated, and re-embedded in new contexts.

Banks (2006) first adopted this critical approach to interrogate the mixed effects of the growth of precarious or casual cultural work in the British city of Manchester. He demonstrated that the expansion of free market values had disembedded cultural workers from stable jobs in particular organizations. But they then sought to embed themselves more deeply in their local communities through new, informal systems of exchange. These new forms of embedding sometimes involved actors securing new networks of production and consumption which served their long-term interests. But sometimes, actors overrode their self-interest because of their deeply-felt sense of obligation to others.

In this way, Banks used moral economy theory to refute the claim that commercialization, and its related privileging of speed, risk and job instability, was wholly "demoralizing" the cultural industries by privileging entrepreneurial individualism, thereby negating "ethics, community and politics" (McRobbie 2002, 523). Thus Banks' work chimes with Hesmondhalgh and Baker's (2011) study of freelancers in magazine journalism, music and television. They argued that such casual workers were prepared to put up with long hours, poor pay and considerable risk and insecurity, in order to pursue the creative autonomy they believed was necessary to produce "good work": defining this as involving both self-realization and public value.

Lee (2012) then draws on both studies in his research into the moral economies of British freelancers working as independent producers of factual television for public service broadcasters—namely the BBC and Channel 4. He highlights freelancers' efforts to negotiate unresolved tensions between a new, neoliberal discourse, which stresses enterprise, commercialism, flexibility and individualism, and an older, more explicitly normative discourse of craft, co-operation and public service. In so doing, Lee identifies an (incomplete and contested) shift from conceptualizations of factual TV production as a kind of moral vocation to a succession of short-term contracts, obtained using the social capital acquired through informal networking.

These studies encourage us to think about the ways in which casual media producers may also be positioned simultaneously "in and against the market" (Goodman 2004, 893). Thus this body of research also speaks to research into the moral economies of digital media production. In particular, Bennett et al.'s (2015) research into the independent companies charged with delivering digital strategies and content to British Public Service Broadcasters (PSBs) is of note. This is because these authors unpick the norms of PSBs in much more detail: explaining that such forms of media production involve legally binding responsibilities which not only have a strong moral core, but also involve legally binding responsibilities. The statutory obligations of PSBs include remaining free of political bias and commercial competition, so their existence provides a profound challenge to the traditional juxtaposition of autonomy and responsibility.

But most importantly, Bennett et al. (2015) illuminate how and why cultural producers working as intermediaries between different sectors tend to blend or hybridize the norms of both. Specifically, they argue that independent production companies create new moral economies by combining the older norms of PSB with value-laden ideas about "networked" digital culture, including the production of multimedia by non-traditional actors (Green and Jenkins 2009; Kennedy 2012). I found that journalists working for other online news outlets, which were not created by PSBs, also sought to draw on normative claims about the special ability of digital media to enable more progressive and open forms of media production.

Although, as Murdock warned (2005), the intrusion of commercial sponsorship and other forms of private funding has reformed such digital communities in ways which undermine the normative principles of open digital sharing in the interests of the public good. Therefore, I join with Murdock (2005) and Hesmondhalgh (2017) in arguing that moral economy theory should not only be used to critique the exchanges taking place within day-to-day media production practice, but should also be used to evaluate the political economies which simultaneously enable and constrain it. In so arguing, I draw on Hesmondhalgh's (2017) conceptualization of international news as a kind of meta-good: that is, a good which enhances our capabilities to think about other goods, including others' capabilities.

Thus it is important that we do not stop at an analysis of the moral economies of media production, but instead consider how they relate to the moral economies of news content. Chouliaraki (2009) argues that the aesthetics and wording of news items work together as textual "moral economies". These, she argues, seek to re/position audiences in relation to distant others, by provoking particular kinds of interpretative, emotional and normative responses.

In addition, Skeggs has written about the moral economies of reality TV programs (2009, 2011), describing how explicit and implicit normative judgements portray participants' voices, appearances and mannerisms as good or bad, worthy or unworthy. In particular, Skeggs reintroduces socio-economic class into her critique: blending moral economy theory with Bourdieu's ideas on cultural capital (1984) in order to examine how the aesthetic tastes of different socio-economic groups are evoked by media producers to serve normative purposes within media texts. Thus, as Skeggs puts it, media texts simultaneously tell and claim.

This work helps to develop Sayer's ideas (2006) about the centrality of normative ideas in interpretative framing: a notion which Stones (2014, 2015) expands upon in detail. Stones suggests that we evaluate news and current affairs texts by asking how they define "the problem" under discussion, and its causes, as well as which actors, structures and powers are seen as relevant to it. A core part of this involves interrogating which normative values, judgments or responsibilities are implied by texts, and which treatments or resolutions are recommended as a result.

Therefore this book seeks to evaluate media effects in several different ways. It assesses the ways in which actors' mutual engagement in moral economies enable them to respond to their obligations to others, and to renegotiate the boundaries between fields. This involves the ways in which they frame their relationship with each other, and any changes in collective understandings of good, appropriate and fair practice in their respective organizations, fields or liminal spheres of activity. But I also interrogate how media producers and other actors frame the people, places and events represented within news texts: so attending to the interplay of narrative frames, aesthetic tastes and normative judgements in the coverage of Africa.

These news texts then have further potential effects, which involve enabling and/or constraining the capabilities of news audiences. These include their ability to engage in critical scrutiny; to hear the voices of those who are neglected and disadvantaged; and to engage in more open and diverse debates about the causes and contexts of suffering (Sen 2010). Therefore, both news production practice and the dissemination of news texts may be seen as emerging from, and having the potential to feed back into, broader political economies.

Using moral economy theory in analysis and evaluation

What I have argued here is that moral economy theory enables greater critical interconnectedness: "joining the dots" between the study of political economy, media production and media texts, which are usually divided from one another. Moral economy theory also helps us to bring together critical insights contained in different academic disciplines. In addition, it helps to combat the fragmented nature of research into NGOs' engagement in newsmaking by enabling us to interrogate exchanges between multiple actors, who positioned in different organizations, locales, and fields of activity, as well as actors who move between different positions, or occupy several different forms of position at the same time.

This helps us get past an outdated binary approach to journalist-NGO relations without losing sight of disparities in power which shape actors' normative perspectives, including scholars' own perspectives. So moral economy theory cannot rid us of the threat of ethnocentricity altogether, but it can minimize the risk of ethnocentricity by encouraging researchers to interrogate their own involvement in socio-economic exchanges with marked normative dimensions. In so doing, moral economy theory highlights the complex mixtures of compliance and resistance, altruism and self-interest, autonomy and responsibility, protection and dominance which shape academic research, as well as journalism.

Moreover, moral economy theory helps to protect scholars from selecting evidence to suit their own (normative) presumptions. This is because it does not proceed from a position of unguarded optimism about new actors' involvement in multimedia production, such as "networked journalism", nor does it carry the heavy, negative load of ideological critiques. Instead, a moral economy approach is well-suited to exploring the potentially mixed effects of NGOs' engagement in news-making, freeing us to develop more nuanced critical strategies in response to the specific challenges thrown up by particular objects of study.

So what does that mean for this study? I started out by outlining three sets of research questions at the start of this book. The first set involved asking: why do journalists use multimedia provided by NGOs in news about Africa? And why do NGO-workers produce, commission or curate it? In order to answer these questions, I examine how multiple actors legitimize exchanges with one another by renegotiating their multiple, value-laden obligations, at the same time as responding to various different economic constraints, values and goals. This analysis includes an attention to the interplay between actors' informal understandings of their moral and political responsibilities, as well as their formal obligations, such as the statutory obligations of PSBs and NGOs' project reporting requirements. In particular, this critical strategy focuses on analyzing the ways in which these legitimizing deliberations construct "trust" between journalists and NGO-workers, which involve emotionally-charged notions of what is good or bad, just or unjust, tolerable and intolerable.

The moral economy research I have discussed here suggests that this "trust" may be facilitated, mediated and/or modified by third parties, including commercial partners and freelancers. It also suggests that we should not assume that these legitimating rationales will be coherent and consistent with one another. Instead, scholars working from a moral economy perspective encourage us to be alert to the potential existence of tensions, contradictions or conflict, which can threaten the "trust" needed to sustain exchange-relations. These include discrepancies between the approaches taken by actors working at local, national and international levels, and the complex relationship/s between notions of autonomy and obligation.

Furthermore, moral economy research makes us alert to the ways in which actors may try to conceptualize "good work" as being simultaneously "in and against the market", in ways which re/shape their working identities, role-perceptions and approaches to branding and marketing. For these reasons, I interrogate the struggles, as well as the forms of collaboration and coopera-tion, between actors. But I also attend to individual actors' engagement in internal dilemmas since this necessitates them making agentive choices about which courses of action to pursue, which can trigger changes in practice.

My second set of research questions involved asking: how does this ma-terial reach journalists, and how it is incorporated into news coverage? This involves a close attention to the various routes via which media may arrive at news outlets, and the ways in which these routes are shaped by different kinds of media practices, as well as other kinds of normative/economic ex-change. Answering these questions also involves analyzing the ways in which actors' (sometimes conflicted) trust in each other re/shapes the actions they take. Thus this critical strategy seeks to illuminate the links between actors' value-laden framing of their relationship with each other within production processes; their understanding of the meanings of external events under con-sideration; and their decision to use particular aesthetics and interpretative frames within media texts.

The third set of questions involved asking: what are the effects of these exchanges on journalism, NGO-work and mediated representations of "Afri-ca" made available to UK audiences? Here, I focus on analyzing any longer-term changes in actors' understandings of what constitutes "good", "appropri-ate" or just "tolerable" practice in their respective area/s of activity, and in the representation of sub-Saharan Africa. Moral economy research suggests that this is likely to involve processes of normative hybridization brought about through boundary-crossing activities, as well as forms of partial disembedding and re-embedding, which cut across organizations, geographic areas and fields of activity. Yet moral economy also alerts us to the possibility that these ex-changes may simultaneously involve the reconstruction of symbolic bound-aries between different kinds of actors, places and activities. So this kind of critical approach is well suited to a complex engagement with boundary work.

Finally, I evaluate the validity of the legitimating rationales used to justify exchanges between NGOs, journalists and others, by interrogating which and whose capabilities were enabled and/or constrained as a result. This, I must stress, is a limited evaluation because I am only able to evaluate the capabil-ities of those who spoke with me, and the potential capabilities afforded to media audiences within the news texts I analyzed. Nonetheless, this is sig-nificant as it is the first evaluation of journalists' and NGO-workers' mutual engagement in news-making which takes account of multiple perspectives. I also hope that others will see, and make use of, the broader theoretical point being made here: that is, the utility of moral economy theory in analyzing and assessing the complex, recursive relationships between multiple political economies, media production practices, and the potential capabilities of audiences.

References

Abdullah, Ibrahim. "Freetown Crowd: The Moral Economy of the 1919 Strikes and Riot in Sierra Leone." *Canadian Journal of African Studies/La Revue Canadienne Des études Africaines* 28, no. 2 (1994): 197–218.

Anyang' Nyong'o, Peter. "Discourses on Democracy in Africa." In *Democratisation Processes in Africa: Problems and Prospects*, edited by Eshetu Chole and Jibrin Ibrahim, 29–42. Dakar, Senegal: CODESIA, 1995.

Appadurai, Arjun. *Modernity at Large: Cultural Dimensions of Globalization*. Public Worlds, vol. 1. Minneapolis, MN: University of Minnesota Press, 1996.

Bailey, Michael, and Des Freedman, eds. *The Assault on Universities: A Manifesto for Resistance*. London: Pluto, 2011.

Banda, Fackson. "Kasoma's Afriethics: A Reappraisal. International Communication Gazette." *International Communication Gazette* 71, no. 4 (2009): 227–42.

Banks, Mark. "Moral Economy and Cultural Work." *Sociology* 40, no. 3 (2006): 455–72.

Beckett, Charlie. *SuperMedia: Saving Journalism so It Can Save the World*. London: Blackwell, 2008.

Beer, Arnold S. de. "News From and in 'the Dark Continent': Afro-Pessimism, News Flows, Global Journalism and Media Regimes." *Journalism Studies* 11, no. 4 (2010): 596–609.

Bennett, James, Niki Strange, and Andrea Medrado. "A Moral Economy of Independent Work? Creative Freedom and Public Service in UK Digital Agencies." In *Media Independence: Working with Freedom or Working for Free*, edited by James Bennett and Niki Strange, 139–58. London, New York: Routledge, 2015.

Berger, Guy. "Theorizing the Media—Democracy Relationship in Southern Africa." *International Communication Gazette* 64, no. 1 (2002): 21–45.

Bhabha, Homi K. *The Location of Culture*. London, New York: Routledge, 1994.

Booth, William James. "On the Idea of the Moral Economy." *American Political Science Review* 88, no. 3 (1994): 654–67.

Bourdieu, Pierre. *Distinction: A Social Critique of the Judgement of Taste*. London: Routledge & Kegan Paul, 1984.

———. *On Television and Journalism*. London: Pluto Press, 1998.

Bourdieu, Pierre, and Loïc J. D. Wacquant. *An Invitation to Reflexive Sociology*. Cambridge: Polity, 1992.

Chouliaraki, Lilie. *The Spectatorship of Suffering*. London: Sage, 2006.

———. "Journalism and the Visual Politics of War and Conflict." In *Routledge Companion to News and Journalism,* edited by Stuart Allan. London: Routledge, 2009.

Christians, Clifford G. "Ubuntu and Communitarianism in Media Ethics." *Ecquid Novi: African Journalism Studies* 25, no. 2 (2004): 235–56.

———. "Utiliarianism in Media Ethics and its Discontents." *Journal of Mass Media Ethics* 2, no. 2–3 (2007): 113–131.

Christians, Clifford G., and Kaarle Nordenstreng. "Social Responsibility Worldwide." *Journal of Mass Media Ethics* 19, no. 1 (2004): 3–28.

Christians, Clifford G., Shakuntala Rao, and Stephen J. Ward. "Toward a Global Media Ethics: Theoretical Perspectives." *Ecquid Novi* 29, no. 2 (2008): 135–72.

Christians, Clifford G., and Michael Traber, eds. *Communication Ethics and Universal Values.* London, New York: Sage, 1997.

Cooley, Alexander, and James Ron. "The NGO Scramble: Organizational Insecurity and the Political Economy of Transnational Action." *International Security* 27, no. 1 (2002): 5–39.

Cottle, Simon, and David Nolan. "Global Humanitarianism and the Changing Aid-Media Field: Everyone Was Dying for Footage." *Journalism Studies* 8, no. 6 (2007): 862–78.

Couldry, Nick. *Listening beyond the Echoes: Media, Ethics, and Agency in an Uncertain World.* Cultural Politics and the Promise of Democracy. Boulder, CO: Paradigm Publishers, 2006.

———. *Media, Society, World: Social Theory and Digital Media Practice.* Cambridge: Polity Press, 2012.

Couldry, Nick, Sonia M. Livingstone, and Tim Markham. *Media Consumption and Public Engagement: Beyond the Presumption of Attention.* Revised and updated edition. Consumption and Public Life. Basingstoke; New York: Palgrave Macmillan, 2010.

De Jong, Wilma, Martin Shaw, and Neil Stammers. *Global Activism, Global Media.* London: Pluto Press, 2005.

De Waal, Alexander. *Famine Crimes: Politics & the Disaster Relief Industry in Africa.* Oxford: James Currey Publishers, 1997.

Fenton, Natalie. "NGOs, New Media and the Mainstream News: News from Everywhere." In *New Media, Old News: Journalism & Democracy in the Digital Age,* edited by Natalie Fenton, 153–68. London: Sage, 2010.

Fourie, Pieter J. "Moral Philosophy as the Foundation of Normative Media Theory: The Case of African Ubuntuism." *Communications* 32, no. 1 (2007): 1–29.

———. "Ubuntuism as a Framework for South African Media Practice and Performance: Can It Work?" *Communicatio: South African Journal for Communication Theory and Research* 34, no. 1 (2008): 53–79.

Franks, Suzanne. *Reporting Disasters: Famine, Aid, Politics and the Media.* London: Hurst Publishers, 2013.

———. "From Pictures to Policy: How Does Humanitarian Reporting Have an Influence?" In *Humanitarianism, Communications and Change,* edited by Simon Cottle and Glenda Cooper, 153–66. New York: Peter Lang, 2015.

Fraser, Nancy. *Justice Interruptus: Critical Reflections on the "Postsocialist" Condition.* New York: Routledge, 1997.

Friberg, Katarina. "Accounts along the Aid Chain: Administering a Moral Economy." *Journal of Global Ethics* 11, no. 2 (2015): 246–56.

Friberg, Katarina, and Norbert Götz. "Introduction to the Thematic Issue 'Moral Economy: New Perspectives'." *Journal of Global Ethics* 11, no. 2 (2015): 143–46.

Frontline Club. *The News Carers: Are Aid Groups Doing Too Much Real Newsgathering?* New York, February 28, 2008. https://www.frontlineclub.com/the_news_carers_are_aid_groups_doing_too_much_real_newsgathering_-_new_york_-_fully_booked/

———. *Embedding with Aid Agencies: Editorial Integrity and Security Risks.* London, February 10, 2015. https://www.frontlineclub.com/embedding-with-aid-agencies-editorial-integrity-and-security-risks/

Frouville, A. Robert. "The Challenge of Moral Economy in Africa." In *Contemporary Perspectives on African Moral Economy*, edited by I.N. Kimambo, G. Hyden, S. Maghimbi, and K. Sugimura, 203–21. Dar es Salaam: Dar es Salaam University Press, 2008.

Gaber, Ivor, and Alice Wynne Wilson. "Dying for Diamonds: The Mainstream Media and NGOs, a Case Study of Action Aid." In *Global Activism, Global Media*, edited by Wilma De Jong, Martin Shaw, and Neil Stammers, 95–109. London: Pluto Press, 2005.

Gallagher, Julia. "Theorising Image—A Relational Approach." In *Images of Africa: Creation, Negotiation and Subversion*, edited by Julia Gallagher, 1–20. Manchester, UK: Manchester University Press, 2015.

Gasher, Mike. "Guest Editor's Introduction." *Aether: The Journal of Media Geography. Special Edition on News* 4 (2009): 1–2.

Gasher, Mike, and Reisa Klein. "Mapping the Geography of Online News." *Canadian Journal of Communication* 33, no. 2 (2008): 193–211.

Goodman, Michael K. "Reading Fair Trade: Political Ecological Imaginary and the Moral Economy of Fair Trade Foods." *Political Geography* 23, no. 7 (2004): 891–915.

Götz, Norbert. "Reframing NGOs: The Identity of an International Relations Non-Starter." *European Journal of International Relations* 14, no. 2 (2008): 231–58.

Granovetter, Mark S. "Economic Action and Social Structure; the Problem of Embeddedness." In *The Sociology of Economic Life*, edited by Mark S. Granovetter and Richard Swedberg, 53–81. Boulder, CO: Westview Press, 1992.

Graybill, Lynn S. "CNN Made Me Do (Not Do) It: Assessing Media Influence on US Interventions in Somalia and Rwanda." Leeds University, 2004. http://ics.leeds.ac.uk/papers/pmt/exhibits/1994/CNNEFfect.pdf.

Green, Joshua, and Henry Jenkins. "The Moral Economy of Web 2.0: Audience Research and Convergence Culture." In *Media Industries: History, Theory and Method*, edited by Jennifer Holt and Ailsa Perren, 213–25. Chichester: Wiley Blackwell, 2009.

Hafez, Kai. *The Myth of Media Globalization.* Cambridge: Polity Press, 2007.

Hallin, Daniel C., and Paolo Mancini. *Comparing Media Systems: Three Models of Media and Politics.* Cambridge: Cambridge University Press, 2004.

———. *Comparing Media Systems Beyond the Western World (Communication, Society and Politics).* Cambridge: Cambridge University Press, 2012.

Hancock, Graham. *Lords of Poverty.* London: Mandarin, 1991.

Hanitzsch, Thomas, Folker Hanusch, Claudia Mellado, Maria Anikina, Rosa Berganza, Incilay Cangoz, Mihai Coman, et al. "Mapping Journalism Cultures across Nations: A Comparative Study of 18 Countries." Journalism Studies 12, no. 3 (2011): 273–93.

Hanitzsch, Thomas, Josef Seethaler, Elizabeth A. Skewes, Rosa Berganza, Incilay Cangoz, Mihai Coman, Basyouni Hamada et al. "Worlds of Journalism: Journalistic Cultures, Professional Autonomy and Perceived Influences across 18 Nations." In The Global Journalist in the 21st Century, edited by David H. Weaver and Lars Willnat, 473–94. London, New York: Routledge, 2012.

Harcup, Tony, and Deirdre O'Neill. "What Is News? News Values Revisited (again)…" Journalism Studies 18, no.12 (2017): 1470–1488.

Hawk, Beverly G. Africa's Media Image. New York, Westport, CT, London: Praeger, 1992.

Hawkins, Virgil. "The Other Side of the CNN Factor: The Media and Conflict." Journalism Studies 3, no. 2 (2002): 225–40.

Hesmondhalgh, David. "Capitalism and the Media: Moral Economy, Well-Being and Capabilities." Media, Culture and Society 39, no. 2 (2017): 202–18.

Hesmondhalgh, David, and Sarah Baker. Creative Labour: Media Work in Three Cultural Industries. Culture, Economy and the Social. London: Routledge, 2011.

Howell, Jude. "The Securitisation of NGOs Post-9/11." Conflict, Security & Development 14, no. 2 (2014): 151–79.

Howell, Jude, and Jeremy Lind. "Changing Donor Policy and Practice in Civil Society in the Post-9/11 Aid Context." Third World Quarterly 30, no. 7 (2009): 1279–96.

Ivarsson, Carolina H. "Moral Economy Reconfigured: Philanthropic Engagement in Post-Tsunami Sri Lanka." Journal of Global Ethics 11, no. 2 (2015): 233–45.

Jones, Ben. "Looking Good: Mediatisation and International NGOs." The European Journal of Development Research 29, no. 1 (2017): 176–91.

Kasoma, Francis P. "Media Ethics or Media Law: The Enforcement of Responsible Journalism in Africa." Ecquid Novi 15, no. 1 (1994): 26–42.

———. "The Foundations of African Ethics (Afriethics) and the Professional Practice of Journalism: The Case for Society-Centred Media Morality." Africa Media Review 10 (1996): 93–116.

Keat, Russell. Cultural Goods and the Limits of the Market. New York: Springer, 2000.

———. "Every Economy Is a Moral Economy," 2004. http://www.russellkeat.net/admin/papers/39.pdf.

Kennedy, Helen. Net Work: Ethics and Values in Web Design. New York: Palgrave MacMillan, 2012.

Khiabany, Gholam. "Whither Eurocentrism? Media, Culture and Nativism in Our Time." In De-Westernizing Communication Research: Altering Questions and Changing Frameworks, edited by Georgette Wang, 207–21. Abingdon: Routledge, 2011.

Kimambo, I.N., G. Hyden, S. Maghimbi, and K. Sugimura, eds. Contemporary Perspectives on African Moral Economy. Dar es Salaam: Dar es Salaam University Press, 2008.

Koch-Baumgarten, Sigrid, and Katrin Voltmer. Public Policy and the Mass Media: The Interplay of Mass Communication and Political Decision Making. New York: Routledge, 2010.

Lee, David. "The Ethics of Insecurity: Risk, Individualization and Value in British Independent Television Production." *Television & New Media* 13, no. 6 (2012): 480–97.

Lindström, Julia. "The Moral Economy of Aid: Discourse Analysis of Swedish Fundraising for the Somalia Famine of 2011–2012." Working Paper. Södertörn University, 2016. http://www.diva-portal.org/smash/record.jsf?pid=diva2%3A1035935&dswid=1952#sthash.3Q eAHipx.dpbs.

Livingstone, Sonia. "Mediation of Caring." In *Caring in Crisis? Humanitarianism, the Public and NGOs*, edited by Irene.B. Seu and Shani Orgad, 65–71. London, New York: Palgrave Macmillan, 2017.

Lodamo, Berhanu, and Terje S. Skjerdal. "Freebies and Brown Envelopes in Ethiopian Journalism." *Ecquid Novi* 30, no. 2 (2009): 134–54.

Lonsdale, John. "The Moral Economy of Mau Mau: Wealth, Poverty and Civic Virtue in Kikuyu Political Thought." In *Unhappy Valley: Conflict in Kenya and Africa, 2*, edited by B Burman, 315–504. London: Currey Athens, 1992.

Lubeck, Paul M. "Islamic Protest under Semi-Industrial capitalism: Yan Tatsine Explained." *Africa* 55, no. 4 (1985): 369–89.

Lugo-Ocando, Jairo, and Patrick O. Malaolu. "Africa—That Scar on Our Face." In *Blaming the Victim: How Global Journalism Fails Those in Poverty*, Jairo Lugo-Ocando, 85–103. London: Pluto Press, 2014.

Mabweazara, Hayes Mawindi. "When Your 'Take-Home' Can Hardly Take You Home: Moonlighting and the Quest for Economic Survival in the Zimbabwean Press." *African Communication Research* 3, no. 3 (2010): 431–50.

Mafeje, Archie. "Theory of Democracy and the African Discourse: Breaking Bread with My Fellow Travellers." In *Democratisation Processes in Africa: Problems and Perspectives*, edited by Eshetu Chole and Jibrin Ibrahim, 5–28. Dakar, Senegal: CODESIA, 1995.

Maghimbi, S. "Water, Nomadism and the Subsistence Ethic in Maasailand." In *Contemporary Perspectives on African Moral Economy*, edited by I.N. Kimambo, G. Hyden, S. Maghimbi, and K. Sugimura, 63–71. Dar es Salaam: Dar es Salaam University Press, 2008.

Mak' Ochieng, Murej. "The African and Kenyan Media as a Political Public Sphere." *Communicatio* 22, no. 2 (1996): 23–32.

Mano, Winston. "Reconceptualising Media Studies in Africa." In *Internationalising Media Studies*, edited by Daya K. Thussu, 277–94. London: Routledge, 2009.

Massey, Doreen. "Power-Geometry and a Progressive Sense of Place." In *Mapping the Futures: Local Cultures, Global Change*, edited by John Bird, Barry Curtis, Tim Putnam, George Robertson, and Lisa Tickner, 60–70. London: Routledge, 1993.

Mauss, Marcel. *The Gift, Trans. WD Halls*. Oxon: Routledge, 1990.

McLagan, Meg, and Yates McKee. "Introduction." In *Sensible Politics: The Visual Culture of Nongovernmental Activism*, edited by Meg McLagan and Yates McKee, 9–26. New York: Zone Books, 2012.

McRobbie, Angela. "Clubs to Companies: Notes on the Decline of Political Culture in Speeded up Creative Worlds." *Cultural Studies* 16, no. 4 (2002): 516–31.

Mostafanezhad, Mary, and Kevin Hannam. "Introducing Moral Encounters in Tourism." In *Moral Encounters in Tourism*, edited by Mary Mostafanezhad and Kevin Hannam, 1–16. London: Routledge, 2016.

Murdock, Graham. "Building the Digital Commons: Public Broadcasting in the Age of the Internet." In *Cultural Dilemmas in Public Service Broadcasting*, edited by Gregory F. Lowe and Per Jauert, 213–30. Coronet Books, 2005.

Mwangi, Sam Chege. "A Search for an Appropriate Communications Model for Media in New Democracies in Africa." *International Journal of Communication* 4 (2010): 1–26.

Natsios, Andrew. "Illusions of Influence: The CNN Effect in Complex Emergencies." In *From Massacres to Genocide: The Media, Public Policy and Humanitarian Crises*, edited by Robert I. Rotberg and Thomas G. Weiss, 149–68. Washington, DC: Brookings Institution, 2002.

Ndangam, Lilian. "'All of Us Have Taken gombo': Media Pluralism and Patronage in Cameroonian Journalism." *Journalism* 10, no. 6 (2009): 819–42.

Ngũgĩ, wa Thiong'o. *Decolonising the Mind: The Politics of Language in African Literature*. Studies in African Literature. New Series. London: James Currey, 1986.

Nolan, David. "Journalism, Education and the Formation of 'public Subjects'." *Journalism* 9, no. 6 (2008): 733–49.

Nussbaum, Martha C. *Women and Human Development: The Capabilities Approach*. Vol. 3. Cambridge: Cambridge University Press, 2001.

———. "Capabilities as Fundamental Entitlements: Sen and Social Justice." *Feminist Economics* 9, no. 2–3 (2003): 33–59.

Nyamnjoh, Francis B. *Africa's Media: Democracy and the Politics of Belonging*. London: Zed Books, 2005a.

———. "Journalism in Africa: Modernity, Africanity." *Rhodes Journalism Review* 25 (2005b): 3–6.

Ogunyemi, Olatunji. "Representation of Africa Online: Sourcing Practice and Frames of Reference." *Journal of Black Studies* 42, no. 3 (2011):457–78.

Phillips, Angela. "Who's to Make Journalists?" In *Making Journalists: Diverse Models and Global Issues*, edited by Hugo de Burgh, 227–44. London: Routledge, 2005.

Polanyi, Karl. *The Great Transformation: The Political and Economic Origins of Our Time*. 2nd ed. Boston, MA: Beacon Press, 2001.

Posusney, Marsha P. "Irrational Workers: The Moral Economy of Labor Protest in Egypt." *World Politics* 46, no. 1 (1993): 83–120.

Powers, Matthew. "Beyond Boon or Bane: Using Normative Theories to Evaluate the News-Making Efforts of NGOs." *Journalism Studies* 18, no. 9 (2017): 1070–86.

Rajak, Dinah. "'HIV/AIDS Is Our Business': The Moral Economy of Treatment in a Transnational Mining Company." *Journal of the Royal Anthropological Institute* 16, no. 3 (2010): 551–71.

Rao, Shakuntala. "Postcolonial Theory and Global Media Ethics: A Theoretical Intervention." In *Media Ethics Beyond Borders*, edited by Stephen J. A. Ward and H. Wasserman, 90–104. London, New York: Routledge, 2010.

Rao, Shakuntala, and Herman Wasserman. "Global Media Ethics Revisited—A Postcolonial Critique." *Global Media and Communication* 3, no. 1 (2007): 29–50.

———. eds. *Media Ethics and Justice in the Age of Globalisation*. Basingstoke: Palgrave Macmillan, 2015.

Reese, Stephen D. "Globalization of Mediated Spaces: The Case of Transnational Environmentalism in China." *International Journal of Communication* 9 (2015): 2263–81.

Rugendyke, Barbara. "Lilliputians or Leviathans? NGOs as Advocates." In *NGOs as Advocates for Development in a Globalising World*, edited by Barbara Rugendyke, 1–14. London: Routledge, 2007.

Sayer, Andrew. *Realism and Social Science*. London: Sage, 2000a.

———. "Moral Economy and Political Economy." *Studies in Political Economy* 12, no. 2 (2000b): 79–103.

———. "For a Critical Cultural Political Economy." *Antipode* 33, no. 4 (2001): 687–708.

———. "(De-) Commodification, Consumer Culture and Moral Economy." *Environment and Planning D Society and Space* 21, no. 3 (2003): 341–57.

———. "Moral Economy." Paper published by the Department of Sociology, Lancaster University, 2004. http://www.comp.lancs.ac.uk/sociology/papers/sayer-moral-economy.pdf.

———. "Moral Economy as Critique." *New Political Economy* 12, no. 2 (2007): 261–70.

———. "Approaching Moral Economy." In *The Moralization of the Markets*, edited by Nico Stehr, Christoph Henning, and Bernd Weiler, 77–97. New Brunswick, NJ: Transaction Publishers, 2010.

———. *Why Things Matter to People: Social Science, Values and Ethical Life*. Cambridge: Cambridge University Press, 2011.

Schön, Donald A. *The Reflective Practitioner: How Professionals Think in Action*. Farnham: Ashgate, 1991.

Schudson, Michael. *The Sociology of News (Contemporary Sociology)*. New York: W.W. Norton and Co., 2003.

Scott, James C. *The Moral Economy of the Peasant*. New Haven, CT and London: Yale University Press, 1976.

Scott, Martin. "Distant Suffering Online: The Unfortunate Irony of Cyber-Utopian Narratives." *The International Communication Gazette* 77, no. 7 (2015): 637–53.

———. "The Myth of Representations of Africa." *Journalism Studies* 18, no. 2 (2017): 191–210.

Sen, Amartya. *Development as Freedom*. Oxford: Oxford University Press, 1999.

———. *The Idea of Justice*. London: Penguin, 2010.

Sesanti, Simphiwe. "The Concept of 'respect' in African Culture in the Context of Journalism Practice: An Afrocentric Intervention." *Communicatio: South African Journal for Communication Theory and Research* 36, no. 3 (2010): 343–58.

Seu, Irene B. "'Doing Denial': Audience Reaction to Human Rights Appeals." *Discourse & Society* 21, no. 4 (2010): 438–57.

———. "'Shoot the Messenger': Dynamics of Positioning and Denial in Response to Human Rights Appeals." *Journal of Human Rights Practice* 3, no. 2 (2011): 139–61.

———. *Passivity Generation: Human Rights and Everyday Morality*, Houndmills, Basingstoke: Palgrave Macmillan, 2013.

Seu, Irene B., and Shani Orgad. *Caring in Crisis? Humanitarianism, the Public and NGOs*. London, New York: Palgrave Macmillan, 2017.

Shaw, Ibrahim Seaga. "Towards an African Journalism Model—A Critical Historical Perspective." *International Communication Gazette* 71, no. 6 (2009): 491–510.

Shivji, Issa G. *Silences in NGO Discourse: The Role and Future of NGOs in Africa*. Nairobi, Oxford: Fahamu/Pambazuka, 2007.

Shutt, Cathy. "A Moral Economy? Social Interpretations of Money in Aidland." *Third World Quarterly* 33, no. 8 (2012): 1527–43.

Silverstone, Roger. *Media and Morality: On the Rise of the Mediapolis*. Cambridge, UK, Malden, MA: Polity Press, 2007.

Siméant, Johanna. "Three Bodies of Moral Economy: The Diffusion of a Concept." *Journal of Global Ethics* 11, no. 2 (2015): 163–75.

Skeggs, Beverley. "The Moral Economy of Person Production: The Class Relations of Self-Performance on 'reality' television." *The Sociological Review* 57, no. 4 (2009): 626–44.

———. "Imagining Personhood Differently: Person Value and Autonomist Working-Class Value Practices." *The Sociological Review* 59, no. 3 (2011): 496–513.

Skinner, David, Mike J. Gasher, and James Compton. "Putting Theory to Practice a Critical Approach to Journalism Studies." *Journalism* 2, no. 3 (2001): 341–60.

Somerville, Keith. *Radio Propaganda and the Broadcasting of Hatred: Historical Development and Definitions*. London: Palgrave Macmillan, 2012.

Stones, Rob. "Social Theory and Current Affairs: A Framework for Greater Intellectual Engagement." *British Journal of Sociology* 65, no. 2 (2014): 293–316.

———. *Why Current Affairs Needs Social Theory*. London, New York: Bloomsbury, 2015.

Thompson, Allan, ed. *The Media and the Rwanda Genocide*. London: Pluto Press, 2007.

Thompson, Edward P. "The Moral Economy of the English Crowd in the Eighteenth Century." *Past and Present* (1971): 76–136.

Tomaselli, Keyan G. "'Our Culture' vs 'Foreign Culture'—An Essay on Ontological and Professional Issues in African Journalism." *Gazette* 65, no. 6 (2003): 427–41.

Turner, Mark, and David Hulme. *Governance, Administration and Development: Making the State Work*. Basingstoke: Macmillan, 1997.

Ward, Stephen J. *Global Journalism Ethics*. Montreal & Kingston: McGill-Queen's University Press, 2010.

———. *Ethics and the Media: An Introduction*. Cambridge: Cambridge University Press, 2011.

Ward, Stephen J., and Herman Wasserman. "Open Ethics: Towards a Global Media Ethics of Listening." *Journalism Studies* 16, no. 6 (2015): 834–49.

Wasserman, Hermann. "Globalized Values and Postcolonial Responses: South African Perspectives on Normative Media Ethics." *International Communication Gazette* 68, no. 1 (2006): 71–91.

———. "Media Ethics and Human Dignity in the Postcolony." In *Media Ethics Beyond Borders: A Global Perspective*, edited by Stephen.J.A. Ward and Herman Wasserman, 74–89. London: Routledge, 2010.

———. "Towards a Global Journalism Ethics via Local Narratives: Southern African Perspectives." *Journalism Studies* 12, no. 6 (December 2011): 791–803.

Willetts, Peter. "What Is a Non-Governmental Organization?" Output from the Research Project on Civil Society Networks in Global Governance, 2006.
http://www.staff.city.ac.uk/p.willetts/CS-NTWKS/NGO-ART.HTM.
Wright, Kate. "Reality without Scare Quotes: Developing the Case for Critical Realism in Journalism Research." *Journalism Studies* 12, no. 2 (2011): 156–71.
———. "Should Journalists be 'Virtuous'? Mainstream News, Complex Media Organisations and the Work of Nick Couldry." *Journalism* 15, no. 3 (2014): 364–81.
———. "Moral Economies: Interrogating the Interactions of Nongovernmental Organizations, Journalists and Freelancers." *International Journal of Communication* 10 (2016a): 1510–29.
———. "'These Grey Areas' How and Why Freelance Work Blurs INGOs and News Organizations." *Journalism Studies* 17, no. 8 (2016b): 989–1009.
Yanacopulos, Helen. *International NGO Engagement, Advocacy, Activism: The Faces and Spaces of Change*. Non-Governmental Public Action Series. Houndmills, Basingstoke: Palgrave Macmillan, 2015.
Zeleza, Tiyambe. "The Moral Economy of Working Class Struggle: Strikers, The Community and the State in the 1947 Mombassa General Strike." *Africa Development/Afrique et Développement* (1995): 51–87.
Zelizer, Barbie. "Journalists as Interpretive Communities." *Critical Studies in Media Communication* 10, no. 3 (1993): 219–37.
———. *Taking Journalism Seriously: News and the Academy*. London: Sage Publications, 2004.
———. "Journalism in the Service of Communication." *Journal of Communication* 61, no. 1 (2011): 1–21.

· 4 ·

PHOTOJOURNALISM, PROFESSIONALISM, AND PRINT NEWSPAPERS

The Independent on Sunday and Christian Aid

Photojournalists are leaving mainstream news outlets in droves. Like many other specialists, they have been squeezed out by cost-cutting, and news cultures which privilege rapidity and multi-skilling over the exercise of time-consuming skills and seasoned judgement (Caple 2013; Wright 2016). But photojournalists also face specific challenges to do with the advent of rapidly-acquired and cost-free User Generated Content (UGC), which may be seen as more authentic and "truthful" by news audiences (Mortensen 2014; Mortensen and Keshelashvili 2013). In addition, new forms of mobile technology and digital software are often believed to make it easy for those without specialist training to produce technically competent and visually attractive images (Ritchin 2009; Solaroli 2015).

The combination of these factors has led to photojournalists being laid off far more frequently than their counterparts in written journalism. For example, the American Society of News Editors stated that whereas 32 per cent of reporters and writers had been sacked since 2000, the numbers of photographers had been cut by 43 per cent (Anderson 2013). Several cases of mass redundancies have also grabbed the headlines in the US, most notably at *The Chicago Sun-Times*, which fired all 28 of its photojournalists in one fell swoop in 2013 (Mortensen 2014). Similar patterns of redundancies have been reported in countries as far apart as Australia (Anderson 2014), Israel (Klein-Avraham and Reich 2016) and Romania (Bardan 2015). Indeed, a recent global study found that most photojournalists are now self-employed (Hadland *et al.* 2015).

The numbers of photojournalists employed as staff by newspapers in the UK are also thought to be plummeting. At a meeting of the National Union of Journalists, former *Guardian* photojournalist, Martin Argles, estimated that although Fleet Street employed 150 photographers in the 1970s, this had dropped to the mid-twenties by 2013 (Argles 2013). This leaves the editorial staff of British newspapers in a very difficult position because they have few (if any) staff photojournalists left, and much lower budgets with which to commission freelancers.

Yet photographs are more important than ever before, even for "legacy" newspapers which don't publish much extra material online. Tabloidization means that even broadsheets publish more images, and these tend to be larger in size, in order to attract the dwindling numbers of people willing to purchase print newspapers (Conboy 2006; Sparks and Tulloch 2000). In addition, newspapers are expected to produce numerous magazines and supplements, which contain many glossy images, in order to attract advertisers and consumers (Moore 2010; Phillips 2010).

So newspaper staff are obliged to find ways of sourcing large volumes of high-quality images at low or no cost. These pictures also need to be visually distinctive, in order to make newspapers stand out from their rivals. But achieving this difference is extremely challenging, as most newspapers depend on subscriptions to the same photographic agencies as their competitors (predominantly Getty and Corbis), as well as drawing images from the same major news wire agencies (predominantly Thomson Reuters and Associated Press) (Caple 2013; Hallas 2012). Moreover, newspaper staff have very little time to hunt for, or conduct checks on, contributed photos because they are already coping with reduced editorial teams and a vastly increased workload (Fenton 2010; Phillips 2012).

International NGOs (INGOs) have long engaged in highly visual forms of activism, so have a tradition of hiring well-respected freelance photojournalists (Hallas 2012; McLagan and McKee 2012). Many INGOs now offer the photos they have commissioned from freelancers to news outlets free of charge. This clearly offers journalists significant time and cost savings (Gandy 1982). But journalists' deliberations about whether or not to use NGO material also involved complex normative considerations (Wright 2016).

Understanding the normative dimensions of journalists' decision-making about photos is particularly important because photojournalism is often seen as having the ability to stimulate progressive social change (Hallas 2012). So the deliberations of news staff about using INGO-commissioned photojournalism brought about complex interactions between normative and economic values.

Freelance photojournalists' decision to work for INGOs is also characterized by a mixture of economic and normative considerations. These freelancers report that they are poorly paid, as news organizations are able to give them fewer commissions than in the past, and the fees for these commissions have not risen in line with inflation (Hadland *et al.* 2015). So many have diversified their client portfolio in order to make financial ends meet (Hadland *et al.* 2015). But INGO commissions were also of value to freelancers because they tended to involve longer foreign trips. Freelancers said these longer periods of travel enabled them to develop deeper relationships with their subjects, which they thought helped them produce more powerful images (Campbell 2007; Grayson 2014).

In addition, working for NGOs can be a significant source of cultural capital for freelancers, as it enables them to follow in the footsteps of some of the best photojournalists in the world. These include Tim Hetherington, who worked for Human Rights Watch, Didier Lefèvre, who accepted a brief from Doctors without Borders, and Gideon Mendel, who covered a project on HIV-AIDS by the Global Fund to Fight AIDS, Tuberculosis and Malaria (Hallas 2012).

This chapter explains how and why staff working for *The Independent* papers in the UK used photos commissioned by INGOs from freelance photo journalists to sustain their commitment to publishing technically skilled, aesthetically distinctive and thought-provoking photojournalism despite widespread cost-cutting. It outlines how these photos were usually incorporated into the papers, before focusing on a more unusual case, involving journalists' acceptance of a double-page spread of written and photographic material from the international aid agency, Christian Aid.

This "World News" article was a double page spread, which represented a food crisis experienced by Malians fleeing from fighting between governmental and Islamist forces, as well as the food shortages faced by the ethnic Dogon group who lived near the frontline (Hogg 2012). In particular, this chapter will examine how the production and placement of this material depended on trust in the "professionalism" of all of those concerned. This had some progressive aspects, but tended to drive out more radical or alternative approaches, including the INGO's politics of "voice" (Couldry 2010) and related efforts to engage in more collaborative and egalitarian forms of media production.

The Independent newspapers

At the time of writing, Evgeny Lebedev, the Russian owner of *The Independent* papers, had just announced that he would cease producing print copies of the 30 year old daily newspaper, its compact version, the *i*, and *The Independent on Sunday*, in order to focus solely on digital output (Lebedev 2016). But the papers had been very slow to move into online journalism: when this study was conducted in 2012, print media was still the main focus of journalistic production, and this content was simply republished online with minimal changes. However, the papers were in the run-up to a major organizational change, which paved the way towards greater web-centricity. This involved merging the news-desks which produced the *Independent* papers with that which produced the London free paper, *The Standard*: with all four combining to produce multimedia content for online and for a new TV station, *London Live* (Ponsford 2013).

Staff did not know about this until February 2013, but they were aware that further integration was likely, and that this would probably involve job losses because the papers were in serious financial trouble. Indeed, at the time when the study was done in August 2012, the *Independent* publications were losing around £17.5 million per annum (Independent Print Ltd. Company Accounts 2011, 2012). This new uncertainty compounded the effects of previous waves of redundancies, which had led to the papers losing around a third of their editorial staff between 2008 and 2012 (interview with David Randall, Foreign Editor of *The Independent on Sunday*, March 20, 2013).

The Deputy Managing Editor stressed that organizational "efficiencies" were "pushing up staff "productivity" without "anyone having to work harder" (interview with Sean O'Grady, *The Independent* and *The Standard* newspapers, August 14, 2013). But editorial staff told a different story. As in studies of US newspapers, the repeated waves of cuts left *Independent* staff feeling overstretched and stressed, which undermined their trust in their managers, colleagues and their sense of belonging to their news organization (Gade 2004; Reinardy 2010). Photojournalists, who felt particularly undermined by the increase in role-merging and multiskilling, even reported incidents of abuse from their immediate team leaders. For example, one claimed that he was subject to:

> Terrible bullying, workplace bullying (…)
>
> [It] was *absolutely* related to cost-cutting because getting to do good assignments was such a scarce opportunity, that it became much, much easier to pit people against each other.

Indeed, all three of the photojournalists formerly employed by *The Independent* papers chose to take redundancy—a crushing blow for papers which had once led the field in British photojournalism (McCabe 2008).

Picture editors were also concerned about role-merging, which they claimed had not only decimated their numbers, but had shaped a lack of respect for their aesthetic judgement and skills. Indeed, managers routinely redistributed the responsibility for selecting images to others with little or no photographic training. As Ivy Lahon, who was then the Deputy Picture Editor of *The Independent*, put it:

> There is the assumption that, "Oh, the art director could step in and do a bit of that" (…) or we could get a sub [editor] to pick a picture instead. (interview, June 26, 2013)

For these reasons, Lahon decided to take redundancy, moving to become a picture editor at Save the Children UK because, she said,

> They really *value* visual expertise there. After all, they know that the difference between one picture and another could be *millions* of pounds. (interview, March 6, 2014)

But Lahon's move was not only shaped by self-interest: she was also dismayed that her own and others' increased workload meant that "basic professional standards" were often not met at *The Independent* papers (interview, June 26, 2013). In particular, she claimed that factual and attribution errors were "slipping through the net too often", especially close to publication deadlines when time was tight.

Thus Lahon painted a picture of a decline in notions of skilled professionalism which involved not only specialist expertise, but also the ability to carry out the practices fundamental to the job (Örnebring 2016). Such approaches to professionalism involve making implicit links between notions of quality control and the trustworthiness of journalism (Örnebring 2016), which is needed to make other normative goals possible. In particular, Lahon's concerns can be seen to relate to an ethics of truth-telling, which is central to notions of occupational professionalism (Aldridge and Evetts 2003; Waisbord 2013).

It is common to view occupational professionalism as different from organizational professionalism, which involves the "discourse of control used increasingly by managers [which] …incorporates hierarchical structures of authority, the standardization of work practices… target-setting and performance review" (Evetts 2006 cited in Örnebring 2009, 4). But Lahon took a far more nuanced line: arguing that skilled professionalism was necessary to meet normative standards and managerial objectives (interview, March 6, 2014). These included constructing *The Independent's* distinctive brand and sustaining the papers' reputation and positioning within the journalistic field, at a time of fierce commercial competition. So the connections between truth-telling, quality and skilled professionalism can serve to link occupational to organizational professionalism (Örnebring 2016); although there can also be tensions or conflicts between them (Aldridge and Evetts 2003).

However, *Independent* staff refrained from any collective discussion of how to navigate their multiple obligations. This was because they worried that senior managers would blame them personally for errors: making them more vulnerable during the anticipated rounds of redundancies. So although some individuals expressed trust in each other, most said that there was a general atmosphere of distrust at the papers, which made them unwilling to engage openly with their peers about the problems they were facing. Instead, journalists and picture editors quietly devised what they thought were short-cuts or "work-around" solutions, so that they could meet managerial directives regarding efficiency, without being found wanting in other ways.

Such approaches were underpinned by a widespread acceptance of the damaging effects of market forces on the papers. As David Randall, the Foreign Editor of *The Independent on Sunday*, put it,

> If we made *board* games or sprockets, we would have been shut down *years* ago: years and years ago. So I fully *understand* that these cuts are necessary (…)
>
> We don't have an entitlement to be subsidized in perpetuity by multi-millionaires in order to do the kind of journalism… for which there is not *apparently* an economic demand. (interview, March 10, 2013)

Indeed, journalists believed that the business model of all print newspapers had been irretrievably "broken" by the provision of free journalistic content, especially online, so there was no point lobbying for other means of funding or management (interview with David Randall, March 10, 2013). Thus how and why *Independent* staff used INGO-commissioned photos was shaped by a combination of the papers' socially liberal perspectives with the harsh, right-wing economic approaches shaping journalists' and picture editors' editorial labor.

This meant that *Independent* staff frequently used photos commissioned from well-known freelancers by large UK-based international aid agencies, as well as environmental and wildlife INGOs, whose normative values they felt were in keeping with *The Independent*. But these images were used to solve production crises brought about by managerial efficiencies. For example, *Independent* picture editors said that they kept INGO-provided photos about long-running issues on file to deal with quiet news weeks, like the one sampled, as cuts to commissioning meant that very few off-agenda items would be coming in and they didn't want to be left with "holes in the paper" (interview with Ivy Lahon, June 26, 2013).

Differently sized images contributed by INGOs were also used to plug gaps in the layout of *The Independent* when last-minute adverts were placed, which the paper couldn't afford to turn down. So about once or twice a month, picture editors said they used INGO pictures as "space-fillers" (interview with Ivy Lahon, June 26, 2013). Yet their managers claimed they would never countenance such a thing: maintaining that the "efficiencies" had not affected "editorial standards" (interview with Sean O'Grady, *The Independent* and *The Standard* newspapers, August 14, 2013).

Using INGO-commissioned photos in these ways involved the creation of new obligations, which constrained journalists' professional autonomy in some ways (Örnebring 2016). As the Sunday Picture Editor explained, these exchanges were founded on an understanding that the photos would be used within a certain time frame—with six months being the maximum limit (interview, June 12, 2013). However, picture editors thought that it was worth entering into this obligation because such images did not go on the internal lists of images commissioned by *Independent* staff. This meant that they weren't faced with a situation where "everyone moans at you that the pictures are too old" (interview with Sunday Picture Editor, June 12, 2013). Thus INGO-commissioned photos enabled picture editors to cope with the production crises produced by role-merging, whilst also minimizing the risk of personal censure, at a time when further redundancies were anticipated (Banks *et al.* 2000).

Finally, Randall, the Foreign Editor of *The Independent on Sunday*, outlined a third way in which INGO-commissioned photos were used (interview, March 20, 2013). This, he said, involved them being "pitched" by INGO press officers to the paper's reporters via personal phone calls and emails, along with "news stories". He then said that the reporter would "flesh this [pitch] out" by conducting a number of "their own" interviews, as was "right and proper" for "professional" journalists., Randall stressed that this form of skilled production was appropriate to the Sunday paper because their reporters had "a bit more time" and were better placed to fulfil *Independent* journalists' commitment to relatively long-form, "independent", "campaigning" and "investigative" journalism.

This approach clearly had ethical and other normative dimensions, which were related to organizational branding and market differentiation (Aldridge and Evetts 2003; Örnebring 2016). But it is debatable how "independent" such forms of reporting could really be. For instance, a press officer from WaterAid was found to have "pitched" what he said was an "exclusive story" to an *Independent on Sunday* reporter (interview with WaterAid press officer, August 24, 2012). However, the press officer admitted that this "exclusive story" was actually a single aspect of the INGO's report released a week before the general embargo date (2012, discussed in interview with WaterAid press officer, August 24, 2012). Although the article did contain quotes from a number of other people (Morrison 2012), the interpretative frame used in the article did not change from that pitched by WaterAid.

All of these practices involved "information subsidies" which allowed *Independent* journalists to work faster and more cheaply (Gandy 1982). But the operation of these subsidies was not straightforward, as it was modified by *Independent* journalists' willingness to invest some of their own time and energy to gesture towards the kinds of distinctive, ethical and skilled journalism which they valued (Örnebring 2016). The complex operation of these information subsidies was also shaped by the efforts of news staff to minimize risk to their own professional reputations, at a time of chronic job insecurity (Banks *et al.* 2000). So journalists and picture editors used INGO material to save time and money, but also to renegotiate the links and tensions between different kinds of "professionalism".

The Independent on Sunday: case study

The exchanges outlined above help to contextualize "habits of thinking, mental models and linguistic paradigms" which underpin the main case study (Schein 2004, 13). This involved a complete form of "news cloning" (Fenton

2010): that is, journalists' incorporation of a double-page spread of written and photographic material from Christian Aid, which was published as a "World News" lead in *The Independent on Sunday* (Hogg 2012). But it was unusual for journalists to accept both written and visual material from an INGO—so unusual, in fact, that no organizational route had been established for dealing with such a submission. In these circumstances, the informal, interpersonal relationships which press officers at INGOs often have with their former journalistic colleagues became very important (Fenton 2010). As Andrew Hogg, Christian Aid's Head of Media, explained,

> What I did in the end was I phoned a mate at *The Independent* (…) and said I have just got back from Mali, I've got a good piece, are you interested?
> And (…) I was told by my mate to send it to [the Foreign Editor of *The Independent on Sunday*.] He said "Put *his* name on it!"
> [Thumps desk for emphasis] (interview, Nov 7, 2012)

Christian Aid's offer appealed to David Randall, the Foreign Editor, because he knew Tom Pilston, the freelance photojournalist hired by the INGO, who had previously been a member of staff at *The Independent*. This gave Randall faith in the high quality of Pilston's work, which he expressed as his "professionalism". As he explained,

> In the first email, Hogg said that Tom Pilston was the photographer who had gone with him. Now Tom is an ex-*Independent* photographer so you know, if I see that *he* has done the pictures, I needn't worry about the quality of them.
> Obviously one *does* worry when its people taking pictures with their mobile phones, however many bloody megapixels they think they've got (…) It is not just technical quality; Tom has also got an *eye*. He's a *professional* photographer as opposed to someone snapping something with their iPhone. (interview, March 10, 2013)

The kind of skilled professionalism described here (Örnebring 2016) involved both technical abilities and aesthetic understanding, which Randall went on to explain, could only be acquired through years of training and experience. The Picture Editor of *The Independent on Sunday* agreed that Pilston's "professional" pictures were good enough to use for "big spread", and not just a small item in a "column"—unlike other kinds of contributed photos whose poor quality became apparent when they were blown up (interview, June 12, 2013). Thus Pilston's photos not only subsidized the efforts of news staff to fill pages (Gandy 1982), they also helped to sustain *The Independent's* distinctive brand and market positioning as a publisher of high quality photojournalism (McCabe 2008).

However, the Picture Editor stressed that she also "trusted" Pilston's "professionalism", in the sense of having faith in his commitment to upholding occupational ethics (Aldridge and Evetts 2003). Indeed, she took Pilston's involvement in the Christian Aid piece as a "guarantee" that what was depicted was not staged, faked or exaggerated (interview, June 12, 2013). This was important to her because senior managers insisted that it was possible for staff to process large volumes of images for the papers swiftly, without cutting back on fact-checking (interview with Sean O'Grady, *The Independent* and *The Standard* newspapers, August 14, 2013). But the Sunday picture editor insisted that:

> You haven't got *time* to double check everything, which is why I'd avoid something from an *unknown* source, from a *suspect* source.
> I would rather avoid that altogether rather than try to check and check and check and *check*. I need to be able to take stuff on *trust* nowadays. (interview, June 12, 2013)

So Pilston's employment by Christian Aid offered the Picture Editor a specific kind of "information subsidy" (Gandy 1982), a "verification subsidy" (McPherson 2015). This enabled her to address the responsibilities of both organizational and occupational professionalism in some, limited ways, despite the presence of powerful constraining factors (Aldridge and Evetts 2003). But, most of all, the Sunday picture editor stressed that Pilston's "professionalism" meant that he had the ability to produce "beautiful" and "un-clichéd" photos with the power to make audiences respond emotionally (Sontag 2008). Pointing to the image reproduced overleaf, she elaborated on this, saying:

> It shows that this, this, sort of, family are *obviously* struggling, and it's very sad, but *beautiful*. I mean, A shot it *beautifully*: there's this lovely light coming in, good colors. And when, when the reader *turns* to this, they will think it's strong and it's heart-rending but without being that sort of bleeding-heart aid agency thing *again* (…) (interview, June 12, 2013)

The Picture Editor's discussion of this photograph was illuminating because it involved considerations relating to the visual differentiation of the paper, and other kinds of market-related concerns. In particular, she stressed her responsibility to appeal to their highly educated, "intelligent readers" without alienating them, saying that she

> …needed to be careful to avoid that "very much sort of *hit* in the guts photography [because] that might actually make some people go "I *really* don't need this on a Sunday morning." (interview with Sunday Picture Editor, June 12, 2013)

Figure 4.1: Malians displaced by fighting, photographed by Tom Pilston for Christian Aid

Source: Tom Pilston/Christian Aid/Panos

Pilston's work was perfect because he deliberately aestheticized suffering: drawing from the traditions of social documentary photography published in current affairs magazines in the 1960s and 1970s (interview with Tom Pilston, February 22, 2013). He also said he used light coming in from the side to generate a soft effect which evoked European portraits by "Old Masters". The ethics of aestheticizing suffering have long been questioned in scholarship about photography (Sontag 2003). But news staff thought that the aesthetically skilled, intertextual nature of Pilston's pictures helped to make other kinds of normative objectives possible. Specifically, both picture editors stressed that they believed that such "sophisticated" and "professional" photojournalism would "draw the reader in and make them ask questions, rather than giving them obvious answers" (interview with Ivy Lahon, June 26, 2013).

The written article provided by Christian Aid was also judged to be of "professional quality" by the Foreign Editor, Randall, who praised its "skilled", "crisp" news writing and "tight" structure which suited the Sunday broadsheet well (interview, March 10, 2013. This was perhaps unsurprising because it had been written by Andrew Hogg, who had been employed as the news editor of

two Sunday broadsheets—*The Observer* and *The Sunday Times*—before he became Christian Aid's Head of Media. But Randall was unaware of this: he was
largely focused on the "information subsidies" which the piece provided for
him (Gandy 1982). In particular, he was very pleased that he needed to spend
very little time on it because it needed only "a very light sub-edit" before it
could be published.

Saving time was important to Randall because of the ways in which role-
merging had drastically increased his workload. As he explained,

> You know, I am looking after the foreign pages of *The Independent on Sunday*, but
> that's about a twelfth of what I do in a week.
>
> I write comment pieces, I get ideas for features, I quite often write them—I've
> just done a big thing on cars. The first three pages of the Features section I write, big
> breaking stories, I write home stories sometimes.
>
> On a Saturday, I write a good deal of the news headlines(…) I'm also acting Dep-
> uty Editor of the paper and I write pieces for the magazine from time to time.
>
> Ten years ago, *The Independent on Sunday* had a foreign editor who did nothing but
> edit foreign copy, and he might have written himself but *only* in his field. That's *not*
> the case now. (interview, March 10, 2013)

Randall also saw the written article provided by Christian Aid as helping
him to differentiate his paper from others without spending any money
(Gandy 1982). He stressed what a "great catch" it would be to get a piece
from a rarely covered location like northern Mali (interview with David
Randall, March 10, 2013). He then added that he could not have afforded
to send his own Africa correspondent or one of the paper's regular stringers on such a trip, unless it was an "obvious lead" which would "run for
several weeks".[1]

Thus using INGO-produced content helped Randall respond to his professional obligations in several different ways. It helped him publish what he
regarded as skilled, high-quality work (Örnebring 2016), whilst also helping
him to fulfil his organizational obligations to produce more material, faster,
and more cheaply (Aldridge and Evetts 2003). At the same time, INGO-
produced content helped Randall respond to the ethical demands of occupational professionalism regarding geographic diversity, which had long concerned him (Aldridge and Evetts 2003).

Randall stressed that he had often been "troubled" by the "skimpy" geographic spread of *Independent* journalists and regular freelancers, as this meant
that he was unable to offer "the kind of geographic coverage [that] the Editor
of the World pages on a national daily newspaper *should* be able to provide"

(interview, March 10, 2013). He had first tried to address the paper's lack of geographic diversity by sourcing new freelancers in unusual locations, but Randall struggled to build trusting relationships with them because of his time-poverty. As he put it,

> *Ideally*, you still want to meet [freelancers] if that's possible …because you want to find out if they've got two *heads* on them! Or they're *barking* [mad]!
>
> An email and sometimes a phone call can't always tell you that (…) But it's getting harder and harder to [meet in person].

However, Randall rejected any possibility of using what he called "citizen journalism" which he dismissed in scathing terms, seeing it as being characterized by "sloppy" writing and "emotional incontinence". He not only saw it as unskilled or "low quality" work which risked damaging the paper's brand, he also saw it as being ethically problematic, as such material often failed to distinguish between facts and feelings or opinions. Next, Randall looked into a different option: exploring the possibility of using material from an organization which showcased work by journalists in what he called "the developing world". In this way, he hoped to diversify the range of places and perspectives in his foreign news coverage, as well as "championing the underdog".

Randall was personally committed to this normative mission because of his own working class background, and because of the paper's history of campaigning journalism. However, Randall complained that this clearing-house had not been run by a "professional" journalist, with "national print experience", so the whole process became far too time-consuming. Indeed, Randall said it had involved a "constant dribble" of long, unsolicited phone calls and the submission of low-quality copy, which needed extensive rewriting before it could be published.

So the material offered by Christian Aid offered Randall a way of resolving tensions between his professional obligation to uphold occupational ethics regarding truth-telling and geographic diversity, as well as enabling him to respond to his professional commitment to publish skilled, high-quality work. At the same time, this exchange helped Randall to fulfil his professional responsibility to deliver large volumes of appropriate and distinctive, content for his organization in quick, cheap ways (Aldridge and Evetts 2003; Örnebring 2016). Thus *Independent* journalists' "trust" in INGO material was not simple, passive or unthinking (Franks 2008a, 2008b). Rather, it emerged from their agentive renegotiation of complex social obligations, relating to the economic and normative values shaping work at *The Independent* papers.

One intriguing factor shaping journalists' deliberations involved their previous experience of working with major aid agencies. For example, Randall spoke of his experience of volunteering to do press work for the Disasters Emergency Committee, which coordinates joint appeals by the UK's major aid agencies. Meanwhile, other members of staff likened their use of NGO images to their collaboration on the paper's Christmas appeal. But even these experiences were related to "norms, values and discursive practices of markets" (Davis 2010, 133) which dominated editorial labor at the *Independent* papers. Indeed, Randall ultimately legitimized his "trust" in the INGO's article like this:

> In cases like *that* [points to Christian Aid article] I don't go and send someone to double check what Andrew [Hogg] has written.
>
> You know he is there, tied to his agency and if it turns out that he's made a third of it up, and that emerges then he'll lose his job and his agency will suffer *big* time. And none of *them* can afford that either.
>
> So that is my *insurance* policy.

So although Randall's "trust" in INGOs had marked normative dimensions, it operated negatively: that is to say, it was far less focused on trying to achieve something good than on minimizing the risk of negative consequences (Banks *et al.* 2000). Furthermore, rather than "trusting" INGOs to represent something other than the market (Fenton *et al.* 1999), this "trust" actually relied upon conceptualizing aid-workers as paid professionals, who also needed to minimize reputational risks, in order to preserve their own positioning within their respective markets (Banks *et al.* 2000). Whilst such reasoning clearly relates to a laudable desire to avoid causing harm by disseminating falsehood, this form of professionalism risks squeezing out alternative values and more inclusive approaches to news-making.

Christian Aid

Christian Aid has long been known for its (relative) radicalism in NGO-work. Supporters of the aid agency have historically tended to be older members of the Church of England, politicized in the 1960s, who were attracted by Christian Aid's commitment to working in partnership with local NGOs to deliver humanitarian aid. In addition, Christian Aid has long been known for its advocacy work, including its commissioning of in-depth research, which it uses to expose and challenge the unjust structures perpetuating poverty and suffering. So we can position this INGO as within the "alchemical" tradition of humanitarian work (Orgad 2013).

However, Christian Aid's supporters have been gradually dying off, so the INGO has had to make its own "efficiencies", including cutting a third of its communications staff in spring 2012, and merging the marketing, media and advocacy teams into one Communications department. For these reasons, staff at Christian Aid were worried for their own futures. Many were also concerned about what this restructure might mean for the organization's normative values, especially after Steven Buckley was appointed to head the new Communications department, as he had a background in commercial marketing.

David Pain, the senior manager overseeing the organizational restructure, was aware of the extensive internal debate about these changes (interview, May 7, 2013). He justified them by arguing that Christian Aid needed to raise more money from the public if it was to avoid becoming overly dependent on governmental contracts, which often served their objectives rather than the needs of beneficiaries (interview, May 7, 2013). Pain also argued that merging the fundraising, media and advocacy teams into one Communications department would enable Christian Aid to develop deeper, more complex and more egalitarian partnerships with the organization's financial supporters, the in-country agencies with whom it works, and the people whom it tries to help. To reflect this normative framing, he even changed his title to the Director of Supporter and Community Partnerships.

However, Pain knew that North/South partnerships are often criticized for being largely symbolic, allowing Northern-based INGOs to be associated with the culturally rich ideals of "bottom-up" democratic participation, without having to make any of the attendant economic or political sacrifices (Anderson 2007; Lister 2003). So he introduced organizational processes to make it easier for in-country program directors to request attention from the media team at Christian Aid's headquarters in London, as well as giving them the right to "sign-off" on any media items press officers created (interview, May 7, 2013). As he explained,

What we're looking for is to strengthen the voice of our partners, who are close to
people living in poverty, to strengthen their influence in the world (…)

So we're interested in (…) making sure that what we say is based on their experience.

Those kinds of values are *very* important for us.

Pain's approach was grounded in a politics of "voice" (Couldry 2010; Sen
2010), which he described as having emerged from his study of liberation
theology in South Africa. In particular, Pain elaborated on the ways in which
his reading of Freire (2014) had helped him to understand the ways in which
black, poor people had become "their own agents of change" towards the end
of apartheid. But such an approach also had strategic uses: enhancing Christian Aid's moral authority (Slim 2002), as well as its appeal to donors looking
to support charities committed to socio-economic justice.

Christian Aid's Program Director in Mali, Yacouba Kone, applauded
what he called Pain's "devolution of power", which he said had influenced
his decision to request media coverage from the aid agency's headquarters (interview, March 22, 2013). But Buckley, the Communications Director with
the background in commercial marketing, said that Kone's request had only
been granted because a West Africa appeal was already in progress, and he was
fairly sure that the boost it would give to fundraising would at least cover costs
(interview, March 8, 2013). For his part, Andrew Hogg, the Head of Media
who wrote the article, asserted that the speed of news production meant that
extensive editorial consultation with in-country staff was usually impossible,
and that any consultation would be likely to be belated and "largely cosmetic"
(interview, November 7, 2012).

In this case, news production processes were speeded up even more because of security risks. Hogg and Pilston, the freelance photographer, were
obligated by the Malian government to stay no more than one night in any
given place because of concerns that jihadi militia would try to abduct foreign
visitors. However, Hogg was also resistant to the idea of in-country directors
making editorial changes on point of principle. He saw writing articles as a
"professional journalistic exercise" in which others should not interfere (interview with Andrew Hogg, November 7, 2012). His position on this was shaped
to some degree by notions of occupational ethics regarding truth-telling and
independent critical judgement (Aldridge and Evetts 2003). In particular, he
stressed that he would not be dissuaded from "writing about what he saw",
even if others wanted him to "take bits out or water it down".

But Hogg also had a strong desire to be recognized by other journalists for producing high-quality work (Örnebring 2016). This became obvious after he failed to get the piece in *The Sunday Times*, because he then targeted *The Independent on Sunday*, even though he knew it had relatively few readers. He argued that he did this because getting a piece into a broadsheet at all meant that the piece had "passed a kind of professional litmus test" of editorial quality. Professional recognition from other journalists was especially important to Hogg because he believed that this cultural capital would help to safeguard his personal autonomy. This was not only under threat from the devolution of editorial power to Christian Aid's overseas partners, but was directly and persistently challenged by Buckley, the new Head of Communications, who was his new line manager. Indeed, Buckley was very outspoken about his wish to

> (…) rein in *some* members of our staff in the press office who have sort of considered themselves *journalists* first and foremost, rather than press officers. (interview, March 8, 2013)

The tensions between Buckley and Hogg were exacerbated by a fundamental disagreement about the INGO's media strategy.[2] This is because the enculturation of Buckley in commercial marketing made him keen to target more popular outlets, arguing that it was necessary for Christian Aid to help them produce softer genres, such as features, in order to fundraise and engage in mass awareness-raising (interview, March 8, 2013; see also Powers 2014). However, he stressed that the commitment to justice underpinning Christian Aid's "brand" meant that he wouldn't allow fundraisers to use what he considered to be "undignified" images of "a small child looking up into the camera and *very* literal expressions of need", in order to raise as much money as possible.

Nevertheless, Hogg's targeting of *The Independent on Sunday* was not simply a matter of strategic self-interest and professional respect. This is because he was convinced that although those who paid for a broadsheet newspaper might be fewer in number, but they were more likely to be "readers with impact", socio-economic elites "with more interest [and] potentially more involvement in international affairs" (interview with Andrew Hogg, November 7, 2012). He also felt that the framing of the story as "news" connoted an appropriate level of importance and urgency, and that providing long-form news was particularly appropriate to an INGO seeking to explain and challenge the structural causes of poverty. So his prioritization of particular kinds of high-quality output involved normative aims and media strategies which were unlike those of many communications workers in other aid agencies (Powers 2014).

Indeed, Hogg's approach had much more in common with the approaches taken by other former editors and correspondents at Human Rights Watch, which will be discussed in more detail the next chapter. In both INGOs, highly experienced international journalists sought to fulfil their moral/political obligations to others by engaging in time-consuming, investigative journalism, as a means of pressing policy-makers and other elites to intervene. These approaches had been powerfully shaped by their shared experiences of covering the Bosnian War of 1992–1995. Like those at Human Rights Watch, Hogg said that this conflict had "shaken [him] to the core" (interview, November 7, 2012), by effectively collapsing the symbolic distance between him and those he was reporting upon (Shaw 1996). As he put it,

> Bosnia was a bit like looking at a model of a society, a functioning *twentieth century* society, in which somebody had ripped the *roof* off (…) and suddenly *everything* was exposed. Everything that we take for granted in a functioning, orderly world had disappeared.
>
> The *truly* [thumps table] remarkable thing about it was that it was happening to *white* [thump] *Europeans* [thump]. That I can only explain is as some kind of *indictment* of oneself, but it is absolutely true.
>
> I had covered conflicts before: I was in Algeria, Israel, Afghanistan, and Iraq. *None* of them had the emotional power of Bosnia (…) because it was so similar to the world that one lived in.
>
> And I can only see that as a searing indictment of myself. (interview, November 7, 2012)

This experience, together with the re-emergence of his Christian faith, led to Hogg becoming partially dis-embedded from mainstream news: describing its increasing commercialization as privileging speed, triviality and sensationalism at the expense of more worthwhile research and investigative work. He finally made his decision to leave the news industry after being obliged to stake out the home of a British politician who was "in trouble for having an affair with a choirboy". When threatened by locals, he retreated to his car, only to reflect that he would "want to beat up me too—what I was doing was morally bankrupt". Thus Randall's description of Pilston as an "old-school professional" was laden with normative approval and a degree of nostalgia for what he saw as journalism's better days. Although Randall also had a shrewd understanding of the ways in which Pilston's "beautiful" photographs would help to sustain the "legacy values" of *The Independent* brand at a time of widespread cost-cutting.

Beauty, professionalism, and the concerned photographer

By constructing beautiful photographs through intertextual conversations with other media and art forms, Pilston sought to "reflect something from within [news audiences'] existing framework of knowledge" in order to engage, and communicate with them about the lives of distant others (Lugo-Ocando and Eldridge 2015, 104). However, the coding and decoding of these visual texts relied upon the aesthetic traditions and tastes associated with privileged Northern media consumers (Gupta 1986; Hall 1997; Walker 1997). It therefore reinforces the exclusion of sub-Saharan photojournalists, who complain that their representational approaches rarely feature in mainstream news outlets (Jayawardane 2017; Richardson 2017).

But no one at Christian Aid questioned whether this aesthetic approach conflicted with the INGO's commitment to facilitating more empowering and egalitarian North/South partnerships. Instead, Christian Aid's Editor, Joseph Cabon, explained that the INGO had chosen to visually brand itself using photojournalism, and related forms of social documentary photography, because of the connections between such aesthetic forms and socio-economic justice (interview, March 1, 2013). Cabon did not have to ask Pilston to conform to these aesthetic styles because he framed his relationship with Pilston in terms of a different kind of professionalism, pertaining to the "concerned photographer" (Capa 1968).

In particular, Cabon stressed that he had chosen Pilston for the assignment his belief in the photographer's commitment to affective/moral responsibilities towards vulnerable subjects, characterized by a "special sensitivity and humanity" (García and Palomo 2015, 42). As he put it,

I see something like 80–100 new photographers every year who come to show me their portfolio fresh out of college (…)

But a *real*, a *professional* photojournalist—their work is something else. They treat the people they photograph with *so* much respect; they *feel* for them…

You *have* to be able to feel something. Otherwise the camera is just literally, you know, a machine that has had its shutter clicked (…)

So it's about the person's head and their *heart*—that's what I look for. (interview, March 1, 2013)

Pilston welcomed the picture editor's framing of his relationship to the INGO in this way (interview, February 22, 2013). But framing their relationship in terms of fellow "professionals" engaged in the production of a particular photographic genre also meant that when Pilston was less willing to challenge Cabon when there was a disagreement about which shot to short-list. Instead, Pilston said that he "trusted" that the Picture Editor had simply a different interpretation of which photo contained the "decisive moment" (interview, February 22, 2013). The term used here is significant because "the decisive moment" was a phrase used by the famous French photographer, Henri Cartier-Bresson, who argued great photography

> (…) recognize[s]—simultaneously and within a fraction of a second—both the fact itself and the rigorous organization of visually perceived forms that give it meaning. [Capturing the decisive moment] requires putting one's head, one's eye, and one's heart on the same axis]. (1952, 191)

There are obvious problems with this logic: for if there can be disagreement about what constitutes the "decisive moment", then how can it exist outside of the photographer's subjective judgement? Why should only professional photographers have the special sensitivity necessary to identify it? In addition, the notion of a transcendental "moment" evades any consideration of the historical, geographical and cultural contexts shaping the codes employed by the photographer, as well as viewers of their photographs (Hall 1997). But what is perhaps most important here is the way in which the transcendentalism evoked by this normative rationale inhibits any considerations about Cabon's use of photography in relation to his branding and promotion of a particular organization—Christian Aid.

Thus Pilston was on firmer ground when he argued that being overruled by a specialized and "professional" picture editor at an INGO could be "better than what happens in news organizations" because of last-minute cropping, which is not carried out by picture editors but by subeditors and layout staff (interview, February 22, 2013). That meant, he said, that "any Tom, Dick or Harry can hack away at your work and they don't have a *clue* what they're doing". Indeed, that is precisely what happened when Pilston's pictures went through a "final cut" by page designers at *The Independent on Sunday*, who cropped one of his shots severely. Both Pilston and Cabon were furious about the crop reproduced overleaf: arguing that it made the subject look as if he was begging. But neither thought it was worth damaging their future relations with staff at the newspaper by raising the issue with them.

Figure 4.2: Malian villager, photographed by Tom Pilston for Christian Aid

Source: Tom Pilston/Christian Aid/Panos

Finally, framing the relationship between Christian Aid and the photojournalist in terms of his "professionalism" meant that no questions were raised about this freelancer syndicating his photos via a photographic agency after the period of exclusive usage stipulated by the INGO expired. Pilston said he often did this because INGOs offered him the opportunity to do "good work", but they tended to "pay a bit less" than newspapers for foreign assignments (interview, February 22, 2013). So he tried to find ways of generating a secondary stream of income in order to fulfil his family obligations: arguing that no matter how morally or politically valuable NGO work was, "my kids still need to go to school and eat and be clothed and stuff".

However, Pilston knew that the news organizations which republished these photos often attributed them to freelancers alone, rather than naming the INGOs who had hired them. Thus syndication had potentially important effects which Pilston did not explore: helping to mask the role/s played by the INGO to news audiences, as well as remediating images in ways which those represented had not necessarily consented to (Wright 2016).

What happened to Christian Aid's politics of voice?

The dominance of value-laden ideas about visual beauty and "professionalism" at Christian Aid meant that the politics of voice, which had originally influenced its organizational restructure, was marginalized within news production processes. To begin with, communications managers never really defined what giving others' "voice" might mean, or how it might relate to a politics of listening in practice (Tacchi 2008). In addition, little thought was given to how a politics of "voice" might relate to issues of accountability, participatory approaches to aid-work and/or collective struggles for recognition (Honneth 1996; Ricoeur 2005). Instead, "voice" tended to be treated as a self-evident, and rather vague, good, which was largely synonymous with people in need being offered the chance to "tell their own stories" (Wright 2018).

Thus the possibility that local people might object to being interviewed by INGO communications officers, or might prioritize the pursuit of other goods, was never considered (Nayel 2013). Communications staff were also not given any guidance about how to embed the abstract principles of "voice" within actual media production processes (Wright 2018). In particular, the INGOs' communications staff had little understanding of the complexities of oral interpretation. Like many others in professional journalism, Hogg, Christian Aid's Head of Media, conceptualized "fixing" an interpreter as a largely logistical issue, akin to booking flights, travel permits or a driver (interview, November 7, 2012; see also Bielsa and Bassnett 2009). So he spent very little time briefing the two Malian interpreters. Indeed, the main instruction which Hogg gave them[3] involved asking them to "translate word for word", rather than paraphrasing what interviewees had said.

Thus Hogg not only failed to distinguish between text-based and oral practices, he also treated both as a kind of "technical relay" in which meaning could be easily transferred from one language to another (Palmer 2007, 13). So he radically underestimated the challenges posed by oral interpretation, which involves complex forms of selection and re-contextualization in real-time. Any acts of inter-linguistic mediation also involve negotiating the subtle interplay of dominance, collaboration, hybridity and resistance (Venuti 1998). This is especially tricky in conflict and post-conflict situations (Palmer 2007) as well as in other contexts in which speakers are acutely aware of the ways in which they need to be "storied" by others, in order to receive benefits upon which they are dependent (Baker 2006). Such acts of mediation are made even more complex when they involve interpreting between speakers whose cultures and languages have been structured in relation to one another by violent and oppressive colonial histories (Bassnett and Trivedi 1999; Spivak 1998; Venuti 1998).

Yet Abdourahamane Keita, the person chosen to interpret between Bambara and French, had received no training in oral interpretation at all. Instead, he usually evaluated agricultural projects for Christian Aid in the regional town of Mopti. Keita explained that as a relatively privileged Bambara man, he had a strong moral obligation to help his countrymen, including his ethnic brothers, who were going hungry during food crises (interview, March 29, 2013). But Hogg and Pilston's approach to aid was alien to him, and he said that this made it difficult for him to interpret for them. In particular, Keita said did not understand many of the technical terms and acronyms used by the British visitors, such as IDPs (Internally Displaced Persons).

But the main problem which Keita experienced involved trying to mediate between the European visitors and those suffering from food shortages. He stressed that this involved far more than translating words—it involved trying to bridge very different and unequal worlds of experience. Indeed, he said he really didn't "know *how* to translate the *context*…the situation of these *desperate* people and their emotions". Part of this difficulty stemmed from the tendency of displaced people to lapse into short, colloquial phrases laden when trying to describe their reaction to events which were painful to them. These often carried powerful, but culturally specific meanings. For example, Keita described one man as using the phrase, "U y'e lanɔgɔ": a saying in Bambara which he said "means something like a total destruction and humiliation … on economic, social and cultural levels" (interview, March 29, 2013).

But Hogg, who had travelled from London, was already frustrated by the cumbersome double-interpretation, from Bambara to French, and then from French to English, so he begged the interpreter to "stop digressing" because this slowed the interpretation process down even more (interview, November 7, 2012). Keita was also worried about antagonizing these important visitors from London, whom he thought might tell his boss that he couldn't do his job properly (interview, March 29, 2013). So he abandoned his earlier tactic of elaborating on culturally-specific terms and giving additional examples in order to try and aid the visitors' understanding. Instead, Keita just used words which were "roughly similar" in French, although he knew that this did not really convey the connotations of cruelty, shame and the destruction of social order. Thus "U y'e lanɔgɔ" was interpreted as "I felt bad".

Nevertheless, some of the most significant obstacles to giving voice to others were created by the unintended effects of the very North/South partnerships which the aid agency sought to foster. This was because Christian Aid had invited the mayor of Mopti to host a meeting to welcome Hogg and Pilston, partially out of respect for his role in leading local communities, and partially in order to ensure his continued cooperation in safety measures and in securing access to the displaced people living within the district. But this mayor managed to alienate many of the displaced people who had gathered to meet the British visitors, because he did not speak Songhaï, their native language, and refused to speak in Bambara, which most of them also spoke.

Instead, the mayor stressed the formality of the occasion and his own high status by using the prestige language at his disposal, French (interview with Yacouba Tangara, GRAT Program Director, April 2, 2013). However, few of the displaced Malians present spoke French, especially those from poorer backgrounds; the handful who did, resented being addressed in a colonial language, particularly in the context of receiving white British visitors (interview with Abdourahamane Keita, March 29, 2013). A serious row ensued, during which many of those who had initially been willing to participate changed their minds (interview with Abdourahamane Keita, March 29, 2013; interview with Andrew Hogg, November 7, 2012).

A final example of the ways in which the very North/South partnerships which Christian Aid sought to foster undermined the agency's ability to give voice to local people involved how they were approached by Christian Aid's partners in Mali, APH and GRAT. Hogg, the Head of Media, was aware that this could be problematic because people in need might feel pressurized to agree because of their dependence on such agencies (interview, November 7, 2012). But no detailed discussion took place about how to avoid this coercion at a managerial level. Instead, Christian Aid's Program Director in Mali simply asked staff at these agencies to arrange participants to be waiting for the Head of Media and the photographer: a course of action which was shaped by his own time-poverty, but also by his own commitment to Christian Aid's egalitarian ethos (interview with Yacouba Kone, March 22, 2013).

Unfortunately, in the absence of any detailed discussion, APH and GRAT framed their requests for media participation in terms of their own organizational interests and prior experiences of mediatized donor reporting (Jones 2017; Krause 2014). This meant that Yacouba Tangara, the Program Director at GRAT told displaced Malians near Gao that they needed to meet the British visitors because they "had to" make the "people who support Christian Aid" know "that they have done the right thing [in] paying for this [project]" (interview, April 3, 2013).

Likewise, Mamadou Tangara, the Project Manager at APH, explained that his previous experience of mediatized donor reporting had influenced the way in which he approached Dogon beneficiaries, who lived near the military front (interview, May 15, 2013.) So he asked for their participation by stressing that they needed to show to donors "that the monies given to the project had been rightly given, and rightly used". Indeed, Tangara stressed that he had had a "very hard job" to persuade the Dogon people to come and meet the British visitors because it was harvest-time and, given the threat to their food supply posed by nearby fighting, they had not wanted to waste a whole day on a media-related visit.

Thus partnerships with in-country agencies, which were conceptualized by Christian Aid's senior managers as supporting a politics of "voice", ended up being semi-coercive, and the INGO's efforts to fulfil its moral/political obligations to local people were subverted to try and demonstrate the INGO's effectiveness to international donors instead. In such circumstances, the accounts which subjects were able to give are likely to have been very limited (Couldry 2010). So it is perhaps unsurprising that the news article which Christian Aid produced (Hogg 2012) framed a food crisis as the main problem and the key actor as Christian Aid's Malian Program Director, in keeping with the INGO's West Africa fundraising appeal.

However, Hogg's intention to influence the political decision-making of elites, as well as his commitment to skilled, journalistic "professionalism" (Örnebring 2016) meant that he was also careful to research and explain several, inter-related causes of the crisis. This involved explaining that it had been shaped by fighting between the Malian government and Islamist secessionists which had displaced people, disrupted agricultural production and food supplies. The article also drew attention to the way in which the lack of rains had led to poor harvests, which had in turn led to high food prices which few Malians could afford because of widespread and long-term poverty in the country. Hogg's piece (2012) even indicated that international markets had exacerbated these problems. So although there were many aspects of the article's production which were highly problematic, the finished piece still had considerable explanatory power.

Moral economy: a coda

The production process discussed here involved forms of "news cloning" (Fenton 2010), "information subsidies" (Gandy 1982) and the dominant forms of "media logic" (Cottle and Nolan 2007) which pushed out more radical, alternative approaches to both journalism and NGO-work. But what I hope to have demonstrated here is the dynamic and complex nature of such processes, which can be better understood by conceptualizing them as moral economies. In particular, this case shows that even when a news outlet is in dire financial straits, the trust needed to enable exchanges of material with an INGO is constructed through actors' mutual, agentive renegotiation of multiple, value-laden obligations to others.

Actors consistently articulated this in terms of their deliberations about their responsibility to uphold different forms of "professionalism". But although the different sorts of professionalism they described could be complementary, but they could also be in tension or conflict with one another. So the construction of trust between the INGO and news outlet required the careful, mutual renegotiation of multiple, sometimes conflicting, "professional" obligations—it was anything but passive and unthinking (Franks 2008a, 2008b).

This moral economy was constructed, in part, through journalists' and NGO-workers' mutual trust in a specialized freelancer, who had worked for *The Independent* and Christian Aid. But this moral economy was also shaped by much broader changes in the political economies of news and aid organizations, which led to the restructuring of actors' day-to-day practices and the erosion of trust in senior managers. Specifically, organizational restructures at both the news outlet and the NGO had involved role-merging and multi-skilling, which had effectively pushed out the forms of journalistic specialism valued by these media producers. These organizational restructures were shaped by a combination of economic and normative factors, including cost-cutting, legitimized by notions of efficiency, and fundraising, justified by ideas of transnational partnership. So we can see moral economies and political economies related to one another in complex, recursive ways in this production process.

By identifying each other as fellow "professionals", the "old hands" involved in this case gained normative affirmation and reassurance of their social status, at a time when their perspectives and values were under siege within their own organizations. The trust created through this production process also enabled actors to gain some limited autonomy, as it enabled them to find ways of doing the kinds of work they valued, despite the presence of powerful constraining factors. To put it another way, media producers used exchanges with each other to try and work around the problems caused by organizational restructuring, rather than explicitly discussing them with their immediate colleagues or bosses. In so doing, media producers can be seen to have become partially disembedded from their own organizations, and partially re-embedded in new exchange-relations with each other which cut across journalism and NGO-work.

But to what extent did this moral economy enable the capabilities of others? At a very basic level, the monies raised through this kind of news coverage may have provided the Malians displaced by war to have adequate food and shelter. Yet the dominance of notions of "professionalism" meant that the more radical politics of voice within the INGO were not significant values-in-action. Quite the opposite: rather than being empowered, local people came close to being coerced, and what they had to say was either constrained by the way in which they were approached by field workers, or lost in translation. Nevertheless, the final article did enhance the ability of news audiences to understand some of the root causes of this particular crisis, without giving the impression that the aid organization either could, or should, provide the only solution to suffering.

Notes

1. The trip cost £7–8,000, but could have been far more time-consuming and therefore more expensive because it involved negotiating progress roadblock by roadblock. This was the main reason why Christian Aid decided to do the piece themselves, rather than offering to embed a journalist from a news outlet with them, as they would usually be required to file within five days, and this couldn't be guaranteed.

2. Both actors have since left Christian Aid, Buckley of his own volition to take another job whilst Hogg took redundancy during a subsequent wave of cuts in 2015, which involved merging the internal and external communications teams.

3. One of these interpreters was a Malian employed by Christian Aid, whilst the other was a Malian school teacher who had volunteered to help its local Malian partners, Groupe de Recherche et d'applications techniques (GRAT) and Actions de Promotion Humaine (APH). Unfortunately, the latter became displaced by fighting and could not be traced.

References

Aldridge, Meryl, and Julia Evetts. "Rethinking the Concept of Professionalism: The Case of Journalism." *The British Journal of Sociology* 54, no. 4 (2003): 547–64.

Anderson, Fay. "Chasing the Pictures: Press and Magazine Photography." *Media International Australia* no. 150 (2014): 47–55.

Anderson, Ian. "Global Action: International NGOs and Advocacy." In *NGOs as Advocates for Development in a Globalising World*, edited by B Rugendyke, 71–95. London: Routledge, 2007.

Anderson, Monica. "At Newspapers, Photographers Feel the Brunt of Job Cuts'." *Pew Research Center*, November 11, 2013. http://www.pewresearch.org/fact-tank/2013/11/11/at-newspapers-photographers-feel-the-brunt-of-job-cuts/.

Argles, Martin. "'The Future of Photography." Speech given at meeting of National Union of Journalists' London Photographer's Branch. June 15, 2013.

Baker, Mona. *Translation and Conflict*. London; New York: Routledge, 2006.

Banks, Mark, Andy Lovatt, Justin O'Connor, and Carlo Raffo. "Risk and Trust in the Cultural Industries." *Geoforum* 31, no. 4 (2000): 453–64.

Bardan, Alexandra. "The Dual Model of the Digital Photo Journalist: A Case Study on Romanian Photojournalism beyond the Economic Crisis." *Journal of Media Research* 8, no. 1 (2015): 19–40.

Bassnett, Susan, and Harish Trivedi, eds. *Post-Colonial Translation: Theory and Practice*. Translation Studies. London, New York: Routledge, 1999.

Bielsa, Esperanca, and Susan Bassnett. *Translation in Global News*. London: Routledge, 2009.

Campbell, David. "Geopolitics and Visuality: Sighting the Darfur Conflict." *Political Geography* 26, no. 4 (2007): 357–82.

Capa, Cornell. *The Concerned Photographer* vol 1. First edition, second printing edition. New York: Grossman Publishers, 1968.

Caple, Helen. *Photojournalism: A Social Semiotics Approach*. New York: Palgrave Macmillan, 2013.

Cartier-Bresson, Henri. *The Decisive Moment: Photography by Henri Cartier-Bresson*. New York: Simon and Schuster, 1952.

Conboy, Martin. *Tabloid Britain: Constructing a Community through Language*. London: Routledge, 2006.

Cottle, Simon, and David Nolan. "Global Humanitarianism and the Changing Aid-Media Field: Everyone Was Dying for Footage." *Journalism Studies* 8, no. 6 (2007): 862–78.

Couldry, Nick. *Why Voice Matters: Culture and Politics after Neoliberalism*. London: Sage, 2010.

Davis, Aeron. *Political Communication and Social Theory*. Communication and Society. London: Routledge, 2010.

Fenton, Natalie. "NGOs, New Media and the Mainstream News: News from Everywhere." In *New Media, Old News: Journalism & Democracy in the Digital Age*, edited by Natalie Fenton, 153–68. London: Sage, 2010.

Fenton, Natalie, Andrew Passey, and Les Hems. "Trust, the Voluntary Sector and Civil Society." *International Journal of Sociology and Social Policy* 19, no. 7/8 (1999): 21–42.

Franks, Suzanne. "Aid Agencies: Are We Trusting Too Much?" *The Political Quarterly* 79, no. 3 (2008a): 316–18.

———. "Getting into Bed with Charity." *British Journalism Review* 19, no. 3 (2008b): 27–32.

Freire, Paulo. *Pedagogy of the Oppressed.* 30th anniversary edition. London: Bloomsbury, 2014.

Gade, Peter J. "Newspapers and Organizational Development: Management and Journalist Perceptions of Newsroom Cultural Change." *Journalism & Communication Monographs* 6, no. 1 (2004): 3–55.

Gandy, Oscar H. *Beyond Agenda Setting: Information Subsidies and Public Policy.* Norwood, NJ: Ablex, 1982.

García, Virginia Guerrero, and Bella Palomo. "The Crisis of Photojournalism." *Communication and Society* 28, no. 4 (2015): 33–48.

Grayson, Louise. "The Role of Non-Government Organisations (NGOS) in Practising Editorial Photography in a Globalised Media Environment." *Journalism Practice* 8, no. 5 (2014): 632–45.

Gupta, Sunil. "Northern Media, Southern Lives'." In *Photography/Politics*, edited by Jo Spence, Patricia Holland, and Simon Watney, 162–66. London: Comedia /Photography Workshop, 1986.

Hadland, Adrian, David Campbell, and Paul Lambert. *The State of News Photography: The Lives and Livelihoods of Photojournalists in the Digital Age.* Oxford: Reuters Institute for Journalism, Oxford University, September 22, 2015.

Hall, Stuart. *Representation: Cultural Representations and Signifying Practices.* London: SAGE, 1997.

Hallas, Roger. "Photojournalism, NGOs and the New Media Ecology." In *Sensible Politics: The Visual Culture of Nongovernmental Activism*, edited by Meg McLagan and Yates McKee, 95–114. New York: Zone Books, 2012.

Hogg, Andrew. "Mali: Five Million Face Starvation." *Independent on Sunday*, August 19, 2012. http://www.independent.co.uk/news/world/africa/mali-five-million-face-starvation-8060073.html

Honneth, Axel. *The Struggle for Recognition: The Moral Grammar of Social Conflicts.* Cambridge, MA: MIT Press, 1996.

Independent Print Ltd. *Directors Report and Financial Statements for the Period Ended 2 October 2011.* London: Companies House, 2011.

———. *Report and Financial Statements up to 30 September 2012.* London: Companies House, 2012.

Jayawardane, M. Neelika. "*The Problem with Photojournalism and Africa.*" *Al Jazeera.com*, January 18, 2017. http://www.aljazeera.com/indepth/opinion/2017/01/problem-photojournalism-africa-170118085812572.html

Jones, Ben. "Looking Good: Mediatisation and International NGOs." *The European Journal of Development Research* 29, no. 1 (2017): 176–91.

Klein-Avraham, Inbal, and Zvi Reich. "Out of the Frame: A Longitudinal Perspective on Digitization and Professional Photojournalism." *New Media & Society* 18, no.3 (2016): 429–446

Krause, Monika. *The Good Project: Humanitarian Relief NGOs and the Fragmentation of Reason.* Chicago; London: University of Chicago Press, 2014.

Lebedev, Evgeny. "Independent Closure: Evgeny Lebedev's Letter to Staff." *The Guardian*, February 12, 2016. http://www.theguardian.com/media/2016/feb/12/independent-closure-evgeny-lebedevs-letter-to-staff.

Lister, Sarah. "NGO Legitimacy Technical Issue or Social Construct?" *Critique of Anthropology* 23, no. 2 (2003): 175–92.

Lugo-Ocando, Jairo, and Scott Eldridge 11. "Visual Journalism and Global Poverty." In *Blaming the Victim: How Global Journalism Fails Those in Poverty*, Jairo Lugo-Ocando, 104–123 London: Pluto Press, 2015.

McCabe, Eamonn. "Photography in Newspapers." In *Pulling Newspapers Apart: Analysing Print Journalism*, edited by B Franklin, 181–203. New York: Routledge, 2008.

McLagan, Meg, and Yates McKee. "Introduction." In *Sensible Politics: The Visual Culture of Nongovernmental Activism*, edited by Meg McLagan and Yates McKee, 9–26. New York: Zone Books, 2012.

McPherson, Ella. "Surmounting the Verification Barrier Between the Field of Professional Human Rights Fact-Finding and the Non-Field of Digital Civilian Witnessing," 2015. https://www.repository.cam.ac.uk/handle/1810/248302.

Moore, Martin. *Shrinking World: The Decline of International Reporting in the British Press 1979–2009.* London: Media Standards Trust, 2010.

Morrison, Sarah. "How £11bn Pledged for Water Never Arrived." *The Independent on Sunday*, August 19, 2012.

Mortensen, Tara Buehner. "Blurry and Centered or Clear and Balanced?" *Journalism Practice* 8, no. 6 (2014): 704–25.

Mortensen, Tara Buehner, and Ana Keshelashvili. "If Everyone with a Camera Can Do This, Then What? Professional Photojournalists' Sense of Professional Threat in the Face of Citizen Photojournalism." *Visual Communication Quarterly* 20, no. 3 (2013): 144–58.

Nayel, Moe Ali. "Palestinian Refugees Are Not at Your Service." Text. *The Electronic Intifada*, May 17, 2013. https://electronicintifada.net/content/palestinian-refugees-are-not-your-service/12464.

Orgad, Shani. "Visualizers of Solidarity: Organizational Politics in Humanitarian and International Development NGOs." *Visual Communication* 12, no. 3 (2013): 295–314.

Örnebring, Henrik. "The Two Professionalisms of Journalism." Working Paper. Reuters Institute for the Study of Journalism, 2009.

———. *Newsworkers: A Comparative European Perspective.* London: Bloomsbury Publishing, 2016.

Palmer, Jerry. "Interpreting and Translation for Western Media in Iraq." In *Translating and Interpreting Conflict*, edited by Miriam Salama-Carr, 13–28. Amsterdam, New York: Rodopi, 2007.

Phillips, Angela. "Old Sources, New Bottles." In *New Media, Old News: Journalism and Democracy in the Digital Age*, edited by Natalie Fenton, 87–101. London: Sage, 2010.

———. "Faster and Shallower: Homogenisation, Cannibalisation and the Death of Reporting." In *Changing Journalism.*, edited by Peter Lee-Wright, Angela Phillips, and Tamara Witschge, 81–98. London: Routledge, 2012.

Ponsford, Dominic. "Independent on Sunday Editor Axed amid Moves to Merge Independent and Standard Editorial Teams." *Press Gazette*, February 12, 2013. http://www.pressgazette.co.uk/independent-sunday-editor-axed-amid-moves-merge-independent-and-standard-editorial-teams.

Powers, Matthew. "The structural organization of NGO publicity work: Explaining divergent publicity strategies at humanitarian and human rights organizations." *International Journal of Communication* 8 (2014): 90–107.

Reinardy, Scott. "Downsizing Effects on Personnel: The Case of Layoff Survivors in US Newspapers." *Journal of Media Business Studies* 7, no. 4 (2010): 1–19.

Richardson, Whitney. "Who Is Telling Africa's Stories?" *The New York Times*, January 10, 2017. https://lens.blogs.nytimes.com/2017/01/10/who-is-telling-africas-stories/

Ricoeur, Paul. *The Course of Recognition*. Harvard: Harvard University Press, 2005.

Ritchin, Fred. *After Photography*. New York: Norton, 2009.

Schein, Edgar H. *Organizational Culture and Leadership*. 3rd ed. Hoboken, NJ: Wiley, 2004.

Sen, Amartya. *The Idea of Justice*. London, New York: Penguin, 2010.

Shaw, Martin. *Civil Society and Media in Global Crises: Representing Distant Violence*. New York: Pinter, 1996.

Slim, Hugo. "By What Authority? The Legitimacy and Accountability of Non-Governmental Organisations." *The Journal of Humanitarian Assistance* 10 (2002). https://www.gdrc.org/ngo/accountability/by-what-authority.html

Solaroli, Marco. "Toward a New Visual Culture of News." *Digital Journalism* 3, no. 4 (2015): 513–32.

Sontag, Susan. *Regarding the Pain of Others*. New York: Picador, 2003.

———. *On Photography*. London, New York: Penguin, 2008.

Sparks, Colin, and John Tulloch, eds. *Tabloid Tales: Global Debates over Media Standards*. Critical Media Studies. Lanham, MD: Rowman & Littlefield, 2000.

Spivak, Gayatri. "Can the Subaltern Speak?" In *Marxism and the Interpretation of Culture*, edited by Cary Nelson and Lawrence Grossberg, 271–315. London: Macmillan, 1998.

Tacchi, Jo Ann. "Voice and Poverty." *Media Development* 1 (2008): 12–15.

Venuti, Lawrence. *The Scandals of Translation*. London; New York: Routledge, 1998.

Waisbord, Silvio. *Reinventing Professionalism: Journalism and News in Global Perspective*. Cambridge: Polity Press, 2013.

Walker, John A. "Context as a Determinant of Photographic Meaning." In *The Camerawork Essays: Context and Meaning in Photography*, edited by Jessica Evans, 52–63. London, New York: Rivers Oram Press.

Wright, Kate. "'Helping Our Beneficiaries Tell Their Own Stories?' International Aid Agencies, the Politics of Voice and the Pitfalls of Interpretation within News Production." *Global Media and Communication*, 2018 Online First DOI:10.1177/1742766518759795.

———. "These Grey Areas": How and Why Freelance Work Blurs INGOs and News Organizations. *Journalism Studies* 17, no. 8 (2016): 989–1009.

· 5 ·

WAR CRIMES, WITNESSING, AND PUBLIC SERVICE TELEVISION

Channel 4 News and Human Rights Watch

When journalists testified in the international tribunals which followed the bloody conflicts in Bosnia and Rwanda, it threw into question long-held convictions about the merits of journalistic "objectivity" in the U.S. and Europe (Tumber 2008). Journalists acting as witnesses for the prosecution of war crimes and genocide were viewed as particularly problematic within Public Service Broadcasting, because of such news organizations' statutory obligations regarding impartiality. Lindsey Hilsum, who is now the International Editor for *Channel 4 News*, but who was then a freelancer at BBC World Service Radio, acted as a witness at the International Criminal Tribunal for Rwanda. She argued that testifying about the mass killings of Tutsis might have compromised her role as a journalist, but that she had a greater responsibility "as a human being" to help prosecute those who ordered the killings (cited in Gjelten 1998, 18). Meanwhile, Tom Gjelten, a correspondent at the US-based National Public Radio (1998), tried to resolve the conflict between his statutory obligations and his moral and political responsibilities by differentiating between journalistic "objectivity" and political "impartiality."

But the response given by the BBC's foreign correspondent, Martin Bell (1997) is perhaps the most famous. He wrote an article, defending a "journalism of attachment" (1997, 7), which "cares as well as knows" and "will not stand neutrally between good and evil, right and wrong" (1997, 8). But others argue that "attached" journalism is dangerous, as journalists following this approach may select evidence that fits their preconceptions, excluding dissenting voices and risking reducing the complexity of war to simplistic moral tales (Hume 1997; Ruigrok 2008). In addition, there is a risk that emotive and partisan news coverage may lead to poorly informed political decisions, including military intervention (Brock 1993; Hurd 1996).

Such arguments rely on the belief that news journalism exerts a powerful influence over policy-makers. The most common model of this is the "CNN Effect", which assumes that the blanket news coverage broadcast by rolling satellite TV channels is able to influence public opinion, which then prompts democratically elected politicians to respond. However, research carried out from the late 1990s onwards suggests that news coverage may be more likely to reinforce public support for politicians' pre-existing intentions, rather than changing policy-makers' minds (Gilboa 2005; Hawkins 2002; Livingston and Eachus 1995).

So it seems advisable to take a more cautious critical stance to media influence, considering the complex ways in which it may interact with other causal factors. Nevertheless, discussions about the political effects of "attached" journalism continued to take place in mainstream journalism throughout the 1990s and 2000s, spreading to discussions about the news coverage of other military conflicts—most notably the American wars in Afghanistan and Iraq (Ruigrok 2010). Indeed, recent obituaries for Marie Colvin, the veteran war correspondent killed in Syria, remained full of these kinds of ideas (Pratt 2012; Zahra 2012).

The longevity of ideas about the morality of "attached journalism" has been shaped by a broader "affective turn" in European and North American societies (Clough and Halley 2007), which has led to journalists' positioning personalized anecdotes before facts and employing emotional language throughout their reports (Wahl-Jorgensen 2013). This often involves outsourcing emotional labor to interviewees (Wahl-Jorgensen 2013), but sometimes journalists write in emotive, confessional ways about their own experiences (Coward 2013; Richards and Rees 2011). Such approaches reconstruct journalists' moral authority in new ways, but they also serve commercial aims. These include helping journalists to differentiate their news outlets from competitors, and sell their content more effectively in a harsh media market (Green and Maras 2002; Illouz 2007).

In television news, more emotive, "attached" forms of journalism are closely related to a shift towards correspondent-led reporting, particularly in the coverage of warfare (Rodgers 2012). Such forms of reporting are not only believed to enhance audiences' emotional engagement in news, but also their trust in its credibility (Rodgers 2012). This is because these kinds of journalism forge powerful conceptual links between the eye-witness, truth telling, and the visual image as evidence: all of which have their roots in judicial practices (Chouliaraki 2009; Joyce 2013; Peters 2001; Tagg 1999). Tensions between emotive and value-laden subjectivity and reporting factual truth are then managed through reference to notions of "bearing witness", which involve the physical act of seeing, but also recognizing atrocity in a deeper, ethico-political sense (Ellis 2000; Frosh and Pinchevski 2008; Kurasawa 2009).

To be more specific, "witnessing" entails the reporter being compelled to speak out against suffering: calling for "truth telling, at the same time as sanction[ing] an interpretation of what is being witnessed" (Zelizer 2000, 10). Such practices have deep, cultural roots in Judeo-Christian traditions of testifying (Felman and Laub 1992). But television is often thought to be a powerful, contemporary way of enabling witnessing: involving not only the reporters' testimony, but also enabling news audiences to act as secondary witnesses. A key issue here is the liveness of television, which enables audiences to be co-present temporally with those who are suffering (Ellis 2000). Indeed, they may even be positioned as complicit in the perpetuation of such suffering, unless they also speak out (Chouliaraki 2006; Peters 2001).

Thus the immediate act of bearing witness and acts of secondary, mediated witnessing both involve powerful moral/political obligations. These relate to the suffering of distant others and to an imagined, broader community or public (Chouliaraki 2006, 2010; Frosh and Pinchevski 2001). For these reasons, witnessing can be seen to produce new forms of publicity, structured around a "cultural politics of legitimacy", which justifies TV journalists and news audiences gazing upon the suffering of distant others (Allan and Zelizer 2004, 5; see also van Oppen 2009).

Human rights INGOs have been quick to capitalize on these shifts in journalistic norms: producing and curating large quantities of video, which they offer to TV programs, as well as presenting as evidence in politico-legal settings (Allan 2015; Gregory 2012). The uncut nature of much of this video is particularly interesting because it simulates liveness, evoking that sense of co-presence with those suffering (Ellis 2000; Peters 2001). Its unedited nature also means that such video appears to lack artifice, enhancing its credibility by evoking forms of citizen witnessing (Allan 2013; Chouliaraki 2006). So how and why TV reporters use the video provided by human rights INGOs is very important in understanding transnational practices of "witnessing", which involve international human rights groups, journalists and other kinds of activists (Kurasawa 2009).

The case study discussed in this chapter examines a production process involving freelance film-makers, journalists at the British public service broadcaster, *Channel 4 News*, and three human rights INGOs. Foremost amongst these was Human Rights Watch (HRW), which commissioned and curated video footage used in two TV reports broadcast by *Channel 4 News* in the spring and summer of 2012 (Miller 2012a, 2012b). But significant forms of indirect influence were also exerted by Amnesty International and Invisible Children Inc., whose video, *Kony 2012*, went viral in the same year.

Both TV pieces were long, investigative and seemingly correspondent-led reports about conflict in the Democratic Republic of Congo. But they were highly personalized and prosecutory in tone: stressing the impunity of a single military general accused of human rights abuses, in order to prompt indignant denunciation (Boltanski 1999). This general was Bosco Ntaganda, who had been charged with multiple war crimes and crimes against humanity by prosecutors at the International Criminal Court (ICC), but who had not yet been arrested. Following the broadcast of these TV reports, in March 2013, Ntaganda handed himself in and his trial commenced at The Hague three years later. At the time of writing in 2017, no verdict had been given.

Channel 4 News

Channel 4 is a UK-based public corporation, which uses cross-subsidization to fund its public service output, including *Channel 4 News*. Like the BBC, *Channel 4 News* has legal obligations to provide UK citizens with programs "of high quality" which deal with "national and international matters" (OFCOM 2004, Annex 1.2) and which must be presented with "due impartiality" (OFCOM Broadcasting Code 2011, section 5). These responsibilities were built into the terms of Channel 4's license at its inception in 1982 and are underpinned by the UK's Broadcasting Acts of 1981 and 1990, as well as the Communications Act of 2003 (Brown 2007; Hobson 2008). But Channel 4 was set up to provide an alternative to the BBC and ITV. So, despite its relatively low budget, *Channel 4 News* has additional responsibilities to "demonstrate innovation, experiment and creativity", to appeal to "the tastes and interests of a culturally diverse society", and "to exhibit a distinctive character" (Communications Act 2003 Section 265).

However, the extent to which Channel 4 fulfils its public service obligations is coming under increasing scrutiny. After the station faced a financial crisis in 2007–2008, its executives agreed to be cross-questioned on an annual basis by the UK parliamentary select committee for Culture, Media and Sport (interview with Inquiry Manager, Houses of Parliament, July 17, 2013).[1] At these parliamentary sessions, Channel 4 executives insisted that *Channel 4 News* was at "the absolute epicenter" of their public service commitments (David Abraham, speaking to Culture, Media and Sport Committee 2010, Evidence 17). But the channel's managers still asked Independent Television News (ITN), the non-profit-making company which makes *Channel 4 News*, to make ten per cent cuts to the news program's budget, as part of a wider package of financial "efficiencies" (Channel 4 2009).

60 editorial staff were made redundant in 2009–2010, most of whom had been working on related programs on satellite channels (interview with Broadcast Officer for the National Union of Journalists, July 25, 2013). Managers claimed that this would help to protect the core evening program (Channel 4 2009). But staff disputed this, arguing that it underestimated how much these journalists had contributed to the main program (Holmwood 2009). At the same time, it was widely understood that Channel 4 had serious, ongoing financial problems, which were exacerbated when the reality TV show, *Big Brother*, moved to Channel 5 in 2010, causing Channel 4 to lose significant advertising revenue (Culture, Media and Sport Committee 2011). The election of a pro-market Conservative government in 2015 led to greater political pressure regarding the channel's financial viability. Indeed, the UK's Culture Secretary even considered the part-privatization of the channel, although this idea was later abandoned (Bond 2017).

But even back in 2012, when this study was conducted, Channel 4 journalists were under considerable pressure. They were required to work with far fewer staff, but they still needed to prove that their program fulfilled its public service remit to channel executives, UK politicians and the UK public, in order to renew its contract with ITN. One way in which *Channel 4 News* did this was by citing its popularity amongst hard-to-reach ethnic groups and younger age ranges (Channel 4 Annual Reports 2007–2012). This claim began to look shaky as program's audience figures declined. The steepest decline of all was amongst 16–34 year olds—precisely the age group that channel executives had always claimed the program could attract (Culture, Media and Sport Committee 2011, Evidence 20). The program was roundly criticized for this by the select committee meeting held in 2011 (Culture, Media and Sport Committee 2013, Evidence 10). So at the time when this study was conducted, journalists were thinking hard about how to make the program's content more accessible and appealing, especially to younger viewers, as well as fulfilling their other obligations as a public service broadcaster.

Thus, as the program's Editor, Ben de Pear, explained, Channel 4 journalists had "learned to box clever" to meet their multiple responsibilities (interview, November 23, 2012). In order to meet their public service remit to be different to other news outlets, Channel 4 journalists made an effort to report upon places and topics rarely covered by other outlets. They also tended to use longer, "investigative" reports which, the Editor explained, were cheaper than airing many short, live two-ways with multiple reporters in different locations. This managerial strategy shaped the division of labor on the program, as the Editor tended to allocate international news stories to correspondents with previous connections to places. This was because de Pear thought that these reporters would have not only have "greater knowledge" of the issues involved, but also a greater "emotional attachment" to those who lived there. He reasoned that this was far more appealing and "convincing" to viewers, especially younger ones, and was therefore "gold" for the program.

The Editor's approach was strongly influenced by the BBC's former correspondent, Martin Bell, whose experiences of covering the Bosnian civil war led him to advocate for a "journalism of attachment" (Bell 1997, 7). Like Bell, de Pear and other Channel 4 journalists argued that the rigorous and persistent pursuit of "objective" fact could (and should) be separated from emotional and moral neutrality (Hilsum 2011a; interview with Jonathan Miller, November 29, 2012). Although the program's International Editor, Lindsey Hilsum, said she was keen to move beyond the good guys/bad guys rhetoric, which characterized some "attached" reporting in Bosnia, she argued that this stance had shaped her warm appreciation of human rights INGOs (2011b). In particular, she said that she relied upon "in-depth reporting" done by groups like Amnesty International and Human Rights Watch, as the program could not afford to produce these kinds of briefings itself (2011b).

The program's Foreign Affairs Correspondent, Jonathan Miller, also spoke about human rights organizations as allies, conceptualizing them as engaged in similar forms of thorough, independent and original "human rights reporting" as journalists (interview, November 29, 2012). As he put it,

You know we [Channel 4 journalists] have to check our sources. We don't believe anybody telling us anything, we test it. We have to be challenging of those who make allegations no matter how sympathetic we might feel towards them.

We have to try and reinforce and back up different sources and what we are told about them. You can't just lap out of the hands of the UN Security Council expert group on Rwanda or DRC [Democratic Republic of Congo].

We have got to have our own information and by going to these places and by interviewing people in the way that I and Human Rights Watch have done. That way, we are getting many, many sources on the same story.

The fuzziness of the term "reporting" is interesting here: serving to blur the lines between journalism and human rights work in ways which justify Channel 4 journalists' close relations to human right INGOs, despite the program's statutory obligations regarding impartiality. When asked about this, Miller changed tack: insisting that his insisted that his "human rights reporting" was not partial, but was instead characterized by its persistence. He said:

I know all about the necessity of impartial, objective journalism…

What I think is important [to stress is that]…in the work that I have done on Sri Lanka, or Eastern Congo—and indeed, a lot of the other human rightsy sort of stories that I have done around the world—the difference is simply the *persistence* of the journalism.

That's what makes it campaigning journalism…

It's not like I am coming at this from a particular … a particular political *place*. (interview, November 29, 2012)

Indeed, Miller was much keener to talk about the moral, rather than the political, implications of his work: describing his approach to journalism as having been powerfully influenced by his parents, who had been Christian missionaries. Even though he didn't share their religious faith, Miller kept a statue of the Virgin Mary on his desk, and described himself as sharing his parents' "zeal" for "challenging injustice". Yet injustice is a political, not a moral, judgement and to frame justice in terms of human rights is to make specific political claims (Nash 2009).

It is therefore problematic that journalists working for a program with statutory obligations to be independent and impartial, regarding themselves as carrying out the same kinds of work as human rights organizations. However, journalists should not be blamed too much for taking this approach as they took their lead from their managers. Indeed, even Channel 4 executives tried to demonstrate the program's public service value by listing the journalistic awards given to it by Amnesty International—including a number given to Miller himself (Channel 4 Annual Reports 2007–2012). So it is perhaps unsurprising that Miller and other Channel 4 journalists regarded their association with human rights organizations as consonant with their public service commitments.

Fostering long-term, trusting relations with talented freelancers offered Channel 4 journalists a different way of addressing their multiple obligations at a time of cost-cutting. Freelancers with expertise in particular geographic areas were especially highly valued, helping to sustain the program's reputation for "ground-breaking" investigative reports (interview with Ben de Pear, November 23, 2012). This semi-casualized approach to news production was not only shaped by financial constraints, but also by broader changes in the channel's political economy, which were also informed by normative values.

This is because the former Labour government led by Tony Blair strongly encouraged the public service broadcaster to engage more comprehensively with freelancers, linking freelancing with "creative risk-taking" (interview with Ben de Pear, November 23, 2012). This led the program to set up its Independents Fund in 2008 (interview with Ben de Pear, November 23, 2012). However, freelancers who specialize in particular media and/or geographic regions are not wholly "independent" media producers because they are reliant on commissions from other kinds of clients, including INGOs (Wright 2016a, 2016b), as happened in this case study.

Freelancers

A freelance film-maker, A, was commissioned in 2011 by Human Rights Watch (HRW) to make a film about the Congolese general, Bosco Ntaganda, in order to campaign for his arrest and extradition (Human Rights Watch 2012). The film project involved A travelling to the DRC to conduct interviews with Ntaganda's alleged victims, which the INGO had set up, as well as attempting an undercover interview with Ntaganda himself—although the camera on that occasion had not worked. A also incorporated other footage into the film, which she had been given by HRW communications managers. This included a clip of archive footage from 2008, which showed Ntaganda appearing to give orders on a walkie-talkie, whilst walking at the head of a group of heavily armed men in army fatigues.

This video clip had been originally filmed by two other freelance film-makers (B and C) in the village of Kiwanja, on the day that a massacre of 150 civilians occurred there. B and C took the footage to one of HRW's fieldworkers, who identified Ntaganda using the INGO's database of images, disproving the general's claim to have been elsewhere at the time (interview with B and C, October 19, 2012; interview with HRW field researcher, May 2, 2013). The HRW fieldworker then told her Washington-based communications managers about the video, and they decided to buy the rebroadcasting rights from B and C, so that a clip of the footage could be used in the film about Ntaganda prepared by A.

When A completed this assignment, she decided to email the Editor and Foreign Affairs Correspondent at *Channel 4 News* about it, because she knew that they had also reported on the Kiwanja massacre. As she put it,

> I knew that Ben [de Pear] had been producing Jonathan [Miller] when they did the Kiwanja film in 2008 (…)
>
> So when I sent the proposal saying "Here is the man responsible for the Kiwanja massacres" to them, I was pretty sure it would be like, "Oh my God, we've got to do this. We have the footage, we were *there*." (interview with A, October 26, 2012)

In the course of this email, A not only let de Pear and Miller know about the existence of footage placing Ntaganda in Kiwanja on the day of the massacre, she also let them know that she had access to footage of interviews with Ntaganda's alleged victims, which she had conducted for HRW. Finally, she offered to perform for *Channel 4 News* what she had failed to achieve for HRW—that is, to record an exclusive, undercover interview with Ntaganda himself.

By pitching in this way, A demonstrated why freelancers play such a significant role in news outlets' adoption of INGO-provided multimedia, for she not only made use of her personal contacts, she also used her insider knowledge of the program's privileging of persistent, correspondent-led reporting. In addition, her pitch played into the way in which the program tended to reuse its own award-winning footage, in order to accumulate further cultural capital. As the Kiwanja report produced by *Channel 4 News* had been given an award by Amnesty International, Channel 4 journalists were predisposed to view the massacre as a "human rights issue" (interview with Jonathan Miller, November 29, 2012).

Finally, A used her detailed knowledge about these two Channel 4 journalists to tap into their passionate sense of personal responsibility to witness on behalf of those whose bodies they had filmed. This sense of responsibility blended embodied forms of eye witnessing with the moral/political act of bearing witness embedded in co-presence, as well as ideas about mediated forms of secondary witnessing (Frosh and Pinchevski 2008; Peters 2001). For example, the Foreign Affairs Correspondent reflected on his experience of reporting on the massacre like this:

> You just got the sense that a terrible, terrible thing had happened and that you were . . . you were just *there* and you had to . . . the . . . the public-service journalist instinct just cuts in and you think . . . this is something I *have* to be here to report. This is really *important*.
> And so there was almost a sense of sort of evidence gathering on a crime scene; there was never going to be any police doing that.
> We . . . we were there as witnesses. . . .
> In a sense, we still *are*. (interview with Jonathan Miller, November 29, 2012)

The kind of public service journalism Miller describes here does not rely on official rationales about the TV program's enablement of national democratic practice through independent, impartial journalism. Rather, it draws from cosmopolitan ideas about the purposes of denouncing crimes against humanity in relation to a global public, constructed partially through international law, but also via the international media (Nash 2009; Volkmer 1999). Thus Channel 4 journalists can be seen to have become partially dis-embedded from national publics, and related legal obligations regarding independence and impartiality, whilst being partially re-embedded in trusting relations with other moral "witnesses" in an imagined, global public. However this dual process of disembedding/re-embedding was only partial because Miller also stressed that British audiences had a "right to know" that their taxes were being given by the British government to Ntaganda's alleged supporters, the Rwandan government, in the form of international development aid (interview, November 29, 2012).

Channel 4 journalists were also motivated by their eagerness to get an exclusive with Ntaganda himself. Unfortunately, despite the Channel's extensive precautions, a violent attack by Congolese militia forced A and Channel 4 journalists to cease their attempts to get an undercover interview with Ntaganda—forcing them to withdraw entirely from the country for security reasons (interview with A, October 26, 2012). But Miller then managed to secure an interview with the new Prosecutor General at the International Criminal Court (ICC), which was included in the first report (Miller 2012a). Following the outbreak of the Ntaganda-led M23 rebellion later in 2012, the program commissioned a Ugandan freelancer to try and conduct interviews with the rebels following Ntaganda. But Miller and de Pear decided not to use that material because it was poorly shot and the questions "were not hard enough" (interview with Jonathan Miller, November 29, 2012). Thus Channel 4 journalists were forced to use rather more wire agency material than they would have liked, in addition to their own archive footage of the Kiwanja massacre, and the victim interviews conducted by A for HRW (interview with Jonathan Miller, November 29, 2012).

Like other freelancers who work for news organizations and INGOs (Wright 2016b), A justified repurposing her work by arguing that she felt a strong, personal responsibility to continue to specialize in this geographic area (interview, October 26, 2012). But she said she could no longer survive financially by acquiring commissions relating to it from news organizations alone. So, she argued, working for INGOs and news organizations enabled her to produce the kinds of knowledge she valued, allowing her to spend extended periods of time seeking out those who were suffering and engaging in a radical politics of listening (Couldry 2006). As she put it,

> If I can draw on different commissions [from news organizations and INGOs] …I have more control to be able to do the things that I am passionate about and that make me want to get out of bed in the morning.
>
> I think it came from going to Bosnia which was my first film that I worked on, listening to extraordinary testimonies from people who aren't normally heard, and finding things out that aren't widely known about.
>
> Why? Because knowledge is power. And maybe we can use that knowledge to make the world a better place; maybe we can help people's lives … maybe we can help stop wars [pause]. If we can, we *should*.
>
> Well [pauses and spreads hands expressively] …maybe [laughs in self-deprecating manner].

Thus A's normative approaches were not the same as those of Channel 4 journalists, but they complemented each other sufficiently to enable the construction of trust. As the Foreign Affairs Correspondent put it, "we trusted [A's] integrity", as well as her journalistic prowess (interview with Jonathan Miller, November 29, 2012). This trust enabled Channel 4 journalists' exchanges with A, but these exchanges also legitimized their non-attribution of video that HRW had commissioned or curated (Miller 2012a).

Only a "veiled" attribution to HRW appears (Van Leuven *et al.* 2013, 442), in the form of clip with Anneke van Woudenberg, who was then the INGO's Senior Congo researcher, and whom Miller said he positioned as "the expert" (Miller 2012a, 2012b, discussed in interview with Jonathan Miller,

November 29, 2012). Miller went on to defend his lack of explicit attribution by saying,

> I would not ordinarily [miss out an explicit attribution to an INGO] other than for the fact that [the freelancer, A] was a trusted friend and colleague.
> So I trusted her journalism . . . and had no reason to disbelieve that the interviews she had done were not genuine.

Likewise, the program's Editor said that he had not carried out any independent checks of the footage of Ntaganda at Kiwanja because he "trusted" B and C, the two freelancers who had shot it (interview with Ben de Pear, November 23, 2012). He then went on to frame the program's use of this material as a "direct deal" with those freelancers, insisting on paying them, even though Channel 4 journalists knew that HRW had already purchased the rebroadcasting rights.[2]

Like A, the two other freelancers, B and C, said that their decision to engage with HRW had been shaped by their long experience of working in the Democratic Republic of Congo. As B explained, his reflections about this had caused him to depart from the principles of political impartiality he had been obliged to observe as a BBC correspondent (interview, October 19, 2012). As he put it,

> I think I have ended up going *way* beyond my role as a "journalist" [indicates inverted commas with fingers].
> Now I think ... maybe I am (...) I must be (...) a sort of a (...) an *activist* now (...)
> I know there is a kind of school in journalism which teaches you to keep a distance. I know what those people say.
> But I think, somehow (...) you *are* involved (...) And the longer you are involved, especially in one place, the more you can't *deny* that(...)
> And one day you just say to yourself, "*Yes*. I am a part of this now."

Later on in the interview, B went on to explain how his Jewish heritage had also shaped his engagement in mediated activism, which appeared to involve a form of bearing witness, despite considerable personal risk (Felman and Laub 1992). He said:

> From an early age I knew about the Shoah and the *heroes* of those times, and about the importance of *resistance*. So I believe that *sometimes* you have to decide which side you take (...) That means it is up to *you*; it is part of your *duty* to take a stand (...)
> I mean after a massacre we covered I called [one of the generals he thought was responsible] and said "Let us come [to you], so we give you the opportunity to challenge our reports."

And the guy received me into his living room and he was like, "How come there are fifty journalists in town (…) and you, *you* are the only one who saw massacre? What's *wrong* with you? You have special *eyes*? You have special *glasses*? Who do you think you *are?*" [Gesticulates and points aggressively].

Meanwhile, C was in the car with her head down, so the armed men outside the house couldn't see her, editing the next piece on the laptop (…) and I was, like, trying to play it diplomatically with this guy who ended up giving us an interview, and denying that the massacre had happened.

We ran it intercut with more footage we had of all of those bodies! We *got* him! [Laughs]

So both sets of freelance film-makers decided to work with HRW as part of their broader engagement in mediated forms of political activism (McLagan and McKee 2012). But freelancers were used to give *Channel 4 News* the appearance of critical independence and political impartiality to audiences, masking the multiple subsidies which the program received from the INGO (Gandy 1982). Indeed, treating their use of this material as a "direct deal" with freelancers meant the program didn't need to attribute anyone else at all, as the contributions made by freelancers were not normally mentioned on-air, unless they voiced the report (interview, B. de Pear, November 23, 2012). This lack of attribution served the interests of *Channel 4 News* well, as the editor explained:

Attributing footage to other people weakens the journalism—always. Because people think "Oh right, so it isn't your story; it's their story."

So it is something you try and avoid doing. (interview with Ben de Pear, November 23, 2012)

Human Rights Watch

Journalists' non-attribution of video commissioned and/or curated by HRW presented the INGO's communications managers with a serious dilemma regarding their conflicting responsibilities. These communications managers didn't see the primary purpose of their engagement with journalism as being fundraising, so they were less concerned about the lack of organizational branding than aid workers might have been (Powers 2014). But most were uncomfortable with the program's non-attribution of material that they had commissioned. This was because HRW's communications managers were former correspondents and senior producers, who regarded themselves as having a "residual responsibility" to uphold "high standards" in international news production, including attribution (interview with Emma Daly, HRW's Communications Director, February 28, 2013).

However, after some internal debate, HRW staff decided not to do anything about *Channel 4 News'* non-attribution of their work because they were worried that this might damage HRW's relations with the program. In particular, they were concerned that this would prevent them from carrying out their greater obligation—to "bear witness with the aim of making change" (interview, E. Daly, February 28, 2013). Indeed, HRW's Deputy Executive Director, who was also a very senior former journalist, claimed that non-attribution could actually be an advantage when it came to political advocacy, as it meant that "a chorus of voices" appeared to be "saying the same thing" (interview with Carroll Bogert, April 28, 2013).

The existence of this debate is interesting: indicating that former journalists who move into INGO communications do not, as has been previously claimed (Fenton 2010), continue to see themselves as journalists, rather than NGO-workers. Instead, like the Head of Media at Christian Aid, HRW managers can be seen to have become partially dis-embedded from the mainstream news industry, following prolonged postings abroad. They often described feeling dislocated or alienated from the commercialized values of journalistic colleagues after returning from covering violent and sustained oppression. For example, HRW's Deputy Executive Director, Carroll Bogert, described her long-term postings in China, Southeast Asia and the Soviet Union as shaping her revulsion for commercially-driven, populist approaches like this:

> When I was at *Newsweek*…the highest praise that you could get from our Editor in Chief was "Ooh nothin' but readers!"
>
> We were a magazine, we had to *sell* (…) So at *some* level, you ended up trying to write stories that people wanted to read (…) rather than what *matters*. (interview, April 8, 2013)

However, for most of the communications managers at HRW, the Bosnian war of 1992–1995 was a much more significant formative event in their journey from the news industry into human rights work. This was because their experience of it had involved new forms of embedding with others. The first of these involved physical closeness to those whose lives were threatened, which triggered a new sense of moral-political obligation to speak out on their behalf. As Daly explained,

In Vietnam, you know people were going out to the front and then coming back and, yes, Saigon got attacked and I guess Phnom Penh as well. But it wasn't the same [as Bosnia].

There wasn't the same proximity, I think, where you were *living* with people who were under attack all the time (…)

You *felt* (. . .) more of a sense of duty to the people you were reporting on. (interview, February 28, 2013)

Journalists also tended to become embedded in new, trusting relationships with peers who were reporting on Bosnia for other news organizations. This included taking responsibility for each other by offering security tips, companionship and comfort during difficult times. HRW's Media Director, Pierre Bairin, summarized the effects of this, saying: "The press corps over there was quite small and tight… I mean [the war] went on for *years*" (interview, February 15, 2013). Finally, journalists working in Bosnia also became embedded in trusting exchanges with human rights workers, so that moving into human rights work at a later date seemed to "make perfect sense [because] we had *already* done a lot of work together on the ground" (interview with Emma Daly, February 28, 2013).

Thus a disproportionately large number of former journalists posted in Bosnia have moved into major human rights organizations. Indeed, these former journalists actively helped to recruit each other. This is how it worked: when Carroll Bogert, who was then HRW's Deputy Executive Director, needed to fill the Communications Director post, she sought the advice of Laura Silber, who had been the Balkans correspondent for *The Financial Times*, before joining the Soros Institute, which is HRW's biggest donor (interview with Carroll Bogert, April 8, 2013). Silber recommended Daly, who had previously been the Balkans Correspondent for *The Independent*, as well as Steve Crawshaw, who had been the paper's East Europe Editor, for a different post (interview with Emma Daly, February 28, 2013).[3] Daly then recruited Bairin, her former colleague and friend, who had previously been working in Bosnia for CNN's Christiane Amanpour—one of the correspondents who defended her practice of partial journalism by distinguishing between objectivity and political neutrality (Amanpour 1996).

These former journalists had the cultural and social capital to be able to clone international news very effectively (Fenton 2010), but they didn't see themselves as doing so. Instead, they regarded themselves as resisting the trend towards fast, populist and profit-driven forms of journalistic production. Bairin in particular criticized the rise of "cheap stunts" and "personality-driven" broadcast journalism, which formed part of his broader critique of live satellite TV (Bromley 2010; Cushion 2010). As he put it,

> The problem with all this live, live, live business (…) is that most of the time what you watch on these news networks you know beforehand (…)
>
> They don't pick up the phone and actually *talk* to somebody, or find something *out*.
>
> They just, like, rehash something that you already know by looking at the Internet. It's so *lame*. But they don't have time for anything else (…)
>
> *All* that effort, all that stress, for *what*? What *exactly* do we *learn*? (interview, February 15, 2013)

In contrast, Bairin described HRW as engaging in "proper reporting", which enhanced the ability of journalism to serve a greater "public purpose", rather than being driven by profit. Likewise, Bogert stressed that although she and her communications staff still "thought like journalists", they had joined the INGO because "the *yardstick* by which HRW defines or decides what it's going to work on is *not* a yardstick of the *market*" (interview, April 8, 2013). Thus HRW staff regarded themselves as challenging commercially-driven news by disseminating knowledge about the plight of vulnerable and abused people, so reinstating the protective function of journalism (Sen 2010).

But in some ways, HRW staff were complicit in the hurried and uncritical re-versioning of others' material which they criticized mainstream journalists for. This is because material gathered by A was not only used to make a film about Ntaganda, it was also used to create the first "test run" of the INGO's now well-established electronic distribution lists (interview with Pierre Bairin, February 15, 2013). Bairin explained that he had designed these distribution lists to mimic wire agency feeds, including "shot lists," "cut-away" shots and "exclusive" unedited footage: everything which a TV journalist might need to edit together a news report quickly and easily. The purpose of modelling these distribution lists on wire agency feeds was also to enhance journalists' trust in the credibility of the footage. As Bairin put it,

> The more "finished" it looks, the more contrived and controlled, the less [broadcast journalists] [will] trust what they see as raw and direct.

However, Bairin stressed, these "raw" clips had been carefully selected to prevent journalists from telling stories other than "the one that we want telling". In addition, despite Bairin's criticisms of commercialized personality-driven journalism, he complied with the personalization of news coverage himself: focusing on Bosco Ntaganda and his lavish lifestyle, rather than finding ways to enable a discussion of the broader causes of the M23 rebellion.

These forms of complicity with mainstream news norms were justified using metaphors of consumption, which positioned HRW as part of a media food chain. As Bogert, HRW's Deputy Executive Director, explained, the INGO had to "produce the right *food*... kind of like plankton... so we can feed the bigger *fish*" (interview, April 8, 2013). The kinds of "fish" that HRW sought to "feed" were elite, rather than populist, news outlets (Powers 2014). As Bogert went on to explain:

> I don't think [media influence] works through public mobilization on an issue. So we don't make any effort whatsoever to get on *Good Morning America* because, although millions and millions and millions of people watch it, but we don't think *policy makers* watch it.
>
> We have no public outreach function here...What we do is to raise a fuss in the media, and the media are a *stand-in* for public opinion in some ways.

So ultimately, HRW's senior management legitimized the INGO's complicity with mainstream news norms in terms of their ability to exert pressure on Northern policy-makers through elite news media (Miller 2013; see also Davis 2007, 2010). Such a model reconceptualizes news as a kind of simulation of "public opinion" (Lippmann 2012 [1922]; Schudson 2003), but this justified concentrating interpretative power in the hands of former journalists from Europe and North America (Fenton 2010). Indeed, it led to the privileging of particular kinds of former journalists: namely, senior journalists with extensive experience of elite-oriented forms of international news, including those who have served as foreign correspondents, editors and bureau chiefs.

Thus the approach taken by HRW's communications managers needs to be distinguished from the approaches taken by the managers of other human rights INGOs, like WITNESS, which focuses on grassroots activism (Allan 2015; Gregory 2010). However, many of HRW's in-country researchers were unhappy with the journalistic identities, roles and practices, which they felt were being foisted upon them by the communications managers who dominated the INGO's head office (interview with Carroll Bogert, April 28, 2013). These field-workers stressed that they were not journalists making news, but INGO-workers engaged in witnessing abuses and advocating on behalf of victims (interview with Carroll Bogert, April 28, 2013; interview with HRW field researcher, May 2, 2013). However, freelance film-makers' lack of organ-

izational embedding meant that they were completely unaware of this con-
troversy, and the role they played in re-enforcing communication managers'
dominance within the INGO (interview with A, October 26, 2012; interview
with B and C, October 19, 2012).

"This could be our own Kony"

Nevertheless, the elitism of HRW communications managers was modified in this production process by the indirect influence of another human
rights INGO, with a far more populist approach. This was Invisible Children Inc., which disseminated a video pressing for the prosecution of the
Ugandan rebel, Joseph Kony. The video, *Kony 2012*, went viral in January
2012. Indeed *Kony 2012* rapidly became the most successful video viral of
all time, achieving over forty million views on *YouTube* in only four days
(Gregory 2012; Harding 2012). *Kony 2012* came out several months after
the program commissioned A to get an undercover interview with Ntaganda. So the video viral didn't shape the program's initial decision to pursue
the story. But it did shape journalists' decision to persist in "telling the Bosco story" throughout 2012, even though security concerns had forced them
to leave the Democratic Republic of Congo (interview with Jonathan Miller, November 29, 2012).

Like many other journalists (Nothias 2013), the Editor at *Channel 4
News*, Ben de Pear, said that he and the correspondent were "*intensely* an-
noyed" by Invisible Children's "very glamorous, *shiny* production" of a video
"riddled with inaccuracies and over-simplifications" (interview with Ben
de Pear, November 23, 2012). De Pear didn't comment upon other, well-
documented objections to *Kony 2012*: namely, the way in which it infan-
tilizes Ugandans, using this to foreground the heroism of American media
activists (Madianou 2013; Nothias 2013). Instead, he explained that his
background at *Sky News* had also made him value accessible, "strong [and]
simple storytelling" (interview with Ben de Pear, November 23, 2012).
So he was keen to capitalize upon the popularity of *Kony 2012*, which he
thought could help the program address its falling audience ratings, particularly amongst younger viewers.

Indeed, de Pear was convinced that Bosco Ntaganda "could be our own
Kony", given that Ntaganda also conscripted child soldiers, and given the
popular resonance of his chilling nickname amongst Congolese locals—"the

Terminator". So, he reasoned, the program had a strong rationale for continuing to report on Ntaganda, whom he described as another "indicted war criminal" in a different part of Africa, who was also charged with the conscription of children. But Ntaganda was a better target, de Pear argued, because he was "hiding in plain view" and still causing suffering, unlike Kony who was a "spent force and, frankly, God knows where by now". Thus *Kony 2012* provided the main "news-peg" for the first report on Ntaganda (Miller 2012a).

The second piece had a different news peg: the mass displacement of civilians, which occurred following outbreak of the M23 rebellion in May 2012 (Miller 2012b). But its narrative frame changed very little: it also focused on Bosco Ntaganda as the main "problem", recommending his arrest and swift extradition to The Hague as the "solution". So the script explains the outbreak of the M23 rebellion like this:

> Bosco went on the run four months ago; fearing arrest after Congo's President backed the ICC, saying Bosco should be tried for war crimes. Hundreds of soldiers loyal to him followed him into the bush (…)

This highly selective treatment of the causes of the M23 rebellion seems to bear out criticisms of "attached journalism" (Hume 1997; Ruigrok 2008). In particular, the piece avoids discussing the rebels' political grievances. This is a striking omission given that the M23 rebellion was so-called because members of the National Congress for the Defense of the People believed that the DRC's president, Joseph Kabila, had broken the terms of a peace treaty signed on March 23, 2009 (United Nations News Service 2013). This included Kabila's mishandling of his own election in 2011, which was widely seen as lacking in credibility by international observers, as well as the President's political opponents (International Peace Information Service 2012).

Yet Ntaganda is identified as the one who broke a deal: getting a "plum job" in the Congolese army, only to become a "turncoat general" (Miller 2012b). Indeed Ntaganda is repeatedly Othered: described not just as a criminal, but as a bringer of "chaos", whose conscription of children symbolizes his destruction of social order (Coundouriotis 2010; Macmillan 2009). He is labelled not just as a "greedy" and opportunistic "warlord", but as "the Terminator"—an inhuman assassin, rather than a rebel commander (Miller 2012a, 2012b). These moral judgements are underpinned by the visual aesthetics of the piece, which include journalists using digital software to lower the brightness of an agency-provided still of Ntaganda and his followers at the corner: creating a vignette of Ntaganda's head and shoulders in a manner reminiscent of a police "mug-shot".

Figure 5.1: Bosco Ntaganda screengrab from *Channel 4 News* report

Source: Thomson Reuters

The unedited video clip of Ntaganda at Kiwanja on the day of the massacre, which was curated by HRW, forms a relatively small proportion of the overall piece. But it plays a pivotal role structurally. This is because it ties together new material with the program's archive coverage of the Kiwanja massacre, in which journalists are positioned as working with Congolese civilians to bear witness to the massacre. The correspondent, Jonathan Miller, is clearly positioned in shot, listening intently to eyewitnesses' accounts, before following a local man who reveals the evidence of the massacre; repeatedly using the motif of opening doors to show viewers the bodies (see image reproduced opposite). Thus although the language of "witnessing" is not explicitly used, it is evoked visually, with journalists offering viewers sights which serve as evidential "proof", not just of Ntaganda's criminality, but of his wickedness, and the need to speak out against it.

Figure 5.2: Kiwanja still from *Channel 4 News* report

Source: Jonathan Miller

However, I want to take a moment here to stress that I do not intend to imply that Ntaganda and his fellow fighters are simply innocent victims of imperialistic misrepresentation. I also acknowledge that there are strong arguments in favor of portraying massacres as emotionally and ethically repellent—so helping to construct and safeguard global communities of civility (Nash 2009). However, these TV reports portray "the persecutor" as a single individual, in ways which risk minimizing the responsibility of audience members for perpetuating warfare (Boltanski 1999, 58). Thus they mark a shift away from the program's earlier representations of Congolese conflict, which discussed media audiences' complicity in the conflict, given their heavy reliance on the minerals smuggled and fought over by Congolese militia (Miller 2007).

Moreover, framing the cause of the M23 rebellion in terms of a single "bad" individual risks closing down the possibility of discussing the fighting as an expression of political agency, no matter how abhorrent the violence may have been. The combination of these two factors risk *Channel 4 News* edging towards constructing the M23 rebellion as African "barbarism" (Atkinson 1999; Marthoz 2007). However, the correspondent made a valid point when he argued that it was often difficult to convey complexity to a mass audience as a public service broadcaster. As he put it,

All public service journalists are involved in trying to strike a balance between pre-senting engaging television which keeps a million viewers keeping watching, and actually delivering meaningful investigative television which enlightens people as to something which is happening, often in some terribly depressing parts of the world. (interview with Jonathan Miller, November 29, 2012)

It is a reasonable argument: if only the most erudite policy experts watch in-ternational news then it can hardly lay claim to publicity. Nor is a seven min-ute news report able to convey the same level of complexity as an academic article or book. However, Channel 4 journalists did not primarily set out to provoke or inform collective, public action, despite Miller's earlier comments about wanting to warn British taxpayers about where their money was going. Instead, Channel 4 journalists tended to agree with HRW's communication managers that it was more effective to place pressure on elite policy-makers through news journalism (Miller 2007, 2013). This, they argued, could even happen in the process of news production, rather than as a result of viewing TV reports. For example, de Pear said,

[Policy-makers] don't want to come across as (…) hiding something when they are giving an interview. So normally we find that just booking an interview time with someone in a position of authority means they'll try to do something about what you are going to ask them about, before they even do the interview
You know the classic line is "Well, it's funny you asked me about that because just this morning I was speaking to the country director (…)" or (…), you know.
It's a way of making things *happen*. (interview, November 23, 2012)

In this case, journalists wanted to pressurize named policy-makers at the UK's Department for International Development, whom they knew watched the program. Specifically, they wanted to persuade them to cease aid to the Rwan-dan government, which was alleged to be backing the M23 rebellion. The aim of this strategy was not to try and stop the M23 rebellion as such, but to iso-late Ntaganda, thereby increasing the likelihood of his arrest (interview with Jonathan Miller, November 29, 2012). This was why the program repeatedly stressed Rwanda's role in enabling the M23 rebellion, obliquely referring to the Rwandan President, Paul Kagame, as the "darling of Western aid donors" (Miller 2012b). Thus the populism evoked by allusions to *Kony 2012* was used to appeal to viewers, in ways which helped the program respond to statutory obligations regarding its publicity. But this populism also served to evoke the notion of public opinion through a kind of "morality play", in order to place pressure on elite policy-makers (Miller 2013).

This risk of inter-elite insularity was exacerbated by the way in which media producers at both HRW and *Channel 4 News* tended to treat external events in a selective manner, citing them as evidence of the efficacy and normative value of their respective approaches (Hume 1997; Ruigrok 2008). These events included the UK government's decision to suspend aid to Rwanda in late 2012 and Ntaganda's surrender in March 2013. Indeed, the fieldworker, who had initially described herself as being "skeptical" about the dominance of journalistic norms and identities in HRW, described herself as "won over" to their "way of thinking" following Ntaganda's arrest: concluding that maybe the production of news journalism "could be an effective form of advocacy" (interview, May 2, 2013). Yet these media producers did not reflect upon whether news coverage might have contributed to Ntaganda's decision to rebel in the first place. This seems remarkable as the report broadcast by *Channel 4 News* shortly before the fighting began stressed the determination of the Congolese President and the ICC's Prosecutor-General to seek out and arrest Ntaganda (Miller 2012a).

The only person who reflected upon the potentially harmful, unintended consequences of news coverage was the freelance filmmaker, A. She explained that her extensive work in the Democratic Republic of Congo had made her question the effects of a "journalism of attachment" (Bell 1997). As she put it,

> The militias have publicly said that if they are unhappy with their situation once they have been absorbed into the Congolese military—they still haven't been paid or they don't have any food or they haven't got the responsibility they wanted or whatever—then they go and rape women, because it is reported.
>
> Then there is an international outcry and the Congolese government, instead of saying "We must stop this to prevent them from doing it again," says, "We must hush it up and ask them what they want."
>
> So one becomes kind of strangely complicit in a way. But I don't want to stop reporting things because that's important too (…)
>
> You know, they [Channel 4 journalists] call it the "journalism of attachment" or something.
>
> But I don't know. I don't have the answers. (interview, October 26, 2012)

A explained that her reluctance to ascribe to "attached" forms of reporting had also been shaped by her experiences of working as a documentary-maker during the Bosnian war—but on the Serbian side (interview, October 26, 2012). Describing a day when she had waited with a pathologist whilst Serbs identified the bodies of their children, husbands and wives, she said:

That really influenced me because I saw Serbs as *people*. But if I ever talked about it and said "Yes, Serbs lost some people as well" it was just not countenanced [by other journalists] because horrible things were happening to many more Muslims.

So I think maybe…when you're frightened and you're being shot at and you are having to report really horrible things, maybe your sort of emotional band-width narrows and you … can't be sympathetic to the people who are doing the killing, because their loved ones are being killed too, even if that's in much smaller numbers.

A's wariness of dehumanizing those positioned as "oppressors" gestures not only to the potentially problematic nature of "attached journalism", but also points towards another problem. That is the inherent contradiction between the discourse of human rights and the dehumanization of aggressors, like Bosco Ntaganda (Douzinas 2007). Unfortunately, her positioning as a freelancer meant that A didn't feel able to discuss her ambivalence with anyone else in the production process, lest she undermine her relationships with members of staff who could offer her commissions in future. Thus freelancing facilitated, rather than challenged, normative and organizational changes already under way at both the INGO and news outlet: with the former remodeling itself as a kind of news wire agency, while journalists at the latter reconstructed public-service journalism as including "witnessing" and "human rights reporting."

Moral economy: a coda

So what were the benefits of employing a moral economy perspective here? Firstly, moral economy theory enabled us to think beyond binary approaches to NGO-journalist relations, in order to enable us address multidirectional forms of influence. So we can, for instance, consider the roles played by freelancers, as well as the cumulative impact of Amnesty International's award-giving practices, and the influence of a popular video viral produced by Invisible Children Inc. In so doing, moral economy theory enabled us to see how problematic it is to attempt to evaluate INGOs' influence on journalism in terms of how much NGO material journalists use, how speedily they process it, or how many other sources they included (Davies 2008; Van Leuven et al. 2013).

Instead, we came to understand how Channel 4 journalists used small amounts of NGO commissioned and curated material in order to respond to their multiple obligations. Their statutory and moral obligations modified crude economic imperatives to work faster and more cheaply: causing journalists to invest considerable amounts of time and energy in seeking other sources. Nonetheless, Human Rights Watch, and other human rights organizations, were still able to exert considerable interpretative influence on the narrative framing of consecutive TV reports.

The interactions of journalists and NGO-workers also seem to have had long-term effects, as their exchanges with one another shaped their reinterpretation what constituted "good work" in their respective fields. These reinterpretations deepened the normative synergies or correspondences between their organizations. Channel 4 journalists came to see public service journalism as involving "attached" forms of "human rights reporting". This involved witnessing to a global, imagined public, whilst also seeking to pressurize elite policy-makers in the UK government. Meanwhile, communications managers at Human Rights Watch regarded themselves as engaging in "proper reporting", which resisted commercial imperatives in ways which had important, public value. Although, on closer examination, it was more accurate to view these communication managers as partially resisting, and partially complying with, commercially driven journalism.

In addition, both the news and non-governmental organization appeared to be moving towards an understanding of media effects which involved trying to exert influence on policy-makers within the production process itself, as well as via the dissemination of news texts. This involved both journalists and NGO-workers emphasizing the validity of inter-elite pressure or contestation as an effective means of mediated advocacy and/or public service journalism. Thus, this moral economy can be seen to have involved complex forms of partial disembedding and re-embedding, which reconstructed journalists' and NGO-workers' ideas about their respective responsibilities, as well as enhancing some of their abilities, at the expense of others.

But what of the capabilities of vulnerable Congolese civilians caught up in the M23 conflict? It may be argued that this moral economy had a protective function, as well as enabling voice (Sen 2010) by disseminating knowledge about the experiences of Ntaganda's alleged victims. This news production process also enabled the dissemination of visual evidence which placed Ntaganda at the scene of a massacre, despite his claims to be elsewhere. This is only one, limited form of justice, but this "verification subsidy" (McPherson 2015a, 2015b) did enhance news audiences' ability to better scrutinize Ntaganda's claims (Sen 2010).Yet at the same time, the personalized, Othering nature of these TV reports meant that viewers were less able to scrutinize other kinds of claims, relating to the political causes and contexts of the M23 conflict. Finally, the way in which this moral economy used trust in freelancers to justify non-attribution meant that viewers were unable to scrutinize the political effects of the program's exchanges with human rights organizations, or vice versa.

Notes

1. This crisis was caused by the expenses the channel incurred during the course of the digital switchover and the loss of advertising revenue caused by audience fragmentation and the global economic crisis (Channel 4 Annual Reports 2008, 2009).
2. HRW paid the freelancers £800 for four minutes of footage. B said that *Channel 4 News* knew which 20 seconds it wanted because of HRW's prior investment and only paid them £400. Although he had wanted more, they "bartered him down" (interview with B and C, October 19, 2012).
3. Crawshaw has since moved on to other senior roles at Amnesty International.

References

Allan, Stuart. *Citizen Witnessing*. Cambridge: Polity Press, 2013.
———. "Visualizing Human Rights: The Video Advocacy of WITNESS." In *Humanitarianism, Communications and Change*, edited by Simon Cottle and Glenda Cooper, 197–210. New York: Peter Lang, 2015.
Allan, Stuart, and Barbie Zelizer. "Rules of Engagement: Journalism and War." In *Reporting War: Journalism in Wartime*, edited by Stuart Allan and Barbie Zelizer, 3–21. London and New York: Routledge, 2004.
Amanpour, Christiane. "Television's Role in Foreign Policy." *Quill*, April 1996, 16–17.
Atkinson, Philippa. "Representations of Conflict in the Western Media: The Manufacture of a Barbaric Periphery." In *Culture and Global Change*, edited by Tim Skelton and Tracey Allan, 102–8. London: Taylor and Francis, 1999.
Bell, Martin. "TV News: How Far Should We Go?" *British Journalism Review* 8, no. 1 (1997): 7–16.
Boltanski, Luc. *Distant Suffering: Morality, Media and Politics*. Cambridge Cultural Social Studies. Cambridge: Cambridge University Press, 1999.
Bond, David. "Proposal to Privatise Channel 4 Dropped." *Financial Times*, March 28, 2017. https://www.ft.com/content/9732f444-13ce-11e7-80f4-13e067d5072c.
Brock, Peter. "Dateline Yugoslavia: The Partisan Press." *Foreign Policy*, 1993.
Bromley, Michael. "'All the World's a Stage': 24/7 News, Newspapers, and the Ages of Media." In *The Rise of 24-Hour News Television*, edited by Stephen Cushion and Justin Lewis, 31–49. New York: Peter Lang, 2010.
Brown, Maggie. *A Licence to Be Different: The Story of Channel 4*. London: BFI, 2007.

Channel 4. "Channel 4 Television Corporation Report and Financial Statements 2008." London: Channel 4, 2008. http://www.channel4.com/media/documents/corporate/annual-reports/CH4_Report2008_Full.pdf.

———. "Channel 4 Television Corporation Report and Financial Statements 2009." London: Channel 4, 2009. http://www.channel4.com/media/documents/corporate/annual-reports/C4_Annual_Report_09.pdf.

———. "Channel 4 Corporation Report and Financial Statements." London: Channel 4, 2011. http://www.channel4.com/media/documents/corporate/annualreports/Ch4_Annual_Report_2011.pdf.

———. "Channel 4 Television Corporation Report and Financial Statements 2012." London: Channel 4, 2012. http://www.channel4.com/media/documents/corporate/annual-reports/Ch4_Annual_Report_2012.pdf.

Chouliaraki, Lilie. The Spectatorship of Suffering. London: Sage, 2006.

———. "Witnessing War: Economies of Regulation in Reporting War and Conflict." The Communication Review 12, no. 3 (August 31, 2009): 215–26.

———. "Ordinary Witnessing in Post-Television News: Towards a New Moral Imagination." Critical Discourse Studies 7, no. 4 (2010): 305–19.

Clough, Patricia Ticineto, and Jean Halley. The Affective Turn: Theorizing the Social. Durham, NC, London: Duke University Press, 2007.

Couldry, Nick. Listening beyond the Echoes: Media, Ethics, and Agency in an Uncertain World. Boulder, CO: Paradigm Publishers, 2006.

Coundouriotis, Eleni. "The Child Soldier Narrative and the Problem of Arrested Historicization." Journal of Human Rights 9, no. 2 (2010): 191–206.

Coward, Rosalind. Speaking Personally: The Rise of Subjective and Confessional Journalism. London, New York: Palgrave Macmillan, 2013.

Culture Media and Sport Committee: "Channel 4 Annual Report. Tenth Report of Session 2010-12." London: UK government, November 22, 2011. http://www.publications.parliament.uk/pa/cm201012/cmselect/cmcumeds/1175/1175.pdf.

Culture Media and Sport Select Committee. "Channel 4 Annual Report 2011." House of Commons, April 2013. http://www.publications.parliament.uk/pa/cm201314/cmselect/cmcumeds/509-i/509i.pdf.

Cushion, Stephen. "Rolling Service, Market Logic: The Race to Be Britain's 'Most Watched News Channel.'" In The Rise of 24-Hour News Television, edited by Stephen Cushion and Justin Lewis, 113–31. New York: Peter Lang, 2010.

Davies, Nick. Flat Earth News: An Award-Winning Reporter Exposes Falsehood, Distortion and Propaganda in the Global Media. London: Chatto and Windus, 2008.

Davis, Aeron. The Mediation of Power: A Critical Introduction. London: Routledge, 2007.

———. Political Communication and Social Theory. Communication and Society. London: Routledge, 2010.

Douzinas, Costas. Human Rights and Empire: The Political Philosophy of Cosmopolitanism. London: Routledge-Cavendish, 2007.

Ellis, John. Seeing Things: Television in the Age of Uncertainty. London: I.B. Taurus, 2000.

Felman, Shoshana, and Dori Laub. *Testimony: Crises of Witnessing in Literature, Psychoanalysis and History*. New York: Routledge, 1992.

Fenton, Natalie. "NGOs, New Media and the Mainstream News: News from Everywhere." In *New Media, Old News: Journalism & Democracy in the Digital Age*, edited by Natalie Fenton, 153–68. London: Sage, 2010.

Frosh, Paul, and Amit Pinchevski, eds. *Media Witnessing: Testimony in the Age of Mass Communication*. Basingstoke: Palgrave Macmillan, 2008.

Gandy, Oscar H. *Beyond Agenda Setting: Information Subsidies and Public Policy*. Norwood, NJ: Ablex, 1982.

Gilboa, Eytan. "Global Television News and Foreign Policy: Debating the CNN Effect." *International Studies Perspectives* 6, no. 3 (2005): 325–41.

Gjelten, Tom. *Professionalism in War Reporting*. Washington, DC: Carnegie Commission on Preventing Deadly Conflict, 1998.

Green, Lelia, and Steven Maras. "From Impartial Objectivity to Responsible Affectivity: Some Ethical Implications of the 9/11 Attacks on America and the War on Terror." *Australian Journal of Communication* 29, no. 3 (2002): 17.

Gregory, Sam. "Kony 2012 through a Prism of Video Advocacy Practices and Trends." *Journal of Human Rights Practice* 4, no. 3 (2012): 463–68.

———. "The Participatory Panopticon and Human Rights: WITNESS's Experience Supporting Video Advocacy and Future Possibilities." In *Sensible Politics: The Visual Culture of Nongovernmental Activism*, edited by Meg McLagan and Yates McKee, 517–549. New York: Zone Books, 2012.

Harding, Lucy. "Kony 2012 in Review." *Journal of Human Rights Practice* 4, no. 3 (2012): 461–62.

Hawkins, Virgil. "The Other Side of the CNN Factor: The Media and Conflict." *Journalism Studies* 3, no. 2 (2002): 225–40.

Hilsum, Lindsey. "No More Good Guys." *British Journalism Review* 22, no. 13 (2011a): 5–7.

———. "The New News Ecology." Speech at the Panel at One World Media Week, London, 12 May 2011b.

Hobson, Dorothy. *Channel 4: The Early Years and the Jeremy Isaacs Legacy*. New York: IB Tauris 2008.

Holmwood, Leigh. "Channel 4 News Staff Condemn Cuts." *The Guardian*, August 14, 2009, sec. Media. http://www.theguardian.com/media/2009/aug/14/channel-4-news-cuts.

Human Rights Watch. *Bosco Ntaganda: Wanted for War Crimes*. 2012. https://www.hrw.org/video-photos/video/2012/05/13/bosco-ntaganda-wanted-war-crimes.

Hume, Mick. *Whose War Is It Anyway? The Dangers of the Journalism of Attachment*. London: Inform Inc., 1997.

Hurd, Douglas. "Why Foreign Policy Cannot Be Dictated by Blind Emotion." *The Evening Standard*, July 16, 1996.

Illouz, Eva. *Cold Intimacies: The Making of Emotional Capitalism*. Cambridge: Polity Press, 2007.

International Peace Information Centre. "Mapping Conflict Motives: M23." Antwerp: International Peace Information Centre, November 2012. http://www.ipisresearch.be/publications_detail.php?id=390.

Joyce, Daniel. "Media Witness: Human Rights in an Age of Digital Media." *Intercultural Human Rights Law Review (St. Thomas University)* 8 (2013): 231.

Kurasawa, Fuyuki. "A Message in a Bottle Bearing Witness as a Mode of Transnational Practice." *Theory, Culture & Society* 26, no. 1 (2009): 92–111.

Lippmann, Walter. *Public Opinion.* Courier Corporation, 2012.

Livingston, Steven, and Todd Eachus. "Humanitarian Crises and US Foreign Policy: Somalia and the CNN Effect Reconsidered." *Political Communication* 12, no. 4 (1995): 413–29.

Macmillan, Lorraine. "The Child Soldier in North-South Relations." *International Political Sociology* 3, no. 1 (2009): 36–52.

Madianou, Mirca. "Humanitarian Campaigns in Social Media: Network Architectures and Polymedia Events." *Journalism Studies* 14, no. 2 (2013): 249–66.

Marthoz, Jean-Paul. "African Conflicts in the Global Media." In *The Media and Conflicts in Central Africa*, edited by Marie-Soleil Frère, 221–39. Boulder, CO: Lynne Rienner, 2007.

McLagan, Meg, and Yates McKee. "Introduction." In *Sensible Politics: The Visual Culture of Nongovernmental Activism*, edited by Meg McLagan and Yates McKee. New York: Zone Books, 2012.

McPherson, Ella. "Advocacy Organizations' Evaluation of Social Media Information for NGO Journalism the Evidence and Engagement Models." *American Behavioral Scientist* 59, no. 1 (2015a): 124–48.

———. "Surmounting the Verification Barrier Between the Field of Professional Human Rights Fact-Finding and the Non-Field of Digital Civilian Witnessing," 2015b. https://www.repository.cam.ac.uk/handle/1810/248302.

Miller, Derek M. "The Morality Play: Getting to the Heart of Media Influence on Foreign Policy." In *Foreign Correspondence*, edited by John M. Hamilton and Regina G. Lawrence, 89–104. London: Routledge, 2013.

Miller, Jonathan. *Congo's Tin Soldiers.* Channel 4 News, 2007. http://www.youtube.com/watch?v=1UN44Lj4KwY.

———. Report on Bosco Ntaganda, *Channel 4 News*, 2 April 2012a

———. Report on displacement caused by M23 rebellion, *Channel 4 News*, 13 August 2012b

Nash, Kate. *The Cultural Politics of Human Rights: Comparing the US and UK.* Cambridge: Cambridge University Press, 2009.

Nothias, Toussaint. "'It's Struck a Chord We Have Never Managed to Strike': Frames, Perspectives and Remediation Strategies in the International News Coverage of Kony2012." *Ecquid Novi: African Journalism Studies* 34, no. 1 (2013): 123–29.

OFCOM. Channel 4 Licence. (2004). http://licensing.ofcom.org.uk/binaries/tv/c4/c4drl.pdf.

———. "The OFCOM Broadcasting Code," February 2011. http://stakeholders.ofcom.org.uk/broadcasting/guidance/programme-guidance/bguidance/.

Oppen, Karoline von. "Reporting from Bosnia: Reconceptualising the Notion of a 'journalism of Attachment.'" *Journal of Contemporary European Studies* 17, no. 1 (2009): 21–33.

Peters, John Durham. "Witnessing." *Media, Culture and Society* 23 (2001): 707–23.

Powers, Matthew. "The Structural Organization of NGO Publicity Work: Explaining Divergent Publicity Strategies at Humanitarian and Human Rights Organizations." *International Journal of Communication* 8 (2014): 90–107.

Pratt, David. "Herald Scotland." *The Brave Face of Journalism*, February 26, 2012. http://www.heraldscotland.com/opinion/13048505.The_brave_face_of_journalism/.

Richards, Barry, and Gavin Rees. "The Management of Emotion in British Journalism." *Media, Culture & Society* 33, no. 6 (September 1, 2011): 851–67.

Rodgers, James. *Reporting Conflict*. London, New York: Palgrave Macmillan, 2012.

Ruigrok, Nel. "Journalism of Attachment and Objectivity: Dutch Journalists and the Bosnian War." *Media, War & Conflict* 1, no. 3 (2008): 293–313.

———. "From Journalism of Activism towards Journalism of Accountability." *International Communication Gazette* 72, no. 1 (2010): 85–90.

Schudson, Michael. *The Sociology of News*. New York: WW Norton and Co, 2003.

Sen, Amartya. *The Idea of Justice*. London: Penguin, 2010.

Tagg, John. "Evidence, Truth and Order: A Means of Surveillance" In *The Photography Reader*, edited by Liz Wells, 244–73. London, New York: Routledge, 1999.

Tumber, Howard. "Journalists, War Crimes and International Justice." *Media, War & Conflict* 1, no. 3 (2008): 261–69.

UK Government. Communications Act (2003). http://www.legislation.gov.uk/ukpga/2003/21/contents.

United Nations News Service. "UN Envoy Welcomes End of M23 Rebellion.," November 5, 2013. http://www.un.org/apps/news/story.asp?NewsID=46423#.VjeLZrfhCUk.

Van Leuven, Sarah, Annelore Deprez, and Karin Raeymaeckers. "Increased News Access for NGOs? How Médecins Sans Frontières' Press Releases Built the Agenda of Flemish Newspapers (1995–2010)." *Journalism Practice* 7, no. 4 (2013): 430–45.

Volkmer, Ingrid. *News in the Global Sphere: A Study of CNN and Its Impact on Global Communication*. Luton: University of Luton Press, 1999.

Wahl-Jorgensen, Karin. "The Strategic Ritual of Emotionality: A Case Study of Pulitzer Prize-Winning Articles." *Journalism* 14, no. 1 (2013): 129–45.

Wright, Kate. "Moral Economies: Interrogating the Interactions of Nongovernmental Organizations, Journalists and Freelancers." *International Journal of Communication* 10 (2016a): 1–19.

———. "These Grey Areas": How and Why Freelance Work Blurs INGOs and News Organizations. *Journalism Studies* 17, no. 8 (2016b): 989–1009.

Zahra, Farwa. "The Express Tribune Blog." *Marie Colvin's Journalism of Attachment*, February 24, 2012. http://blogs.tribune.com.pk/story/10359/marie-colvins-journalism-of-attachment/.

Zelizer, Barbie. *Remembering to Forget: Holocaust Memory Through the Camera's Eye*. University of Chicago Press: Chicago, 2000.

ONLINE SLIDESHOWS, "SELLING IN", AND MORAL EDUCATION

BBC News Online and Save the Children

Online news offers journalists exciting opportunities to tell stories in new, multimodal ways, the most common of which is the photo slideshow (Caple and Knox 2012; Jacobson 2010; Lillie 2011). These slideshows are frequently found on sites claiming to offer "global" news to international audiences, and involve a sequence of images, minimal text, and sometimes, music or audio (Engebretsen 2014; Roosvall 2014). In war reporting, they tend to be presented as "hard news" (Caple and Knox 2012), but otherwise, they are usually framed as softer "human interest" items which focus on the personal experiences of one individual or a small group of individuals (Engebretsen 2014). These kinds of frames have often been seen as depoliticizing and decontextualizing suffering (Cottle and Nolan 2007). But they cater to online audiences' preference for personalized and emotionally compelling stories, as well as visually arresting multimedia (Sambrook *et al.* 2013).

Audience popularity is of vital commercial importance to most online news sites because news managers use metric data proving how many users visit the site, and how much they interact with it, to attract potential advertisers (Currah 2009). Attracting more advertisers is particularly important at a time when online adverts are worth far less than print adverts. However, audience metrics have a complex relationship with the production of news about Africa—they don't tend to drive which stories journalists cover, or how they cover them, in isolation (Bunce 2015). Instead, algorithmic data tends to interact with other considerations relating to normative values, organization-al branding and market positioning in order to shape journalists' approach to media production (Bunce 2015).

Photo slideshows which represent actors from the Global South are particularly interesting as they may be framed as appealing, human interest items, but they don't tend to be obvious "clickbait". Instead, they generate potentially complex meanings through the relationship/s of images, text, and audio to one another (Engebretsen 2014): constructing value-laden notions of "globality" or "humanity" in ways which reconstruct audiences' imagined relationships with distant others (Roosvall 2014). Yet this "moral education" (Chouliaraki 2008) also has commercial purposes: encouraging brand loyalty by forging emotive and normative attachments between the consumer and the news outlet (Ghodeswar 2008; McDowell 2011).

In addition, photo slideshows are often used to visually differentiate news sites from their competitors (Caple 2013), helping to compensate for the lack of original written content on most news sites (Redden and Witschge 2010). Slideshows can also be used to create the impression of a broad geographic spread of international coverage (Mellese and Müller 2012), despite the re-duction in the numbers of correspondent posts and foreign bureaux (Franks 2013). This is important because many overseas users are attracted by the promise of distinctive, high-quality and comprehensive international cover-age (Newman and Levy 2012). Finally, human interest slideshows tend not to date as quickly as hard news so can remain on the site, accomplishing all of these objectives, long after any accompanying "hard news" stories have had to be replaced.

Thus producing online slideshows enhances journalists' abilities to ad-dress multiple commercial and normative objectives, at the same time as en-gaging in new story-telling techniques. However, producing slideshows is a logistical nightmare for online journalists because the aesthetic conventions of slideshows are derived from photographic galleries and photo essays (Ca-ple and Knox 2012). So constructing them necessitates using large volumes of technically and aesthetically sophisticated forms of photography, whose coherence is usually aided by the vision of a single, specialized photographer (Caple and Knox 2012; Engebretsen 2014). Yet most newspapers have made their own photojournalists redundant during successive rounds of cost-cutting (Anderson 2014; Hadland et al. 2015; Klein-Avraham and Reich 2013), and broadcasters, like the BBC, never had many to start with. Online journalists also lack the budgets needed to commission specialized photojournalists and, given the aesthetically sophisticated nature of most online slideshows, it is difficult to construct them using cheaper pictures taken by untrained reporters, or User Generated Content (UGC).

For these reasons, most photo slideshows published by online news outlets are compiled using images taken from the major wire agencies, such as Thomson Reuters, and photographic agencies, like Getty (Roosvall 2014). But this is hardly ideal if journalists want to use online slideshows to visually distinguish their site from rivals, as most major news organizations subscribe to exactly the same photographic agencies and wire feeds (Caple 2013). Moreover, trawling through wire feeds and the image banks of photographic agencies takes online journalists a significant amount of time and effort. This is difficult, given that they are expected to produce, and continually refresh, very large volumes of material on a 24/7 basis (Redden and Witschge 2010). The labor-intensive nature of producing photo slideshows therefore risks taking up so much time that journalists are unable to sustain another key selling point of online news outlets—that is, its ability to break, and continually update, news (Allan 2006).

Major US and UK-based international aid agencies have been swift to respond, by subsidizing news outlets' production of photo slideshows. They regularly commission well-known freelance photojournalists from Europe and North America in order to provide picture editors and/or regional editors with galleries of beautiful images, representing the areas in the Global South where they are active. In so doing, these INGOs draw upon their longstanding traditions of employing photographic images to fundraise and engage in mass awareness-raising or public education (Fehrenbach and Rodogno 2015; McLagan & McKee, 2012; Powers 2014). Although international aid agencies have also been criticized for their willingness to adopt immediately appealing, personalized and emotive human interest frames, in order to enhance their organizational brands and stimulate financial giving (Cottle and Nolan 2007). So there is a marked synergy or compatibility between the approaches taken by these kinds of INGOs and online outlets purporting to offer "clickable" global news.

This chapter examines how commercial, normative and editorial values interacted with one another during a specific production process involving journalists at one of the most visited news sites in the world, *BBC News Online*, and one of the most heavily commercialized international aid agencies, Save the Children UK. This production process was collaborative: involving a member of staff from Save the Children providing the photos, whilst the BBC journalist conducted an audio interview with a former child soldier[1] who had fought in the civil war in South Sudan (Crowley and Fleming 2010a). To be more specific, the BBC journalist, who was in South Sudan in order to gather material in the run-up to the country's independence, agreed to be embedded with the INGO on a side-trip to the rural area where the boy lived.

But this side trip was only given the green light by BBC managers because Save the Children were also offering another, even more technically sophisticated piece, which they thought would appeal to online users. This was an interactive 360° degree image with embedded audio clips, representing adults from the boy's village who had fled the war, but who had returned after peace was declared (Crowley and Fleming 2010b). BBC journalists saw portraying these rarely represented actors and places as helping them meet their statutory obligations to uphold Reithian public service principles regarding the education of media audiences. But they also thought that Save the Children's proposal would help them to publish the kind of immediately attractive content which could be easily promoted to the editors of the main global news page on the website, as well as to international news audiences. Indeed, the pieces were regarded so favourably by senior BBC journalists that they were republished two years later in the summer of 2012, as part of a special report of archive material marking the anniversary of South Sudan's independence.

Meanwhile, press officers at Save the Children saw the "clickability" of both pieces as helping them promote their organizational voice by reaching a very large media audience. They thought this would help them to consolidate their relations with existing donors: so securing their fundraising base. But they also felt a strong sense of moral obligation to engage in forms of mediated advocacy which would educate those who didn't already know about the situation in South Sudan, including the experiences of child soldiers (Powers 2014). Thus the trust needed to trigger these exchanges emerged from marked correspondences or complementarities between the aims, values and obligations of the INGO and the news organization.

However, this production process was also characterized by significant tensions within the INGO, and between the INGO and the news organization, which threatened to derail the production process altogether. This is because actors' values, objectives and obligations partly competed with one another, as well as having some partial complementarities. Thus this case study contrasts with those in previous chapters as it illuminates the formation of a very shaky and uncertain form of trust, which emerged from considerable compromise and conflict. So this chapter speaks to other work about the potential instability of INGO-journalist coalitions (Orgad 2013; Waisbord 2011). In particular, it shows that even the most unstable and conflict-ridden exchanges between journalists and NGO-workers may still have important and long-lasting effects: bringing about new interactions between sets of economic and normative values, in ways which entrench the capabilities and perspectives of some actors at the expense of others.

BBC News Online and public-commercial hybridity

The BBC is a public corporation whose existence is justified in British law by notions of its normative value to the British public, including its obligations to provide high-quality international news to British people which is independent from, and impartial to, political and commercial interests (Department of Culture, Media and Sport 2006). Indeed, the body to which the BBC is most immediately accountable, the BBC Trust, announced that it would be conducting a major investigation into the impartiality of the Corporation's output only ten days before the sample was taken (Plunkett 2012). Nevertheless, at the point of renewing its Charter in 1996, the Corporation was obliged to accept that one of its core objectives should be to generate income through commercial activities, in order to supplement the license fee. So it has become an odd kind of public-commercial hybrid (discussed in Steemers 1999, 2005).

The hybrid at the heart of the hybrid, as it were, is *BBC News Online*, which, since 2007, has allowed advertising on the international-facing English language site, *BBC News.com*, whilst remaining advert-free to British users, in accordance with the terms of the BBC Agreement. When the former Director General, Mark Byford, took this decision he tasked the Head of Global News, Richard Sambrook, with setting up a committee to find ways of "ensuring a clear divide between editorial and commercial decision-making", so that the "public trust in the authority of the BBC's journalism" was not endangered (interview, April 14, 2014).

Sambrook said that this involved creating a raft of organizational policies and structures in order to deal with "enormous internal tensions". He then expanded on this, saying

> Worldwide [the commercial arm of the BBC] had always wanted to make the site as
> commercial as possible (…)

> Basically, they thought they could make a fortune from it. But they didn't always understand the editorial sensitivities involved.
>
> They just kept pushing and *pushing* (…) So this is why you had the committee set up, and reviews and panels and reports and things… It was to keep Worldwide honest, really.

But the BBC experienced a 16 per cent drop in income after a Conservative-led government froze its license fee in the settlement of 2010, as well as obliging the Corporation to pay for other services previously subsidized directly by the British government. The cost-cutting this necessitated compounded previous budget reductions at *BBC Online* of 25 per cent, which Mark Thompson, the BBC's then Director General, enacted in March 2010, in order to try and ward off attacks by the Corporation's commercial rivals and the Conservative party, which has a long history of ideological opposition to state-supported public service broadcasting (Hendy 2013; Tumber 2011).

One of the effects of this was to make generating revenue from the advertising placed on the international version of *BBC News Online* more important, although David Moody, the Head of Strategy at BBC Worldwide, explained that this was still a "drop in the ocean" compared to the revenue generated by the license fee (interview, January 24, 2014). Moody clarified this by releasing figures which have not been previously been made public: saying that his projections suggested that the advertising income of the site in 2014 would be around 60 million dollars, having risen from 50 to 55 million dollars in 2012, when the sample for this study was taken. But back in 2009, advertising income was a relatively low twenty to twenty four million dollars, because, Moody said, the effects of the global recession combined with the relative newness of the BBC brand to US advertisers had made for a "tough couple of years".

However, as Moody went on to explain, increasing advertising spend on the site had been very difficult because of the very strict rules about which adverts could be placed around hard news and because few advertisers wanted to place promotions near "depressing" and "unpredictable" news coverage anyway (interview, January 24, 2014). Instead,

> What people tend to want in advertising is the stuff *around* news, which tends to be (…) if we think about the traditional newspaper format, the stuff you would find in the features section.

In particular, Moody had argued that advertisers were looking to "associate their brand" with "up-beat" features

(…) around Business, around Finance, around Health and Well-being, around Motoring—all the things that in their extreme form would be in what the *Financial Times* publishes in "How to Spend" on a Saturday.

For these reasons, Moody said that BBC Worldwide had been allowed to move into editorial commissioning, albeit in consultation with BBC News. Indeed, he complained that BBC journalists simply didn't make enough of the kinds of lifestyle items popular with advertisers, so Worldwide was "having to" spend money commissioning these kinds of features from "the market": stressing that these Worldwide-commissioned features now comprised "an increasingly large part—often the majority" of the features on *BBC News.com* (interview, February 17, 2014). Thus the "clear divide between editorial and commercial decision-making", instituted by Sambrook's committee back in 2007 (interview with Mark Byford, April 14, 2014), appears to have become eroded.

This helps to contextualize the case study because one of the policies developed by Sambrook's committee involved banning adverts from NGOs after a test case regarding Oxfam. Accepting adverts from NGOs was found to be "inappropriate", along with accepting adverts from "other political…lobby or pressure groups": with both potentially damaging public perceptions of the BBC's impartiality and independence (BBC Strategic Approval Committee 2009, 10). Yet the Africa Editor of *BBC News Online*, Joseph Winter, regularly accepted photographic galleries commissioned by major US and UK-based aid agencies because of his increasing time and financial poverty, following the cuts in 2010. He described the loss of a post on the Africa desk as leaving him and his remaining producer:

> (…) just *flying* around [smiling] (…) like a blue-arsed fly
> I mean, Africa is a *very* busy patch *most* of the time (…)
> And now? [Shrugs] *Much* more so. (interview with Joseph Winter, May 7, 2013)

Winter's response to this change in his working conditions was to concentrate his energies on the production of news, which he re-framed as "our core job", even though news stories were not always the most frequently viewed items. As he put it,

> If there's some huge story, I don't know Boston marathon bombings or 9/11 or, you know, those kind of things, that's when (…) we come into our own.
> That's our *real* (…) when people really come to our sites in huge numbers, so we have to give them the news. That's *really* public service journalism.

Thus, much like journalists at *Channel 4 News*, Winter's efforts to justify his use of NGO-provided material resulted in him reconstructing notions of public service journalism. The visual compartmentalization of NGO-provided images in the Watch/Listen section of the site further enabled Winter to argue that accepting aid agencies' material did not affect the "real" public service journalism carried out at *BBC News Online*. But he also used another legitimating rationale, arguing that:

> The big aid agencies often come up with very good photos; very strong, powerful photos (…) I'm looking for emotion, artistry, you know, just a (…) a *powerful* picture that tells a story (…)
> If we were to be offered pictures that weren't very good, we wouldn't use them. But mostly they're *really* good.

Underpinning this judgement were particular tastes which involved privileging the aesthetic traditions of Northern elites (Gupta 1986). This begs the question of whose version of the "global" is being presented in such slide-shows, and whose moral order it relates to (Denčik 2013). But online journalists did not reflect on such complex questions about media effects. Instead, they were largely preoccupied with avoiding compassion fatigue (Moeller 1999). As Winter put it, he didn't want to "wear out audiences" by publishing photos of suffering which had "shock value", at least outside of major "emergencies", as he assumed that online users would "just tune out that stuff after a while" (interview, May 7, 2013).

Winter couldn't use in-house photographers to accomplish this because *BBC News Online* only had access to two, and neither were usually available for travel outside the UK (interview with Joseph Winter, May 7, 2013). So Winter was attracted by aid organizations' habit of hiring what he called "really good freelancers", whose fees and travel costs he could not afford himself. However, aid agencies also enabled Winter to save time and money in other ways, because they were prepared to shoulder the burden of health and safety precautionary procedures. BBC journalists stressed that the health and safety forms necessary to send freelancers to hostile environments had become prohibitive. Many mentioned that the paperwork had dramatically increased, following an event in 2003, in which a freelancer was thought to have contracted the ebola virus in the Democratic Republic of Congo, and had to be evacuated by air to emergency medical facilities in another country, at great expense.

But journalists also spoke about the ways in which INGOs helped them manage other kinds of risks by supervising freelancers (Banks *et al.* 2000). Many said they were mindful of an incident in 2011, in which a freelancer was found to have faked film footage for a *Panorama* documentary. This necessitated the Corporation having to give back a journalistic award, which mortified BBC journalists and news managers. Thus the approach taken by journalists at *BBC News Online* contrasted sharply with journalists at *Channel 4 News* and *The Independent* papers, who saw the involvement of trusted freelancers as a guarantee of the veracity of the material and the ethical nature of production processes.

Winter's approach was also different from those of other journalists in previous cases, in that it was strongly shaped by his obligations to uphold the Corporation's Editorial Guidelines. These guidelines are shaped by the BBC Agreement, which sets out the Corporation's obligations to the British public. The guidelines don't deal with journalists' use of written or multimedia provided by INGOs, but with the involvement of BBC staff in joint fundraising appeals. The Corporation hosts a number of such appeals, including Children in Need night and Red Nose Day, as well as the joint appeals for international aid organizations, led by the UK's Disasters Emergency Committee (DEC). These kinds of agreements have led to a tendency in the Corporation to conceptualize international aid agencies as beneficent "charities", rather than political actors (Franks 2013; Lindström 2016), unless their charitable work entails them intervening in conflicts which are politically sensitive for the Corporation.

Indeed, the BBC's editorial guidelines were rewritten at the request of the BBC Trust, as part of its response to complaints about its refusal to take part in the DEC appeal for Gaza in 2009 (Thomas and Hindman 2012). So the guidelines now stress that all BBC staff should be careful to maintain their "impartiality and independence" when dealing with "charities" (BBC Editorial Guidelines 16.4.57–16.4.58). But the only further guidance which is given involves BBC staff making sure that any "arrangements do not give the impression that the BBC is promoting the charity or endorsing it above other charities working in the same field" (BBC Editorial Guidelines 16.4.57–16.4.58).

For these reasons, BBC Online journalists decided not accept any material from INGOs which were "into full-on political lobbying like human rights and environmental groups", or which might have "party political links" (interview with Joseph Winter, May 7, 2013). Winter was in charge of taking these decisions for the Africa page, but as he didn't have time to research smaller organizations, this meant that he tended to accept material from major international aid agencies in the US and UK, whose work he was familiar with. Although he stressed that he spread his acceptance of material out amongst them, as

> Otherwise we get complaints from all the other aid agencies, saying, you know (…) "You're giving undue prominence to one aid agency over another."

Winter was also meticulous about attributing NGO content, and tried to retain some critical independence through a variety of different measures. This included insisting that aid agencies gave him a large collection of photographs to choose from—around 30 to 40 shots. This meant that he could select and order photos into a sequence for a slideshow, as well as rewriting the captions underneath. Although he admitted that the changes he made were sometimes "quite minimal" (interview with Joseph Winter, May 7, 2013).

So BBC journalists' efforts to meet their statutory responsibilities, as articulated in the editorial guidelines, clearly modified the operation of the "information subsidies" provided to the website by international aid agencies (Gandy 1982). However, these practices also served as a way of legitimizing BBC journalists giving international aid agencies repeated advantages in the framing of sub-Saharan Africa. This seems likely to have cumulative political effects, including normalizing and legitimizing Northerners' intervention in the continent's affairs (Lugo-Ocando and Malaolu 2014).

Winter's geographic expertise meant that he was aware of this problem, saying that he was uneasy about using so many photos from aid agencies, in case it entrenched Africa's dependence on foreign aid (interview, May 7, 2013). Nevertheless, the way in which the editorial guidelines were written meant that he did not see this concern as undermining the Corporation's collective obligation to remain politically impartial. Instead, like the Africa Editor at *The Guardian*, he said his worries about using NGO photos were "personal concerns": arguing that his organizational responsibilities to produce enough material for the Africa page trumped any "private worries" he might have.

However, Winter was prepared to speak out about his resentment of the amount of time and effort involved in producing slideshows and "special reports". These were curated collections of archive material, the purpose of which was to provide background about a particular country and/or theme, in an "engaging" manner, rather than as "dry analysis" (interview with BBC Online Africa producer, November 16, 2012). Photo slideshows using images provided by aid agencies were well-suited to this purpose because of their aesthetic and interactive qualities, but also because their human interest framing meant they didn't become outdated as quickly as news items. So journalists' production of special reports was subsidized to a significant extent by aid agencies. Although trawling through archives and curating related material still took far more time than Winter wanted, which he thought risked taking his attention away from breaking news.

Another reason why Winter disliked special reports was that he suspected that their construction was not driven by editorial priorities. As he put it,

> To be honest, [the Special Collections] are a pain, you know. They take a lot of time, fiddling around, putting them in, making them look nice, and not many people click on them (...) But, erm, (...) you know, the thing to say is, who decides *when* we do them is important (...)
>
> There has been, if not exactly *pressure*, then *talk* of experiments about advertisers, because (...) if there's a special event coming up then there's so many adverts around it. And if there's a special page, then (...) for example, banks operating in South Sudan, you know, the likes of them *may* like to advertise around that so the page has to look really snazzy. (interview with Joseph Winter, May 7, 2013)

Two things are worth highlighting here. Firstly, these frank remarks contradict Winter's earlier claim that the use of aid agency photos did not impinge upon the "real" journalism at *BBC News Online*. The production of slideshows and Special Reports using these kinds of photos clearly did impinge on the time he had to engage in other journalistic tasks, including attending to breaking news. Secondly, Winter claimed that the visual aesthetics of slideshows were thought to help the site attract advertisers—even if they did not boost audience clicks. Thus Winter appeared to be hinting at another way in which increased financial pressure was eroding the Corporation's division between editorial and commercial decision-making.

Child soldiers, "selling in", and moral education

Slideshows constructed using aid agency images were also bound up with other kinds of commercialized, promotional practices, which structured BBC journalists' relationship with each other (Davis 2013). This was because the kinds of visually distinctive images provided by international aid agencies helped Africa Online journalists to persuade the editors in charge of the main index pages to link to African coverage. Winter's junior colleague, talked about this in detail: describing this internal negotiation as a form of "selling". As she put it,

I think [international aid agencies] are often able to provide that something a bit *different* we are always looking for [*sic*]. For example, these [indicates new photos provided by another major aid agency] got quite a big push on the site (…)

You know, when it comes to clicks, it's often a question of whether you get quite good promotion on the front pages. So at *Online* you are always trying to sort of *sell* your story to (…) the World index, the international front page [and] the UK-facing front pages.

You're always trying to get these features onto those front pages, so that they get the most hits (…)

[So] If you are Desk Editor that day, you will call up those Editors to try and push it to those front pages. (interview with BBC Online Africa producer, November 16, 2012)

Indeed, this producer used the same metaphors of promotional "pushing" or "selling" to describe the whole chain of relationships involved in the production of slideshows. This began with aid agencies' approaches to her, continued through her relations with the main editors at *Online*, and ended with the act of persuading as many online users as possible to click on the material in question. At each stage, she described the kinds of material most likely to be successfully "sold" as being highly visual, emotive and personalized items (Sambrook *et al.* 2013). Such an approach involved her taking a much more broad-brush approach to audience metrics than her editor, Winter, who insisted that relatively few online users clicked on these particular slideshows. In contrast, the junior producer said,

When you are on *Online*, you've got all the statistics you can see what people are clicking on and you have to try and sell your story in a way that people will read them [*sic*] (…)

I mean, you get daily [algorithmic] reports and when you go on [to the site] you can even see the most popular stories. So there's always loads of statistics about what works well.

To really *sell* the story you need to get personal in [*sic*]. So you are always trying to find you know the *human story* (…)

So the 360° photo which Save gave us was a good sell because it had ordinary people just telling their own stories.

And [the former child soldier] featured in the slideshow] was *perfect*. I mean he is *really* easy to sell, isn't he?

You know, a boy soldier (…) [Tails off and gesticulates].

He's got a personally strong story, so you can always find lots of little emotive ways of getting people to click on it.

At the time when this material was republished, the most obvious example of the popularity of representations of African child soldiers was the video viral,

Kony 2012. This was produced by the US-based INGO, Invisible Children Inc. about those forced into military service by the Ugandan rebel, Joseph Kony (Gregory 2012). But although this helped shape the decision to repub-lish the slideshow in 2012, the viral did not shape its original production, which occurred two years earlier, in 2010. Instead, the "human interest" rep-resentation of the boy soldier was intricately bound up with broader, market-ized processes of promotion, both inside and outside the BBC. Indeed, the boy himself was described as a commodity which was "easy to sell".

This marketized approach has been long discussed in relation to human-itarian dilemmas: with aid workers often being torn between the need to "bankroll intervention" and between their consciousness of the potentially damaging long-term effects of commodifying suffering (Kennedy 2009). But the notion of "selling in" has rarely been discussed in relation to journalism. Although this also risks marginalizing otherness and politics: appealing to the tastes of the largely Northern socio-economic elites consuming *BBC News Online*, without challenging them in any profound fashion (Calhoun 2003; Cheah 2013).

Yet it would be wrong to describe this slideshow as involving a decisive shift away from a Reithian model of "telling people what they need to know", and towards a wholly commercialized model which offers some, privileged people "what they want—when, where and how they want it" (Lee-Wright 2010, 74). This is because the producer working on the Africa page repeat-edly legitimized her approach in terms of her commitment to the Reithian mission to educate (Born 2004; Küng-Shankleman and Küng 2000). In fact, she argued that the "whole point" of her work was to try to get as many *On-line* readers as possible to read items about Africa because then, "they should understand at least *some* of the issues involved" (interview with BBC Online Africa producer, November 16, 2012).

Unfortunately, there isn't much evidence to suggest that media audienc-es really do use online news to learn about the suffering of distant others, including its causes and contexts (Scott 2015). But the junior producer on the Africa page hoped to achieve a kind of moral education, which involved forging imaginary and empathetic relations between these others and the socio-economic elites comprising *BBC Online's* audience through new me-dia(Chouliaraki 2008). In so doing, Fleming tended to elide legitimating ra-tionales for photo slideshows and other kinds of interactive multimedia, such as the 360° image about the other villagers, which included audio inserts. In particular, she argued that both kinds of aid agency material engaged online audiences in more active ways and helped them "understand what it's like to *be*" those represented (interview with BBC Online Africa producer, November 16, 2012). Indeed, she said she would love to publish more interactive media projects which allowed *Online* readers to "move around" within and between digital scenes "as if they were really there". But the time and effort needed to host them on the site was prohibitive, so, she concluded, slideshows would "have to do, most of the time."

This producer's approach was partially shaped by her own background in public relations at the BBC and her reluctance, like others in this study, to confront the ways in which white, relatively privileged, African-born journalists tended to control the representation of poor black Africans (interview, November 16, 2012). However, the producer's approach was also shaped by the interaction of two very different subcultures within BBC News. These were *BBC News Online* and World Service Radio, which both she and Winter had previously worked for.

The Africa Online team also sat alongside journalists working for the African sections of World Service Radio—a whole floor away from the rest of the *Online* team. As online journalists' workload means that they are increasingly unable to leave their desks (Fenton 2010), who they sit alongside has become very important. But it is also important to note that this new seating arrangement was a relatively recent development, as the African services had only just moved into the BBC's new Broadcasting House. Previously they had been located in Bush House, on the other side of London to the rest of the *Online* team.

The overall editor of *BBC News Online*, Steve Herrmann, explained that the Africa Online team had been physically embedded within the African sections of World Service Radio in order to help mitigate the loss of the third Africa *Online* post (interview, June 10, 2013). Herrmann also described this form of embedding as encouraging a more "efficient" transfer of knowledge from the "experts" in African services to staff working on the website. However, the enculturation of Winter and his junior colleague in the African Services meant that they saw it differently. They argued that this seating plan helped them bring an "African service ethos" to bear on online news norms (interview with Joseph Winter, May 7, 2013). In particular, they stressed that creating "human interest" media items for online should enable "ordinary Africans' voices to be heard" (interview with Joseph Winter, May 7, 2013; interview with BBC Online Africa producer, November 16, 2012).

Previous research about BBC World Service Radio has identified a distinct working culture, which existed up until the departure of news staff from Bush House in 2012 (Gillespie and Webb 2013). This working culture, it is argued, was structured by cosmopolitan norms derived from the station's diasporic origins, its multiple language services, extensive network of local reporters, and unusually mixed audiences (Gillespie and Webb 2013). Specifically, World Service listeners have tended to contain two main groups: regular listeners belonging to socio-economic elites, and short-wave audiences, who tune in more sporadically, especially when facing "acute political, economic, ecological and human rights crises" (Baumann and Gillespie 2007, 6).

The need to bear both kinds of audiences in mind when creating radio programming is thought to have shaped the emergence of particular values regarding journalists' role of helping disempowered others be heard by elites (Gillespie and Webb 2013). Although journalists' actual practices didn't always up to such high ideals, as they were also shaped by the station's colonial heritage, mainstream forms of journalistic gatekeeping, and over-optimistic visions of the ability of digital technology to foster communicative empowerment (Ogunyemi 2011).[2]

Thus BBC Online journalists refused to carry an interview by Save the Children with the boy soldier because of their formal obligations regarding impartiality and independence, but also because of their informal sense of moral responsibility to act as guardians of others' voices (interview with BBC Online Africa producer, November 16, 2012). However, the producer's insistence that she be allowed to do the interviewing on the trip set her on a direct collision course with the humanitarian multimedia officer at the INGO, who saw enabling others' voices as the responsibility of aid-workers. In order to clarify the nature of this argument, it is necessary to explain its roots in an internal conflict, which took place within Save the Children itself.

Save the Children UK, humanitarianism, and "voice"

Save the Children UK prioritizes raising money to provide humanitarian relief to alleviate the suffering of others, often in disasters, crises or other emergencies. It can therefore can be positioned as a "chemical" aid agency, as opposed to an "alchemical" agency which prioritizes exposing and explaining the structural causes of suffering (Orgad 2013). Indeed, Save the Children is widely seen as one of the most heavily commercialized agency in the sector (Parker 2015), and is often criticized by more alchemically-minded aid-workers, such as those at Christian Aid, for using what they regard as degrading imagery in order to raise as much money as possible.

But one of the agency's most senior managers, Gareth Owen, who was in charge of delivering aid at Save the Children UK said he wanted to resist this commercialization, which he also saw as squeezing out the organization's normative values (interview, March 1, 2013). One of the ways in which he did this was to take the opportunity afforded by an organizational restructure to change the name of his department from "Emergencies", which he argued was synonymous with fundraising, to "Humanitarian". He said that his purpose in so doing was to try and "mainstream the humanitarian gene back into (…) this big beast that has largely forgotten all that stuff".

Owen was particularly concerned about what he described as the ways in which the INGO's press officers engaged with media organizations. As he put it,

> You know, the usual thing was that Save would hire a freelancer in the moment to go out and shoot some pictures of kids in day three of an earthquake and all the rest of it. And that was the sort of tried and trusted way of sort of gathering a certain amount of material (…)
>
> But (…) it was (…) normally from a fundraising perspective or from a (…) a very *simple* media perspective.
>
> And we [in the Humanitarian department] wanted (…) to create a more honest relationship with the public who support us. I felt, and others felt, that [Save UK] had started to *spin* excessively through media because of fundraising. (interview with Gareth Owen, March 1, 2013)

In contrast, Owen said he wanted to engage with media organizations in order to "educate the public" by enabling local people's values and perspectives to be heard and by illuminating their agency and resourcefulness (interview, March 1, 2013). These are all classic instances of giving "voice" to others (Couldry 2010). Owen also felt passionately about "teaching people" about what he called the "brokenness" of the aid system, which kept failing to prevent acute crises from happening. Thus the way in which Owen related humanitarianism to journalism involved a "definite form of politics" (Nolan and Mikami 2013, 62), which was not too far away from more radical, alchemical approaches to humanitarianism, which involve a critical engagement with states and markets (Calhoun 2008; Orgad 2013).

The broader implications of this are interesting as NGO-workers involved in delivering aid have historically tended to view mediation as a necessary evil, needed to fund humanitarian work (Nolan and Mikami 2013). But here we have a very experienced aid-worker, who not only saw media production as a form of humanitarian work, but who even appointed a Humanitarian multi-media producer, in order to offer media audiences the kind of moral education he believed was important (Chouliaraki 2008). Owen decided that this person should be skilled in producing video and photographs because he knew that visual images were in great demand in mainstream news—especially online.

However, in order to prevent this person from being swallowed up by the press team, Owen thought it necessary to take some precautionary steps. The first of these involved situating the post in Nairobi, rather than in London, embedding it within the agency's team of rapidly deployable emergency response personnel. Secondly, Owen deliberately appointed someone who wasn't a former journalist, but an experienced photographer who had always worked for aid agencies, as he thought that this person would be more likely to share his normative values (interview with Gareth Owen, March 1, 2013).

This Multimedia Officer took the photographs for the slideshow and in the 360° image: describing his interest in such work as powerfully shaped by his experience of learning French, as well as the extended period he had spent living in Francophone countries. He said that both of these experiences had made him interested in how a politics of voice might intersect with issues of oral and intercultural interpretation. For example, he described how, as a white American from the mid-West, immersion in another language had

(…) broke open my mind to see that the concepts you understand the world with are actually largely tied to your native language.

Once you jump outside that you learn (…) that there are all these different ways that we can see and understand reality, understand our culture, understand ourselves, our relationship to the world.

So for me it is *always* been about how to balance how to empower someone to voice *their* reality with all its differences (…)

But at the same *time*, trying to figure out where is this space of commonality amidst all these differences, so that I can enable an audience who might be millions of miles away to understand. (interview, August 31, 2012)

However Owen had deliberately appropriated commercialized discourses of efficiency in order to convince Save's commercially-minded former Chief Executive, Jasmine Whitbread, to allow him to introduce the post (interview with Gareth Owen, March 1, 2013). This meant that the field trips undertaken by the Humanitarian Multimedia Officer were funded via a complicated cost-recovery system, levied across all of the departments in the organization. So, as Owen explained, the Multimedia Officer "effectively cost nothing" (interview, March 1, 2013). But this meant that each department in the organization felt entitled to "bid" for the Multimedia Officer to provide multimedia for them: arguing that his ability to fulfil multiple briefs on single trip was central to his "value for money" for the organization (interview with Multimedia Officer, August 31, 2012).

This phrase is interesting because it tends to involve conceptualizing accountability in terms of financial auditing (Couldry 2010). So it did not prompt a more rigorous interrogation of which and whose values should shape media production and which kinds of obligations should ensure that this was carried out responsibly. Instead, the line manager of the Multimedia Officer, Hannah Reichardt, assumed that her responsibility was to get "as much good content for a variety of different stakeholder groups as possible" (interview, November 22, 2012). Unfortunately, both she and the Multimedia Officer found that this meant that trips risked becoming "overstuffed". This tended to squeeze out the more challenging and innovative forms of media which Owen had wanted to produce (interview with Multimedia Officer, August 31, 2012).

In addition, close links between fundraising targets and large media audiences meant that the agency's press officers were entitled to disrupt commissions already agreed with the Humanitarian Multimedia Officer, if a more popular media outlet evinced an interest in his work. On the South Sudan trip, Kathryn Rawe, Save's Media Manager for Africa, obliged him to drop an arrangement he had made to do a short film about a former child soldier for The *Guardian.co.uk* as part of a year-long "Child's Eye" series. Instead, she wanted him to collaborate with *BBC Online* to produce an audio slideshow (interview with Kathryn Rawe, November 16, 2012).

This change of plan came about when Rawe managed to get the producer at *BBC News Online* interested in the 360° slideshow. She also mentioned the possibility of doing a piece about a former child soldier during that conversation as she thought that the BBC's news site would be "a better home" for it (interview with Kathryn Rawe, November 16, 2012). Rawe defined a "better" outlet solely in terms of audience numbers. Reaching a mass audience, she argued, was the best way to engage in more effective fundraising in the long-term, even though the emotional "pull" of these pieces was unlikely to result in new donations. This was because Rawe thought that this approach was likely to enable the INGO to consolidate its relations with existing donors, and "prime the ground" for the next emergency appeal. However, when she talked about these fundraising strategies, she stressed not just commercial imperatives, but also her moral obligation to raise as much money as she could to help those in need (see also Daynes 2017).

In addition, Rawe thought that reaching a large audience would enable her to meet her responsibility to meet the public education objectives of Save the Children (Powers 2014). She interpreted these objectives as involving mass awareness raising, rather than providing more detailed contextual explanations, because the purpose of this education was, she thought, to stimulate audiences to act to relieve suffering, which she primarily thought of in terms of financial giving, but which she knew could involve other actions as well. These objectives meant that she was willing to make considerable editorial compromises with popular outlets, including tabloids with whose politics she did not agree. As she put it,

> You can get the story that's exactly how you want it to be on a specialized blog or something and maybe *five* people will read it (…) and they already *know* a lot about child soldiers (…)
>
> *Or* you can maybe make some compromises and get it in a much bigger outlet read by people who might know nothing it, and the difference you can make with that is far greater.

BBC News Online is no tabloid, but it is one of the most popular news sites in the world (Jones and Salter 2011), so it was a very desirable target for Save's press officers. However, this change of plan occurred very late in the day, when the Humanitarian Multimedia Officer was already out on the trip. He was opposed to the BBC producer doing the interviewing because he argued that he was better placed to empower and protect such a vulnerable child, because of the training he had received through the INGO (interview with Multimedia Officer, August 31, 2012). The Multimedia Officer also objected in principle to a BBC journalist "walking in and just basically *hijacking* the piece" after he had already had lengthy negotiations with *The Guardian*.

These negotiations included reaching an agreement that the piece would use subtitles rather than being dubbed over with an English voice: something which the Humanitarian Multimedia Officer felt very strongly about because of his conviction that empowering children's "voices" was an "embodied process" (Couldry 2010, 8). As he explained,

There are things that come through when somebody is speaking, so that even if you
don't understand their language, you can hear *them*—their intonation, inflection,
hesitations.
All these sorts of verbal-emotional cues (…)
That *matters* (….) (interview, August 31, 2012)

So initially, the multimedia officer refused to allow the BBC journalist to conduct the interviews with South Sudanese subjects (interview with Multimedia
Officer, August 31, 2012; interview with Kathryn Rawe, November 16, 2012).
Indeed, both parties had to call their respective managers back at headquarters to resolve the stand-off. The producer's managers at *BBC News Online*
supported her, agreeing that it would damage public perceptions of the Corporation's independence and impartiality if they accepted an interview carried
out by an INGO-worker, when it was possible for a BBC journalist to do it
(interview with BBC Online Africa producer, November 16, 2012).

Save's Head of News, Sarah Jacobs, also backed up the decision made by
press officer, Kathryn Rawe, arguing that it was a "no brainer" to compromise
and "go with *BBC Online*" because

The BBC was *the* go to place for global news then.
So in terms of readership and spread and all of that it was just basic *maths* (…)
You see, the main thing we are trying to do is get *our* voice heard in the most
influential and most widely read spaces. (interview, March 19, 2013)

Thus a radical politics of giving voice to a marginalized child soldier was effectively co-opted by those wishing to promote Save the Children's organizational voice.

"Selling in" or "selling out"?

Rawe and Jacobs, who were both located in Save's press office, did not see this
as a problem because they tended to conceptualize their relationships to journalists and media audiences in a very different way to those working in the
humanitarian department. Much like the producer at *BBC News Online*, they
saw themselves as "selling in" stories in order to reach the largest target market (interview with Sarah Jacobs, March 19, 2013; interview with Kathryn
Rawe, November 16, 2012). So they privileged promotional processes which
hinged upon on the easy, popular appeal of "human interest" stories. This
approach seemed commonsensical to them, but had actually emerged from

previous professional experiences, which predisposed them to blend media populism with marketing.

Both described themselves as having become used to "selling" their stories to news outlets as freelance journalists, in ways which led them to stress their immediate appeal to a mass audience (interview with Kathryn Rawe, November 16, 2012; interview with Sarah Jacobs, March 19, 2013). Jacobs had also been on the receiving end of freelancers' sales pitches as a commissioning editor for the *You* magazine, an advert-heavy, magazine supplement which accompanies the tabloid, *The Mail on Sunday*. Whilst Rawe had previously worked as a public affairs officer for South West Trains: an experience which she said had made her acutely aware of how to use news media to improve public awareness of her organization's brand. As Rawe put it,

> I always have a double agenda of getting the message we want publicized out there, and getting our name linked to it.

But the press office's decision to instigate a last-minute change of plan, together with the overloading of the South Sudan trip in the name of "value for money" meant that the Humanitarian multimedia officer and the South Sudanese press officer, Anthony Lodiong, didn't have much time to prepare. So neither spent much time briefing the junior, South Sudanese field worker tasked with interpreting between Dinka and English (interview with Multimedia Officer, August 31, 2012; interview, Anthony Lodiong, June 9, 2013). This was an important omission because this field worker did not have any training in oral interpretation. Yet the task he was asked to perform was an exceptionally difficult one: interpreting for a child who had been forced to join a military group in an unstable post-conflict situation, as well as mediating between languages and cultures bound together by colonialism (Baker 2006; Bassnett and Trivedi 1999; Wright 2018).

These potential problems were exacerbated by the unequal structuring of the boy's relationship with Save the Children and with the fieldworker tasked with interpretation. This was because the field worker was an assistant on one of the INGO's cash transfer schemes, which the boy's family were financially dependent upon (interview with Field Worker, May 15, 2013). The field worker also claimed that he had not been aware that the interviews and pictures of the boy and others in his village were to be used in two multimedia items for a news outlet. Indeed, he said that he had not been aware that the BBC producer was a journalist. He thought she was a replacement for Kathryn Rawe, the press officer, who had fallen sick earlier in the trip.

So, much like the field-workers in other case studies, the field worker asked the boy, his family and the other villagers to participate in ways which would have been more in keeping with an internal project or donors' report than a news piece. He approached the villagers by saying that he needed them to have their photos taken and do interviews for Save the Children, as "we want to make something that we are doing for them even better" (interview with Field Worker, May 15, 2013). The field worker later regretted this bitterly because he felt that he had gained the villagers' acceptance under false pretenses: arguing that they had "trusted" him as a worker for Save the Children on the cash transfer scheme and as a fellow Dinka, "a brother (...) the same to them" (interview, May 15, 2013).

The field worker explained that the villagers would have felt obliged to help a member of Save the Children prepare an internal report, because of the norms of reciprocity. But they had no such obligation to give interviews to a journalist for a news outlet, and "would not have wanted to make an interview *world-wide*" because exposing their poverty in this way would be undignified. He therefore felt that he had inadvertently enabled an unjust exchange, which risked disrupting his harmonious, respectful relations with his kin. This made him deeply uneasy because he understood humanitarian aid to involve reciprocal sharing during times of hardship. He left Save the Children shortly afterwards.

It is worth stressing here that Save the Children does have detailed ethical policies about the need to obtain informed consent, especially when children are involved (interview with Kathryn Rawe, November 6, 2012). In accordance with these policies, Save staff had made a point of speaking with the boy, his family and community leaders in order to get permission to take photographs and record interviews (interview with Multimedia Officer, August 31, 2012). However, the haste and miscommunication produced by the last-minute re/structuring of this production process, combined with the row between the INGO-worker and the journalist, meant that no one had made sure that the interpreter understood the projected outcomes and audiences. As a result, the boy, his family and his broader community were inadvertently misled about the purposes of media participation. So, despite INGO-workers and journalists both intending to enable others' voices, South Sudanese subjects were denied a very basic form of voice—the ability to give informed and meaningful consent.

Indeed, the boy, his parents and the other villagers did not even know that they had been speaking to a journalist until a month later, when the South

Sudanese field worker next returned to their village (interview with Field Worker, May 15, 2013). This was long after the slideshow had been published on one of the most popular news sites in the world. This is not just a problem of disempowerment and disrespect, it also involves potential security risks to subjects as their names, faces, location and relationship to different military groups were published without their knowledge at a time when peace in South Sudan was still very fragile. Indeed, the country lapsed back into civil war in 2013, less than a year after both pieces were republished by *BBC News Online*. By 2016, the UN had begun to warn that genocide was likely in the country.

For these reasons, I did not challenge Save the Children's decision not to permit me to republish photographs from the slideshow, as five years had elapsed between the writing of this book and field workers approaching the boy and his parents for their consent to be depicted. I also welcome the IN-GO's efforts to deal with constructive criticism by adopting the interpretation guidelines I produced together with other experts (Wright 2018). However, I would point out the that images of the boy soldier and the villagers are still publicly available on *BBC News Online*. I would also point to the ongoing difficulties with linguistic interpretation highlighted in Save's subsequent re-search (Warrington and Crombie 2017). This found that media participants in Jordan, Bangladesh and Niger "only had a vague idea of the purpose of media production" (Warrington and Crombie 2017, ix), so there are clearly ongoing problems with obtaining informed consent.

What then of the audio slideshow which was the main focus of this pro-duction case study? Audio of the former child soldier speaking in Dinka was woven seamlessly in and out of an English voice-over, to give online users some indication of his embodied voice—although this compromise was far from the Humanitarian Multimedia Officer's original plan. The Africa Editor at *BBC News Online*, Winter, justified this decision on the grounds that he had a responsibility to make the piece "easier" for online audiences to con-sume, because "if they find it hard work, they're just going to click on some-thing else" (interview, May 7, 2013). The primacy of the BBC in enabling this boy's voice is also stressed in the introductory text, which states that he "tells the BBC" about his feelings and difficulties feeding his family.

This family, the oral narrative explains, consists of the boy's disabled fa-ther, mother and six younger siblings. But their collective dependence on cash hand-outs from Save the Children is not mentioned until near the end of the piece—long after most online users would have clicked away. The image accompanying this oral comment shows the boy receiving banknotes in an envelope from a seated, South Sudanese man, along with other queuing villagers. So INGO branding does exist in the text of the slideshow, as well as in the attribution, but the intervention of journalists ensured that the promotion of Save the Children's brand did not dominate it.

Instead, the main focus of the slideshow's narrative involves the problems faced by the boy in the wake of his abduction by Arab raiders, which the written text describes him as being "angry" about. This emotion is emphasized in the oral speech of the child who voiced the former child soldier's interview, who says that the Arab soldiers "beat" him. So "the boy" says he "chose" to "fight them" by joining the South Sudanese army to fight for "self-determination", before deciding to leave because he needed to go home to look after his family. But these very strong, assertive oral statements exist in tension with the written text which introduces the slideshow, because this describes the boy and other former soldiers who served in the civil war, as in "recovery".

The photographs produced by Save the Children also tend to portray this former child soldier as a traumatized and isolated victim (Coundouriotis 2010; Macmillan 2009). He is usually depicted alone, gazing into the distance in a disassociated fashion. On those occasions when he is portrayed in the same frame as others, he is positioned at a distance from them, looking out of shot in a distressed fashion. Indeed, even after he talks about his anger at being "beaten" by Arab soldiers, and his "rescue" by his father, the image shown is of him crying, alone. Finally, no images are used of this teenager as a soldier, even when he talks about his desire to take up arms against his oppressors, as images of child soldiers tend to appall and repel Northern audiences, so could never, as Linfield wryly remarks, be used in a "Save the Children ad" (2010, 143). Instead, when the boy discusses his time in the South Sudanese army, the image chosen to accompany this oral narrative is of him in about as passive a position as it is possible to achieve—he is depicted sleeping.

Indeed, the only photo which depicts this former child soldier with any kind of weaponry is the first image in the sequence, which appears when "he" is talking about leaving the South Sudanese army. Here, the boy is depicted holding a spear, which is positioned in the immediate foreground of the photo, connoting violence. But the photo has been tightly cropped, so that the sharpness of the spear is suggested, but never shown. Thus rather than the different forms of media involved in this online slideshow building meaning by complementing one another (Caple 2013), they appear to be in tension with one another.

So the slideshow both challenges and reproduces narratives about African child soldiers as isolated, traumatized victims requiring Northerners' help

(Coundouriotis 2010; Macmillan 2009). This ambivalence emerged from the marked tensions which characterized the relationship of BBC News Online to Save the Children, as well as the relationship between the humanitarian and media teams within the INGO: making it unclear what online audiences are meant to learn about child soldiers, and how they should re/imagine their relationship to them (Chouliaraki 2008).

Moral economy: a coda

The use of a critical approach informed by moral economy theory in this case steered us away from juxtaposing commercial and normative aims in too simplistic a manner. Indeed, it shows us that moral and economic concerns are inseparable: with both working together to inform donor and audience relations, organizational branding, media populism, and ideas of efficiency or value for money. Moral economy theory therefore helps us to avoid caricaturing the relationship between journalists and international aid agencies by demonstrating that promotional logics were at play on both sides. Yet these promotional logics were imbricated in different normative ideas relating to humanitarianism and public service journalism, as well as moral education.

So the news outlet and the NGO had partially complementing normative/economic approaches, which led them to privilege the production of particular sorts of "'clickable'" images with a strong human interest focus. However, moral economy theory also shows how and why serious tensions emerged from actors' differing conceptualizations of their responsibilities to others. In particular, it is worth noting that the internal conflict within Save the Children was not simply shaped by a clash between the INGO's advocacy and fundraising objectives (Powers 2014), nor was it simply a conflict between long-serving aid-workers and newly recruited former journalists (Fenton 2010). Instead, it emerged from a combination of factors, which all related to differing ideas of responsibility. These included the marketized approaches to accountability espoused by senior managers; the growing dominance of certain kinds of former journalists who felt obligated to get the biggest audience possible for media; and the efforts of more radical aid-workers to take responsibility for safeguarding the voices of South Sudanese subjects.

Internal tensions within the BBC were more muted, and were managed by journalists' interpretation of the Corporation's Editorial Guidelines. These conceptualized aid agencies as politically neutral "charities", stressing the need to avoid giving the impression of preferring one over another, rather than tackling the broader political implications of repeatedly giving them definitional advantages. As these guidelines were written in response to an argument about a DEC appeal, this finding supports Franks' (2013) claim that joint fundraising has led to BBC journalists privileging aid agencies in the coverage of Africa.

However, moral economy theory helps to demonstrate that journalists' approaches to aid agency material were also shaped by other causal factors. In particular, this case highlights the broader erosion of the Corporation's divide between commercial and editorial decision-making. This erosion, together with a blend of the norms dominating BBC Online and the African services at BBC World Service Radio, meant that journalists were able to legitimize routinely accepting multimedia from aid agencies, whilst still being barred from taking their adverts.

Nevertheless, BBC journalists did exercise a measure of critical independence in their day-to-day practice: expending time and energy by conducting interviews, selecting images and rewriting text themselves. Thus BBC journalists' attempts to be seen to meet their statutory responsibilities, as articulated through their internal editorial guidelines, effectively modified how these kinds of INGO-provided "information subsidies" were operationalized (Gandy 1982). Yet BBC journalists' attempts to renegotiate the boundary between journalism and NGO-work in this way brought them into direct conflict with the Humanitarian multimedia producer at Save the Children UK, because he also felt he needed to exert editorial control in order to meet his obligations to others. Moral economy theory therefore helps us to analyze why conflicts between INGOs and news outlets occur, as well as helping us to interrogate the tensions and arguments which occur within organizations.

But perhaps the most interesting insight enabled by the model of the moral economy relates to the effects of this exchange. For even though these exchange-relations were marked by tension, doubt, and conflict, they still had long-lasting effects: shaping BBC journalists' repositioning of international aid organizations as enabling new forms of global public service journalism. Meanwhile, at Save the Children, the attempt of radicals in the Humanitarian department to use "value for money" as a kind of Trojan horse backfired badly: rather than smuggling their version of "alchemical" humanitarianism back into the organization, their work (and their ideals) were coopted to support the dominant status quo.

So, what about the capabilities of others? Despite optimistic claims about the special ability of new media to facilitate learning about the suffering of distant others, audience research shows that few online users actually use new media in that way (Scott 2015). It is also questionable how much audiences really learn from human interest items (Cottle and Nolan 2007), especially when these reproduce their own aesthetic values (Gupta 1986). Moreover, the attention of online audiences tends to be very fragmented, so there may not be as strong a correlation between online coverage and monies raised, as there is in broadcast (Cooper 2015).

Thus it isn't clear how much these kinds of online slideshows enhance the ability of those suffering to secure their subsistence needs through aid agencies' fundraising, or enable audiences to better understand their plight. What we do know is that the boy, his parents and villagers were not given the most basic form of voice—informed consent—during the production process. Dinka people were therefore used to construct the globality of *BBC News Online* and the organizational voice of Save the Children UK in the name of moral education, without anyone seriously interrogating the validity of this claim.

Notes

1. The name of this child has been removed from this chapter, given the security situation in South Sudan
2. The UK government's desire to extend its soft power may also become an increasingly important shaping factor in future, given Foreign and Commonwealth Office's recent explanation of its rationale for funding 11 new language services in conflict-prone areas (Abubakar 2016).

References

Abubakar, Abdullahi. "Speaking in Tongues: BBC World Service Expansion Aims to Extend British Soft Power." *City University*, November 25, 2016. https://theconversation.com/speaking-in-tongues-bbc-world-service-expansion-aims-to-extend-british-soft-power-69022

Allan, Stuart. *Online News: Journalism and the Internet.* Buckingham: Open University Press, 2006.

Anderson, Fay. "Chasing the Pictures: Press and Magazine Photography." *Media International Australia* 150, no. 1 (2014): 47–55.

Baker, Mona. *Translation and Conflict.* London, New York: Routledge, 2006.

Banks, Mark, Andy Lovatt, Justin O'Connor, and Carlo Raffo. "Risk and Trust in the Cultural Industries." *Geoforum* 31, no. 4 (2000): 453–64.

Bassnett, Susan, and Harish Trivedi, eds. *Post-Colonial Translation: 97. Theory and Practice.* Translation Studies. London, New York: Routledge, 1999.

Baumann, Gerd, and Marie Gillespie. "Diasporic Citizenships, Cosmopolitanisms, and the Paradox of Mediated Objectivity: An Interdisciplinary Study of the BBC World Service." 2007. http://www.open.ac.uk/socialsciences/diasporas/publications/bbcws_180407_paper.pdf.

BBC. "BBC Strategic Approval Committee," December 1, 2009.

———. "Editorial Guidelines." BBC. Accessed February 17, 2010. http://www.bbc.co.uk/editorialguidelines/.

Born, Georgina. *Uncertain Vision: Birt, Dyke and the Reinvention of the BBC.* London: Secker & Warburg, 2004.

Bunce, Mel. "Africa in the Click Stream: Audience Metrics and Foreign Correspondents in Africa." *African Journalism Studies* 36, no. 4 (2015): 12–29.

Calhoun, Craig. "The Class Consciousness of Frequent Travellers: Towards a Critique of Actually Existing Cosmopolitanism." In *Debating Cosmopolitics*, edited by Daniele Archibugi and Mathias Koenig-Archibugi, 86–116. London, New York: Verso, 2003.

———. "The Imperative to Reduce Suffering: Charity, Progress and Emergencies in the Field of Humanitarian Action." In *Humanitarianism in Question: Politics, Power, Ethics*, edited by Michael N. Barnett and Thomas George Weiss, 73–97. Cornell Paperbacks. Ithaca, NY: Cornell University Press, 2008.

Caple, Helen. *Photojournalism: A Social Semiotics Approach.* New York: Palgrave Macmillan, 2013.

Caple, Helen, and John S. Knox. "Online News Galleries, Photojournalism and the Photo Essay." *Visual Communication* 11, no. 2 (2012): 207–36.

Cheah, Pheng. "'The World Is Watching': The Mediatic Structure of Cosmopolitanism." *Journalism Studies* 14, no. 2 (2013): 219–31.

Chouliaraki, Lilie. "The Media as Moral Education: Mediation and Action." *Media, Culture & Society* 30, no. 6 (2008): 831–52.

Cooper, Glenda. "'Give Us Your F***ing Money': A Critical Appraisal of TV and the Cash Nexus." In *Humanitarianism, Communications and Change*, edited by Simon Cottle and Glenda Cooper, 67–78. New York: Peter Lang, 2015.

Cottle, Simon, and David Nolan. "Global Humanitarianism and the Changing Aid-Media Field: Everyone Was Dying for Footage." *Journalism Studies* 8, no. 6 (2007): 862–78.

Couldry, Nick. *Why Voice Matters: Culture and Politics after Neoliberalism.* London: Sage, 2010.

Coundouriotis, Eleni. "The Child Soldier Narrative and the Problem of Arrested Historicization." *Journal of Human Rights* 9, no. 2 (2010): 191–206.

Crowley, Colin, and Lucy Fleming. "Audio Slideshow: Ex-Child Soldier in Sudan." BBC, May 4, 2010a, sec. Africa. http://news.bbc.co.uk/1/hi/world/africa/8599293.stm.

———. "Panoramic Photo: Sudan Homecoming." BBC, December 4, 2010b, sec. Africa. http://news.bbc.co.uk/1/hi/world/africa/8609304.stm.

Currah, Andrew. *What's Happening to Our News: An Investigation into the Likely Impact of the Digital Revolution on the Economics of News Publishing in the UK*. Oxford: Reuters Institute for the Study of Journalism, 2009.

Davis, Aeron. *Promotional Cultures: The Rise and Spread of Advertising, Public Relations, Marketing and Branding*. Cambridge: Polity Press, 2013.

Daynes, Leigh. "Communicating Suffering: A View from NGO Practice." In *Caring in Crisis? Humanitarianism, the Public and NGOs*, edited by Irene B. Seu and Shani Orgad, 119–23. London, New York: Palgrave Macmillan, 2017.

Denčik, Lina. "What Global Citizens and Whose Global Moral Order? Defining the Global at BBC World News." *Global Media and Communication* 9, no. 2 (2013): 119–34.

Department for Culture, Media and Sport. Broadcasting: An Agreement Between Her Majesty's Secretary of State for Culture, Media and Sport and the British Broadcasting Corporation (2006). http://www.bbccharterreview.org.uk/pdf_documents/BBCAgreement_Cm6872_july06.pdf.

Engebretsen, Martin. "The Soundslide Report." *Nordicom Review* 35, no. 1 (2014): 99–113.

Fehrenbach, Heide, and Davide Rodogno, eds. *Humanitarian Photography: A History*. Cambridge: Cambridge University Press, 2015.

Fenton, Natalie, ed. *New Media, Old News*. London: Sage, 2010.

Franks, Suzanne. *Reporting Disasters: Famine, Aid, Politics and the Media*. London: Hurst Publishers, 2013.

Gandy, Oscar H. *Beyond Agenda Setting: Information Subsidies and Public Policy*. Norwood, NJ: Ablex, 1982.

Ghodeswar, Bhimrao M. "Building Brand Identity in Competitive Markets: A Conceptual Model." *Journal of Product & Brand Management* 17, no. 1 (2008): 4–12.

Gillespie, Marie, and Alban Webb. *Diasporas and Diplomacy: Cosmopolitan Contact Zones at the BBC World Service (1932–2012)*. London, New York: Routledge, 2013.

Gregory, Sam. "Kony 2012 through a Prism of Video Advocacy Practices and Trends." *Journal of Human Rights Practice* 4, no. 3 (2012): 463–68.

Gupta, Sunil. "Northern Media, Southern Lives'." In *Photography/Politics*, edited by Jo Spence, Patricia Holland, and Simon Watney, 162–66. London: Comedia/Photography Workshop, 1986.

Hadland, Adrian, David Campbell, and Paul Lambert. *The State of News Photography: The Lives and Livelihoods of Photojournalists in the Digital Age*. Oxford: Reuters Institute for Journalism, Oxford University, September 22, 2015.

Hendy, David. *Public Service Broadcasting*. New York: Palgrave Macmillan, 2013.

Jacobson, Susan. "Emerging Models of Multimedia Journalism: A Content Analysis of Multimedia Packages Published on Nytimes.com – Atlantic Journal of Communication." *Atlantic Journal of Communication* 18, no. 2 (2010): 63–78.

Jones, Janet, and Lee Salter. *Digital Journalism*. London: Sage, 2011.

Kennedy, Denis. "Selling the Distant Other: Humanitarianism and Imagery—Ethical Dilemmas of Humanitarian Action." *The Journal of Humanitarian Assistance* 28 (2009) https://tufts.edu/jha/archives/411

Klein-Avraham, Inbal, and Zvi Reich. "A Bleak Picture: How News Organizations Missed the Potential of Digitization to Improve Photojournalism." Paper given to the International Communication Association, London, 17-21 June, 2013.

Küng-Shankleman, Lucy, and Lucy Küng. *Inside the BBC and CNN: Managing Media Organisations*. London and New York: Routledge, 2000.

Lee-Wright, Peter. "Culture Shock: New Media and Organizational Change at the BBC." In *New Media, Old News: Journalism and Democracy in the Digital Age*, edited by Natalie Fenton, 71–86. London: Sage, 2010.

Lillie, Jonathan. "How and Why Journalists Create Audio Slideshows: An Exploratory Study of Multimedia Adoption." *Journalism Practice* 5, no. 3 (2011): 350–65.

Lindström, Julia. "The Moral Economy of Aid: Discourse Analysis of Swedish Fundraising for the Somalia Famine of 2011–2012." Working Paper. Södertörn University, 2016. http://www.diva-portal.org/smash/record.jsf?pid=diva2%3A1035935&dswid=1952#sthash.3Qe AHipx.dpbs.

Linfield, Susie. *The Cruel Radiance: Photography and Political Violence*. Chicago: University of Chicago Press, 2010.

Lugo-Ocando, Jairo, and Patrick O. Malaolu. "Africa—That Scar on Our Face." In *Blaming the Victim: How Global Journalism Fails Those in Poverty*, Jairo Lugo-Ocando, 85–103. London: Pluto Press, 2014.

McDowell, Walter S. "The Brand Management Crisis Facing the Business of Journalism." *International Journal on Media Management* 13, no. 1 (2011): 37–51.

McLagan, Meg, and Yates McKee. "Introduction." In *Sensible Politics: The Visual Culture of Nongovernmental Activism*, edited by Meg McLagan and Yates McKee, 9–26. New York: Zone Books, 2012.

Mellese, Mastewal Adane, and Marion G. Müller. "Mapping Text-Visual Frames of Sub-Saharan Africa in the News: A Comparison of Online News Reports From Al Jazeera and British Broadcasting Corporation Websites." *Communication, Culture & Critique* 5, no. 2 (2012): 191–229.

Moeller, Susan. *Compassion Fatigue: How the Media Sell Disease, Famine, War and Death*. New York: Routledge, 1999

Newman, Nic, and David Levy. *Reuters Institute Digital News Report 2012*. Oxford: Reuters Institute for the Study of Journalism, 2012.

Newman, Nic, David Levy, and Rasmus K. Nielsen. *Reuters Institute Digital News Report 2015*. Oxford: Reuters Institute for the Study of Journalism, 2014.

Nolan, David, and Akina Mikami. "'The Things That We Have to Do': Ethics and Instrumentality in Humanitarian Communication." *Global Media and Communication* 9, no. 1 (2013): 53–70.

Ogunyemi, Olatunji. "Representation of Africa Online: Sourcing Practice and Frames of Reference." *Journal of Black Studies* 42, no. 3 (2011): 457–78.

Orgad, Shani. "Visualizers of Solidarity: Organizational Politics in Humanitarian and International Development NGOs." *Visual Communication* 12, no. 3 (2013): 295–314.

Parker, Ben. Speech at "Humanitarian News: changes, challenges and prospects" conference, City University, London, October 21, 2015.

Plunkett, John. "Stuart Prebble to Lead BBC Impartiality Review." *The Guardian*, August 2, 2012. http://www.theguardian.com/media/2012/aug/02/stuart-prebble-lead-bbc-impartiality-review.

Powers, Matthew. "The Structural Organization of NGO Publicity Work: Explaining Divergent Publicity Strategies at Humanitarian and Human Rights Organizations." *International Journal of Communication* 8 (2014): 90–107.

Redden, Joanna, and Tamara Witschge. "A New News Order? Online News Content Examined." In *New Media, Old News*, edited by Natalie Fenton, 171–86. London: Sage, 2010.

Roosvall, Anna. "The Identity Politics of World News: Oneness, Particularity, Identity and Status in Online Slideshows." *International Journal of Cultural Studies* 17, no. 1 (2014): 55–74.

Sambrook, Richard, Simon Terrington, and David Levy. *The Public Appetite for Foreign News in TV and Online*. Oxford: Reuters Institute for the Study of Journalism, 2013.

Scott, Martin. "Distant Suffering Online: The Unfortunate Irony of Cyber-Utopian Narratives." *The International Communication Gazette* 77, no. 7 (2015): 637–53.

Steemers, Jeanette. "Between Culture and Commerce: The Problem of Redefining Public Service Broadcasting for the Digital Age." *Convergence: The International Journal of Research into New Media Technologies* 5, no. 3 (1999): 44–66.

———. "Balancing Culture and Commerce on the Global Stage." In *Cultural Dilemmas in Public Service Broadcasting*, edited by Gregory F. Lowe and Per Jauert, 213–50. Goteborg, Sweden: NORDICOM, 2005.

Thomas, Ryan J., and Elizabeth Blanks Hindman. "'People Will Die because of the BBC': British Newspaper Reaction to the BBC Gaza Appeal Decision." *Journalism* 13, no. 5 (2012): 572–88.

Tumber, Howard. "Business as Usual: Enough of Phone Hacking, Let's Attack the BBC." *Television & New Media* 13, no. 1 (2011): 12–16.

Waisbord, Silvio. "Can NGOs Change the News?" *International Journal of Communication* 5 (2011): 142–65.

Warrington, Siobhan with Crombie, Jess. *The People in the Pictures: Vital Perspectives on Save the Children's Image-Making*. London: Save the Children UK, 2017.

Wright, Kate. "'Helping Our Beneficiaries Tell Their Own Stories?' International Aid Agencies, the Politics of Voice and the Pitfalls of Interpretation within News Production." *Global Media and Communication*, 2018. Online First DOI 10.1177/1742766518759795.

· 7 ·

DIGITAL DIALOGUE, INTERNATIONAL DEVELOPMENT, AND BLOGGING

The Guardian and Internews

Can NGOs foster greater social inclusion by facilitating digital conversations between marginalized people and wealthy media audiences living far away? Some critics say that they can—and should (Beckett 2008; Beckett and Mansell 2008). Their work draws from Castells' theory of the networked society (2000) in order to reposition NGOs, audiences and other media actors as "produsers", who continually create and consume digital media discourse in collaboration with each other (Deuze 2008; Gillmor 2006). International news is seen as being a key site for such fluid and multidirectional exchanges, with proponents of "networked" journalism claiming that it enables new, digital dialogues which move beyond the dichotomies of "North" and "South", "information rich" and "information poor" (Beckett and Mansell 2008, 99).

These forms of "networked journalism" involve reconceptualizing the role of journalists: viewing them as facilitators who enable collective deliberation by filtering, curating, linking and contextualizing others' contributions (Jarvis 2006; van der Haak *et al.* 2012). But this implies a very different approach to factual truth: privileging forms of ongoing learning, in which the act of knowing is never complete (Jarvis 2009, discussed in Robinson 2011). Thus the exchanges involved in "networked journalism" rely upon different forms of trust facilitated by "transparency"—a term encompassing value-laden notions of openness, honesty and accountability (Kovach and Rosenstiel 2001; Singer 2007).

"Transparency" involves two separate, but potentially interlinked strands (Karlsson 2010). These are *disclosure transparency*, in which news producers explain how journalistic coverage has been produced, and *participatory transparency*, in which audience members become involved in media production (Karlsson 2010). Both forms of transparency involve their own defensive rituals, which may be viewed as replacing those pertaining to objectivity (Tuchman 1972, discussed in Karlsson 2010). But on closer examination, both forms of transparency are deeply problematic.

Disclosure transparency rests on the notion that journalists must explain the norms shaping their selection and presentation of information (Karlsson 2010, 2011). But the nature of collective norms is that they tend to be so deeply ingrained that they remain unexamined or implicit (Schein 2004). So it may be difficult for journalists to identify the norms shaping their work, let alone explain them in a transparent fashion to others. In addition, it is unclear how much journalists need to disclose to construct audiences' trust in the journalistic coverage they produce. There is, as Marsh so eloquently put it, "no end to what could be relevant" (2010).

Participatory disclosure is problematic because journalists still tend to control who participates, as well as the limits and conditions of their participation. This control often remains unstated, hidden from the audience's view. Indeed, even journalistic outlets which have been specifically designed to facilitate participatory and fluid forms of North/South digital dialogue have been found to be powerfully shaped by the dominant norms of newsrooms in the US and UK (Braun and Gillespie 2011; Ogunyemi 2011). In addition, deep material and economic inequalities continue to seriously constrain media participation in ways which journalists, and media audiences, may not fully realize.

For example, the growth mobile of phone ownership in sub-Saharan Africa is often touted as enabling far greater media participation (Beckett 2008; Sambrook 2010). But mobile signals are still very patchy and the smartphones needed to access the internet are expensive. This means that mobile access to the internet remains largely confined to urban, socio-economic elites (Mabweazara 2010; Pew Research Center 2015). Gender inequality also means that men tend to have more access to the internet than women (International Telecommunications Union 2017). Furthermore, internet use requires literacy, particularly in the English language, which dominates the websites of most major media organizations (Curran *et al.* 2012). All of this makes it very difficult for actually existing forms of networked journalism to live up to the ideals of open and inclusive participation.

Blogs are a particularly interesting case in point because they are often seen as playing a special role in stimulating inclusive, transparent and trusting forms of digital dialogue (Allen 2008; Lasica 2003; Singer 2007). This is because blogging has emerged from oppositional forms of activism, and has retained its informal, personalized style, as well as its strong associations with the formation of participatory communities (Kahn and Kellner 2004; Keller 2012; Moyo 2011; Thorsen 2013). But blogs about Africa can be sites of political oppression, as well as subversion and resistance (Allan 2014; Somolu 2007).

International NGOs (INGOs) also tend to produce blogs, drawing upon ideals about empowering the voices of the poor and oppressed (Cooper 2015). But in practice, these blogs tend to privilege the voices of wealthy Northerners (Cooper 2015). Indeed, both INGOs and news outlets have been accused of appropriating bloggers' free labor, to enhance their organizational brands and increase the interactivity of their websites, whilst simultaneously controlling the perspectives and values in circulation within media discourse (Cooper 2015; Deuze and Fortunati 2010).

Such critical concerns relate to arguments about the operation of participatory communication within international development. Although participatory communication operates carries a powerful normative charge, connoting inclusiveness and empowerment, its exact meaning and relationship to international development is often unclear (Mody 2003; Scott 2014a). Notions of "participation" and "development" can also be co-opted in ways which are ineffective or even harmful, serving only to entrench the norms and systems of the established world-order (Escobar 1999, 2012). In particular, many critics remain concerned that the recent plethora of media development INGOs operating in sub-Saharan Africa effectively export Northern journalistic ethics and modes of media ownership, which may be inappropriate or unsustainable within sub-Saharan countries (Berger 2010; LaMay 2009). This latter point relates to other, more specific concerns about the growing numbers of wealthy Northern entrepreneurs funding media production in and about Africa via private trusts and foundations (Berger 2010; Bunce 2016: LaMay 2009).

The production case study explored in this chapter involved blending notions of networked journalism, participatory communication, and international development with foundation funding, freelancing and donor reporting. In the course of analyzing this production process, I interrogate a paradox: namely, how and why ideas about participation, inclusiveness and transparency masked a very narrow system of exchange-relations, constructed through the intersection of trusting on and offline conversations.

Practically speaking, this production process involved two freelancers from Europe and the US producing a donor report for the US-based INGO, Internews. This praised one of its projects, which supported and trained refugees to run their own radio stations, so helping them communicate with one another and relevant aid agencies in Chad, after fleeing fighting in Darfur. But at the same time, the freelancers produced a blog for a news outlet—the Global Development section of *The Guardian* website—about exactly the same project.[1] This used much of the same written material, as well as a single still photograph. But the freelancers' obligations to the INGO were not mentioned in the blog at all. In addition, both the INGO and the news outlet are funded by the same private donor—the enormously wealthy Bill and Melinda Gates Foundation—which is widely accused of using media outlets to promote privatized notions of international development (Birn 2014; Curtis 2016; Martens and Seitz 2015; Paulson 2013).

The Guardian online

The Guardian is the world's second most popular English language newspaper online, outstripped only by *The New York Times* (Alexa.com 2017). Although the broadsheet is based in the UK, its overseas audiences are growing rapidly, especially in the US and Australia, where little left-leaning media previously existed. It is renowned for taking a web-centric approach to journalism early on, which involves producing large volumes of content quickly, publishing free-to-access digital material before print editions, and experimenting with innovative, web-specific genres (Collis *et al.* 2011). In particular, it has been seen as the chief pioneer of blogs written by non-journalists (Eastment 2005; Thurman and Walters 2013).

The Guardian's journalism has also been highly influenced by the ideas about the potential of online and social media to enable progressive forms of "networked" or process-oriented journalism (Beckett 2008; Jarvis 2009). As Sheila Pulham, the Managing Editor of *Guardian.co.uk*, put it,

> [*The Guardian's* approach] involves wanting to have as many views as possible and to move away from the kind of "us to them" model of journalism.

So I suppose, we're there in the center, and there's everything else around us and we want to make sure that communication is going in multiple directions, because I think the internet has helped people to realize that, on any given subject, the world expert in that is not necessarily sitting in this building.

It might be a particular individual somewhere else in the world or it might be a combination of the shared knowledge of the wider community, whatever that is, and you know, the more people you speak to or the more people you allow to speak, the better the answer you get. (interview, May 6, 2013)

Such an approach has important epistemological implications, with knowledge being conceptualized not as a single, stable "truth", but as a much more provisional, "best answer" based on the available evidence and a broad range of perspectives (Jarvis 2009; Hornmoen and Steensen 2014). This approach has served to legitimize *The Guardian's* more open, participatory approaches to journalistic production, including its early adoption of User Generated Content (UGC), its experiments with crowdsourcing, and its practice of leaving stories open for audience comments (Daniel and Flew 2010; Singer and Ashman 2009). In addition, such epistemological and normative approaches have shaped *Guardian* journalists' collaborative work with others to break major news stories. These include reporting on UK MPs' fraudulent claiming of expenses in 2009; Edward Snowden's evidence regarding the surveillance tactics of the American National Security Agency in 2013; and the widespread tax evasion enabled by the Panamanian offshore law firm, Mossack Fonseca in 2016.

The Guardian's approach to networked journalism emerged from the interaction of specific economic and cultural values. As the former Director of International and Business Development at Guardian News and Media, Stella Beaumont, explained in the mid-1990s the "cool and avant-garde element of *The Guardian's* staff" began working with journalists at the US-based *Wired* magazine on niche commercial projects (interview, May 10, 2013). So, she said, they became "immersed in the culture of the web." But these operations remained largely separate from *The Guardian* newspaper, and its Sunday edition, *The Observer*, until another British broadsheet, *The Daily Telegraph*, geared up its own online operation in 1999. *BBC News Online*, which was launched in 1997, was also rapidly expanding at this time. So Beaumont said that *The Guardian's* management became concerned that other news organizations were "coming to eat our lunch" in term of audience share, just as new job sites, such as *monster.co.uk*, were threatening the paper's recruitment advertising revenue.

For these reasons, senior managers took a decision to integrate their internet operations with the papers and to rebrand their own website in ways which reinforced their unity. Indeed, participants didn't really talk about *The Guardian's* internet operations as having normative potential until they described the boom in US traffic which was triggered by the 9/11 bombings of the World Trade Center in New York. As Beaumont, who launched the *Guardian US* site in the same year, said

> The liberal left in America had absolutely nowhere else to go because at *that* time, even *The New York Times*, you know, which is probably *the* most left of center of the American newspapers, was feverishly patriotic (…)
>
> You would never really hear a dissenting voice about America and foreign policy *anywhere* other than on *The Guardian* website.
>
> And, so (…) that's the time the traffic really started to take off in the US, and the Second Gulf War added even more to that. That's when we thought—yeah, this is a *good* thing to be doing; this is *important*. As well as, you know the business side of it.

Likewise, Pulham, the Managing Editor of the *Guardian.co.uk*, said that it was during this period that "we really started to see the moral value of challenging the powerful" through *The Guardian's* website, because it "suddenly had this incredible ability to wield substantial geo-political influence" in relation to "*the* global superpower" (interview, May 6, 2013).

Yet the paper has been in serious financial trouble for many years now. By 2016, its annual operating losses were over 58.5 million pounds, which resulted in senior managers at the Guardian Media Group taking the decision to cut 250 posts—a hundred of which were editorial staff (Martinson 2016). This comes on top of previous waves of cuts, including those taking place in 2010–2011, which led to the number of editorial staff employed at *The Guardian* and *Observer* to be cut by around a third. Like other newspapers, *The Guardian's* financial problems stemmed from a combination of factors, including falling circulation figures, the rising costs of print and the migration of advertising online, where adverts are worth far less. Indeed, Beaumont, the former Business Head, said that a still advert placed on *The Guardian's* website was worth around a tenth of its former print value (interview, May 10, 2013).

The recession which followed the global economic crash of 2009 then led to advertising revenue plunging to a "frightening degree" (interview with Stella Beaumont, May 10, 2013). Despite this, *The Guardian* pursued an aggressive expansionist policy, launching a US edition in 2011, and then an Australian edition in 2013. Senior managers also chose to keep its online content free of charge: a decision which was shaped by *The Guardian's* web-centric approach. As Beaumont put it,

> The whole *Guardian* strategy and philosophy was being "of the web", not just "on the web", and if you are "of the web" and you live and breathe and, you know, it is part of your ecosystem, then you don't charge. (interview, May 10, 2013)

This strategy was enabled by the subsidies provided by the not-for-profit Scott Trust, which was founded on a bequest left by the paper's long-serving editor, C.P. Scott, who wanted to sustain the paper's journalism free from commercial or political interference in perpetuity (*Guardian Media Group* website n.d.; Starkman 2013). By 2016, *The Guardian* was in danger of "burning through" the financial safety net provided by Trust because of its ongoing operational losses, so the introduction of some paid-for content was starting to be considered (Mance 2016). But prior to that, one of *The Guardian's* business strategies was to try and stem unsustainable losses by acquiring commercial "partners", who were willing to pay a premium to sponsor subsites based around lifestyle content, specialist interests and "professional communities" (interview with Sheila Pulham, May 6, 2013). Private trusts and foundations also provided a small but significant stream of income: 3.8 million out of a total of 214.5 million pounds of revenue in 2017 (personal correspondence with Sheila Pulham, November 6, 2017).

The Gates Foundation and the Global Development sub-site

One of the most generous and best-known of these philanthropic foundations is the Bill and Melinda Gates Foundation—the world's largest charitable foundation (Bishop and Green 2008). Its support enabled the creation of the Global Development sub-site in 2010, via an initial sponsorship deal, which was worth 2.5 million dollars (Ribbens 2011)—"a s**t ton of money" given *The Guardian's* financial state (Salmon 2011). The stated purpose of the Global Development subsite was to monitor progress towards the UN's Millennium Development Goals (MDGs). A second three-year deal with the Gates Foundation commenced in 2015, which was worth a further two and a half million dollars (Harrow and Pharaoh 2017). But this was framed by a new mission—to track the transition of the (largely unachieved) Millennium Development Goals into Sustainable Development Goals.

Madeleine Bunting, the journalist who initiated the deal, claimed that the sub-site would foster better "understanding" of the aid industry, as well as explaining "big problems" with multiple causes "through powerful stories of individual lives" (2010). She then positioned the Global Development site as "taking over" from *The Guardian's* three year immersive, virtual reality project with AMREF, which purported to depict the development of a Ugandan village called Katine (Bunting 2010). However, the Katine project was controversial. It has been criticized for facilitating the mediatization of aid: encouraging media teams to become more dominant within development organizations, as well as re/shaping INGO-workers' perceptions of accountability in ways which point upwards towards media audiences and donors, rather than downwards, towards local people (Jones 2017). So legitimizing the Global Development subsite as an extension of the Katine project is potentially problematic.

Accepting funding from the Gates Foundation is also controversial because Bill Gates and other US entrepreneurs have been accused of using their philanthropic donations to shape media discourse in ways which privilege their own definitions of the nature, purpose and goods afford by international development (Bunce 2016; McGoey 2015; Scott 2014b; Wilkins and Enghel 2013). These definitions, the argument goes, prioritize globalized, privatized and technocentric interventions over addressing structural socio-economic inequalities, including those caused by capitalism itself (Birn 2014; Martens and Seitz 2015; Paulson 2013). Thus some critics see wealthy "philanthrocapitalists" as lowering resistance to their companies' expansion into emerging Southern markets (Birn 2014; McGoey 2015).

The Gates Foundation has become a particular focus of critical/political attention because it is explicitly committed to enabling others to tell "success stories" about aid, most notably through its "Aid is Working: Tell the World" project (Grand Challenges 2012, discussed in Paulson 2013). This forms part of a raft of "advocacy and policy" projects worth more than $1 billion, which include funding media organizations and journalists' training programs (Birn 2014; Doughton and Helm 2011). Indeed, the Gates Foundation is a prolific media funder, not only giving money to *The Guardian*, but also supporting Spain's *El Pais* newspaper; the African Media Institute; the *Global Health* magazine; the *US Global Health Policy* Portal and a number of American broadcasters, including ABC, NBC, PBS and Viacom (Doughton and Helm 2011; Fortner 2010; Paulson 2013). Thus the Gates Foundation risks making mediatized discourse, "an echo chamber" in which its values and activities go unchallenged (Marc Cooper quoted in Doughton and Helm 2011).

However, most of this debate has taken place in the US, so the influence of the Gates Foundation on *The Guardian* has come in for comparatively little critical scrutiny. Some journalistic pieces have been published which accuse *Guardian* journalists of either excluding criticism of the Gates Foundation and/or of publishing overtly fawning coverage, such as its profile of Melinda Gates (Doughton and Helm 2011; Fortner 2010). But Alan Rusbridger, who was the Editor of *The Guardian* at the time when the Gates deal was struck, argued that the Gates sponsorship enabled journalists to report on important, long-term stories about social justice and internationalism, which don't nec-essarily have a mass audience or fit with conventional news values (discussed in Fortner 2010).

In addition, the current Managing Editor of *The Guardian*, Sheila Pul-ham, defended the paper's acceptance of Gates' money by stressing how "transparent" they had been about it (interview, May 6, 2013). Pulham went on to stress that the Foundation made no efforts to influence specific stories, so *Guardian* journalists remained "editorially independent" (interview, May 6, 2013). Thus the approach taken by the Gates Foundation to its sponsorship of *The Guardian* Global Development site appears to contrast with the more di-rective approach it has taken to other media organizations: for example, jour-nalists on PBS' *Newshour* program claim that the foundation provided them with a list of "potential story subjects" (Doughton and Helm 2011). However, Browne (2010), Feldman (2007) and Fortner (2010) have all argued that the financial incentives provided by liberal foundations and trusts, and the social relationships in which these incentives are embedded, tend to lead to the nat-uralisation of pro-market ideologies and elite-centered systems of commercial globalization—even when no explicit editorial intervention is involved.

The site's Managing Editor, Sheila Pulham, argued that these dangers could be minimized by seeking sponsorship "partners" with whom *The Guard-ian* "shares values", saying

> Well, it's all around "fit" between them and us. So, for example, if the North Korean government came along and wanted to do a human rights project with us (...) we might be a little *skeptical*. [Chuckles]
>
> But there is often common ground between our values and those of *some* founda-tions and companies. (interview, May 6, 2013)

Yet a foundation's ability to influence journalists' thinking may actually be greatest when its goals and cultural norms overlap with those of the recipient news organization. Edmonds (2002) has argued that this can create a kind of a "benevolent fog" which makes it more difficult "for editors and journalists to draw the distinction between accepting a grant and accepting a funder's point of view."

My own research found evidence that Gates' sponsorship of the Global Development sub-site had had a powerful effect on the rest of the news organization. Large numbers of photographs provided by NGOs were found on *The Guardian's* Africa page, which had originated in the Global Development section. A respondent on the commissioning desk explained that this was in keeping with Global Development's "particularly open approach to NGOs" (interview, August 29, 2013). Such material is automatically cross-listed to *The Guardian's* Africa page through electronic tagging. But material produced by the Global Development team sometimes dominated the Africa page, especially on quiet news weeks, when the absence of obvious leads and cost-cutting meant that the Foreign Desk was unable to commission many items. For example, in the sample studied, items from the Global Development site comprised over two thirds of the material published on the Africa page for four out of seven days.

The respondent on the commissioning desk said this was not unusual, but she was uncomfortable with the prominence of INGO-provided material in the site's coverage of Africa, saying that she thought it emerged from "a kind of ideology" or

> (...) a theory about Africa that sort of stereotypes it in a very particular way as this needy, desperate continent that wants us great benevolent Western powers to help it. I am personally opposed to that stereotyping (...) I think it's demeaning. (interview, August 29, 2013)

This person described these views as arising from her "political (...) progressive" values, and years of experience covering the continent. However, much like other Africa specialists she didn't think it was worth challenging colleagues over this, saying that these were just her "personal opinions" and that she was "not involved" in the Global Development site at all, even though "we do sometimes run their pieces in the paper".

The norms shaping the production of the Global Development site also spilled over into *The Guardian's* Sunday edition, *The Observer*. For example,

Paul Webster, the paper's Deputy Editor, justified using INGO-provided photos in his paper, saying:

> The old rules that govern the relationship between media organizations and charities have changed. They're changing all the time.
>
> You know, *The Guardian*, clearly, has a part of its website [the Global Development section] sponsored by charity [the Gates Foundation] (…) That's a thing you wouldn't have seen 25, 30 years ago. (interview, 30 April, 2013).

But the frequent use of INGO-provided photos at Guardian News Media was also shaped by the large numbers of pictures required by web-centric approaches to journalism. James Powell, who had been put in charge of innovative uses of pictures on the website, in addition to his old job as deputy picture editor for *The Observer*, put it like this:

> It's not just finding one image for a story like I used to do. It's about doing a whole gallery for the story.
>
> It's also (…) doing audio slideshows, choosing pictures of the day, choosing the 20 pictures of the week (…)
>
> So [my working remit is] broader, *much* broader now. The web is a *machine* that needs feeding quite a lot! [Laughs]. (interview, May 16, 2013)

Powell stressed that it was impossible to do this without some kind of "outside help" as most of the organization's photojournalists had been cut. By the time of interviewing, *The Guardian* only had two staff photographers left—a sharp fall from the six members of staff and six contract photographers employed in the 1980s (Martin Argles, former Guardian photographer, speaking at National Union of Journalists meeting, June 29, 2013). Meanwhile *The Observer*, had no full-time staff photographers left at all—although it had a few more on day-a-week contracts (interview with James Powell, May 16, 2013).

Powell knew that some of these part-time journalists worked on commission for INGOs. He was largely sanguine about this: viewing it as a pragmatic solution for colleagues whom he could no longer afford to pay full-time or to send on many foreign trips. He saw little conflict of interest because he knew these photographers personally and "trusted their ethics". Indeed, as far as Powell was concerned, the arrangement worked well because these photojournalists often came in and pitched INGO-commissioned photos, saving him a considerable amount of time, as well as money (Gandy 1982).

But most of the NGO-provided photos on *The Guardian's* website did not arrive via this route. Instead, the bulk appeared to have been either solicited by, or offered to, the Community Coordinator for the Global Development.

This person was not a journalist, but had previous experience of working for an INGO. So she had very good working relations with British and European INGOs, which she kept up through informal meetings in London. Although she tried to bring in smaller African NGOs when big umbrella events were happening, this was difficult and infrequent.

The Community Coordinator knew this wasn't ideal, so said she tried to be "transparent" about where the material on the Global Development site came from. But this didn't address the bigger problem: that is, that the version of international development disseminated by *The Guardian* was defined, to a very significant degree, by private, non-governmental organizations. Thus relatively informal, off-line conversations, facilitated by physical proximity, existing social links and cultural similarities, shaped digital dialogue in a manner which was far less open, inclusive and fluid than *Guardian* managers claimed.

Freelancers

Similar kinds of trusting, off-line conversations seem to have shaped the interactions between commissioning editors working for the Global Development sub-site and their regular freelancers, who were often physically present in the same office (Gollmitzer 2014). For instance, the freelance journalist, D, described how she and a freelance photojournalist, E, got the commission to produce the blog like this:

> What happened is that I do [a regular item on the "Global Development" site] And so I chat to [this editor] quite a lot and s/he knows that I go off and do these other kinds of projects, so I have done various things for them in the past on other trips that I have done (…)
>
> Anyway, in a conversation about my work for the World Service Media Trust with [this editor], I mentioned that I was going to Chad as well with [another news-related INGO] Internews and I said "Don't you think it would be quite interesting to do maybe a feature on these radio stations manned by refugees from Darfur?"
>
> Because I know that they are always looking out for…some kind of a development angle. (interview, August 30, 2012)

The freelancer admitted that she was not entirely clear what editors at the Global Development section meant by "a development angle": suggesting that they appeared to be keen on exploring "how people are working to improve their own situations" (interview with D, August 30, 2012).[2] Whilst this didn't necessarily involve NGOs, D said that "there's definitely a symbiosis" which occurs between INGOs and the Global Development site, because of "their special funding" from the Gates Foundation. Indeed, she admitted that she "didn't know where they drew the line [between NGO-work and journalism] really".

But although other INGOs ask freelancers to pitch for them (Polly Markandya, speaking at Frontline Club 2015), that did not happen in this case. Instead, D pitched this story of her own accord, stressing that photos could also be provided by E, the freelance photographer she would be travelling with. D's reasoning here was influenced by editors' reluctance to spent much money or time on foreign trips, including evaluating health and safety risks. As she put it,

> I think the way that [commissioning editors] operate is that if you can go to them and say, "Do you want a piece on Chad? It won't cost you anything. It will just arrive in your inbox in a perfectly formed package and you don't have to do anything.
>
> You don't have to take any responsibility for me; you don't have to do anything. You will just get that piece." Of course they are going to say "Yes."
>
> But if you go to them and say "I want to go to Chad but, you know, you have to do my risk assessment. You have to pay my flight you know—blah di blah." They're just going to go "What?" and they won't do it.
>
> So I think the reason I get to do what I do is because I can go to them and say "Listen, I will deliver this and you will not hear from me until the piece arrives in your inbox"
>
> (…) You know, the bottom line is that you just don't cause anybody any problems. And that's what I realized, so that's what I'm doing.

Thus this freelancer transferred the "information subsidies" provided by Internews to *The Guardian*, without any direct intervention by the Gates Foundation or the INGO (Gandy 1982). These indirect information subsidies were significant, even though the material was not offered free of charge. This is because Internews hired D and the freelance photojournalist, E, to travel to Chad for several weeks in order to produce a donor report about the radio station, which had been run in Chad for refugees fleeing the conflict in Darfur. This trip cost the INGO over £12,000, including the freelancers' fees. But *The Guardian* paid the freelancers just £90 for the blog and £45 for the use of a single, still image.

However, the trust underpinning these exchanges had more than economic and interpersonal dimensions. It was also shaped by a kind of dovetailing or complementarity between the normative aims of the news outlet and the INGO. Journalists at the Global Development subsite wanted to foster fluid and pluralistic forms of digital dialogue and participatory approaches to international development. Whilst those at Internews claimed to "empower local media" in the Global South to "give people the news and information they need"; "the ability to connect"; and "the means to make their voices heard" (Internews n.d.). Yet, ironically, this production process was characterized by a marked lack of inclusiveness and plurality.

Although Internews had trained Darfuri journalists living as refugees in Chad for years, they weren't given the opportunity to produce media representations of themselves and their activities for donors. Instead, two Northern freelancers were commissioned to produce the report, which involved a very expensive and lengthy trip. Indeed, one of the freelancers was flown from Latin America to Washington DC, to pick up visas, before flying on to Chad—a distance of more than 12,000 kilometers. This seems even more remarkable given that the manager who commissioned the freelancers, Deborah Ensor, had a background in participatory community journalism (interview, January 18, 2013). However, Ensor maintained that these freelancers were better placed to produce "high quality" work which would not only appeal to donors, but which was appropriate for a "journalistic institution" like Internews, which sought to uphold "independent journalism the world over".

This conceptualization of freelancers as "independent" is particularly interesting because it was also used to legitimize freelancers undertaking a commission for *The Guardian* at the same time as producing the legacy report for Internews. In *The Guardian* blog, the biographical details list the author as an "independent journalist", refraining from mentioning any commitment to Internews. Whilst Deborah Ensor, the senior manager at Internews, defended her decision to allow D and E to pitch to *The Guardian* like this:

> When I hired a journalist like D to document the project, I was hiring her to document our project for us, not with the intent that I wanted her to write a story for her media house, because I don't believe that's how journalism should work.
>
> I mean she asked me. She said "Would you mind if I sold a story about this to *The Guardian* or to whoever else was interested?" And I was very happy. I said, "Yes, please go for it!"
>
> She can interview me if she wants, and I can choose to speak or not to speak with her, but I had no intention to review it. I never even saw it before it went in, because it's the same to me as any journalist doing any piece, right?
>
> I don't have the right to do that. I mean she is an *independent* journalist. So I didn't have a desire to (…) to (…) shape her (…) her story. I *didn't* shape her story, right? (interview, January 18, 2013)

But although staff at Internews did not prompt, proof-read or sub-edit the blog which freelancers produced for The Guardian, they did fund and organize the Chad trip. They also briefed the freelance journalists about what they wanted to achieve, and set up interviews and photo-shoots for them to produce the original donor report. So the freelancers remained uncomfortable that the time and financial costs shouldered by Internews were not indicated in the strap-line of the blog (interview with D, August 30, 2012; interview with E, June 13, 2013). Nevertheless, they insisted that they had fulfilled their "ethical" obligations by being "transparent" about their situation to the INGO and The Guardian (interview with D, August 30, 2012). Like other freelancers in this book, they were also deterred from challenging news outlet's non-attribution of the INGO because of the precarious nature of freelancing. As E put it,

> Sometimes as a freelancer, you don't want to mess up your relationship with an editor you want to work with in future. It's not always an easy power relationship. (interview, June 13, 2013)

This finding is important for two reasons. Firstly, it demonstrates that some actors may regard the demands of "transparency" as having been largely fulfilled by engaging in disclosure within the production process itself, even if that disclosure is never published (Karlsson 2010). Secondly, it shows that when editors and former journalists working in INGOs are challenged on their lack of plurality and inclusiveness, they tend to duck away from these kinds of legitimizing rationales: stressing freelancers' independence instead. As previously discussed in relation to the Channel 4/Human Rights Watch case, this strategic defense allows journalists and INGO-workers to deny the ways in which freelancing is blurring the boundaries between journalism and NGO-work, whilst acting in ways which foster greater boundary-crossing.

Freelancers also tended to exaggerate their critical autonomy (Edström and Ladendorf 2012; Frölich et al. 2013; Ladendorf 2013). For instance, D began by claiming that her loyalty to Internews ended with the contract, so she had "editorial control as a journalist" over The Guardian blog (interview, August 30, 2012). Whilst the photojournalist, E, said "I don't think that our reporting was in any way swayed by the fact that Internews was paying for our trip" (interview, June 13, 2013). Yet, when challenged, both freelancers took a much more nuanced line: outlining in detail the complex, internal conversations they had with themselves about what they were doing and why they were doing it (Wright 2016).

Freelancers' accounts of these internal conversations focused upon their efforts to square their commitments to journalism with their engagement in what they knew was essentially promotional work (Frölich *et al.* 2013; Obermaier and Koch 2015). Normative values were central to their deliberations, but they didn't involve a decisive shift from occupational norms to more fluid forms of personal morality (Ladendorf 2013; Mathisen 2017). Instead, freelancers combined moral, political and economic values in new and complex ways.

For instance, E said that she had decided to take commissions from NGOs and news organizations as she was deeply committed to specializing as a photojournalist and that she had learned as a college student that there were no longer many staff photojournalist posts in mainstream news. So she worked for NGOs and news organizations to "make financial ends meet" and in order to do the kinds of work she valued (interview with E, June 13, 2013). But moral values were also very important to E, as she stressed that her chosen career had been shaped by her desire to do something "good" as a practicing Christian. As she put it,

> I'm a person with faith (…) I don't want to sell nuclear weapons because I think that's wrong.
>
> I don't want to work in a bank. I don't want to…I just want to do something that makes the world a better place (…)
>
> Try not to waste your life away, you know? (interview with E, June 13, 2013)

E then went on to say that her religious faith had led her to become committed to "liberal" political values. These had also shaped her commitment to photojournalism, because she believed that it had the ability to prompt collective action (interview with E, June 13, 2013). As she explained,

> [I want to make images] that are so powerful that when people see them, they stop and, really (…) *see* it, and they react to it. They say "Wow, that's something. Wow, that's sad."
>
> Then they engage in (…) compassion-induced action.
>
> That means, they see [the photo] and they say "What can I do about it?" And they pick up that pen and they write a letter to the congressman or they share it on their social media site or they write that cheque; they figure out where they can go and volunteer.

E said that her thinking about such matters had been formed by the time she had spent studying photojournalism and NGO campaigning at an American university (interview, June 13, 2013). In particular, she had been very influenced by Moeller's work on compassion fatigue (1999), arguing that it demonstrated that advocacy was not just an "NGO-type goal", but also a journalistic one. As in other cases, this finding shows that journalists don't necessarily pull INGOs towards professional norms of impartiality (Fenton 2010). Instead, they construct common ground between NGO-work and journalism, by blending notions of journalistic campaigning and NGO advocacy.

Nevertheless, E stressed that she wanted to avoid sliding too far into producing PR, and tried to achieve this by upholding the occupational standards of photojournalism on her work for NGOs. As she put it,

> When I shoot for NGOs, I apply *New York Times* ethics to that (…) You know, absolutely nothing posed, nothing manipulated (…)
> The ethical standards of a news photograph—absolutely no Photoshopping or touching up.
> I've seen NGO photographers who put NGO T-shirts on people and have them standing in lines as if they are getting their rice.
> I won't do that. I don't think that would be ethical for a journalist.

Unlike E, D had not worked for an INGO before. So she said was in a "bit of a strange space", in which she was still working out how to negotiate tensions between her commitment to journalistic ethics and her efforts to make a living as a regional specialist (interview with D, August 30, 2012). Her commitment to regional specialism was shaped by her desire for greater autonomy in order to pursue work which she enjoyed and valued. These values were predominantly political for D. For instance, she said,

> I just wanted to be freer to do the kind of journalism that I think needs to be out there (…) because most people in the world know fuck all about his region.
> It's like (…) it's not even on the *map* for them.
> And that's (…) well, it's not right, is it?

But D was also keen to use freelancing as a way of managing her domestic life in a manner which was consistent with her caring responsibilities, which also related to her moral values. As she put it,

> I met my boyfriend and now we are getting married, so I am not in a position to just clear off somewhere else [on a foreign posting] for long periods of time—that's not exactly *loving* or *fair* on him (…)

But [if I took a newsroom job] I would be doing night shifts, I would be doing very long 12 hour shifts: leaving the house really early and getting back late at night.

I thought if we want children (…) I don't want to be dropping them off at childcare at six in the morning in the middle of winter and working really hard in a loud, pressured environment.

That would be *miserable*. And what kind of a parent could I be to those children?

So I thought I could maybe mix childcare with [freelancing] (…) and just reduce the number of trips I do. (interview, August 30, 2012)

Thus, like other freelancers, D became freelance in order to escape the oppressive aspects of a staff job at a major news organization, in order to fulfil her (current and future) caring responsibilities (Mathisen 2017; Wright 2016).

D began trying to resolve the tensions between these moral/political obligations and her commitment to journalistic ethics by reflecting critically on the nature of knowledge, saying:

Who can ever be impartial about anything, you know? I'm a white western woman who has worked in Chad as a journalist. So if I go to look at a radio station, I have absolutely got a viewpoint on how it should be. I am *never* going to be impartial.

I'll try my best to be *honest* about what I have seen. But I don't really believe that you can get a piece that's completely free from all the kinds of ideas and values which you bring to a story—just by being *yourself* really. (interview, August 30, 2012)

However, although D stressed the importance of "honesty" as a particular kind of disclosure transparency, she ultimately found this an unsatisfactory resolution. Like E, she then moved towards discussing what she would and would not do as a means of demonstrating her ability to exercise some, limited forms of critical independence as a freelancer. For instance, she said that she would have refused to write a "very positive" donor report or a largely supportive blog if she "found (…) enormous corruption within the Internews project or that something terrible that was happening" (interview with D, August 30, 2012). She also argued that she could exercise some autonomy by only working for organizations whose work she valued, saying:

I choose carefully who I work for, they have to be doing something *really* worthwhile. Then (…) I don't have too many problems writing what they want me to write.

Indeed, D saw working for Internews as involving far fewer ethical dilemmas than working for other NGOs because they supported local journalists. As she explained,

I'm a journalist and I have worked in Chad and I've seen how difficult it is to operate there and I think anyone that's trying to help journalists and trying to promote that (…) [is doing worthwhile work].

When I meet other journalists in Chad, there is definitely a sense of solidarity there. (interview, August 30, 2012)

So freelancers negotiated their multiple obligations to others in ways which recombined moral, political and economic values. But occupational ethics and role-perceptions remained a dominant feature of D and E's deliberations—with both continuing to identify strongly as "journalists", rather than as PR officers for INGOs.

Internews

D and E weren't sure why Internews had hired two freelance journalists to prepare their donor report: confessing that they thought the assignment was "a little bit random" (interview with D, August 30, 2012; see also interview with E, June 13, 2013). But D and E's commission from Internews was far from random. It was tightly structured in a similar manner to D's commission from *The Guardian*, as it depended on informal conversations facilitated by physical proximity and existing social and cultural links. This is because D was recommended to Deborah Ensor, who was then Internews' Vice President for Africa, Health and Humanitarian Programs, by Ian Noble, who was working as the country director for Chad at Internews. Noble had been introduced to D at a friend's party in the Chadian capital of N'djamena and they got talking because they were both brought up in the same small, English town (interview with D, August 30, 2012; interview with Ian Noble, March 28, 2013).

But Noble stressed that his "trust" in D was powerfully shaped by a sense of their "shared values" (interview, March 28, 2013). Like D, Noble had also been a radio journalist who had become "disenchanted" with his former employer, Radio France Internationale. In particular, he had been increasingly frustrated by the internal politics and cost-cutting in the news organization, which he said was making it harder and harder for journalists to meet the people they were reporting upon. Noble regarded this situation as particularly problematic because he saw working "in the field" as indicative of a deep commitment to authentic North/South relationships, saying it involved

(...) connecting with people in real, concrete situations, dealing with the real issues
that have to do with their lives, rather than doing it at several removes from a com-
fortable newsroom in Paris or London or Washington. (interview, March 28, 2013)

Thus Noble saw D, who also wanted to find ways to continue to work "in
the field", as "sharing that feeling of concern and commitment towards other
people" to "try to help them to have a better life" (interview with Ian Noble,
March 28, 2013). For these reasons, Noble saw D as a normative ally as well as
a personal friend. However, D's journalistic background was important to Noble, because he thought that her longstanding service as a BBC correspondent in Chad gave her the language skills, logistical experience and regional
expertise she needed to produce a "credible" donor report for Internews. This,
Noble argued, was important because Internews staff needed to have "trust"
in the "credibility" of their own organization, which would be undermined if
the INGO produced an "advertorial" about its work. Noble then expanded on
this, saying

> We believe we are a credible organization—by credible, I mean we are a media and
> development organization and we are training people and supporting all kinds of
> journalistic principles and ethics all the time in the various countries around the
> world that we work in.
>   So I believe, and we all believe at Internews, that we should be endorsing the same
> principles when it comes to [the representation of our own work].

Therefore Noble's decision to recommend D to Ensor involved complex ar-
ticulations of a particular form of trust—credibility—which rested upon his
double location of authenticity "in the field" and in professional journalism.
So although Noble was personally very interested in postcolonial politics, he
didn't reflect upon whether the Darfuri journalists working on the Chad project should have been enabled to prepare the report themselves.

This finding seems to speak to research about the spread of former journalists and newsroom norms into non-governmental work: illustrating how and
why the alterity of media development INGOs in particular may be undermined (Cottle and Nolan 2007: Fenton 2010). However, Internews' engagement in mediatized forms of donor reporting was also shaped by the short-term
nature of donor funding for particular INGO "projects" (Jones 2017; see also
Krause 2014). This is because the kind of donor report which D and E were
hired to create was a "legacy" report about what the project had achieved. The
project was about to close because Internews had been forced to withdraw
after donors had refused to renew their support for it. These donors included

bilateral and multilateral agencies, as well as a number of private trusts and foundations, although not the Gates Foundation.

As Ensor explained, having to close a project was not unusual because grants were given on an increasingly insecure, short-term basis (interview, January 18, 2013). Although Internews had run the radio project for seven years (2005–2012), she said that the INGO had never been sure that the radio stations would be funded from year to year. This, Ensor argued, had made it very difficult for the INGO's managers to shift what had originally been envisaged as a short-term humanitarian project aimed at providing information to refugees, into a sustainable development project, run by the refugees themselves. Indeed, now that the INGO had lost its donor funding and been forced to withdraw, everyone who was involved was worried that the radio stations would not survive—leaving vulnerable refugees without the communication systems they had come to depend upon.

Donors' short-term funding practices had also made it impossible for the INGO to carry out traditional project evaluation of the radio stations, as this would have involved bringing in experts to carry out staged evaluations over the planned lifetime of the project (interview with Deborah Ensor, January 18, 2013). So Ensor found herself in a very difficult situation. She knew that demonstrating "impact and accountability" in a "transparent manner" was "incredibly important" in securing new streams of funding. But she couldn't pursue established routes to doing that because of the short-term nature of that funding. In any case, Ensor argued, some donors didn't actually read detailed project evaluations, tending to have much more positive, emotional responses to multimedia content. As she put it,

> Sometimes you put out a boring academic report and you kind of hope they'll read it (…) But you produce some amazing photos and people look at the photos and say "Wow, these are so beautiful!"

For these reasons, Ensor's thinking about "transparency" and "accountability" became bound up with mediatized forms of project reporting, directed upwards towards international donors, rather than downwards towards local journalists. Similar conclusions have been reached by other studies about the effects of using multimedia projects and SMS text messaging in project reporting (Jones 2017; Madianou et al. 2016). What this case adds to those studies are understandings about the ways in which such reporting practices involve a small pool of trusted, freelance journalists and photojournalists, many of whom are from the UK and North America.

Ensor's utilization of mediatized reporting strategies led her to ask her staff to put together a list of between five and ten pre-vetted and rapidly deployable freelancers who could carry out these kinds of project evaluations (interview with Deborah Ensor, January 18, 2013). This list already included E, the freelance photojournalist suggested by D, as E had previously carried out a similar "assessment" for Internews in the Daadab refugee camp in Kenya (interview with Deborah Ensor, 18 January, 2013). Once more, this opportunity arose from an informal conversation when a member of Internews' staff, met E at a social event in Venezuela where she is based, although she is originally from the USA (interview with E, June 13, 2013). Thus, on the basis of Noble's recommendation, D's friendship with E, and Ensor's previous experience of E's work, the pair were given the Chad commission, even though this involved E making a very expensive and logistically complicated trip to Chad.

Ensor insisted that Internews had respected the freelancers' "journalistic independence" by giving them a "light touch" briefing, which consisted of her emailing them eight bullet points in an email (interview, January 18, 2013). But the main thrust of this briefing involved tasking freelancers with creating a positive piece about what the project had achieved (interview with D, August 30, 2012). This included stressing that Internews had done its best to help local journalists create a sustainable basis for the future—even though the freelancers knew that Internews staff feared that the radio stations would not survive the INGO's departure. In addition, Ensor insisted that D and E's "standards as independent journalists" had been maintained because they "could have said we are uncomfortable doing this for you" if they had got there and believed that "the project was garbage" (interview, January 18, 2013). But she went on to make it clear that if D and E had prepared a critical assessment of the project for Internews, or had written a critical blog about it, then they would not have been hired again.

Thus intertwining ideas about D and E's independence, credibility and authenticity as journalists were used by staff at Internews to sidestep the problematic lack of inclusiveness in this production process. Indeed, the main purpose of freelancers' work for Internews was to produce "beautiful", uplifting images and a "magazine style" report, in keeping with the tastes of Northern elite donors (interview with Deborah Ensor, January 18, 2013; see also Gupta 1986). D and E were so successful at doing this that Ensor later planned to use their work at a special event for bilateral and multilateral donors in Washington DC, including representatives from the US State Department, USAID, the UN's High Commission for Refugees and the UK's Department for International Development. As she explained,

> We'll hang up the pictures—E's pictures are really stunning—and we will hand out this beautiful magazine piece that D wrote.
>
> Then we are going to have a very interactive kind of panel discussion with donors (…) to talk about what we achieved.
>
> We want to make the case, you know, in a *soft* way, that this is really important (…) I mean (…) it was a beautiful project that did tremendous things
>
> (…) So it's almost like a kind of *love* letter to the project and to the people who supported it.

Thus the purpose of the media produced by freelancers was to trigger donors' feelings of enjoyment and "love" for the project they had supported, as well as feelings of being "loved" by the INGO. Such forms of assessment did not confront them with the problems caused by their short-term approach to funding. Needless to say, the conversations stimulated in this way were likely to be very limited in scope, excluding many different perspectives or values, as the discussion event was geared towards celebrating donors' role in the success of this particular form of international aid, rather than critiquing it.

The actual blog which D and E produced using recycled photographic and written materials from the Internews donor report was also very positive. It promotes Internews' work by describing the radio stations it set up as "flourishing". This claim is supported visually by a vibrantly-colored action shot, depicting the agency of the refugee reporters (reproduced overleaf). In addition, the photograph is taken at an angle, which enhances the sense of dynamism and movement in the picture. The viewer's gaze is then directed towards the two refugees via this diagonal angle, which is reinforced by strategically placed globes on the desks of what appears to be a school classroom. In this way, the photograph makes visual links between dynamism, participatory media, globality, and the production of knowledge: all of which help to construct Internews' brand, as well as that of *The Guardian* Global Development site.

The success of the radio stations is then established in the written text using anecdotal evidence and direct, personal quotes, including one from a woman who found out from the radio that she could give birth in hospital. These details complement the informal, personalized nature of a blog, whilst avoiding difficult questions about the inability of Internews to carry out a detailed project evaluation because of donors' short-term approach to funding. However, the piece does contain some veiled criticisms of donors' funding practices, which Internews did not feel able to make in the course of its own project reporting. Although the donors who pulled out are not named, the blog mentions that funding for refugee projects in the region is "getting harder to come by" and that "money will be an enormous challenge" for those seeking to keep the radio stations alive in future.

Figure 7.1: Darfuri refugees depicted by E/Internews

Such muted criticisms do not amount to a critique of the way in which Darfuri refugees have been treated. Nor do they engage with the problematic funding of media development projects and their funding structures in a broader sense, as the author, D, swiftly moves on to discuss the avenues which local journalists planned to pursue to try to generate some income themselves. Thus the blog creates the impression of *The Guardian's* support for participatory and inclusive forms of journalism, whilst avoiding presenting a more serious challenge to international donors, including the Bill and Melinda Gates Foundation, which funds the Global Development site, as well as other projects by Internews.

For these reasons, we must question the validity of the legitimating rationales which actors used. The grounding of this production process in value-laden concepts of transparency, inclusivity and journalistic independence facilitated and legitimated a remarkably narrow system of trusting exchanges. These not only concentrated interpretative control within the hands of

American and European journalists, rather than Darfuri refugees living in Chad, but they also privileged Northern aesthetic traditions in order to please British and American donors and make them feel "loved."

Moral economy: a coda

The model of the moral economy is geared towards enabling an analysis of how and why multiple effects emerge, allowing critics to better pinpoint how and why specific people's capabilities are enabled or constrained. This helps us to move beyond the crude forms of intentionality often implied in PR theory (e.g. Davies 2008), for unlike the other INGOs discussed in this book, Internews staff did not set out to place their material in, or to influence the narrative framing of, mainstream news. Nor was there any conspiracy in which the Gates Foundation attempted to use its funding of news outlets to give greater credibility to an INGO it supported. Nevertheless, the embedding of freelancing in multiple, trusting social exchanges created an almost entirely closed system in which certain values, perspectives and approaches to international development dominated.

Reversioning the material commissioned by the INGO as a blog for a news outlet enhanced freelancers' ability to make a living doing the kinds of specialized work they valued. This transaction enhanced the ability of the INGO to promote its work within the international development sector, although this had not been the original intention of INGO staff. Whilst journalists at *The Guardian's* Global Development site received indirect but significant "information subsidies" (Gandy 1982), which helped them to stimulate the kinds of networked journalism with professional communities which they valued, for normative and economic reasons.

The media text which was produced certainly avoided positioning all Africans as helpless victims, whilst shedding some light on the experiences of Darfuri refugees in Chad. But the largely celebratory, positive tone of the blog, which was derived from the donor report, inhibited harsher and more far-reaching criticisms of the ways in which Dafuri refugees have been treated. Thus, although no personnel from the Gates Foundation were directly involved in this production process, it benefited indirectly: gaining an increased ability to support its claim that, on the whole, international "aid works" (Paulson 2013). So the blog did not provide any serious challenge to Gates' privatized approaches to international development.

The application of moral economy theory to this case therefore helps us to explore the unintended effects of production processes. It also enables us to challenge the commonly held belief that INGOs and major international news organizations collude in propagating pessimistic representations of Africa: representing the continent as doomed to failure unless rescued by benevolent Northerners (Franks 2013; Lugo-Ocando and Malaolu 2014). Instead, it builds on more recent work which shows that development INGOs differentiate themselves from other kinds of INGOs, and try to attract jaded donors, by stressing their role in enhancing the capabilities of poor people in the Global South (Dogra 2012). Although these INGOs may not always express unalloyed hope for the future of the continent (Nothias 2014), their concentration on the empowering nature of "good projects" (Krause 2014) risks inhibiting critiques of unjust transnational structures—including the funding of media development itself (Berger 2010; LaMay 2009).

Thus the production of this blog brought about unintended forms of hypocrisy: creating narrowness in the place of inclusivity and participation, opacity instead of transparency. But rather than simply blaming individual media producers, it is important to understand how the moral economy in which they were embedded related recursively to broader political economies. In particular, I want to stress the problematic nature of private foundation funding in journalism, which constrained the ability of those working at Guardian News Media to facilitate dialogue about international development in ways which weren't dominated by northern INGOs. I also want to highlight the ways in which cost-cutting in mainstream news forced those wishing to engage in regional or media specialism into freelancing: the precarious nature of which necessitated them taking commissions from multiple clients, whilst inhibiting them from discussing any ethical problems with others.

Finally, I want to emphasize the problematic nature of short-term project funding in INGO-work, which predisposed INGO-workers to avoid challenging donors about the difficulties this caused in international development. Instead, they were incentivized to replace critical dialogue with feel-good forms of mediatized project reporting to international donors. Therefore, this moral economy rested upon the intersection of particular economic structures which, when combined with normative ideas about progressive, participatory and dialogic media production, effectively towed both journalism and NGO-work towards far less inclusive, radical and sustainable approaches to international development.

Notes

1. The reference to this piece has been removed at the request of the freelancers concerned.
2. Unfortunately, the editor in this case declined an offer to participate in this study.

References

"Alexa – Top Sites by Category: News." Accessed August 22, 2017. https://www.alexa.com/topsites/category/Top/News.

Allan, Joanna. "Privilege, Marginalization, and Solidarity: Women's Voices Online in Western Sahara's Struggle for Independence." *Feminist Media Studies* 14, no. 4 (July 4, 2014): 704–8.

Allen, David S. "The Trouble with Transparency: The Challenge of Doing Journalism Ethics in a Surveillance Society." *Journalism Studies* 9, no. 3 (2008): 323–40.

Argles, Martin. "The Future of Photography." Speech given at meeting of National Union of Journalists' London Photographer's Branch June 15, 2013.

Beckett, Charlie. *SuperMedia: Saving Journalism so It Can Save the World.* London: Blackwell, 2008.

Beckett, Charlie, and Robin Mansell. "Crossing Boundaries: New Media and Networked Journalism." *Communication, Culture and Critique* 1, no. 1 (2008): 92–104.

Berger, Guy. "Problematising 'media development' as a bandwagon gets rolling." The *International Communication Gazette* 72, no.7 (2010): 547–65.

Birn, Anne-Emanuelle. "Philanthrocapitalism, Past and Present: The Rockefeller Foundation, the Gates Foundation and the Setting (s) of the International Global Health Agenda." *Hypothesis* 12, no. 1 (2014). http://www.hypothesisjournal.com/?p=2503

Bishop, Matthew, and Michael F. Green. *Philanthrocapitalism: How the Rich Can Save the World and Why We Should Let Them.* New York: Bloomsbury Press 2008.

Braun, Joshua, and Tarleton Gillespie. "Hosting the Public Discourse, Hosting the Public: When Online News and Social Media Converge." *Journalism Practice* 5, no. 4 (2011): 383–98.

Browne, Harry. "Foundation-Funded Journalism: Reasons to Be Wary of Charitable Support." *Journalism Studies* 11, no. 6 (2010): 889–903.

Bunce, Mel. "Foundations, Philanthropy and International Journalism." *Ethical Space* 13, no. 2/3 (2016): 6–15.

Bunting, Madeleine. "Guardian Launches Site to Explore Aid | Media | The Guardian." *The Guardian*, September 20, 2010. http://www.theguardian.com/media/2010/sep/20/guardian-aid-website-bill-gates.

Castells, Manuel. *The Rise of the Network Society.* 2nd ed. Information Age, vol. 1. Oxford: Blackwell, 2000.

Collis, David J., Peter Olson, and Mary Furey. "The Guardian: Transition to the Online World'." *Harvard Business School*, July 16, 2011.

Cooper, Glenda. "Hurricanes and Hashtags: How the Media and NGOs Treat Citizens' Voices Online in Humanitarian Emergencies." *Interactions: Studies in Communication & Culture* 6, no. 2 (2015): 233–44.

Cottle, Simon, and David Nolan. "Global Humanitarianism and the Changing Aid-Media Field: Everyone was Dying for Footage." *Journalism Studies* 8, no. 6 (2007): 862–78.

Curran, James, Natalie Fenton, and Des Freedman. *Misunderstanding the Internet.* Communication and Society. London: Routledge, 2012.

Curtis, Mark. *Gated Development: Is the Gates Foundation Always a Force for Good?* London: Global Justice Now! January 2016. http://www.globaljustice.org.uk/sites/default/files/files/resources/gated-development-global-justice-now.pdf.

Daniel, Anna, and Terry Flew. "The Guardian Reportage of the UK MP Expenses Scandal: A Case Study of Computational Journalism." In *Record of the Communications Policy and Research Forum 2010*, 186–94. Sydney: Network Insight Pty. Ltd., 2010. http://eprints.qut.edu.au/39358/.

Davies, Nick. *Flat Earth News: An Award-Winning Reporter Exposes Falsehood, Distortion and Propaganda in the Global Media.* London: Chatto and Windus, 2008.

Deuze, Mark. "The Professional Identity of Journalists in the Context of Convergence Culture." *Observatorio (Obs*)* 2, no. 4 (2008). http://www.obs.obercom.pt/index.php/obs/article/viewArticle/216.

Deuze, Mark, and Leopoldina Fortunati. "Journalism without Journalists." In *News Online: Transformation and Continuity*, edited by Graham Meikle and Guy Redden, 164–77. Basingstoke: Palgrave Macmillan, 2010.

Dogra, Nandita. *Representations of Global Poverty: Aid, Development and International NGOs.* Library of Development Studies, vol. 6. London; New York: I.B. Tauris; Palgrave Macmillan, 2012.

Doughton, Sandi, and Kristi Helm. "Does Gates Funding of Media Taint Objectivity?" *Seattle Times*, February 19, 2011. http://seattletimes.com/html/localnews/2014280379_gatesmedia.html.

Eastment, Diana. "Blogging." *ELT Journal* 59, no. 4 (2005): 358–61.

Edmonds, Rick. "Getting Behind the Media: What Are the Subtle Trade-Offs for Foundation-Funded Journalism?" *Philanthropy March/April*, 2002.

Edström, Maria, and Martina Ladendorf. "Freelance Journalists as a Flexible Workforce in Media Industries." *Journalism Practice* 6, no. 5–6 (2012): 711–21.

Escobar, Arturo. "Discourse and Power in Development: Michel Foucault and the Relevance of His Work to the Third World." In *Theoretical Approaches to Participatory Communication*, edited by Thomas L. Jacobson and Jan Serveas, 309–35. Cresskill, NJ: Hampton Press, 1999.

———. *Encountering Development: The Making and Unmaking of the Third World.* 2nd ed. Princeton, Oxford: Princeton University Press, 2012.

Feldman, Bob. "Report from the Field: Left Media and Left Think Tanks—Foundation-Managed Protest?" *Critical Sociology* 33, no. 3 (2007): 427–46.

Fenton, Natalie. "NGOs, New Media and the Mainstream News: News from Everywhere." In *New Media, Old News: Journalism & Democracy in the Digital Age*, edited by Natalie Fenton, 153–68. London: Sage, 2010.

Franks, Suzanne. *Reporting Disasters: Famine, Aid, Politics and the Media*. London: Hurst Publishers, 2013.

Frölich, R., Thomas Koch, and Magdalena Obermaier. "What's the Harm in Moonlighting? A Qualitative Survey on the Role Conflicts of Freelance Journalists with Secondary Employment in the Field of PR." *Media Culture and Society* 35, no. 7 (2013): 809–29.

Frontline Club. *Embedding with Aid Agencies: Editorial Integrity and Security Risks*. London, 2015. https://www.frontlineclub.com/embedding-with-aid-agencies-editorial-integrity-and-security-risks/

Gandy, Oscar H. *Beyond Agenda Setting: Information Subsidies and Public Policy*. Norwood, NJ: Ablex, 1982.

Gillmor, Dan. *We the Media: Grassroots Journalism by the People, for the People*. Beijing: O'Reilly, 2006.

Gollmitzer, Miriam. "Precariously Employed Watchdogs?" *Journalism Practice* 8, no. 6 (2014): 826–41.

Gupta, Sunil. "Northern Media, Southern Lives'." In *Photography/politics*, edited by Jo Spence, Patricia Holland, and Simon Watney, 162–66. London: Comedia /Photography Workshop, 1986.

Harrow, Jenny, and Cathy Pharoah. "Philanthropic Journalism Funding in the UK." London: Journalism Funders Forum, 2017. https://journalismfundersforum.com/uploads/downloads/jff_london_report.pdf.

Hornmoen, Harald, and Steen Steensen. "Dialogue as a Journalistic Ideal." *Journalism Studies* 15, no. 5 (2014): 543–54.

International Telecommunications Union. "ICT Facts and Figures," 2017. http://www.itu.int/en/ITU-D/Statistics/Documents/facts/ICTFactsFigures2017.pdf.

Internews (n.d.). *What We Do*. https://www.internews.org/.

Jarvis, Jeff. "Networked Journalism." *BuzzMachine*, July 5, 2006. http://buzzmachine.com/2006/07/05/networked-journalism/.

Jones, Ben. "Looking Good: Mediatisation and International NGOs." *European Journal of Development Research* 29, no. 1 (2017): 176–91.

Kahn, Richard, and Douglas Kellner. "New Media and Internet Activism: From the 'Battle of Seattle' to Blogging." *New Media & Society* 6, no. 1 (2004): 87–95.

Karlsson, Michael. "Rituals of Transparency: Evaluating Online News Outlets' Uses of Transparency Rituals in the United States, United Kingdom and Sweden." *Journalism Studies* 11, no. 4 (2010): 535–45.

———."The immediacy of online news, the visibility of journalistic processes and the restructuring of journalistic authority." *Journalism* 12, no.3 (2011):279–95.Keller, Jessalynn Marie. "Virtual Feminisms: Girls' Blogging Communities, Feminist Activism, and Participatory Politics." *Information, Communication & Society* 15, no. 3 (2012): 429–47.

Kovach, Bill, and Tom Rosenstiel. *The Elements of Journalism: What Newspeople Should Know and the Public Should Expect*. New York: Three Rivers Press, 2001.

Krause, Monika. *The Good Project: Humanitarian Relief NGOs and the Fragmentation of Reason.* Chicago; London: University of Chicago Press, 2014.

Ladendorf, Martina. "Freelance Journalists' Ethical Boundary Settings in Information Work." *Nordicom Review* 33, no. 1 (2013): 83–98.

LaMay, Craig L. *Exporting Press Freedom.* New Brunswick, NJ: Transaction Press, 2009.

Lasica, Joseph D. "Blogs and Journalism Need Each Other." *Nieman Reports* Fall (2003): 70–74.

Lugo-Ocando, Jairo, and Patrick O. Malaolu. "Africa—That Scar on Our Face." In *Blaming the Victim: How Global Journalism Fails Those in Poverty,* Jairo Lugo-Ocando, 85–103. London: Pluto Press, 2014.

Mabweazara, Hayes. "Newtechnologies and Journalism Practice in Africa: Towards a Critical Sociological Approach," 2010. http://researchrepository.napier.ac.uk/id/eprint/2756.

Madianou, Mirca, Jonathan Corpus Ong, Liezel Longboan, and Jayeel S. Cornelio. "The Appearance of Accountability: Communication Technologies and Power Asymmetries in Humanitarian Aid and Disaster Recovery." *Journal of Communication* 66, no. 1 (2016): 960–81.

Mance, Henry. "Guardian to cut £54m of costs and introduce paid-for content." *Financial Times,* Jan. 25, 2016.
https://www.ft.com/content/83512944-c35e-11e5-808f.-8231cd71622e

Martens, Jens, and Karolin Seitz. *Philanthropic Power and Development: Who Shapes the Agenda?* Bonn: Global Policy Forum, 2015.

Martinson, Jane. "Guardian Media Group to Cut 250 Jobs in Bid to Break Even within Three Years." *The Guardian,"* March 17, 2016. http://www.theguardian.com/media/2016/mar/17/guardian-media-group-to-cut-250-jobs.

Mathisen, Brigit R. "Entrepreneurs and Idealists: Freelance Journalists at the Intersection of Autonomy and Constraints." *Journalism Practice* 11, no. 7 (2017): 909–24.

McGoey, Linsey. *No Such Thing as a Free Gift: The Gates Foundation and the Price of Philanthropy.* London: Verso, 2015.

Mody, Bella. *International and Development Communication: A 21st-Century Perspective.* New York: Sage Publications, 2003.

Moeller, Susan D. *Compassion Fatigue: How the Media Sell Disease, Famine, War and Death.* New York, London: Routledge, 1999.

Moyo, Last. "Blogging down a Dictatorship: Human Rights, Citizen Journalists and the Right to Communicate in Zimbabwe." *Journalism* 12, no. 6 (2011): 745–60.

Nothias, Toussaint. "'Rising', 'Hopeful', 'New': Visualizing Africa in the Age of Globalization." *Visual Communication* 13, no. 3 (2014): 323–39.

Obermaier, Magdalena and Thomas Koch. "Mind the gap: Consequences of inter-role conflicts of freelance journalists with secondary employment in the field of public relations." *Journalism,* 16, no.5 (2015): 615–29.

Ogunyemi, Olatunji. "Representation of Africa Online: Sourcing Practice and Frames of Reference." *Journal of Black Studies* 42, no. 3 (2011):457–78.

Paulson, Tom. "Gates Foundation's Funding of Media and Influence over Public Dialogue." *Humanosphere,* February 13, 2013. http://www.humanosphere.org/basics/2013/02/a-personal-view-behind-the-scenes-with-the-gates-foundations-media-partners/.

Pew Research Center. "Cell Phones in Africa: Communication Lifeline." *Pew Research Center's Global Attitudes Project*, April 15, 2015. http://www.pewglobal.org/2015/04/15/cell-phones-in-africa-communication-lifeline/.

Ribbens, Elisabeth. "Gates Foundation Reaffirms Support for Global Development." The Guardian, October 25, 2011. http://www.theguardian.com/help/insideguardian/2011/oct/25/gates-foundation-reaffirms-commitment-global-development.

Robinson, Sue. "'Journalism as Process': The Organizational Implications of Participatory Online News." *Journalism & Communication Monographs* 13, no. 3 (2011): 137–210.

Salmon, Felix. "Media Buyer of the Day, Gates Foundation Edition." News. *Reuters US Edition*, November 18, 2011. http://blogs.reuters.com/felix-salmon/2011/11/18/media-buyer-of-the-day-gates-foundation-edition.

Sambrook, Richard. *Are Foreign Correspondents Redundant?* Oxford: Reuters Institute for the Study of Journalism, 2010.

Schein, Edgar H. *Organizational Culture and Leadership*. 3rd ed. Hoboken, NJ: Wiley, 2004.

Scott, Martin. *Media and Development: Development Matters*. London: Zed Books, 2014a.

———. "Introduction to the DSA Media and Development Study Group." London, 2014b.

Singer, Jane B. "Contested Autonomy: Professional and Popular Claims on Journalistic Norms." *Journalism Studies* 8, no. 1 (2007): 79–95.

Singer, Jane B., and Ian Ashman. "'Comment Is Free, but Facts Are Sacred': User-Generated Content and Ethical Constructs at the Guardian." *Journal of Mass Media Ethics* 24, no. 1 (2009): 3–21.

Somolu, Oreoluwa. "'Telling Our Own Stories': African Women Blogging for Social Change." *Gender & Development* 15, no. 3 (2007): 477–89.

Starkman, Dean. "No Paywalls, Please: We're The Guardian." *Columbia Journalism Review* 10 (2013).http://archives.cjr.org/the_audit/no_paywalls_please_were_the_gu.php

The Guardian (n.d.). "The Scott Trust." *The Guardian*. http://www.theguardian.com/the-scott-trust.

Thorsen, Einar. "Live Blogging and Social Media Curation: Challenges and Opportunities for Journalism." In *Journalism: New Challenges*, edited by Karen Fowler-Watt and Stuart Allan, 123–45. Poole: CJCR: Centre for Journalism & Communication Research, 2013.

Thurman, Neil, and Anna Walters. "Live Blogging–digital Journalism's Pivotal Platform? A Case Study of the Production, Consumption, and Form of Live Blogs at Guardian. Co. UK." *Digital Journalism* 1, no. 1 (2013): 82–101.

Van der Haak, Bregtje, Michael Parks, and Manuel Castells. "The Future of Journalism: Networked Journalism." *International Journal of Communication* 6 (2012): 2923–38.

Wilkins, Karin Gwinn, and Florencia Enghel. "The Privatization of Development through Global Communication Industries: Living Proof?" *Media, Culture & Society* 35, no. 2 (2013): 165–81.

Wright, Kate. "These Grey Areas": How and Why Freelance Work Blurs INGOs and News Organizations. *Journalism Studies* 17, no. 8 (2016): 989–1009.

· 8 ·

AFRICAN SELF-HELP, CORPORATE SOCIAL RESPONSIBILITY, AND POSITIVE FEATURES

The Observer and the Kenyan Paraplegic Organization

Journalists working for media organizations in the US and UK have long been accused of portraying Africa in overly negative ways (Hawk 1992). Writers, diasporic organizations and sub-Saharan politicians have all condemned their sporadic, decontextualized and crisis-driven coverage of the continent (de Beer 2010a, 2010b; Opuku-Owusu 2003; Wainaina 2005). More recently, social media participants have taken to Twitter to challenge international news organizations over the negative wording of their reports—the most famous example of which was the #SomeoneTellCNN campaign (Nothias 2017; Nyabola 2017). Underpinning these criticisms is the conviction that the overwhelmingly negative news reporting of the continent seriously damages the prospects of people living in sub-Saharan countries (Marthoz 2007; Schorr 2011).

But is news about Africa really so overwhelmingly negative? We can't assume that it is, as academic researchers have tended to make judgements about what such coverage is like on the basis of a narrow range of studies, which also involve a highly selective focus on negative events (Scott 2017). In addition, it seems questionable to imply that all reporting of negative events in sub-Saharan countries is necessarily problematic as entirely positive "sunshine journalism" is usually regarded as little more than elite-led propaganda (Kuper and Kuper 2001). Moreover, negativity is a core news value and other continents are often presented far more negatively than Africa (Nothias 2016; Scott 2009). So it may be wiser to critique Afropessimism, which involves journalists not only selecting negative events to cover, but also using racialized stock stereotypes and totalizing strategies to make doom-laden predictions about the future of the entire continent (Nothias 2013a).

However, journalists reporting on sub-Saharan countries for Northern news outlets are alert to criticisms that their coverage is overly negative and disempowering, and many try to respond (Bunce et al. 2017; Nothias 2017). How they respond is shaped by a number of factors, including their privileging of new or counterintuitive angles; increases in funding for business journalism; and the repositioning of the world's largest wire agencies in relation to one another (Bunce 2017a). A more immediate trigger was the publication of McKinsey's *Lions on the Move* report (Roxburgh et al. 2010), which waxed lyrical about the continent's economic prospects. So, in 2011–2012, we saw a peak in positivistic journalistic coverage about the continent (Bunce 2017b).

These kinds of coverage are often described as constructing "Africa Rising" narratives (Bunce et al. 2017; Nothias 2014). Such media items tend to be upbeat, magazine features which express "hope" for Africa's future and employ a sleek, professionalized aesthetic: often depicting African subjects who appear to directly return the viewer's gaze, or uplifting, wide-angle shots of open horizons (Nothias 2014). These features praise African entrepreneurialism, self-help and rapid economic growth (Nothias 2014). But they also highlight different forms of cultural renaissance, as well as the spread of media technology, especially mobile phones (Nothias 2014). However, rather than constituting greater diversity, they tend to invert Afropessimism: with journalists only selecting positive events for coverage and utilizing racialized stock characters. Indeed, the little boy depicted flying the rainbow-colored, Africa-shaped kite on the now famous cover of *The Economist* was actually Photoshopped to darken his skin (2011, discussed in Nothias 2014).

Most significantly of all, these pieces continue to measure African countries' "progress" in terms of their capitulation to neoliberal policies and Northern conceptualizations of economic growth, before using totalizing strategies in order to make optimistic predictions for the future of the entire continent(Nothias 2014). So these "Africa Rising" narratives marginalize other ways of measuring progress, including the redistribution of wealth and the sustainability of economic growth (Biney 2013). This potentially lowers discursive resistance to the growing dominance of multinationals. Indeed, related forms of business journalism may even portray emerging markets as "the final frontier" for Northern businesses, encouraging them to engage in a new "scramble for Africa" (Bunce 2017b).

Classic "Africa Rising" features about the continent's economic growth are now much less common, following the publication of a second, less glowing McKinsey report (2016, discussed by Bunce 2017b). But journalists continue to draw from the visual, linguistic and conceptual repertoire established during this period, blending these textual characteristics with those of other kinds of positivistic narratives about the continent. For example, development INGOs have sought to distinguish themselves from the negative depictions of Africa disseminated by humanitarian agencies by constructing media campaigns which stress the agency and dignity of sub-Saharan people (Dogra 2012; Orgad 2015).

Some humanitarian agencies have also responded to criticisms of their use of degrading "aid porn" by utilizing positivistic narratives. For instance, Oxfam ran a glossy "See Africa Differently" campaign, which celebrated the variety and beauty of sub-Saharan landscapes (Scott 2017). These campaigns seem to usher in a welcome change in perspective, but they also further INGOs' strategic objectives: re-legitimizing their relationships with poor people in the Global South in ways which may appeal to jaded Northern donors (Dogra 2012).

Numerous positivistic media campaigns have also been created by African governments and businesses in an attempt to rebrand their countries, including Ethiopia, Ghana and Kenya (Fanta 2015; Fisher 2015; Kimani 2015; Tuwei and Tully 2017). Such campaigns, which often involve the use of social media, are explicitly designed to "talk back" to old imperialistic narratives, which positioned Africans as weak, passive and unable to help themselves (Flamenbaum 2017; Kimani 2015). These media campaigns tend to emerge from the related interactions of different groups of actors, including commercial PR firms, businesses and governments (Kimani 2015; Tuwei and Tully 2017). So they are designed to achieve many different strategic objectives, including re/constructing political legitimacy and securing political support within sub-Saharan countries, at the same time as attracting greater cultural recognition and economic investment from outside (Tuwei and Tully 2017).

Thus even when journalists publish or broadcast more positive features about sub-Saharan countries, they participate in complex discursive struggles about the meaning/s of Africa, which are believed to have important implications for the re/distribution of political and economic resources (Gallagher

2015). Yet when the British journalists in this study talked about using images provided by small, sub-Saharan NGOs to construct more positive, empowering representations of Africans "helping themselves", they tended to see this as much less risky than using material from international NGOs based in the US and UK. This was because they perceived sub-Saharan NGOs as being "simpler" and less "commercialized" than their wealthier, international counterparts (Magee 2014).

For these reasons, the British journalists I interviewed (Wright 2014) thought that it was "empowering" to use material from small sub-Saharan NGOs to construct relatively short, light features about African self-help, which had a strong human interest focus. These features tended to be about entrepreneurial and/or mediated forms of activity. But journalists did this relatively rarely: only using photos provided by these NGOs when they were sufficiently technically accomplished to be published, as well as being composed in what they thought was an aesthetically pleasing manner. Curiously, they never questioned how such small, poor NGOs had managed to achieve this despite their lack of financial and cultural capital. Nor did British journalists question how such small NGOs had managed to capture their attention, when this is notoriously difficult for smaller NGOs, given the volume of material available online (Thrall et al. 2014). Instead, journalists tended to praise the emancipatory potential of social media, without which they would not have been aware of these NGOs or able to acquire their pictures.

In particular, these journalists seemed unaware of the growth of Corporate Social Responsibility (CSR) programs in emerging sub-Saharan markets, and their implications for social media activity. CSR programs in African countries are still in their infancy, so are often conducted on a relatively informal or ad hoc basis (Visser and Tolhurst 2010). They may be shaped by many different normative values and cultural contexts, which vary from country to country (Visser and Tolhurst 2010). But they tend to be the province of medium to large companies, as the need in many sub-Saharan countries is so great that philanthropic giving and economic empowerment are seen as the right thing to do, as well as having a PR purpose (Visser 2006; Visser and Tolhurst 2010).

Multinational companies or those with foreign investors and partners seem to be particularly keen on CSR programs (Visser and Tolhurst 2010): using their engagement with multiple stakeholders, including local NGOs, to construct their social legitimacy within sub-Saharan countries (Gruber and Schlegelmilch 2015; Idemudia 2014; Muthuri and Gilbert 2011). Such programs tend to involve hybridizing local and foreign values and related conceptualizations of social responsibility, but there is little agreement about whose moral and ethical frameworks are more dominant (Idemudia 2014). There is also little agreement about the extent to which CSR accommodates or re/shapes development agendas (Banerjee 2008; Hamann and Acutt 2003).

What we do know is that multinational companies working in African countries tend to engage in "proximate" forms of CSR. This means that they generally support projects which are in line with company objectives; focus on addressing problems related to the companies' core business; and/or affect communities close to the companies' area of operation (Ponte *et al.* 2009). These forms of CSR tend to take the form of philanthropic action, such as when companies step in to provide public services which the nation state has a limited capacity to provide (Idemudia 2014; Gruber and Schlegelmilch 2015; Rajak 2010; Visser 2006). But they may also involve the provision of other services through volunteering, and this can involve complex collaborations between multiple partners (Gruber and Schlegelmilch 2015; Idemudia 2014).

As this chapter shows, commercial companies are increasingly bringing in commercial advertising, PR and marketing agencies to work with sub-Saharan NGOs to develop sophisticated marketing campaigns on a *pro bono* basis. In particular, the case study explored here demonstrates why and how the telecommunications giant, Safaricom, worked with others on a CSR project with a small, sub-Saharan NGO, in order to produce a highly mediated fundraising campaign. The campaign, which was created in collaboration with the Kenyan Paraplegic Organization, was designed to provoke a social media storm, which resulted in many different news outlets picking up the story. These included the international news outlets *Al-Jazeera*, *BBC News Online*, *The New York Times* and *The Huffington Post*, as well as one of Kenya's leading newspapers, *The Standard*.

The journalists working for these organizations all produced short, upbeat human interest features which alluded to notions of African self-help, the spread of social media and/or mobile technology. Thus although this chapter is about the production of a feature for the British broadsheet, *The Observer* (Kiberenge 2012), the specific norms, practices and political economies of this news outlet were not as dominant as they were in other cases. Instead, *Observer* journalists' use of a still image from this NGO campaign was shaped by their broader efforts to produce better journalism about the continent, which combined with the promotional principles underpinning the mutual engagement of the NGO and commercial businesses in CSR.

Safaricom, Scangroup, and the Kenyan Paraplegic Organization

Like many other African NGOs, the Kenyan Paraplegic Organization (KPO) lacked the financial and cultural capital needed to produce its own multimedia or to target news outlets in a segmented manner (Fenton 2010). So the NGO's leader, Tim Wanyonyi, approached a senior executive at Safaricom, (Kenya's largest mobile phone provider, and an affiliate of the Vodafone group), to ask him if the company would consider supporting the NGO in order to help it fundraise. As with other case studies, this pivotal encounter was made possible by interpersonal connections, socio-economic and cultural similarities and geographic proximity. This is because Wanyoni, who was then a lawyer, first approached the Safaricom executive in charge of the CSR scheme at a barbecue held by mutual friends in an affluent suburb of Nairobi.

However, this social encounter was also enabled by journalism, as the reason why the Safaricom executive was open to meeting Wanyoni was that he had already read about the shooting incident which had made him a paraplegic in Kenyan newspapers (interview with Safaricom Executive, April 23, 2013). Wanyonyi and others at KPO had also seen journalistic coverage of Safaricom's support for other NGOs, including the way in which the company had spearheaded the "Kenyans for Kenya" fundraising campaign the year before (interview with Zack Kimotho, April 26, 2013). The company's mobile cash transfer platform, M-PESA, had played a central role in that campaign: enabling Kenyans living in the country and abroad to donate millions of dollars to relieve those starving in the north of the country (Buku and Meredith 2013).

The idea for a low-cost mobile cash transfer scheme was originally investigated by researchers at Vodafone/Safaricom, and supported the UK's Department for International Development, as this was originally conceptualized as aiding microfinance (Omwansa and Sullivan 2012). However, after Safaricom launched M-PESA[1] in 2007, it rapidly expanded its range of applications beyond microfinance, so that it is now one of the most successful mobile banking tools in the developing world (Jack and Suri 2011). M-PESA has a particularly strong penetration in Kenya, where it is used by 80 per cent of rural households (Aker and Mbiti 2010), as well as young, wealthy and educated urbanites (McKay and Kaffenberger 2013). Indeed, the growth of M-PESA has driven Safaricom's expansion and greatly increased its revenue streams by encouraging a rapid growth mobile phone uptake (Morawczynski 2010).

Using M-PESA in the "Kenyans for Kenya" famine relief campaign therefore helped develop strong, value-laden associations between the mobile banking platform and notions of economic empowerment, corporate responsibility and Kenyan self-help. But it also privileged privatized and technological solutions to the country's serious socio-economic problems. Indeed, we might even think of Safaricom's use of M-PESA in the "Kenyans for Kenya" campaign as a new form of cause-related marketing. Rather than a kind of "brand aid" (Richey and Ponte 2011), which seeks to sell products to Northern consumers as a way of alleviating Africans' suffering (Ponte *et al.* 2009; Richey and Ponte 2013), Safaricom executives embedded the product in the relief effort itself, in ways which enhanced its brand within emerging African markets.

So it is perhaps unsurprising that Safaricom's involvement in the "Kenya for Kenyans" famine relief campaign is consonant with its approach to commercial advertising. Safaricom adverts construct the company's brand by evoking value-laden notions of openness, inclusivity and individualistic forms of upward mobility: all of which are seen as underlying Kenyan people's positive attitude of entrepreneurialism and self-help (Tuwei and Tully 2017). Thus Safaricom may be seen as branding itself via a form of "commercial nationalism" which ties Kenyan identity to consumerism and particular forms of economic development (Tuwei and Tully 2017). Yet this kind of branding also serves to challenge negative, imperialistic narratives which position Africans as helpless and passive, so needing to be rescued by benevolent Northerners (Hawk 1992; Franks 2013; Lugo-Ocando and Malaolu 2014).

Such forms of branding enhanced Safaricom's social legitimacy at a particularly difficult time: the aftermath of a major corruption scandal relating to one of its subsidiaries, Mobitelea, which was registered in the British island of Guernsey (Nguyen 2007; Rice 2007). Allegations against Safaricom executives were investigated by both the Kenyan parliament and the UK's Serious Fraud Office, before being dropped several years later, due to lack of proof. But, interestingly Safaricom's CSR program did not explicitly address issues of corporate probity. Instead, it was structured around ideas about the morality of gift-giving. For instance, Bob Collymore, the company's Chief Executive, is reported to have spoken with other senior managers after the "Kenyans for Kenya" campaign, to stress that being a "socially responsible company" involved staff giving their personal time, energy and skills, not just corporate money (interview Safaricom Executive, April 23, 2013). As the Safaricom executive explained, Collymore had said,

> I have contributed my time and *myself* to put this [campaign] together.
>   If I can have ten more people like this, we could have an impact on society. (interview, April 23, 2013)

This kind of gift-giving was not conceptualized in terms of corporate "giving in kind", but in terms of executives' "contributions as individuals": an approach which the Safaricom Executive said had shaped his personal decision to serve on KPO's Board of Trustees (interview, April 23, 2013). However, other senior executives at Safaricom focused on a different sort of reciprocity: arguing that the company's CSR program was a form of social investment, which would pay ample commercial dividends in terms of investor interest and consumer goodwill in the long-term (Baillie, cited in Kamau and Anami 2010). Thus KPO's campaign was shaped by different kinds of normative approaches and commercialized promotional cultures (Davis 2013), long before the Safaricom Executive approached Scangroup to ask their staff to design a mediated fundraising campaign with KPO and Safaricom on a *pro bono* basis.

Scangroup is a pan-African network of advertising, PR and marketing firms which is based in Nairobi, and which usually handles Safaricom's account. Scangroup includes a number of smaller, African companies like Squad Digital and RedSky advertising, alongside the US-based multinational, Ogilvy and Mather. As advertising executives at RedSky explained, it was not unusual for their commercial clients to ask them to design media campaigns for small African NGOs as part of their CSR programs (interview with Mark Fidelo, April 18, 2013; interview with Mike Miller, May 4, 2013). Indeed, they stressed that this was an increasingly common way for Kenyan and foreign-owned businesses to enhance their commercial brands in sub-Saharan countries. Much of this CSR work was done through social media, as Mike Miller, who was then the Creative Director of RedSky, explained:

> There are so many companies that have jumped on the social bandwagon and do cause marketing [as part of their CSR schemes].
>   It has become *such* a big thing now, especially on Facebook and things like that. (interview, May 4, 2013)

These advertising executives spoke about the sympathy they had for the individual Kenyan paraplegics whom they had met. But ultimately, they legitimized their involvement in CSR media campaigns by conceptualizing the organizational advantages gained by commercial businesses and African NGOs as interchangeable forms of "good". As Mike Miller, RedSky's Creative Director, put it: "There's always a business need to do something good for their own organizations [through CSR], as well as the NGO you are doing good for" (interview, May 4, 2013). However, Miller rapidly abandoned this even-handed win-win approach when a disagreement arose between himself and some of the members of KPO, who were uncomfortable with the kind of campaign he was developing and wanted him to explore alternative approaches.

When this clash occurred, Miller made it clear that he expected to have interpretative control over the campaign, as he explained:

> There was a hiccup in the middle where [some KPO members] got very scared about what they had signed up for (…)
>
> What happened was some [KPO members] thought the idea [for the campaign] was too big and we were asked to do a Plan B.
>
> So I got everybody in a meeting in front of RedSky and did the "Over my *dead* body, this is not going to happen" number (…)
>
> They were just going "What if it doesn't work? [Said in panicky voice]. What if (…) what if?" And I was like, "You *can't* not go with this *now*."
>
> But [some KPO members] still thought it had got out of hand and that, maybe, we were doing the wrong thing (…)
>
> So there was a big fight about ownership.
>
> Yeah (…) there was a lot of bad feeling there. (interview, May 4, 2013)

Miller said he took this hard line in order to preserve his creative autonomy, which he believed was necessary to produce high-quality advertising. In particular, he and the other expats who dominated Scangroup's creative team[2] wanted to design an innovative "360° media campaign", which would span mainstream and social media (interview with Mike Miller, May 4, 2013). In addition to the satisfaction of doing "good work", RedSky creatives stressed that they could use these kinds of innovative campaigns to strengthen their personal portfolios, as well as allowing them to apply for international industry awards, such as Cannes (interview with Mark Fidelo, April 18, 2013; interview with Mike Miller, May 4, 2013). As Miller explained, this was invaluable to creatives in helping them to "brand" and "sell" themselves as individual media workers in a precarious, globalized marketplace (Deuze 2007). As Miller he put it,

> There's a *lot* of people out there struggling with their careers, you know, after the global financial crisis really hit advertising (…)

> As a creative, you're always wanting to do work that gets you noticed, that *brands* you as an innovative thinker, because, on a selfish note, erm, you know (....), you're looking after your own career…
>
> One of the best ways to do that is cause marketing because you can make [those campaigns], sort of (…) beyond the normal. So it's a very common thing in advertising, to use *pro bono* work to showcase how creative you can be.
>
> It's great because you don't have a commercial client breathing down your neck the whole time; you've got a bit more freedom. (interview, May 4, 2013)

Miller went on to argue that being based in a sub-Saharan country, at least in the short-term, was a good solution, because the emerging nature of African economies meant that it was the "last frontier for marketing…You can really make your name here" (interview, May 4, 2013). Miller asserted that his approach was not unusual, for apart from Fidelo, who had settled in Nairobi after a period of globe-trotting, the other creatives with whom he worked were part of an "incestuous" group of itinerant expats who moved wherever work opportunities presented themselves (interview, May 4, 2013). Indeed, by the time Miller was interviewed, he had already moved to Taipei, having previously lived in the UK, Germany, Australia, and Taiwan, as well as Kenya.

Therefore the way in which the KPO campaign was shaped by norms at Safaricom and amongst the expat staff at Scangroup meant that neither considered the possibility of lobbying the Kenyan government to expand the acute care services it already provided to paraplegics through the state-funded clinic in Nairobi (interview with Mike Miller, May 4, 2013). Instead, these actors focused on working together to find a way of raising enough funds for the NGO to build its own new rehabilitation clinic by creating a "saleable event" (Davis 2013, 2) in order to raise money from Kenyans living in Kenya and around the world via M-PESA. To be more specific, Fidelo, another creative at RedSky, had come up with a "concept" which he hoped would stimulate significant donations from Kenyan elites and diasporas, as well as eliciting smaller contributions Kenyan *wananchi*—the mass of poorer individuals who might only be able to afford to donate a one Kenyan Shilling a day (interview with Mark Fidelo, April 18, 2013).

This involved choosing a member of KPO to wheel himself from Nairobi to Johannesburg, over four thousand kilometers away: the distance an individual with spinal injuries had to travel to access long-term rehabilitation services. This "event" was made even more "saleable" (Davis 2013, 2) by using Squad Digital to track this person's progress using GPS technology in order to publish constant *Facebook* updates, Tweets, and embedded photo and video feeds: so causing a "social media storm" which Fidelo hoped would attract the attention of the national and international media (interview with Mark Fidelo, April 18, 2013).

Both Fidelo and Miller then set about finding a "saleable individual" to embed in this "saleable event" (Davis 2013, 2). This involved interviewing a number of possible candidates before selecting Zack Kimotho as the best KPO member for the job. This was because of his level of fitness and determination, but also because he was a black Kenyan, so helped the campaign allude to ideas of black African empowerment. In addition, Kimotho was "relatable" figure for most Kenyans, as Fidelo put it,

> He was a vet before he got shot and he's got two kids. But, you know, he's determined to live his life, and erm (…) that kind of thing was always going to go down well.
>
> Plus, you know, like a lot of people here, he's a very big-hearted fella and wanted to do something to help other people in his condition (…)
>
> And we thought it would be like a secondary er (…) *bonus* if we got somebody, you know (…) who's a good-looking guy. (interview, April 18, 2013)

So there were many different products being "sold" in this kind of cause-related marketing: Kimotho, KPO, the creatives at Scangroup who prepared the campaign, and M-PESA. But Kimotho appeared oblivious to this: stating only he was acutely aware that he had only been able to obtain rehabilitation services because of his privileged professional position, which meant that he was able to afford to travel abroad (interview, 26, April 2013). So, Kimotho said, he felt a strong sense of emotionally-charged moral responsibility, "in [his] heart", to help other paraplegics who "could not make it out" of Kenya to get the help they needed (interview, April 26, 2013).

Kenyan nationalism, Africa Rising narratives, and *The Observer*

Thus although the multimedia produced for this NGO campaign was not designed to be picked up by news outlets, it resonated with contemporary news values, as it was highly personalized, uplifting and had a clear human interest focus (Harcup and O'Neill 2017). Indeed, these expat advertising executives framed the campaign in ways which were designed to persuade media audiences that the key problem was Kimotho having to continue on his arduous, exhausting and dangerous journey. The campaign proposed that the solution to this problem was for audience members to "Bring Zack Back Home" by

donating enough money, via M-PESA, to enable a new paraplegic rehabilitation center to be built in Nairobi (interview with Mark Fidelo, April 18, 2013;
interview with Mike Miller, May 4, 2013).

This media campaign had many of the characteristics of popular forms
of post-humanitarian communication (Chouliaraki 2013). It emphasized the
playful capabilities of digital media; focuses on the positive, but low-intensity
emotions of audiences; and offered media audiences a simple and immediate
"solution" to the problem which could be expedited entirely through communications technology. As such, the "Bring Zack Back Home" campaign might
be expected to be detached from the traditional grand narratives, which link
emancipation to solidarity (Chouliaraki 2013, 9–15). However, despite the
domination of the campaign by the highly individualized commercialized
practices of largely white European and Australian expats, it was legitimized
by notions of Kenyan empowerment and collective self-help.

This was because "Bring Zack Back Home" was conceptualized as "capi-
talizing upon the success of the "Kenyans for Kenya" famine relief campaign"
(interview with Mark Fidelo, April 18, 2013). Indeed, Nick Thiong'o, the account manager at Ogilvy and Mather's office in Nairobi said that he believed
he had been appointed to deal with press enquiries because of his previous
experience on this campaign, which he said would enhance journalists' trust
in him (interview, March 27, 2013). Thiong'o then sought to develop this
association in journalists' minds by pitching the campaign to them in a very
similar manner: arguing that "we Kenyans shouldn't all the time rely on the
government or external donors...to solve problems for us." Thiongo is also a
black Kenyan, and thus was thought to be more appropriate by the creatives
running the campaign than using either a white Kenyan or an expat, given
the highly racialized discourse about economic empowerment, inclusion and
"African" self-help.

But this was not necessarily how journalists in the UK understood the
meaning and value of the campaign. Kenfrey Kiberenge, who is also a black
Kenyan, was on an internship at *The Observer* newspaper in London at the
time (interview, August 28, 2012). This was funded by the David Astor
Trust, which provides paid placements for promising East African journalists, in memory of a former *Observer* Editor (interview with Jim Meyer, David
Astor Trust, November 5, 2012). His friends in Nairobi forwarded him the
campaign via Facebook and Twitter: joking that they needed to start their
own campaign to "Bring Kenfrey Back Home." So he initially came across the
campaign as a kind of in-joke between friends.

But Kiberenge saw the campaign as having important political implications relating to matters of socio-economic injustice. As he explained,

> In Kenya, right now, we do not need to be spending huge amounts of public money to refurbish the parliament.
>
> We have malaria (…), HIV is killing people, cancer is killing people. People who have spinal injuries need a facility to treat them (…)
>
> But our leaders in Kenya, they can afford to fly to South Africa and America, many, many times if they need health treatment.
>
> One senior minister, she had breast cancer and another, a man, was treated for prostate cancer in America. How many Kenyans can afford the air ticket, let alone treatment in the best hospitals in the world?
>
> They fly out of the country because the public taxpayers' money will cover them for health insurance. But these are members of parliament and ministers who are supposed to be championing Kenyan health systems. They know Kenyan hospitals can't help them and they don't deal with it. They are cowards, these MPs and ministers.
>
> I'm looking at this campaign as a way of getting into some of these contradictions, and [the government's] poor priorities—just as a reminder that Kenyans deserve as good as their leaders. (interview, August 28, 2012)

Yet Kiberenge put very little of these political reflections in his pitch to the British editors at *The Observer*, the Sunday edition of *The Guardian* newspaper. This was because he was only an intern and he didn't think it would fit the editorial priorities and other norms shaping work at a UK organization, like the Guardian News Media. Kiberenge was right in this assumption, for reasons he did not fully comprehend at the time. As discussed in the previous chapter, NGO-provided material had begun to be much more acceptable throughout the organization, following the sponsorship of the Global Development section of *The Guardian* website by the Bill and Melinda Gates Foundation. Such material tended to privilege privatized and globalized approaches to international development—not state-driven ones. The Guardian News Media also took a strong digital-first approach to publishing, so that even the editor of the Sunday print edition cited company research about online algorithms showing that readers found human interest stories much more engaging than harder political stories (interview with Paul Webster, April 30, 2013).

But ultimately Kiberenge's ability to pursue the KPO story depended on the way in which the positivistic, national narratives of the Bring Zack Back Home campaign intersected with British journalists' efforts to respond to criticism about their negative and homogenizing coverage of the African continent. As Paul Webster, the Deputy Editor of the paper, explained, he gave Kiberenge permission to go ahead with the story because

When it comes to stories about Africa, we try and include as wide a range as possible so it's not all well, here's another story about a disastrous situation in an African country brought about through war or poverty or what have you.

Reflecting on media trends is part of our effort to have more varied coverage of the continent, which is itself extremely varied and going through some extraordinary, and often very positive, transformations. (interview, April 30, 2013)

In particular, Webster was intrigued by the way in which the Bring Zack Back Home campaign had gone viral, sparking a social media storm which had spread far beyond Kenya's borders. Indeed, senior editors were intrigued that a campaign for small, African NGO had managed to become a top trend on Twitter, under #BringZackBackHome. This social media phenomenon was seen in the senior editors' meeting as offering the paper a way to "do a new take on the spread of mobile phones in Africa", which were seen as "helping Africans to help themselves and each other in really exciting ways" (interview with Lucy Rock, November 23, 2012).

However, such a story was not judged to be sufficiently important or new to merit being a lead news story. Instead, it was used to fill a small slot on page three of the paper, which had become available late in the production cycle. As the duty editor explained, this position which was usually used for stories which were not really "hard news" but more "features...human interest or something cultural—just something different to throw in the mix" (interview with Lucy Rock, November 23, 2012).

Thus expatriate advertising creatives in Nairobi indirectly "sold" notions of African empowerment and progress to British journalists via social media. The duty news editor said that such a "'positive story'" would also help to sell The Observer, as a Sunday newspaper "cannot be all doom and gloom" (interview with Lucy Rock, November 23, 2012). In particular, Rock assumed that doing a story about "an African NGO's use of social media" would be "so different" to other forms of negative news coverage about the continent that it would help to differentiate the paper from its rivals, in print and online.

Yet Observer journalists did not run any checks to see if this was the case. Had they done so, they would have found that Kenya's The Standard (Standard-Digital 2012), Al-Jazeera (Greste 2012) and The New York Times (Gettleman 2012) had already covered the campaign. China's Xinhua news agency also covered it (Mutua 2012), as did BBC News Online (BBC 2012) and The Huffington Post (2012). Thus British journalists treated the material they saw on social media as if it were an "information subsidy" (Gandy 1982) which would help them differentiate their output from that of their rivals—but it was no such thing.

The lack of challenge which the KPO campaign posed to Anglo-American cultural norms and neoliberal market systems also deterred *Observer* journalists from scrutinizing the issues and values concerned. So they not only thought that it was a "light" news story, but also a "simple one (…) one of the most straightforward that we do actually" (interview with Lucy Rock, November 23, 2012). Indeed, the only independent work which Kiberenge was tasked with doing involved continuing to monitor social media feeds, calling the PR person for the campaign to get a higher resolution version of the photo he had already seen on social media, and interviewing Zack Kimotho himself by phone (interview with Kenfrey Kiberenge, August 28, 2012; interview with Lucy Rock, November 23, 2012).

The editor on duty that day didn't conduct any further checks herself because she did not want to offend the Kenyan intern, Kiberenge, by "breathing down his neck": stressing that she respected his editorial independence as a "fully fledged journalist" like everyone else at *The Observer* (interview with Lucy Rock, November 23, 2012). The paper had also merged the roles of the domestic and international news editor, which meant that she was not only very short of time, but she was also painfully aware of how inexperienced she was at covering African news. Indeed, she said that even a junior intern like Kiberenge would "know more about Kenya than I do".

The absence of any more rigorous research was problematic because it meant that journalists were not aware that the campaigners had no plans in place to enable them to do any more than build the clinic. They didn't know how they would fund the cost of equipment, pay the salaries of staff, or support the running costs of the building, so the ability of the campaign to deliver politically progressive effects was sorely limited. Finally, journalists were unaware that the NGO had important political links. The details of these political connections were clearly published on the NGO's website, although this information has since been removed. But in 2012, the site listed Ida Odinga as a member of KPO's advisory panel—the wife of the then Prime Minister, Raila Odinga.

Indeed, Wanyonyi, the head of KPO, stood as an MP for Odinga's party (the Orange Democratic Movement), less than six months later. He's now the MP for Westlands—the constituency in which Safaricom is based. Wanyonyi was active on Twitter in the run-up to the election, and during that period, and his account depicted him smiling in front of a "Bring Zack Back Home" poster. So he appears to have thought that the cultural and social capital amassed during the fundraising campaign would aid his candidacy. But although Wanyonyi agreed to be interviewed for the original research project (Wright 2014), he did not wish to be quoted in a book.

"Dramatizing reality"

Finally, journalists' uncritical use of the KPO photograph and the interpretative frame in which it was embedded was problematic because the KPO campaign—and journalistic stories about it—all depended upon Kimotho's determination to go "all the way" to Johannesburg if necessary (interview with Mike Miller, May 4, 2013). But by the time Kiberenge interviewed him on behalf of *The Observer*, Kimotho had already stopped his journey. Kimotho told Kiberenge that this was a temporary pause, because his health was suffering after two months on the road and Safaricom also needed to apply for a new fundraising license (interview with Kenfrey Kiberenge, August 28, 2012; interview with Zack Kimotho, April 26, 2013). Yet when I spoke to a senior executive at Safaricom, he said that those in charge of the campaign had decided not to resume because donations had tailed off (interview with Safaricom Executive, April 23, 2013). 73 million Kenyan Shillings had been raised—just over 700 thousand U.S. dollars. So Kimotho stopped his journey before he had raised even half of the campaign's financial target.

Moreover, no logistical plans, financial budgets, fundraising licenses or travel permits had ever been put in place to allow Kimotho to continue over the Kenyan border. This was because none of the senior figures at Safaricom or Scangroup had thought that Kimotho would need to go more than a week before enough money had been raised (interview with Safaricom Executive, April 23, 2013; interview with Mike Miller, May 4, 2013). Organizers claimed that the fundraising potential of the campaign had been undermined by the lack of mainstream media coverage inside Kenya after the main launch, as a political crisis had occurred which preoccupied Kenyan journalists: a helicopter crash which had killed the Internal Security Minister, his assistant and six others (interview with Safaricom Executive, April 23, 2013).

But it did not appear that Kimotho was ever made aware that he was taking part in a "pseudo-event" (Cottle and Nolan 2007, 866). He maintained that he had been asked to go all the way to Johannesburg (interview, April 26, 2013). Indeed, Kimotho stressed that he had fully intended to keep going until he had raised enough money to fund a new rehabilitation clinic, so he had felt deeply disappointed to return home. When those in charge of the campaign were challenged about why they had not made the nature of Kimotho's journey clearer, the Safaricom executive, replied using commercialized, "promotional" logic (Davis 2013). He said,

> In *hindsight*, we probably could have explained it better, like in a preamble before the launch, to say *this* is the idea and *this* is the intention. So we are just *dramatizing* it... like in advertising, it is just creative license!
>
> You know you have you see it on the TV; you see someone driving a Toyota and then starting to drive a BMW. It is a dramatization about how BMW is better. He doesn't *really* have a blonde wife and happy blue-eyed kids playing in the surf.
>
> It's not reality, but it's a *dramatization* (...) to move towards an objective. It is a mood, a goal, a feeling.
>
> In our case, that goal was to fundraise, yeah? (interview, April 23, 2013)

For these reasons, the KPO campaign involved very different media strategies to those employed by INGOs. The actors working on this campaign used social media in ways which attracted national and international journalists, but without having to spend time and money tailoring media content to individual outlets (Fenton 2010). They also worked according to promotional norms, rather than journalistic ones, which produced a very different kind of "media logic" (Cottle and Nolan 2007). Although this highly personalized media campaign fitted in easily with the priorities and assumptions of British journalists, its commercial creators did not share journalists' commitment to realism and truth-telling, which is usually central to the normative claims made about news (Wright 2011).

Instead, these commercial actors tended to describe news coverage as a form of "publicity" (interview with Safaricom Executive, April 23, 2013) or advertising "space" (interview with Mike Miller, May 4, 2013) donated by media owners. The lack of insight which journalists had into this epistemological mismatch was alarming, for even when the Deputy Editor at *The Observer* was made aware that the unattributed photo had been taken by advertising and marketing specialists working for an NGO campaign, he claimed that no serious harm had been done. His rationale for this was that the photo (reproduced overleaf) showed Kimotho in his wheelchair in front of a long road, so it was "obvious what it's about" (interview with Paul Webster, April 30, 2013). But even the photo itself was not what journalists took it to be—it was a still taken by an advertising executive during the filming of a staged TV advertisement (interview with Mike Miller, May 4, 2012).

Figure 8.1: Bring Zack Back Home campaign photo

Source: Mike Miller

So what was the article which arose from these production processes actually like? It was produced in 2012, at the height of the trend for "Africa Rising" narratives (Bunce 2017b) and journalists referred to the need to create different and more positive representations of the continent in their editorial deliberations. The article itself also draws from the visual, tonal, linguistic and framing repertoire of "Africa Rising" narratives. The image used depicts an open vista and a single, black individual, Zack Kimotho, who steadily returns the gaze of the viewer (Nothias 2014). The tone of the feature is also consistently upbeat, referring to "hope" three times, as well as focusing on a single, positive stock character: an individual "hero", who is determined to help himself and others (Orgad 2015). No mention is made of structural problems and contexts, including the economic injustices which motivated Kimotho, and Kiberenge's concerns regarding the Kenyan government's unwillingness to fund better health services.

But in other ways, the article does not fit the "Africa Rising" model because it makes no efforts to measure the continent's progress economically, or make positive predictions for its future (Nothias 2014). In fact it makes no reference to "Africa" at all—referring to Kenya and Kenyans throughout. Thus journalists appear to have blended some of the traits of the "Africa Rising" metanarrative with other positivistic narratives about national identity and social media. In particular, it is a Kenyan, rather than an "African" NGO, which is seen as providing the solution to the problem by "organizing the campaign". It is also members of the Kenyan "public", who are said to have "taken to social media to spread the word". So KPO is positioned within the article as being supported by Kenyans *en masse*, who are motivated by an ethics of collective self-help, economic empowerment and gift-giving, facilitated through Twitter.

Moreover, although the article privileges and naturalizes privatized solutions to suffering, celebrating an almost entrepreneurial spirit of self-help, it does not take a strong pro-business line (Bunce 2017b). No mention is made of ideas of Safaricom's engagement with the NGO through its CSR scheme and the only way that readers would become aware of the company's embedding of M-PESA in the campaign was if they clicked on the hyperlink to donate. The engagement of the expat creatives at Scangroup in the production process is also not referred to. Indeed, the photo is not even attributed to the advertising executive who took it for the KPO campaign, but is simply given the byline: "Zachary Kimotho sets out on his journey".

Moral economy: a coda

It's a fascinating case study, but why look at it through the lens of moral economy theory? Why not see the KPO campaign as a new form of cause-related marketing, which doesn't sell products to Northerners in order to "save" Africans, but which embeds people and products within *pro bono* marketing campaigns, in order to develop positive brand associations within sub-Saharan markets? As this chapter shows, the theory about cause-related marketing and "brand aid" is a decent place to start (Ponte *et al.* 2009; Richey and Ponte 2013). But moral economy theory helps us build a much more complex picture of the operation of cause-related marketing and CSR.

Specifically, it illuminates how and why exchanges occur between multiple groups, which bring about the interaction of many different economic goals, and notions of "the good" and "the just". These interactions involve actors' collective renegotiation of their different normative responsibilities and economic interests in ways which construct some symbolic boundaries to

WHO'S REPORTING AFRICA NOW?

do with branding products, people and countries. Yet at the same time they breached boundaries between different geographic locations, social groups and fields of activity (Rajak 2010). So moral economy theory helps us to challenge the assumptions often made by British journalists who think that African NGOs are somehow "simpler" and less commercialized than INGOs.

In particular, we start to see how small, sub-Saharan NGOs which lack the financial and cultural capital to make, commission and place multimedia on their own come to rely on other, more powerful parties. But in so doing, they become bound up with discursive struggles between different groups of elites over positivistic readings of "Africa", and the construction of sub-Saharan identities (Bunce *et al.* 2017; Gallagher 2015; Tuwei and Tully 2017). In this case, such struggles privileged normative ideas about grassroots communication, gift-giving, socio-economic inclusion and counter-hegemonic resistance, at the same time as furthering the economic and political interests of elites.

Much like the last chapter, this hypocrisy was shaped by the increasingly precarious nature of media work, including journalistic internships and the short-term contracts experienced by itinerant advertising and marketing professionals. Therefore, a moral economy perspective encourages us to move past overgeneralized dichotomies between "Africans" and "non-Africans". This chapter also acts as a warning to Northern journalists not to make naïve assumptions about the "simplicity" of multimedia provided by sub-Saharan NGOs, or their supposed lack of commercialism. Indeed, in their desire to avoid negative, homogenous and disempowering depictions of Africa, journalists appear to be seriously failing to scrutinize the nature of positivistic representations of sub-Saharan countries, as well as who benefits from them (Sen 2010).

Even though commercial actors were marginalized in this feature, their capabilities were greatly enhanced by their involvement in the production process. Advertising executives said they were able to seek new, blue-chip clients by including this news coverage in their personal and organizational portfolios as evidence of their international reach. Safaricom was better able to build the brand of M-PESA in relation to value-laden ideas about the relationship of Kenyan nationalism to communications technology and grassroots empowerment. Meanwhile, *Observer* journalists were better able to fill a gap arising late in the production process relatively quickly and easily, despite their lack of specialist staff. But at the same time, they were able to address their normative ideas about their responsibility to produce more diverse kinds of journalism about Africa.

The Kenyan intern was able to use his experience on prestigious British broadsheets to get a good job on a leading broadsheet back home in Nairobi. Whilst the KPO campaign appears to have given its leader, Tim Wanyoni, some cultural and social capital in Westlands, which may have contributed to his success in the Kenyan general election six months later. At the time of writing, the NGO also benefited from being able to use Wanyonyi's parliamentary office as its administrative center. Wanyoni continues to be the NGO's Executive Chairman—even though this raises questions about the extent to which KPO can be said to be a non-governmental organization.

But although the campaign heightened national and international awareness of the plight of Kenyan paraplegics, it does not appear to have enhanced the ability of the poorest Kenyans to obtain rehabilitation services yet. A Tweet was sent by the Bring Zack Back Home campaign in August 2013 saying that construction of the clinic was underway. But when a journalist was sent by Kenya's *The Standard* paper to follow up on the story in 2016, they found that the clinic was nothing more than an empty shell covered with tall grass, which seemed to indicate that little construction work had taken place for some time (Mahungu 2016). No international media outlets reported on this story, even though it was disseminated via social media. So the way in which the KPO campaign privileged the promotional norms of advertising over truth-telling seems to have had long-lasting and problematic effects: inhibiting the ability of international news audiences to scrutinize the nature, values and effects of CSR in Kenya (Sen 2010).

Notes

1. The "M" in M-PESA stands for mobile, and *pesa* is the Swahili word for money.
2. Fidelo and Miller were both white British men and the others in charge of the campaign were a white German woman, a white Australian man, and an Indian man who had been living in Sydney: the film crew were white Kenyans but were working according to the instruction of the expats.

References

Aker, Jenny C., and Isaac M. Mbiti. "Mobile Phones and Economic Development in Africa." *The Journal of Economic Perspectives* 24, no. 3 (2010): 207–32.
Banerjee, Subhabrata Bobby. "Corporate Social Responsibility: The Good, the Bad and the Ugly." *Critical Sociology* 34, no. 1 (2008): 51–79.

BBC. "The Man Pushing Himself across Africa." *BBC*, August 21, 2012. http://www.bbc.co.uk/news/world-africa-19316955.

Beer, Arnold S. de. "News from and in 'the Dark Continent': Afro-Pessimism, News Flows, Global Journalism and Media Regimes." *Journalism Studies* 11, no. 4 (2010a): 596–609.

———. "Looking for Journalism Education Scholarship in Some Unusual Places: The Case of Africa." *Communicatio: South African Journal for Communication Theory and Research* 36, no. 2 (2010b): 213–26.

Biney, Ama. "Is Africa Really Rising?" News. *Pambuzuka News*, September 4, 2013. http://www.pambazuka.org/en/category/features/88748.

Buku, Mercy W., and Michael W. Meredith. "Safaricom and M-PESA in Kenya: Financial Inclusion and Financial Integrity." *Washington Journal of Law, Technology & Arts* 8 (2013): 375.

Bunce, Mel. "The International News Coverage of Africa: Beyond the 'Single Story'." In *Africa's Media Image in the 21st Century: From the "Heart of Darkness" to "Africa Rising,"* edited by Mel Bunce, Suzanne Franks, and Chris Paterson, 17–29. London: Routledge, 2017a.

———. "Africa Rising: The International News Media and the Rebranding of Africa as the 'Final Investment Frontier.'" International Communication Association, San Diego, 28 May 2017b.

Bunce, Mel, Suzanne Franks, and Chris Paterson. *Africa's Media Image in the 21st Century: From the "Heart of Darkness" to "Africa Rising."* London: Routledge, 2017.

Chouliaraki, Lilie. *The Ironic Spectator: Solidarity in the Age of Post-Humanitarianism.* Cambridge: Polity Press, 2013.

Cottle, Simon, and David Nolan. "Global Humanitarianism and the Changing Aid-Media Field: Everyone Was Dying for Footage." *Journalism Studies* 8, no. 6 (2007): 862–78.

Davis, Aeron. *Promotional Cultures: The Rise and Spread of Advertising, Public Relations, Marketing and Branding.* Cambridge: Polity Press, 2013.

Deuze, Mark. *Media Work.* Cambridge: Polity, 2007.

Dogra, Nandita. *Representations of Global Poverty: Aid, Development and International NGOs.* London; New York: I.B. Tauris; Palgrave Macmillan, 2012.

Fanta, Emmanuel. "Mirrors, Mimicry and the Spectre of a Failed State: How the Government of Ethiopia Deploys Image." In *Images of Africa: Creation, Negotiation and Subversion*, edited by Julia Gallagher, 86–104. Manchester: Manchester University Press, 2015.

Fenton, Natalie. "NGOs, New Media and the Mainstream News: News from Everywhere." In *New Media, Old News: Journalism & Democracy in the Digital Age*, edited by Natalie Fenton, 153–68. London: Sage, 2010.

Fisher, Jonathan. "Image Management in East Africa: Uganda, Rwanda, Kenya and Their Donors –." In *Images of Africa: Creation, Negotiation and Subversion*, edited by Julia Gallagher, 63–85. Manchester: Manchester University Press, 2015.

Flamenbaum, Rachel. "A "New Ghana" in "Rising Africa"? In *Africa's Media Image in the Twenty-First Century: From the Heart of Darkness to Africa Rising*, edited by Mel Bunce, Suzanne Franks, and Chris Paterson, 116–125. Abingdon, OXON: Routledge, 2017.

Franks, Suzanne. *Reporting Disasters: Famine, Aid, Politics and the Media.* London: Hurst Publishers, 2013.

Gallagher, Julia. "Theorising Image—A Relational Approach." In *Images of Africa: Creation, Negotiation and Subversion*, edited by Julia Gallagher, 1–20. Manchester: Manchester University Press, 2015.

Gandy, Oscar H. *Beyond Agenda Setting: Information Subsidies and Public Policy*. Norwood, NJ: Ablex, 1982.

Gettleman, Jeffrey. "Kenyan Paraplegic Is on a 2,500-Mile Journey by Wheelchair." *The New York Times*, June 29, 2012. http://www.nytimes.com/2012/06/30/world/africa/kenyan-paraplegic-is-on-a-2500-mile-journey-by-wheelchair.html.

Greste, Peter. "Wheeling across Africa for the Disabled," June 27, 2012. http://www.aljazeera.com/video/africa/2012/06/201262785348857806.html.

Gruber, Verena, and Bodo B. Schlegelmilch. "MNEs' Regional Headquarters and Their CSR Agenda in the African Context." *International Marketing Review* 32, no. 5 (2015): 576–602.

Hamann, Ralph, and Nicola Acutt. "How Should Civil Society (and the Government) Respond To 'Corporate Social Responsibility'? A Critique of Business Motivations and the Potential for Partnerships." *Development Southern Africa* 20, no. 2 (2003): 255–70.

Harcup, Tony and Deirdre O'Neill. "What is news? News values revisited (again). *Journalism Studies* 18, no. 12 (2017): 1470–88.

Hawk, Beverly, G. *Africa's Media Image*. New York, Westport, CT, London: Praeger, 1992.

Idemudia, Uwafiokun. "Corporate Social Responsibility and Development in Africa: Issues and Possibilities." *Geography Compass* 8, no. 7 (2014): 421–35.

Jack, William, and Tavneet Suri. "Mobile Money: The Economics of M-PESA." National Bureau of Economic Research, 2011. http://www.nber.org/papers/w16721.

Kamau, Macharia, and Luke Anami. "Corporate Social Responsibility Now a Priority." *Standard Digital News*, December 21, 2010. http://www.standardmedia.co.ke/article/2000025099/corporate-social-responsibility-now-a-priority?articleID=2000025099&story_title=corporate-social-responsibility-now-a-priority&pageNo=3.

Kiberenge, Kenfrey. "Wheelchair Hero's 2,485 Mile Journey to Raise Funds for Kenya's First Spinal Injury Rehab Unit." *The Observer*, August 19, 2012. https://www.theguardian.com/world/2012/aug/19/zachary-zack-kimotho-kenya-wheelchair

Kimani, Wanja. "Reimagining Ethiopia: From Campaign Imagery to Contemporary Art." In *Images of Africa: Creation, Negotiation and Subversion*, edited by Julia Gallagher, 167–87. Manchester: Manchester University Press, 2015.

Kuper, Andrew, and Jocelyn Kuper. "Serving a New Democracy: Must the Media 'speak Softly'? Learning from South Africa." *International Journal of Public Opinion Research* 13, no. 4 (2001): 355–76.

Lugo-Ocando, Jairo, and Patrick O. Malaolu. "Africa—That Scar on Our Face." In *Blaming the Victim: How Global Journalism Fails Those in Poverty*, Jairo Lugo-Ocando, 85–103. London: Pluto Press, 2014.

Magee, Helen. *The Aid Industry—What Journalists Really Think*. London: International Broadcasting Trust, 2014.

Mahungu, Jacqueline. "Did Zack Come Back Home?" *The Standard*, January 3, 2016. https://www.standardmedia.co.ke/article/2000186919/did-zack-come-back-home.

Marthoz, J.P. "African Conflicts in the Global Media." In *The Media and Conflicts in Central Africa.*, edited by Marie-Soleil Frère, 221–39. Boulder, CO: Lynne Rienner, 2007.

McKay, Claudia, and Michelle Kaffenberger. "Rural vs Urban Mobile Money Use: Insights From Demand-Side Data." *CGAP*, January 23, 2013. http://www.cgap.org/blog/rural-vs-urban-mobile-money-use-insights-demand-side-data.

Morawczynski, Olga. "Saving through the Mobile: A Study of M-PESA in Kenya." In *Advanced Technologies for Microfinance: Solutions and Challenges: Solutions and Challenges*, edited by Arvind Ashta, 148–64. Hershey, NY: Business Science Reference, 2010.

Muthuri, Judy N., and Victoria Gilbert. "An Institutional Analysis of Corporate Social Responsibility in Kenya." *Journal of Business Ethics* 98, no. 3 (2011): 467–83.

Mutua, Peter. "Roundup: Kenya's Disabled Persons to Set up Spinal Injury Rehab Center." *China.org.cn*, August 18, 2012. http://www.china.org.cn/world/Off_the_Wire/2012-08/18/content_26269735.htm.

Nguyen, Katie. "Kenya Watchdog Probes Safaricom Ownership." *Reuters*, March 19, 2007. https://www.reuters.com/article/idUSL1943856320070319.

Nothias, Toussaint. "Definition and Scope of Afro-Pessimism: Mapping the Concept and Its Usefulness for Analysing News Media Coverage of Africa." *Leeds African Studies Bulletin* 75 (2013a): 54–62.

———. "'Rising', 'Hopeful', 'New': Visualizing Africa in the Age of Globalization." *Visual Communication* 13, no. 3 (2014): 323–39.

———. "How Western Journalists Actually Write about Africa." *Journalism Studies* (2016): 1–22. DOI: 10.1080/1461670X.2016.1262748

———. "Mediating the Distant Other for the Distant Audience: How Do Western Correspondents in East and Southern Africa Perceive Their Audience?" In *Africa's Media Image in the Twenty-First Century: From the Heart of Darkness to Africa Rising*, edited by Mel Bunce, Suzanne Franks, and Chris Paterson, 73–82. Abingdon, OXON: Routledge, 2017.

Nyabola, H. Nanjala. "Media Perspectives: Social Media and New Narratives: Kenyans Tweet Back." In *Africa's Media Image in the Twenty-First Century: From the Heart of Darkness to Africa Rising*, edited by Mel Bunce, Suzanne Franks, and Chris Paterson, 113–15. Abingdon, OXON: Routledge, 2017.

Omwansa, Tonny K., and Nicholas P. Sullivan. *Money, Real Quick: The Story of M-PESA*. London: Guardian Books, 2012.

Opuku-Owusu, Stella. *What Can the African Diaspora Do to Challenge Distorted Media Perceptions about Africa?* London: African Foundation for Development, 2003.

Orgad, Shani. "Underline, Celebrate, Mitigate, Erase: Humanitarian NGOs' Strategies of Communicating Difference." In *Humanitarianism, Communications and Change*, edited by Simon Cottle and Glenda Cooper, 117–32. New York: Peter Lang, 2015.

Ponte, Stefano, Lisa Ann Richey, and Mike Baab. "Bono's Product (RED) Initiative: Corporate Social Responsibility That Solves the Problems of 'Distant Others.'" *Third World Quarterly* 30, no. 2 (2009): 301–17.

Rajak, Dinah. "'HIV/AIDS Is Our Business': The Moral Economy of Treatment in a Transnational Mining Company." *Journal of the Royal Anthropological Institute* 16, no. 3 (2010): 551–71.

Rice, Xan. "Kenyan Inquiry into Vodafone's Mystery Partner." *The Guardian*, February 16, 2007. https://www.theguardian.com/media/2007/feb/16/kenya.citynews.

Richey, Lisa Ann, and Stefano Ponte. *Brand Aid: Shopping Well to Save the World*. Minneapolis, MN: University of Minnesota Press, 2011.

———. "Brand Aid: Values, Consumption, and Celebrity Mediation." *International Political Sociology* 7, no. 1 (2013): 107–11.

Roxburgh, Charles, Norbert Dörr, Acha Leke, Amine Tazi-Riffi, Arend van Wamelen, Susan Lund, Mutsa Chironga, *et al.* "Lions on the Move: The Progress and Potential of African Economies | McKinsey & Company," 2010. http://www.mckinsey.com/global-themes/middle-east-and-africa/lions-on-the-move.

Schorr, Victoria. "Economics of Afro-Pessimism: The Economics of Perception in African Foreign Direct Investment." *Nokoko* 2 (2011): 23–62.

Scott, Martin. "Marginalized, Negative or Trivial? Coverage of Africa in the UK Press." *Media, Culture & Society* 31, no. 4 (2009): 533–57.

———. "The Myth of Representations of Africa." *Journalism Studies* 18, no. 2 (2017): 191–210.

Sen, Amartya. *The Idea of Justice*. London: Penguin, 2010.

Standard Digital News. "Bring Zack Back Home," June 13, 2012. http://www.standardmedia.co.ke/ktn/video/watch/2000058360/-bring-zack-back-home.

Thrall, A. Trevor, Dominik Stecula, and Diana Sweet. "May We Have Your Attention Please? Human-Rights NGOs and the Problem of Global Communication." *The International Journal of Press/Politics* 19, no. 2 (2014): 135–59.

Tuwei, David, and Melissa Tully. "Producing Communities and Commodities: Safaricom and Commercial Nationalism in Kenya." *Global Media and Communication* 13, no. 1 (2017): 21–39.

Visser, Wayne. "Revisiting Carroll's CSR Pyramid." In *Corporate Citizenship in Developing Countries*, edited by Esben R. Pedersen and Mahad Huniche, 29–56. Copenhagen: Copenhagen Business School, 2006

Visser, Wayne, and Nick Tolhurst. *The World Guide to CSR: A Country-By-Country Analysis of Corporate Sustainability and Responsibility*. Sheffield: Greenleaf Publishing, 2010.

Wainana, Binyavanga. "How to Write About Africa," Vol. 92, 91—6. London; New York: Granta, 2005.

Wright, Kate. "A Quiet Revolution: The Moral Economies Shaping the Use of NGO-Provided Multimedia in Mainstream News about Africa." Goldsmiths College, University of London, 2014.

———. "Reality without Scare Quotes: Developing the Case for Critical Realism in Journalism Research". *Journalism Studies* 12, no.2 (2011):156–71.

· 9 ·

CONCLUSION

Debates about NGOs' role in the production of African news have been heated. But until now, there has been little systematic research which allowed us to identify its effects on journalism, NGO-work and the representation of the continent. Instead, critics have tended to hypothesize on the basis of limited evidence: drawn either from their personal experiences as practitioners (Beckett 2008; Frontline 2008, 2015) or from studies of aid agencies' participation in the coverage of famines and other crises (Franks 2010, 2013; Lugo-Ocando and Malaolu 2014). This book was designed to address that lacuna: analyzing journalists' use of multimedia provided by a range of different NGOs during a very different kind of news-making period.

This was a "quiet" news week, during which no joint appeals, major conferences or parliamentary sessions were planned which related to a sub-Saharan country. This should not be read as a "normal", "average" or "representative" news week, as there is no such thing in international news production. Instead, I aimed to develop general theory by exploring contrasting cases, which enabled me to test and refine existing hypotheses and working assumptions. In so doing, I also aimed to avoid the kinds of negative cherry-picking which tend to characterize other studies about the media representation of the continent (Scott 2017).

This book is unusual for a further three reasons. First, it avoids the fragmentation of previous research, by attending to the perspectives and practices of multiple actors collectively involved in specific production processes. In so doing, I move beyond organizational boundaries: attending not only to the structuring of journalists' and NGO-workers' interactions with one another, but also interrogating the roles played by other kinds of actors whose agency is not normally addressed in research about NGO-journalist relations. In particular, I illuminate the crucial roles played by freelancers who work for International NGOs (INGOs) and news outlets, as well as syndicating material back and forth between them. But my decision to move beyond the newsrooms and press offices in the Global North also led me to interrogate the ideas, values and practices of those based in sub-Saharan countries, including field workers, business executives, advertising and PR professionals.

Secondly, this book is unusual because it moves the study of NGO-journalist relations in a new theoretical direction: tackling the highly normative character of these kinds of news production using moral economy theory. This involved interrogating why and how multiple actors legitimized economic exchanges with one another as "good work" (Hesmondhalgh and Baker 2011). But I also analyzed how economic and normative values interacted with one another within production processes, and how this related to actors' renegotiation of their responsibilities to others. In so doing, I found that actors' conceptualization of "good work" in their respective areas changed, in ways which had broader implications for the boundaries between journalism, NGO-work and other kinds of activities (Carlson and Lewis 2015; Powers 2015).

Finally, this book is unusual in using moral economy theory to make explicit the grounds upon which I based my own evaluations of these kinds of news-making. This involved taking a decision to move away from conducting normative evaluation according to democratic theory, which is often the default position in journalism studies (Powers 2017). However, I have argued that this risks reinforcing ethnocentric bias and effacing important critical debates about the political effects of NGO work. So, I took an alternative approach to normative evaluation: examining which and whose capabilities were enhanced as a result of news production processes, in so far as these could be ascertained. In this way, I hope to have made a broader contribution to the theorization of media effects: relating this in an interdisciplinary manner to African studies, international development, sociology, and the cultural and creative industries.

How and why do journalists use NGO-provided multimedia in news about Africa?

NGOs are not only important providers of news about Africa during famines, floods and other crises, they also regularly contribute multimedia to news outlets during "quiet" news periods. A total of 23 items containing NGO-provided images and video were found in a single week, with NGOs providing material for the majority of items about the continent in some news organizations. Indeed, NGO material may be used more frequently during quiet news weeks than at some other times, as journalists said they often held this content back to use during such news-making periods, when they knew that little material about the continent would be commissioned by their own news desks.

Like Franks (2010, 2013), I found that widespread cost-cutting in the news industry was a powerful causal factor shaping journalists' decision to use this material in the coverage of Africa. Specifically, news staff were struggling to sustain their African coverage in the face of repeated reductions in staffing, bureaux, travel and commissioning budgets. The rapid growth in digital news production was also found to have dramatically increased journalists' workload, making it much harder for them to source new stories and double-check facts (Fenton 2010b). But what was even more important was the speeding up of journalistic work and the implementation of cost-cutting as role-merging: both of which squeezed out specialized forms of journalistic production (Örnebring 2016). This left journalists struggling to find ways of differentiating their news outlet from competitors.

So journalists' use of NGO material did not involve inclusive and egalitarian forms of "networked journalism", including User Generated Content (Beckett 2008; Beckett and Mansell 2008). Instead, it tended to be shaped by journalists' efforts to cope with the loss of in-house specialism, including different kinds of knowledge, skills and contacts. Yet the ways in which news staff conceptualized the problems caused by their loss of specialism, and what they regarded as appropriate responses to those problems, were powerfully shaped by the collective norms of their individual news outlets.

These collective norms were not static but were continually re/produced in a dynamic fashion through journalists' agentive decision-making within daily news production practice. Journalists' deliberations about the choices they had to make involved them responding to the many different obligations exerted by the specific political economies of their news outlets: for example, through modes of national regulation, media ownership, forms of political and market positioning, as well as through relations with audiences, advertisers and sources. Thus the political economies of news organizations and the collective norms of news outlets were recursively linked to one another in ways which produced considerable heterogeneity.

However, three broad trends were observed. The first of these involves the production of media items which were not lead news stories. Journalists experienced most difficulty in producing these kinds of items, as managers assumed that they merited even less time, attention and planning than leads, so allocated resources accordingly. Thus the kinds of media items incorporating NGO material in a quiet week tended to be very different to the media items using it to represent major famines, hurricanes and other disasters. (Cooper 2009, 2011; Cottle and Nolan 2007; Franks 2008a, 2008b, 2013). Rather than being leading news stories, the media items in this study tended to be lower-ranking, in all but the most resource-poor news outlet. These lower-ranking items included many different genres, such as relatively long investigative news reports, off-agenda features and blogs, as well as visually-driven genres, such as photo slideshows.

The production of these lower-ranking items involved a second trend: that is, journalists' use of NGO material in order to compensate for their loss of geographic specialism. This loss was viewed as highly problematic by journalists working at many different "serious" or "quality" news outlets. This was because they saw offering a wide range of international coverage, which differed from that of their competitors, as an essential part of the normative value of their outlet. Those working for Public Service Broadcasters, like journalists at *BBC News Online* and *Channel 4 News*, also had specific statutory obligations to offer a wide range of international news coverage, which carried strong moral connotations for them (Bennett *et al.* 2015). Whilst other, left-wing journalists at *The Guardian*, *The Observer* and *The Independent* spoke of their professional, moral and political responsibility to find ways of continuing to represent poor and vulnerable people around the world.

So expressing a commitment to cover a wide range of African places played an important, symbolic role in journalistic discourse. Indeed, it may almost be said to be a form of virtue signalling to the journalistic self and others. An interesting comparison can be made here with the coverage of Latin America and the Caribbean—which is now even less frequent than journalism about sub-Saharan countries (GAP 2016; Nothias 2016). Yet the journalists in this study did not talk about the need to increase or improve their coverage of

Latin America or the Caribbean with the same normative fervour. It is easy to assume that the normative values attached to African coverage in British news organizations are driven by the country's colonial legacies—a kind of lingering "White Journalists' Burden", if you will. But in voicing concerns about African coverage, the journalists in this study also tried to express a far more progressive aspiration: that is, their intention to find ways of preventing many of the world's poorest areas from being excluded from the "map" provided by international news (Gasher 2009; Gasher and Klein 2008).

Nevertheless, it is important to stress that journalists' efforts to continue to offer regular coverage of Africa, which differed from that of their immediate rivals, had important market implications. It helped to position news outlets as "quality" products in a fiercely competitive market: so helping them to pursue new, and potentially lucrative, audiences overseas (Bicket and Wall 2009; Wall and Bicket 2009). The representation of poor, non-elite places and people in Africa tended to be particularly important in online journalism: helping to build consumer loyalty in a very competitive international market, by constructing imagined relations between the news brand and value-laden ideas about globality and humanity (Denčik 2013; Roosvall 2013).

These uses of NGO-provided material were also shaped by a third trend: that is, journalists' efforts to cope with their loss of visual specialism. It is no secret that photojournalists have been disproportionately affected by repeated waves of redundancies (Anderson 2014; Bardan 2015; Klein-Avraham and Reich 2016; Mortensen 2014). Even the largest news organizations in this study had no more than two photojournalists on staff, both of whom were not available to go on assignment full-time. Photo commissioning budgets have plunged and picture editors have also left news outlets in their droves: with many of them moving from news outlets to INGOs, including one of the participants in this study. The loss of both geographic and visual specialization can therefore be seen as a kind of double blow to "serious" or "quality" journalism.

This double blow was deeply problematic for journalists working for legacy broadsheets, who were trying to sustain their reputation for disseminating high quality news photography. But journalists working for online news sites struggled even more because they required far higher volumes of visually appealing and technically polished images. So it is perhaps unsurprising that the most dominant form of NGO media used by journalists was the photograph. NGO-provided photos were found in all but one of the instances of NGO-provided multimedia found in African coverage, with the remaining item being a video clip. But, again, journalists were not simply looking for more photos. That could have been more easily accomplished by taking them from the wire and photographic agency feeds, which most major news organizations subscribe to (Caple 2013). Instead, journalists were looking for pictures which would visually differentiate their news outlet from its competitors. They tended to do this by using INGO photographs which were different aesthetically from other kinds of news images, often reflecting on how beautiful they were.

Many of these images had been commissioned by INGOs from freelance photojournalists, who also worked for news outlets. These individuals were known and well-respected by staff journalists: indeed, some of them were even former colleagues. Trust in these freelancers' professionalism, experience and ethical approach often helped persuade news staff to accept INGO-commissioned images. Although journalists who had experienced freelancers faking material tended to be more reassured by INGOs' editorial supervision of these casual media producers. Either way, using INGO-commissioned images tended to be regarded as a pragmatic solution to the problem of funding photojournalism. This was because the privileging of multiskilling and role-merging within news outlets meant that most news staff understood very little about the construction of visual meaning. So they did not consider using INGO-commissioned photos as involving a serious reduction in their editorial control.

Instead, journalists tended to see photos as illustrating what they had written: locating interpretative control in words not visual images, even when the genres they were creating were obviously visually-driven, like photo slideshows. For these reasons, it was common for journalists to accept photos from INGOs, but it was very unusual for them to accept a written article by an NGO-worker. Only the most time and resource-poor outlet in this study did so, with most news staff in other outlets maintaining that "it's ok to take [and NGO's] pictures, but not their words." Yet this approach greatly underestimates the interpretative influence exerted by INGOs through images.

Their failure to understand the importance of visual meaning also inhibited journalists from considering the ethical and political implications of aestheticizing Africans' suffering (Sontag 2003). In particular, journalists did not seem to understand that they were privileging a specific kind of gaze structured by the norms and tastes of socio-economic elites in Europe and North America. This was because the photos commissioned by INGOs tended to be heavily influenced by high-brow traditions of social documentary photography, whose beauty stems from intertextual allusions to other elite aesthetic traditions, including painting by European Old Masters (Gupta 1986). At best, this might be seen as a way of mitigating Otherness: offering kind of aesthetic bridge to the lives of strangers, whose experiences were very different to those of media audiences, instead of using the time-worn device of the mediating aid-worker or celebrity (Orgad 2015). However, these ways of seeing and being seen were structured by the aesthetic tastes of Northern elites (Bourdieu 1984). So the visions of global moral order constructed within these news texts were not those of the people being represented (Cheah 2013; Denčik 2013).

Nevertheless, using photos provided by sub-Saharan NGOs didn't necessarily lead to greater authenticity, diversity or alterity. This was because journalists would only accept images which they thought were of sufficient technical and aesthetic quality, and these did not tend to be produced by the most alternative groups. Indeed, the NGO-provided images which were most popular with journalists in this sample were actually produced by commercial marketing and advertising executives, many of whom were expats, who were working the Kenyan Paraplegic Organization as part of a Corporate Social Responsibility (CSR) scheme.

Even when journalists were informed that the image they had used had been taken from a staged TV advertisement, they still insisted that their use of NGO-provided material was unproblematic. This was partly because they persisted in conceptualizing still images as relatively simple or straightforward media. But they were also convinced that it was progressive to feature stories about Africans' empowerment through social media and mobile phones, drawing explicitly on "Africa Rising" narratives (Bunce et al. 2017; Nothias 2014).

So we can start to talk about the shift of geographic and visual specialization away from news organizations and towards INGOs, which are able to employ highly skilled and experienced specialists on a paid or voluntary basis. Journalists' use of the multimedia produced by these specialists was geared towards trying to differentiate their news output, especially lower-ranking media items, from their competitors. Yet journalists' deliberations about what constituted that "difference" were very limited. Although many were aware of criticisms about the stereotypical and disempowering news about the continent, the pressurized, multi-skilled nature of their work meant that they tended to think of creating "different" representations of Africa in a very narrow ways. These involved providing coverage of less frequently covered African countries; publishing beautiful images; and/or creating upbeat features about African agency, rather than negative news about African victimhood.

Theoretical implications: obligation subsidies, freelancing, and moral economies

By using NGO multimedia, journalists were clearly able to reduce the amount of time and money they spent on the specialized kinds of news production they needed to differentiate their news output from their competitors. But these cases show that it is too simplistic to think of these exchanges as "information subsidies" (Gandy 1982) or even "churnalism" (Davies 2008). This is because journalists didn't just use any material from any NGO which would save them time and money. Instead, they only used material from NGOs which helped them create specific media genres which they valued, but found increasingly challenging to produce in-house.

In particular, journalists at legacy news outlets, with a largely domestic audience, tended to privilege INGOs able to subsidize their production of relatively long (and seemingly correspondent-led) forms of investigative or campaigning journalism. Whilst online journalists, who were focused on securing larger global audiences, tended to privilege INGOs able to help them create popular human interest genres with more immediate human interest appeal, such as blogs and photo slideshows. Although a broader trend was also observed which involved print and online journalists using material from small sub-Saharan NGOs to try and differentiate their African output from what they assumed was the overwhelmingly negative and stereotypical output of others (Scott 2017).

It is tempting to see journalists' legitimizing rationales for these exchanges as *post hoc* justifications. But journalists' normative values often modified economic imperatives relating to cost and time savings, and they usually discussed these modifications in terms of meeting their responsibilities to others. The most striking example of this was at *Channel 4 News*, where journalists felt a strong moral obligation to the victims of a massacre they had witnessed in the Democratic Republic of Congo, as well as having statutory obligations regarding the provision of original, independent journalism. Both of these formal and informal responsibilities worked together to shape journalists' use of very small amounts of INGO-commissioned material in an expensive and time-intensive production process, spanning ten months. This included extensive health and safety preparation, an (aborted) field trip and attempts to commission other sources.

Meanwhile, at *BBC News Online*, journalists' statutory obligations regarding impartiality, which were translated in the Corporation's Editorial Guidelines and managerial directives, meant that journalists insisted on being given large galleries of images, so that they could exercise editorial control via picture selection and ordering. This was the case even though the INGOs who contributed the photos were able and willing to provide BBC journalists with finished slideshows. Journalists at the BBC and elsewhere also conducted their own interviews or, at the very least, rewrote photographic captions, in order to respond to their obligations regarding critical independence.

Furthermore, when journalists sought out material from small sub-Saharan NGOs, they did so in ways which were shaped by a mixture of moral, political and professional obligations. So they were willing to spend time contacting such organizations via social media to request high resolution images. Yet this was much more laborious than using pictures from big wealthy INGOs, whose press officers regularly gave news editors access to large galleries electronically.

Thus journalists' use of NGO material was not only driven by the need to make time and cost savings: instead, it involved complex considerations regarding their statutory obligations and/or their sense of moral, political or professional responsibilities to others. In addition, most of this material was not offered to journalists by NGO press officers, but arrived at the news outlet indirectly, usually via freelancers. These freelancers were sometimes paid by news outlets for the material they had produced even though this had been commissioned by INGOs. Indeed, on one occasion, journalists insisted on paying freelancers for their video footage when they knew that the INGO had purchased redistribution rights, so there was no legal need to do so. Thus freelancing had important normative, as well as operational, functions which related closely to the renegotiation of the boundaries between journalism and NGO-work.

In order to understand this, we need to look more closely at how these forms of liminal freelancing worked. The freelancers in this book tended to take commissions from both INGOs and news outlets—sometimes consecutively, and sometimes at the same time. They also syndicated material from one kind of organization to another, either formally, through a third party agent, or via more informal arrangements (Wright 2016a, 2016b). These boundary-crossing practices were enabled by the cultural capital which these freelancers possessed within journalism as specialists. They were particularly highly regarded by journalists who were uneasy about the growing dominance of multiskilling and generalism in their own newsrooms.

Journalists' respect for freelancers' specialist skills and knowledge tended to go hand in hand with their strong belief in freelancers' ethical integrity as journalists, including their critical independence. Indeed, journalists' belief in freelancers' independence and their use of corresponding formal mechanisms—such as payments and copyright agreements—enabled news staff to conceptualize themselves as doing direct deals with well-respected freelancers, rather than taking multimedia from INGOs. Interestingly, INGO-workers took a similar approach: defending themselves against charges of unduly influencing news outlets, by appealing to the supposed "independence" of freelancers.

Yet the repeated indirect exchanges with INGOs via freelancers were found to predispose journalists to accept INGOs' framing of events: increasing the likelihood that such frames would be perceived as consonant with journalists' own strategic goals, production practices and normative values. So these liminal forms of freelancing deepened the synergies between the INGO and news outlet through repeated, indirect exchanges, whilst enabling journalists and INGO-workers to disavow too close a connection with one another (Wright 2016b). Such processes of disavowal enabled both sides to navigate tensions between their various responsibilities, but were particularly important to journalists with statutory obligations to remain independent.

For all of these reasons, I argue that it is less useful to think of NGOs providing journalists with "information subsidies" (Gandy 1982), than it is to think of them offering journalists "obligation subsidies". I use this term to refer to journalists' ability to negotiate their multiple responsibilities more cheaply and rapidly than they might have done otherwise, rather than simply seeking the greatest time and cost savings. This is because the nature of these responsibilities meant that journalists might still invest some of their own time and money in production processes— including investing in processes which sustained the appearance of editorial independence from NGOs. Thus the notion of "obligation subsidies" takes us towards a much more complex engagement with boundary work (Carlson and Lewis 2015).

In particular, the concept of "obligation subsidies" helps us challenge some of the fundamental assumptions underlying theory about "information subsidies" (Gandy 1982) and "churnalism" (Davies 2008). This is because this concept helps us to understand that NGOs can (and do) exert powerful and long-lasting forms of interpretative influence even when contacts with journalists are indirect; when contributed material forms a relatively small proportion of a report; and when journalists engage actively, and even rigorously, in their own reporting processes. The importance of freelancing in so many of these cases also draws into question the presumptions of NGO intentionality, which underpin much of the related work on PR. For liminal forms of freelancing not only meant that freelancers could pitch multimedia to news outlets which had not been targeted by the NGO, they could also pitch material which the NGO had never intended to be placed in news coverage at all.

In particular, this book examines a case in which freelancers pitched on material which was originally commissioned by Internews for a project report, aimed at institutional donors in North America and Europe. Although executives at Internews were at pains to stress that they commissioned many different kinds of donor reports, a senior manager explained that she sometimes used this kind of "quasi-journalistic" reporting because donors' shrinking funding cycles made it difficult to carry out traditional modes of evaluation, involving staged target setting and planning for sustainability over a period of several years. She also stressed that many institutional donors, including representatives from some of the most experienced bilateral and multilateral agencies, often ignored dry academic reports. Yet, she said, they reacted in a much more positive, emotional manner to media exhibitions featuring the kinds of "high-end" photo-journalism which used to be found in "quality" magazines.

This case appears to be part of a growing trend which deserves greater critical attention, involving the intersection of news reporting and project/donor reporting. This is because some INGO managers, such as those at Human Rights Watch, said they now commission freelancers to go on "dual purpose" trips: creating some kinds of imagery suitable for news audiences, and others more suitable for exhibiting to government donors and/or private trusts and foundations. Whilst other INGO managers, such as those at Save the Children, said that they took a more flexible approach: seeing what material freelancers produced on trips, and then considering reusing it for a variety of different purposes. This included using it in project reports, in marketing literature, or exhibiting it at dinners held for blue chip commercial donors.

So although we can start to move forward by using the concept of "obligation subsidies", ultimately we need to conceptualize NGO-journalist relations as being embedded in much more complex, pluralistic and dynamic exchanges. In this book, I have suggested that moral economy theory provides us with a suitable critical framework with which to do this: enabling us to take seriously the highly normative nature of journalist-NGO interactions, whilst still attending to the recursive relationship between such normative values and multiple, unequally structured political economies.

Here, I have focused on the ways in which moral economy theory illuminates how journalists' re/division of editorial labor is being reshaped by their changing perceptions of who and what they are accountable for, as well as dependent upon (Sayer 2007). Such a critical framework is especially useful in addressing why and how journalists' use of NGO material did not involve a whole-hearted capitulation to market forces, nor did it involve consistent, normatively-driven resistance to them. Rather, journalists' use of NGO-provided material can be seen as being simultaneously "in and against the market" (Goodman 2004, 893).

Previous research conducted from a moral economy perspective has been invaluable in illuminating how the statutory obligations of Public Service Broadcasters relate to powerful moral values (Bennett *et al.* 2015). Whilst studies on the cultural and creative economies helped me to understand how freelancing is structured in relation to individualistic, entrepreneurial norms in a difficult and precarious job market, as well as in relation to older ideas about craft, cooperation, community and public value (Banks 2006; Lee 2012). What my work adds to theirs are understandings about the ways in which moral economies shape exchanges between different kinds of journalists, NGOs and others, which construct particular kinds of imagined relations across national boundaries.

In so doing, these kinds of exchanges are also deeply imbricated in the renegotiation of boundaries between different fields of activity. This boundary work is complex, involving the masking or disavowal of dependence upon NGOs, at the same time as facilitating and legitimizing further boundary-crossing activity. The strategies involved in this work make it very difficult to assess NGO influence through the analysis of texts alone. Moreover, NGO influence is not always exerted in the ways that scholars have come to expect. It may operate through indirect as well as direct exchanges; misunderstandings as well as shrewd evaluations; unintended and unacknowledged effects, as well as deliberate and carefully planned strategies.

How and why do NGOs provide multimedia about Africa to news outlets?

NGO-workers justified their involvement in news production using a range of different normative ideas, which often involved notions of inclusivity and empowerment. For example, the Kenyan NGO and their commercial allies saw themselves as having a responsibility to resist imperialistic constructions of Africans as passive victims; whilst those working for international aid agencies often expressed a sense of obligation to give "voice" to marginalized African people. But NGOs' and INGOs' engagement in media production could be far from inclusive or empowering—so the effects of NGO-workers' engagement in news production were not as progressive as they claimed.

In the Kenyan case, notions of Corporate Social Responsibility focused on businesses' engagement in financial giving and voluntary work; ignoring more complex issues, like financial probity, which might have been more relevant in the aftermath of an international fraud scandal. These value-laden ideas of responsibility interacted with ideas of Kenyan solidarity and self-help, in order to construct forms of commercial nationalism (Tuwei and Tully 2017) which simultaneously marketed the NGO, a commercial cash transfer platform, and expat advertising executives. The fundraising campaign which emerged was visually slick, technically sophisticated, and raised large amounts of money from social and mainstream media audiences. But it ended up disempowering and marginalizing lower-ranking NGO members, who were not happy with the approach which their corporate partners took.

Meanwhile, major INGOs often leaned heavily on low-ranking field staff and in-country partners to secure the participation of local people. Both press officers and their managers reasoned that these field workers were more likely to have pre-existing social relationships with local people, and would be more sensitive to cultural norms, expectations and responsibilities. But although some field workers saw themselves as being part of local and ethnically-based networks of obligation relating to the provision of subsistence (Scott 1976), last-minute changes, overstuffed field trips and misunderstandings about the challenges posed by oral interpretation severely limited the potential progressiveness of this approach. Field workers' own economic interests and their previous experience of donor reporting could also lead to them framing media participation to local people in ways which limited what they could say. Indeed, these factors led to field-workers inadvertently misinforming, or even coercing, local people, despite the existence of detailed organizational policies about informed consent and the protection of vulnerable people.

INGO-workers gave far more consideration to their production of visual imagery than their enablement of voice. The privileging of visual media was found to have been partially shaped by longstanding traditions relating to visual activism (McLagan and McKee 2012); fierce ethical debates about INGOs' use of visual imagery (van der Gaag and Nash 1987); and the importance of visual imagery in organizational branding and marketing. Most INGOs had internal guidelines governing their production and use of images, which participants referred to far more often than the guidelines issued by umbrella bodies (Lidichi 1999). However, these organizational guidelines tended to be rather lacking in detail: outlining the visual styles thought to be in keeping with the INGOs' external image, and urging staff to take more responsibility to avoid the routine use of graphic and sensationalistic images of passive, suffering bodies. None dealt with the problematic dominance of Northern aesthetic traditions in any detail.

Indeed, NGO-workers usually saw their use of Northern traditions of photo-journalism and social documentary photography as far more progressive than sensationalistic "aid porn": arguing that these kinds of aestheticization granted African subjects more dignity, as well as having powerful associations with advocating for social change (Strauss 2005). Such visual traditions depend upon powerful, value-laden ideas about the skilled, experienced and "concerned" photographer (Capa 1968), but these kinds of specialists do not come cheap. Although INGOs are known to recruit former journalists, picture and film editors as staff (Cottle and Nolan 2007; Fenton 2010a), most of their funding is restricted to particular projects or appeals. So it was much easier for even the wealthiest INGOs to buy in freelancers as and when they needed them, than to recruit them to staff positions.

Rather than using this as an opportunity to try out media producers from sub-Saharan countries, many of whom are freelance (Bunce 2010; Jayawardane 2017; Richardson 2017), INGO-workers tended to commission American and European freelancers with whom they had social connections and cultural similarities.This was even found to be the case when an INGO had an explicit remit regarding media participation. Rather than using the in-country journalists whom the INGO had trained and worked with over a period of several years, its communication managers flew in freelancers from over twelve thousand kilometers away. The decision to use these kinds of freelancers was therefore not just shaped by budgetary factors, but also by time pressures and informal social connections, as well as the desirability of using media producers whose work was likely to appeal to Northern media audiences.

For their part, these specialized freelancers regarded INGO commissions favorably because they helped them make financial ends meet, at a time when news organizations were reducing the number of commissions they give out, as well as failing to raise their rates in line with inflation (Brown 2010). But freelancers didn't just accept INGO commissions for economic reasons. Rather, they valued INGO commissions because INGOs funded longer field trips than most news organizations could afford, as well as offering them far more logistical support (see also Grayson 2014; Hallas 2012). This made for a more enjoyable working life and gave them far more health and safety protection than other forms of freelancing (Jaakkola 2015; Palmer 2015). Moreover, as INGO trips tended to be planned further in advance than news trips, taking

INGO commissions made it easier for freelancers with partners and family responsibilities to fulfil their caring obligations to others (Wright 2016b).

But what was most important to these freelancers was the way in which collaborating with INGOs allowed them to address their often passionately-felt normative responsibilities to distant others. In particular, by spending more time with their subjects, these freelancers believed that they could produce images which were more worthwhile and meaningful (Campbell 2007). Freelancers then tended to link this normative difference to the belief that INGOs allowed them more creative freedom as respected specialists. So they saw working for INGOs as "good work" in many different ways (Hesmondhalgh and Baker 2011).

However, although INGOs offered freelancers significant amounts of workplace autonomy, rarely offering explicit directions to media producers on the job, they offered them far less creative autonomy than freelancers, and staff journalists, realized (Hesmondhalgh and Baker 2011). Specifically, INGOs exerted considerable amounts of interpretative influence by selecting freelancers whose aesthetic and normative approaches complemented their own. NGO-workers also arranged subjects' media participation in particular ways and controlled briefing and image selection processes. INGOs were also found to exercise significant amounts of interpretative influence through seemingly casual conversations about practical arrangements, some of which were held on planes or in jeeps, whilst accompanying freelancers to field sites.

As warm working relations had already been established between INGO workers and freelancers by that point, freelancers didn't usually perceive these chats as impinging upon their autonomy. Instead, tensions were more likely to arise during image selection processes, when photographers disagreed about which shots to send to news editors. Yet, when these editorial disagreements did occur, they tended to be diffused by freelancers' perceptions of INGO picture and film editors as fellow specialists, well-versed in the norms and demands of specific media genres, in comparison with multiskilled news editors, who understood little about their craft.

Precarious forms of media production also shaped the boundary-crossing which took place between the fields of NGO-work, commercial PR, advertising and marketing in the Kenyan case. These were not facilitated by liminal forms of freelancing, but by a journalistic internship and the short term contracts of itinerant advertising and marketing expats. These were clearly very different kinds of media workers and the NGO in question had far less power in the production process, because NGO-workers were not paying for the services of casual media

producers. However, much like freelancers, the intern and the advertising executives all chose to engage in media production with NGOs as they thought that
this allowed them greater creative freedom than they would have experienced
otherwise, as well as greater recognition from others in their respective fields.
This in turn allowed them to seek future opportunities in an increasingly competitive international job market. So researchers need to pay far more attention to
the opportunities and restrictions experienced by different kinds of casual media
workers in their mediation of the relationship between NGOs and news outlets.

Theoretical implications: mediated advocacy, news cloning, and media logic

Although the exchanges which NGOs had with news outlets were facilitated and legitimized by casual media workers, it is important that we don't
over-generalize about the effects of this because NGOs adopted very different
media strategies. Like Orgad (2013), I found that the approaches taken by
international aid agencies could be split into two broad camps, pertaining to
the "chemical" and "alchemical" traditions of humanitarianism, although this
division was often quite messy and contested.

Save the Children UK is a good example of a "chemical" aid agency because it focuses on providing immediate relief to those suffering in humanitarian crises. This aid tended to conceptualized by the INGO's press officers
as "charity", with financial giving being a matter of personal moral virtue or
benevolence (Lindström 2016). The media strategies adopted by Save the
Children also came closest to the pattern described by Powers (2014), as its
press officers tended to target popular media because of their commitment to
educating the public about the existence of suffering, in order to prompt them
to give financially. Indeed, the INGO was sometimes criticized by other aid
workers for being overly commercialized.

However, even Save the Children did not prioritize attracting new donors outside of major appeals. Instead, its press officers were more concerned
with consolidating their relationship with existing donors and/or raising
their organizational profile. These activities were believed by press officers
to be consonant with long-term fundraising aims. But they were also seen as
furthering advocacy goals, which involved NGO-workers' passionately felt
sense of responsibility to raise awareness of the existence of particular forms
of suffering—rather than explaining or contextualizing it in any great detail.

Such press officers were not just former journalists (Fenton 2010a), but particular kinds of former journalists: those with experience of freelance, magazine and lifestyle journalism. All of these actors were used to pitching items with immediate, emotive appeal, so perceived their roles in aid agencies as a continuation of their previous careers. Indeed, they frequently stressed the virtue of drawing upon their transferrable skills, knowledge and professional contacts to generate maximum revenue during fundraising appeals.

Outside of major fundraising appeals, Save's press officers turned their attention to creating engaging, but less emotionally intense, forms of visual media—often contributing galleries of photos to online news outlets. These images capitalized on online journalists' need for "clickable", interactive multimedia: using a strong human interest focus to draw attention to the long-running issues facing those who had been displaced by fighting or other crises. However, this media strategy necessitated making editorial compromises which were sometimes unpopular with others in their organization, who took different approaches to the kinds of education which should be carried out through media production.

Indeed, one of the most surprising things about this study was quite how organized and wide-ranging challenges to the press office could be. At Save, tensions over news production not only existed between fundraising and advocacy teams (Orgad 2015), they even extended to those in charge of delivering aid. Nevertheless, press officers were able to co-opt the work of their more radical colleagues because of the broader moral economy in which they all worked. This economy not only involved aid-workers' dependence on public fundraising in ways which privileged targeting mass audiences, it also legitimized such an organizational strategy using powerful, normative ideas about moral virtue and "value for money" (Shutt 2012).

In contrast, a smaller cluster of "alchemical" aid agencies (Orgad 2013) were found to be committed to exposing and challenging the structural causes of suffering in detail. This involved them targeting prestige domestic outlets with niche audiences, such as broadsheets, to try and place long-form investigative or campaigning news reports, which involved far greater contextualization. Christian Aid was a good example of this kind of agency, as it invested a considerable amount of time and energy in investigative research and interviewing. But although the organization was desperately in need of money, and although the INGO's senior managers were more interested in populist approaches, or conceptualized the organization's engagement in media production in terms of egalitarian partnerships, its Head of News was far more oriented towards socio-economic elites. Specifically, he targeted niche media, such as broadsheets, in order to try and influence policy-makers and professional readers whom he thought had more power to effect change.

This finding challenges Powers' work (2014) to some extent, as it shows that there may not be a straightforward split between aid agencies and human rights organizations. Rather, some of those working for alchemical aid agencies may have more in common with human rights organizations, which are better known for pursuing these kinds of elite-oriented media strategies (Powers 2014). However, it is fair to say that the human rights workers in this study, from Human Rights Watch, had a far more precise idea of which policy-makers they wanted to influence and how this influence might be exerted. It is also fair to say the normative values in circulation at Human Rights Watch and Christian Aid were very different: with the former drawing on ideas of entitlement under international law, whilst the latter was more heavily influenced by liberation theology.

Nevertheless, the similarities between the media strategies adopted by "alchemical" aid agencies and human rights organizations may be worth investigating further because these INGOs attracted similar kinds of former journalists. These were former bureau chiefs, senior producers or correspondents with extensive experience of reporting on profoundly unequal conflicts abroad—most frequently in Bosnia. So they had very different professional backgrounds to the former journalists working for "chemical" aid agencies. Rather than conceptualizing their roles in NGOs as a continuation of their career, involving transferrable skills, knowledge and contacts, these former journalists described it in terms of disruption, disorientation and even trauma.

Specifically, these former journalists saw their experiences of reporting in deeply unequal wars as transforming their normative perspectives and creating within them a deep unease with the norms of mainstream journalism. In particular, they pilloried commercially-driven forms of journalism, which privileged speed and entertainment over time-consuming forms of research, travel and interviewing. So these former journalists approached mediated advocacy in a different way to former journalists working for "chemical" aid agencies. This involved them constructing forms of knowledge which simultaneously challenged, and were complicit in, the time-saving, reversioning practices they decried. Thus I argue that it is not sufficient to see former journalists as introducing "media logic" (Altheide and Snow 1979, discussed in Cottle and Nolan 2007) or "news cloning" into NGOs (Fenton 2010a). Instead, we need to examine which

kinds of former journalists are recruited by which kinds of INGOs, as well as
which kinds of news values they bring with them, and, potentially, react against.

Likewise, "media logic" (Cottle and Nolan 2007) and related ideas about
the "mediatization" of NGO-work (Jones 2017) aren't sufficiently detailed
analytical tools to help us understand why leading figures at the Kenyan
Paraplegic Organization were willing to participate in the construction of a
pseudo-event, or why Internews utilized quasi-journalistic approaches to project reporting. After all, commissioning high-end magazine photojournalism
to consolidate relations with American and European institutional donors
is a very different kind of activity to constructing a commercial marketing
campaign in order to generate donations from Kenyans via social and mobile
media. In addition, these two cases both highlight the need to move past
scholars' current fixation on mainstream news audiences as the only targets of
NGOs' engagement in multimedia production: considering its potential uses
and effects in a far more pluralistic and nuanced way.

What I hope to have demonstrated here is that moral economy theory
can provide the critical framework needed to do this: enabling scholars to
explore the structured interactions of journalists, NGOs and others, without
marginalizing the agency, conflict and messy compromises which are often
involved. In particular, moral economy theory helps us to address the highly value-laden nature of such exchanges, including conceptions of "good
work" (Hesmondhalgh and Baker 2011), in ways which don't presuppose
the existence of a stable, coherent ideology. Instead, moral economy helps
us to explore much more mixed and dynamic effects: illuminating how and
why different forms of normative contestation and hybridization may occur,
which have implications for the reproduction of boundaries between organizations and fields, and for the ability of news media to enhance or constrain
the abilities of others.

Effects

But how do we use moral economy theory to interrogate these effects? I have
argued that a moral economy perspective can be used to attend to the ways
in which exchanges between journalists, NGO-workers and others partially disembed actors from their organizational and field-specific contexts, and
partially re-embed them in new exchange–relations with one another (Sayer
2001). These new exchange relations tend to enhance the abilities of par-

ticipants to respond to their multiple obligations to others—although some abilities of some actors were clearly enhanced far more than others. These kinds of exchange-relations also tend to have a momentum of their own: generating new, value-laden obligations, which necessitate actors renegotiating their previous responsibilities in new ways.

Such new responsibilities tend to involve forms of normative hybridization (Bennett *et al.* 2015), which were most apparent when repeated exchanges between similar kinds of journalists and INGOs took place. So, for example, journalists at *Channel 4 News* who used more than one kind of multimedia provided by Human Rights Watch, employed freelancers who also worked for human rights organizations, and benefited from briefings and journalistic awards given by Amnesty International. Over a period of time, through these cumulative exchanges, they had come to regard public service broadcasting as including human rights journalism. This involved them reworking their responses to their statutory obligations regarding impartiality, as well as reconceptualizing their moral responsibilities as involving witnessing to a global public.

At the same time, communications managers at Human Rights Watch, who engaged in repeated exchanges with public service and broadsheet journalists, had come to see themselves as engaging in "proper reporting". They defined this in opposition to commercially driven approaches, arguing that they therefore had much in common with public service broadcasters and other kinds of "quality" news outlets. Yet this involved them reconceptualizing their responsibilities to victims of human rights abuses in ways which privileged targeting elite media, rather than simply publishing research reports or witnessing on their behalf in legal cases. So both human rights workers and Channel 4 journalists described each other as engaged in similar kinds of activities.

However, even one-off exchanges could influence longer-term shifts within the collective norms of NGOs and news organizations. For instance, an isolated incident of *The Independent on Sunday* accepting a full double page spread from Christian Aid was highly influential in a senior news editor's reconceptualization of professionalism: leading to him supposing that there should be "far more scope for that sort of thing" in the future. Getting the article accepted also strengthened the position of the NGO's Picture Editor and Head of News in internal arguments about the collective norms which should shape the organization's communications strategy: enabling them to continue to privilege particular kinds of professionalism over other approaches. This in turn enabled them to resist pressure from immediate managers to focus on more populist outlets, in accordance with fundraising objectives, as well as pressure from senior managers, who wanted them to engage in more collaborative, egalitarian forms of media-making.

Understanding how these forms of partial disembedding and re-embedding operate is, I would argue, crucial to understanding the nature of the "trust" between particular sets of NGOs and journalists (Franks 2008a, 2008b), in ways which go beyond simple allegations of "favoritism" (Frontline Club 2015). Although another key factor in the construction of this trust is the network of informal, interpersonal relations which exists between NGOs and news outlets. These relations tend to be mediated via freelancers with geographic proximity, existing social connections and cultural similarities to key actors, so they tend to entrench insularity. Yet the political effects of this insularity were rarely reflected upon by participants—and was largely hidden from news audiences.

Indeed, NGO-provided multimedia was not clearly attributed in half of the examples in the broader sample: a phenomenon which was shaped by the involvement of freelancers, but also by the highly pressurized nature of news production, which has made errors more common. So whilst these forms of news-making enhanced the abilities of media producers to respond to their various obligations, they tended to inhibit the ability of news audiences to scrutinize the values shaping news texts (Sen 2010). Nevertheless, journalists' use of NGO-provided multimedia did have some progressive effects. Human rights groups, freelancers and public service journalists worked together to expose lies (Miller 2012), whilst "alchemical" aid agencies provided detailed explanations of the structural causes and contexts of suffering (Hogg 2012). Both of these progressive effects involved INGOs' engagement in the production of investigative or campaigning news reports.

However, both were also negative news items about crises in sub-Saharan countries, which have previously been seen as very harmful to African people (Lugo-Ocando and Malaolu 2014). Yet neither made use of time-worn clichés about "darkness", "chaos", "madness" in relation to the conflicts they portrayed, nor did they articulate their causes in terms of "tribalism". They did not treat Africa as a homogenous whole, or make negative predictions about the fate of the whole continent (Nothias 2013). Moreover, although both news stories focused on the need for Northern intervention, they did not portray people living in sub-Saharan countries as helpless and silent victims (Duffield 1996; Kennedy 2009). Indeed, the journalists and NGO-workers involved in the production of these items took pains to mention and/or depict the coping strategies of African individuals and groups.

One of the main ways in which journalists and NGO-workers did this was to include quotes from African subjects about their experiences, thoughts and feelings. Many of the portrayals of Africans' coping actions were fleeting, superficial and highly personalized. However, there were some instances where sub-Saharan people were given the opportunity to discuss their views about the causes and contexts of their suffering, as well as suggesting possible treatments or solutions. Yet these more empowering frames tended to be reserved for "experts", such as legal prosecutors, politicians and the country directors of the INGO in question. So the extent to which these items gave voice to people who are neglected and disadvantaged was limited (Sen 2010)—although, they were no worse than the kinds of framing commonly found in journalists' own representations of Africa (Nothias 2016).

Rather than being more progressive than hard news, "softer" slideshows, blogs and "positive" or upbeat features had somewhat less to recommend them. Using the material provided by NGOs enabled the depiction of a wider range of African places and people than might otherwise have been achieved by journalists alone. That very visibility may have a protective function: helping to raise awareness of the existence of some forms of suffering (Sen 2010). Many quotes from sub-Saharan subjects were used in these piece. Indeed, one was solely the (interpreted) voice of a South Sudanese boy, as even the interviewer's questions were cut out. But although there were instances where sub-Saharan people were able to mention their political views and coping strategies, this was rare, and the main thrust of the quotes involved subjects' personal feelings and experiences, in order to add greater human interest.

It is possible that such human interest pieces may enable more effective fundraising in the long-term. So these media items may enhance others' basic capabilities in future, including their ability to be free from hunger and to access relevant medical facilities (Sen 2010). However, the problem with these kinds of news production was that they tended to involve other kinds of effects, which were the very opposite of what actors involved in production processes claimed. Normative rationales involving transparency and mediated dialogue were used to produce closed representational systems, which inhibited more radical criticism of privatized structures and funding processes. Efforts to educate news audiences about the failings of the aid system, and to illuminate the agency of local people, resulted in an aid agency inadvertently exploiting a vulnerable child.

Finally, rationales about resisting imperialistic oppression were used by expat creatives to marginalize the lower-ranking members of an African NGO, and raise thousands of dollars from ordinary Kenyans to build a clinic which no one ever had any plans to run. Indeed, it is important to stress that rather than aiding public reasoning by providing more diverse or alternative perspectives, the production process involving this small, sub-Saharan NGO appears to have been the most harmful of all. This is because it marginalized the truth-telling function of news, fundamentally undermining its ability to enable scrutiny of the values and interests in question (Sen 2010).

So I wanted to write this book to challenge the assumption that accepting material from a wider range of NGOs would necessarily improve the openness, inclusivity and social engagement of journalism. However, my intention here is not to single out individuals and groups to blame, as participants were usually well-intentioned and working under intense pressure. Indeed, I appreciate their candor and admire their willingness, in many cases, to take on board constructive criticisms. Given the high ideals associated with both journalism and NGO-work, I think it is also realistic to expect that real-world production processes will fall short of normative standards—at least to some degree.

But I do think it is important to highlight the dangerous effects of a combination of broad structural trends. These are the changing nature of project funding in NGO-work, the growth in precarious forms of media production, and difficulties with news funding: all of which are interacting with one another to produce significant changes in the coverage of Africa. I have found that these changes risk further marginalizing the perspectives of those who are already disadvantaged, whilst claiming to empower them. This is because these production processes continue to concentrate interpretative power in the hands of journalists, former journalists and other elites. They therefore tend to entrench elite representational traditions and globalized, privatized approaches to defining the problems of sub-Saharan countries, as well as relevant actors, judgements, contexts and solutions. Thus although some forms of NGO material may some progressive effects, I do not think that NGO content is an adequate substitute for regular, well-funded and rigorously researched journalism about Africa.

Where next?

So where should research in this area go next? In this book, I have developed moral economy theory to help us better understand how moral, political and economic factors work together to produce the "trust" underpinning complex exchange-systems, which cut across geographic borders as well as boundaries between different fields of activity. This trust is clearly tenuous and unstable, as there are tensions and conflicts, as well as complementarities, between the normative values of multiple actors, and their related responsibilities to others.

Indeed, one of the most surprising findings of this study has been how difficult it can sometimes be for NGOs and journalists to work together, even though they are structurally predisposed to do so by changes in their mutual political economies, and by the movement of staff and freelancers between news and non-governmental organizations. But even when such exchanges are short–lived or involve relatively small amounts of content, they can still have significant effects not only on the framing of media texts, but also on actors' understandings of what it is to do "good work" in their respective areas of activity.

But how should such a model be used in future? I want to conclude by out-lining four potential areas for future research, although there are many other potential applications of moral economy theory. Perhaps the most obvious application of a moral economy model would be to explore the roles played by UN agencies and the International Committee of the Red Cross (ICRC) in media production. These large and important organizations have been rather marginalized within the current body of research, which tends to focus exclusively on NGOs. Nevertheless, the multimedia content of these organizations appeared frequently in satellite TV channels and news websites in my sample. It was also apparent from interviews with media producers that journalists and NGO communications officers monitored the media output of UN agencies and the ICRC closely, so these organizations are very much part of the same system of the same news ecosystem.

Likewise, moral economy theory could be used to explore the media pro-duction practices of different kinds of NGOs and activist groups in other sub-Saharan countries— many of whom work in partnership with internation-al aid agencies. I was very aware in my explorations of Malian and Kenyan organizations that I was only scratching the surface of what could be a rich and varied vein of study. Both kinds of research might then be enhanced by using a moral economy perspective to explore the connections between news-making and the growth in mediatized, or even quasi-journalistic, forms of donor reporting to private foundations, bilateral and multilateral agencies. In this way, we might generate new insights into changes in the construction of knowledge and accountability within humanitarian, human rights and/or international development work.

A third, neglected area which begs for further exploration involves the workings of the Emergency Appeals Alliance, which not only includes the UK's Disaster Emergency Committee (DEC) but also sister organizations in other countries, including Japan, Sweden and Germany. Little is known about the kinds of exchanges which these kinds of umbrella bodies have with one another, with their respective, in–country news organizations, and with the new, US-based Global Response Emergency Coalition, which was formed in 2017. Although we do know that the Global Response Coalition has taken a much more welcoming approach to commercial organizations, partnering with giants like Pepsico and Visa, as well as media organizations like Google and Twitter. Applying a moral economy perspective to such a topic seems likely to be useful in interrogating these multiple, cross-border exchanges, as well as helping to assess whether they produce a single, dominant "emergency imaginary" reliant on moral responsibility to the distant stranger (Calhoun 2010)—or whether many different, intersecting imaginaries are in operation.

This leads us towards a third, intriguing topic of study to which moral economy theory could be applied: that is, the increasingly common partner-ships formed between major aid agencies, news organizations and other kinds of commercial business. Aid agencies are increasingly forming partnerships with blue-chip donors, like Barclays Bank and the pharmaceutical giant, GlaxoSmithKline, as well as various private trusts and foundations (Cooper 2015; Jones 2017). But they are also teaming up with other kinds of businesses which specialize in sophisticated forms of media production, in order to en-gage in new forms of fundraising. These include game development firms like Bohemia Interactive, which recently worked with the ICRC to develop the *Laws of War* bolt-on to the PC game, *Arma 3*, including giving share of the profits from the sale of the package to the aid agency. Virtual Reality produc-tion companies, like RYOT and Within (formerly Vrse), have also begun to work with NGOs and UN agencies to create sophisticated VR documentaries, which are regularly used at fundraising galas and diplomatic conferences, as well as being incorporated within news websites. Yet we still know very little about the values and practices shaping these kinds of complex production processes, or what their effects might be.

However, a moral economy perspective teaches us to look beyond the dazzling world of big money and high tech in order to interrogate which (and whose) capabilities are enhanced, and which (and whose) capabilities are constrained by such production processes. So above all, I would like to encourage researchers to use the model I have developed here to illuminate the decision-making of those represented in the media produced by NGOs, UN agencies and other activist groups. Scholars and practitioners currently know far too little about the values and perspectives shaping the deliberative processes of these vital media actors (Warrington and Crombie 2017).

Thus we risk making erroneous assumptions about the kinds of obligations which those portrayed believe themselves to have, the capabilities which they are (and are not) able to exercise in production processes, as well as the effects that media participation has upon them. Therefore my main hope is that the model of moral economy theory I have developed here can be used to address these questions in future. In so doing, we might be able to better explain and evaluate the complex interactions of multiple actors working in various organizations, fields, locations and cultures around the world.

References

Anderson, Fay. "Chasing the Pictures: Press and Magazine Photography." *Media International Australia* 150, no. 1 (2014): 47–55.

Banks, Mark. "Moral Economy and Cultural Work." *Sociology* 40, no. 3 (2006): 455–72.

Beckett, Charlie. *SuperMedia: Saving Journalism so It Can Save the World*. London: Blackwell, 2008.

Beckett, Charlie, and Robin Mansell. "Crossing Boundaries: New Media and Networked Journalism." *Communication, Culture and Critique* 1, no. 1 (2008): 92–104.

Bennett, James, Nicola Strange, and Andrea Medrado. "A Moral Economy of Independent Work? Creative Freedom and Public Service in UK Digital Agencies." In *Media Independence: Working with Freedom or Working for Free*, edited by James Bennett and Niki Strange, 139–58. London, New York: Routledge, 2015.

Bicket, Douglas, and Melissa Wall. "BBC News in the United States: A Super-Alternative News Medium Emerges." *Media, Culture & Society* 31, no. 3 (2009): 365–84.

Bourdieu, Pierre. *Distinction: A Social Critique of the Judgement of Taste*. London: Routledge & Kegan Paul, 1984.

Brown, Maggie. "Why Freelancing is Now a Dead Loss." *British Journalism Review* 21, no. 1 (2010): 61–65.

Bunce, Mel. "'This Place Used to Be a White British Boys' Club': Reporting Dynamics and Cultural Clash at an International News Bureau in Nairobi." *The Round Table* 99, no. 410 (2010): 515–28.

Bunce, Mel, Suzanne Franks, and Chris Paterson. "Introduction: A New Africa's Media Image?" In *Africa's Media Image in the Twenty-First Century: From the Heart of Darkness to Africa Rising*, edited by Mel Bunce, Suzanne Franks, and Chris Paterson, 1–14. London, New York: Routledge, 2017.

Calhoun, Craig. *The Idea of Emergency: Humanitarian Action and Global (dis) Order*. New York: Zone Books, 2010.

Campbell, David. "Geopolitics and Visuality: Sighting the Darfur Conflict." *Political Geography* 26, no. 4 (2007): 357–82.

Capa, Cornell. *The Concerned Photographer* Vol. 1 First edition, second printing edition. New York: Grossman Publishers, 1968.

Caple, Helen. *Photojournalism: A Social Semiotics Approach*. New York: Palgrave Macmillan, 2013.

Carlson, Matt, and Seth C. Lewis, eds. *Boundaries of Journalism: Professionalism, Practices and Participation*. London, New York: Routledge, 2015.

Cheah, Pheng. "'The World is Watching': The Mediatic Structure of Cosmopolitanism." *Journalism Studies* 14, no. 2 (2013): 219–31.

Cooper, Glenda. "When the Lines between NGO and News Organization Blur'. Special Report: NGOs and the News." *Nieman Journalism Lab*, December 21, 2009. http://www.niemanlab.org/2009/12/glenda-cooper-when-lines-between-ngo-and-news-organization-blur/.

———. *From Their Own Correspondent? New Media and the Changes in Disaster Coverage: Lessons to Be Learned*. Oxford: Reuters Institute for the Study of Journalism, 2011.

———. "'Give Us Your F****ing Money': A Critical Appraisal of the TV and the Cash Nexus." In *Humanitarianism, Communications and Change*, edited by Simon Cottle and Glenda Cooper, 67–78. New York: Peter Lang, 2015.

Cottle, Simon, and David Nolan. "Global Humanitarianism and the Changing Aid-Media Field: Everyone Was Dying for Footage." *Journalism Studies* 8, no. 6 (2007): 862–78.

Davies, Nick. *Flat Earth News: An Award-Winning Reporter Exposes Falsehood, Distortion and Propaganda in the Global Media*. London: Chatto and Windus, 2008.

Denčik, Lina. "What Global Citizens and Whose Global Moral Order? Defining the Global at BBC World News." *Global Media and Communication* 9, no. 2 (2013): 119–34.

Duffield, Mark. "The Symphony of the Damned: Racial Discourse, Complex Political Emergencies and Humanitarian Aid." *Disasters* 20, no. 3 (1996): 173–93.

Fenton, Natalie. "NGOs, New Media and the Mainstream News: News from Everywhere." In *New Media, Old News: Journalism & Democracy in the Digital Age*, edited by Natalie Fenton, 153–68. London: Sage, 2010a.

———. ed. *New Media, Old News*. London: Sage, 2010b.

Franks, Suzanne. "Aid Agencies: Are We Trusting Too Much?" *The Political Quarterly* 79, no. 3 (2008a): 316–18.

———. "Getting into Bed with Charity." *British Journalism Review* 19, no. 3 (2008b): 27–32.

———. "The Neglect of Africa and the Power of Aid." *Communication Gazette* 72, no. 1 (2010): 71–84.

———. *Reporting Disasters: Famine, Aid, Politics and the Media*. London: Hurst Publishers, 2013.

Frontline Club. *The News Carers: Are Aid Groups Doing Too Much Real Newsgathering?* New York, 2008. http://www.frontlineclub.com/the_news_carers_are_aid_groups_doing_too_much_real_newsgathering_-_new_york_-_fully_booked/.

———. *Embedding with Aid Agencies: Editorial Integrity and Security Risks.* London, 2015. https://www.frontlineclub.com/embedding-with-aid-agencies-editorial-integrity-and-security-risks/

Gandy, Oscar H. *Beyond Agenda Setting: Information Subsidies and Public Policy.* Norwood, NJ: Ablex, 1982.

GAP – Global Attention Profiles. "Technorati A List Media Attention," July 20, 2016. http://gapdev.law.harvard.edu/.

Gasher, Mike. "Guest Editor's Introduction." *Aether: The Journal of Media Geography. Special Edition on News* 4 (2009): 1–2.

Gasher, Mike, and Reisa Klein. "Mapping the Geography of Online News." *Canadian Journal of Communication* 33, no. 2 (2008). http://cjc-online.ca/index.php/journal/article/viewArticle/1974.

Goodman, Michael K. "Reading Fair Trade: Political Ecological Imaginary and the Moral Economy of Fair Trade Foods." *Political Geography* 23, no. 7 (2004): 891–915.

Grayson, Louise. "The Role of Non-Government Organisations (NGOS) in Practising Editorial Photography in a Globalised Media Environment." *Journalism Practice* 8, no. 5 (2014): 632–45.

Gupta, Sunil. "Northern Media, Southern Lives." In *Photography/politics*, edited by Jo Spence, Patricia Holland, and Simon Watney, 162–66. London: Comedia /Photography Workshop, 1986.

Hallas, Roger. "Photojournalism, NGOs and the New Media Ecology." In *Sensible Politics: The Visual Culture of Nongovernmental Activism*, edited by Meg McLagan and Yates McKee, 95–116. New York: Zone Books, 2012.

Hesmondhalgh, David, and Sarah Baker. *Creative Labour: Media Work in Three Cultural Industries.* Culture, Economy and the Social. London: Routledge, 2011.

Hogg, Andrew. "Mali: Five Million Face Starvation." *Independent on Sunday*, August 19, 2012. http://www.independent.co.uk/news/world/africa/mali-five-million-face-starvation-8060073.html

Jaakkola, Maarit. "Outsourcing Views, Developing News: Changes in Art Criticism in Finnish Dailies, 1978–2008." *Journalism Studies* 16, no. 3 (2015): 383–402.

Jayawardane, M Neelika. "*The Problem with Photojournalism and Africa.*" *Al Jazeera*, January 18, 2017. http://www.aljazeera.com/indepth/opinion/2017/01/problem-photojournalism-africa-170118085814572.html

Jones, Ben. "Looking Good: Mediatisation and International NGOs." *European Journal of Development Research* 29, no.1 (2017): 176–91.

Kennedy, Denis. "Selling the Distant Other: Humanitarianism and imagery—Ethical Dilemmas of Humanitarian Action." *The Journal of Humanitarian Assistance* 28 (2009). https://sites.tufts.edu/jha/archives/411

Klein-Avraham, Inbal, and Zvi Reich. "Out of the Frame: A Longitudinal Perspective on Digitization and Professional Photojournalism." *New Media & Society* 18, no. 3 (2016): 429–46.

Lee, David. "The Ethics of Insecurity: Risk, Individualization and Value in British Independent Television Production." *Television & New Media* 13, no. 6 (2012): 480–97.

Lidichi, Helen. "Finding the Right Image: British Development NGOs and the Regulation of Imagery." In *Culture and Global Change*, edited by Tim Skelton and Tracey Allen, 87–101. London: Routledge, 1999.

Lindström, Julia. "The Moral Economy of Aid: Discourse Analysis of Swedish Fundraising for the Somalia Famine of 2011–2012." Working Paper. Södertörn University, 2016. http://www.diva-portal.org/smash/record.jsf?pid=diva2%3A1035935&dswid=1952#sthash.3Qe AHipx.dpbs.

Lugo-Ocando, Jairo, and Patrick O. Malaolu. "Africa—That Scar on Our Face." In *Blaming the Victim: How Global Journalism Fails Those in Poverty*, 85–103. London: Pluto Press, 2014.

McLagan, Meg, and Yates McKee. "Introduction." In *Sensible Politics: The Visual Culture of Nongovernmental Activism*, edited by Meg McLagan and Yates McKee, 9–24. New York: Zone Books, 2012.

Miller, Jonathan. "Report on Bosco Ntaganda." *Channel 4 News*, August 15, 2012.

Mortensen, Tara Buehner. "Blurry and Centered or Clear and Balanced?" *Journalism Practice* 8, no. 6 (2014): 704–25.

Nothias, Toussaint. "Definition and Scope of Afro-Pessimism: Mapping the Concept and Its Usefulness for Analysing News Media Coverage of Africa." *Leeds African Studies Bulletin* 75 (2013): 54–62.

———. "'Rising', 'Hopeful', 'New': Visualizing Africa in the Age of Globalization." *Visual Communication* 13, no. 3 (2014): 323–39.

———. How Western Journalists Actually Write about Africa." *Journalism Studies* (2016): 1–22. DOI: 10.1080/1461670X.2016.1262748

Orgad, Shani. "Visualizers of Solidarity: Organizational Politics in Humanitarian and International Development NGOs." *Visual Communication* 12, no. 3 (2013): 295–314.

———. "Underline, Celebrate, Mitigate, Erase: Humanitarian NGOs' Strategies of Communicating Difference." In *Humanitarianism, Communications and Change*, edited by Simon Cottle and Glenda Cooper, 117–32. New York: Peter Lang, 2015.

Örnebring, Henrik. *Newsworkers: A Comparative European Perspective*. London: Bloomsbury Publishing, 2016.

Palmer, Lindsay. "Outsourcing Authority in the Digital Age: Television News Networks and Freelance War Correspondents." *Critical Studies in Media Communication* 32, no. 4 (2015): 225–39.

Powers, Matthew. "The Structural Organization of NGO Publicity Work: Explaining Divergent Publicity Strategies at Humanitarian and Human Rights Organizations." *International Journal of Communication* 8 (2014): 90–109.

———. "NGOs as Journalistic Entities: The Possibilities, Promises and Limits of Boundary Crossing." In *Boundaries of Journalism: Professionalism, Practice and Participation*, edited by Matt Carlson and Seth C. Lewis, 186–200. London: New York, 2015.

————. "Beyond Boon or Bane: Using Normative Theories to Evaluate the News-Making Efforts of NGOs." *Journalism Studies* 18, no. 9 (2017): 1070–86.

Richardson, Whitney. "Who Is Telling Africa's Stories?" *The New York Times*, January 10, 2017.

Roosvall, Anna. "The Identity Politics of World News: Oneness, Particularity, Identity and Status in Online Slideshows." *International Journal of Cultural Studies* 17, no. 1 (2013): 55–74.

Sayer, Andrew. "For a Critical Cultural Political Economy." *Antipode* 33, no. 4 (2001): 687–708.

————. "Moral Economy as Critique." *New Political Economy* 12, no. 2 (2007): 261–70.

Scott, James C. *The Moral Economy of the Peasant.* New Haven, CT, London: Yale University Press, 1976.

Scott, Martin. "The Myth of Representations of Africa." *Journalism Studies* 18, no. 2 (2017): 191–210.

Sen, Amartya. *The Idea of Justice.* London: Penguin, 2010.

Shutt, Cathy. "A Moral Economy? Social Interpretations of Money in Aidland." *Third World Quarterly* 33, no. 8 (2012): 1527–43.

Sontag, Susan. *Regarding the Pain of Others.* New York: Picador, 2003.

Strauss, David Levi. "The Documentary Debate: Aesthetic or Anaesthetic? Or, What's so Funny about Peace, Love, Understanding and Social Documentary Photography?" In *Between the Eyes: Essays on Photography and Politics*, edited by John Berger and David Levi Strauss, 3–11 New York: Aperture, 2005.

Van der Gaag, Nikki, and Cathy Nash. *Images of Africa: The UK Report.* Oxford: Oxfam, 1987.

Wall, Melissa, and Douglas Bicket. "Window on the Wider World': The Rise of British News in the United States." *Journalism Practice* 2, no. 2 (2009): 163–78.

Warrington, Siobhan with Jess Crombie (2017). *The People in the Pictures: Vital Perspectives on Save the Children's image-making.* London: Save the Children UK.

Wright, Kate. International Aid Agencies, the Politics of Voice and the Pitfalls of Interpretation within News Production." *Global Media and Communication*, In print.

————. "Moral Economies: Interrogating the Interactions of Nongovernmental Organizations, Journalists and Freelancers." *International Journal of Communication* 10 (2016a): 1–19.

————. "'These Grey Areas' How and Why Freelance Work Blurs INGOs and News Organizations." *Journalism Studies* 17, no. 8 (2016b): 989–1009.

INDEX